Palgrave Macmillan Memory Studies

Series Editors: **Andrew Hoskins** and **John Sutton**

International Advisory Board: **Steven Brown**, University of Leicester, UK, **Mary Carruthers**, New York University, USA, **Paul Connerton**, University of Cambridge, UK, **Astrid Erll**, University of Wuppertal, Germany, **Robyn Fivush**, Emory University, USA, **Tilmann Habermas**, University of Frankfurt am Main, Germany, **Jeffrey Olick**, University of Virginia, USA, **Susannah Radstone**, University of East London, UK, **Ann Rigney**, Utrecht University, Netherlands

The nascent field of Memory Studies emerges from contemporary trends that include a shift from concern with historical knowledge of events to that of memory, from 'what we know' to 'how we remember it'; changes in generational memory; the rapid advance of technologies of memory; panics over declining powers of memory, which mirror our fascination with the possibilities of memory enhancement; and the development of trauma narratives in reshaping the past.

These factors have contributed to an intensification of public discourses on our past over the last 30 years. Technological, political, interpersonal, social and cultural shifts affect what, how and why people and societies remember and forget. This ground-breaking series tackles questions such as: What is 'memory' under these conditions? What are its prospects, and also the prospects for its interdisciplinary and systematic study? What are the conceptual, theoretical and methodological tools for its investigation and illumination?

Matthew Allen
THE LABOUR OF MEMORY
Memorial Culture and 7/7

Silke Arnold-de Simine
MEDIATING MEMORY IN THE MUSEUM
Empathy, Trauma, Nostalgia

Rebecca Bramall
THE CULTURAL POLITICS OF AUSTERITY
Past and Present in Austere Times

Irit Dekel
MEDIATION AT THE HOLOCAUST MEMORIAL IN BERLIN

Anne Fuchs
AFTER THE DRESDEN BOMBING
Pathways of Memory 1945 to the Present

Irial Glynn and J. Olaf Kleist (*editors*)
HISTORY, MEMORY AND MIGRATION
Perceptions of the Past and the Politics of Incorporation

Andrea Hajek
NEGOTIATING MEMORIES OF PROTEST IN WESTERN EUROPE
The Case of Italy

Amy Holdsworth
TELEVISION, MEMORY AND NOSTALGIA

Jason James
PRESERVATION AND NATIONAL BELONGING IN EASTERN GERMANY
Heritage Fetishism and Redeeming Germanness

Sara Jones
THE MEDIA OF TESTIMONY
Remembering the East German Stasi in the Berlin Republic

Emily Keightley and Michael Pickering
THE MNEMONIC IMAGINATION
Remembering as Creative Practice

Amanda Lagerkvist
MEDIA AND MEMORY IN NEW SHANGHAI
Western Performances of Futures Past

Philip Lee and Pradip Ninan Thomas (*editors*)
PUBLIC MEMORY, PUBLIC MEDIA AND THE POLITICS OF JUSTICE

Erica Lehrer, Cynthia E. Milton and Monica Eileen Patterson (*editors*)
CURATING DIFFICULT KNOWLEDGE
Violent Pasts in Public Places

Oren Meyers, Eyal Zandberg and Motti Neiger
COMMUNICATING AWE
Media, Memory and Holocaust Commemoration

Anne Marie Monchamp
AUTOBIOGRAPHICAL MEMORY IN AN ABORIGINAL AUSTRALIAN COMMUNITY
Culture, Place and Narrative

Katharina Niemeyer (*editor*)
MEDIA AND NOSTALGIA
Yearning for the Past, Present and Future

Margarita Saona
MEMORY MATTERS IN TRANSITIONAL PERU

Anna Saunders and Debbie Pinfold (*editors*)
REMEMBERING AND RETHINKING THE GDR
Multiple Perspectives and Plural Authenticities

Estela Schindel and Pamela Colombo (*editors*)
SPACE AND THE MEMORIES OF VIOLENCE
Landscapes of Erasure, Disappearance and Exception

V. Seidler
REMEMBERING DIANA
Cultural Memory and the Reinvention of Authority

Bryoni Trezise
PERFORMING FEELING IN CULTURES OF MEMORY

Evelyn B. Tribble and Nicholas Keene
COGNITIVE ECOLOGIES AND THE HISTORY OF REMEMBERING
Religion, Education and Memory in Early Modern England

Barbie Zelizer and Keren Tenenboim-Weinblatt (*editors*)
JOURNALISM AND MEMORY

Palgrave Macmillan Memory Studies
Series Standing Order ISBN 978–0–230–23851–0 (hardback)
978–0–230–23852–7 (paperback)
(*outside North America only*)

You can receive future titles in this series as they are published by placing a standing order. Please contact your bookseller or, in case of difficulty, write to us at the address below with your name and address, the title of the series and the ISBN quoted above.

Customer Services Department, Macmillan Distribution Ltd, Houndmills, Basingstoke, Hampshire RG21 6XS, England

Space and the Memories of Violence

Landscapes of Erasure, Disappearance and Exception

Estela Schindel
Universität Konstanz, Germany

Pamela Colombo
École des Hautes Études en Sciences Sociales, France

Introduction, selection and editorial matter © Estela Schindel and Pamela Colombo 2014
Individual chapters © Respective authors 2014

All rights reserved. No reproduction, copy or transmission of this publication may be made without written permission.

No portion of this publication may be reproduced, copied or transmitted save with written permission or in accordance with the provisions of the Copyright, Designs and Patents Act 1988, or under the terms of any licence permitting limited copying issued by the Copyright Licensing Agency, Saffron House, 6–10 Kirby Street, London EC1N 8TS.

Any person who does any unauthorized act in relation to this publication may be liable to criminal prosecution and civil claims for damages.

The authors have asserted their rights to be identified as the authors of this work in accordance with the Copyright, Designs and Patents Act 1988.

First published 2014 by
PALGRAVE MACMILLAN

Palgrave Macmillan in the UK is an imprint of Macmillan Publishers Limited, registered in England, company number 785998, of Houndmills, Basingstoke, Hampshire RG21 6XS.

Palgrave Macmillan in the US is a division of St Martin's Press LLC, 175 Fifth Avenue, New York, NY 10010.

Palgrave Macmillan is the global academic imprint of the above companies and has companies and representatives throughout the world.

Palgrave® and Macmillan® are registered trademarks in the United States, the United Kingdom, Europe and other countries.

ISBN 978–1–137–38090–6 hardback

This book is printed on paper suitable for recycling and made from fully managed and sustained forest sources. Logging, pulping and manufacturing processes are expected to conform to the environmental regulations of the country of origin.

A catalogue record for this book is available from the British Library.

Library of Congress Cataloging-in-Publication Data
Space and the Memories of Violence: Landscapes of Erasure, Disappearance and Exception / [editors] Estela Schindel, Universität Konstanz, Germany; Pamela Colombo, École des Hautes Études en Sciences Sociales, France.
    pages cm. — (Palgrave Macmillan memory studies)
Includes bibliographical references.
ISBN 978–1–137–38090–6
  1. Space—Social aspects. 2. Violence. 3. Collective memory—Political aspects. 4. Crimes against humanity. I. Schindel, Estela, editor. II. Colombo, Pamela, editor.
HM654.S637 2014
304.2′3—dc23   2014025907

Transferred to Digital Printing in 2015

Contents

List of Figures	vii
Preface	viii
Notes on Contributors	x

Introduction: The Multi-Layered Memories of Space   1
Pamela Colombo and Estela Schindel

Part I   Spatial Inscriptions of Annihilation

1 Violent Erasures and Erasing Violence: Contesting Cambodia's Landscapes of Violence   21
James A. Tyner

2 Polish Landscapes of Memory at the Sites of Extermination: The Politics of Framing   34
Zuzanna Dziuban

3 Spaces of Confrontation and Defeat: The Spatial Dispossession of the Revolution in Tucumán, Argentina   48
Pamela Colombo

4 Subterranean Autopsies: Exhumations of Mass Graves in Contemporary Spain   61
Francisco Ferrándiz

Part II   The Representation of Violence: Spatial Strategies

5 Faces, Voices and the Shadow of Catastrophe   77
Jay Winter

6 The Cartographer. Warsaw, 1: 400,000   91
Juan Mayorga (English translation by Sarah Maitland)

7 'All Limits Were Exceeded Over There': The Chronotope of Terror in Modern Warfare and Testimony   105
Kirsten Mahlke

vi *Contents*

8   The Concentration Camp and the 'Unhomely Home':
    The Disappearance of Children in Post-Dictatorship Argentine
    Theatre   119
    Mariana Eva Perez

Part III Haunted Spaces, Irrupting Memories

9   'The Whole Country Is a Monument': Framing Places of Terror
    in Post-War Germany   135
    Aleida Assmann

10 Haunted Houses, Horror Literature and the Space of Memory
    in Post-Dictatorship Argentine Literature   150
    Silvana Mandolessi

11 Counter-Movement, Space and Politics: How the Saturday
    Mothers of Turkey Make Enforced Disappearances Visible   162
    Meltem Ahıska

12 An Orderly Landscape of Remnants: Notes for Reflecting on
    the Spatiality of the Disappeared   176
    Gabriel Gatti

13 A Limitless Grave: Memory and Abjection of the Río de la Plata   188
    Estela Schindel

Part IV Spaces of Exception, Power and Resistance

14 Spatialities of Exception   205
    Pilar Calveiro

15 Imaginary Cities, Violence and Memory: A Literary Mapping   219
    Gudrun Rath

16 Occupied Squares and the Urban 'State of Exception': In,
    Against and Beyond the City of Enclaves   231
    Stavros Stavrides

17 'Memory, that Powerful Political Force'   244
    Interview with David Harvey

Index   254

Figures

1.1	Mugshot of Keat Sophal, arrested on 13 April 1977. She was detained for 99 days until she was executed on 22 July	22
1.2	Tuol Sleng Security-Center, Phnom Penh, Cambodia	28
2.1	Elżbieta Janicka, *Sobibór, 250,000* (4 July 2003); from the cycle *The Odd Place*	36
2.2	Museum-Memorial Site in Bełżec	42
2.3	Sobibór Death Camp Memorial Site	43
3.1	Villages founded by the military during the dictatorship and towns where research was conducted (Tucumán, Argentina)	53
5.1	Dix, Otto. *Transplantation*	82
5.2	Picasso, Pablo. *Guernica*	83
5.3	Kiefer, Anselm. 'Breaking of the Vessels' in the collection of the Saint Louis Art Museum	85
5.4	BB83_04456 – Holland House library after an air raid, 1940	86
5.5	Jewish Museum in Berlin	87
9.1	Map of Germany with the borders of 1937, showing the sites of concentration camps	137
9.2	Collective excavation at the site of the former Gestapo headquarters (1985)	140
9.3	Flyer of "Aktion Hotel Silber"	142
9.4	'Audioweg Gusen'. The present Gartenstraße in Gusen in which, between 1940 and 1945, the Barracks from the camp Gusen I were located	147
12.1	Scale model of the 'Casa Grimaldi' clandestine detention centre, Santiago de Chile, December 2007	180
13.1	Reconstruction of the Portrait of Pablo Míguez, by Claudia Fontes	189
13.2	Drawings on the River, by Jorge Velarde	196

Preface

The production of this book was funded by the European Research Council under the European Union's Seventh Framework Program through the research group *Narratives of Terror and Disappearance* (FP/2007–2013, ERC Grant Agreement No. 240984 NoT), based at the University of Konstanz. This source also granted the main funding for the international symposium that gave origin to the present volume. The symposium, entitled *Spatialities of Exception, Violence and Memory*, took place in Madrid between 1 and 3 February 2012, at the Residencia de Estudiantes and the Centro de Ciencias Humanas y Sociales, belonging to the Spanish National Research Council (CCHS-CSIC). Further sponsorship was awarded by the Spanish Ministry of Science and Innovation (MICINN, Acción Complementaria FFI2011-14371-E), the research groups *The Politics of Memory in Contemporary Spain* (Plan Nacional I+D+i CS02009–09681) and *Philosophy after the Holocaust* (Plan Nacional I+D+i FFI2009–09368) and the Max Planck Research Prize *Geschichte+Gedächtnis* from the University of Konstanz.

For their support in different phases of this project, we would like to extend our deepest thanks to Aleida Assmann, Francisco Ferrándiz, Manuel Reyes Mate, Concha Roldán, José Antonio Zamora and, especially, to Kirsten Mahlke who, as director of the NoT research group, provided us with institutional and financial backing throughout this process, from the conception of the symposium to the materialization of this book. Kirsten stood permanently at our side with her intellectual openness and creativity, offering us constant motivation and advice and, above all, her trust in this project.

We would also like to mention our colleague, Rosario Figari-Layús, whom we thank for her skilful suggestions and organizational help during the encounter in Madrid, as well as the late Asunción Gaudens Cros, who designed the poster that publicized the symposium. Jorge Morales, alongside Victor Pareja and Cristina Ramos, gave us an invaluable logistic support at the CSIC. We also thank Carlos Agüero, Amanda Demitrio, Julia Blanco, Carmen Domench, Marije Hristova, Paula Martos, Pedro Ochoa, Nicolás Oviedo and Gemma Vidal for their voluntary assistance during those days.

We are most grateful to the series editor, Andrew Hoskins, and to everyone at Palgrave who guided and assisted us through the different stages of putting this book together. Special mention must go to Felicity Plester and Chris Penfold.

A big '*gracias*' goes to Sophie Oliver, Philip Derbyshire and Philippa Page, who provided their patience and language skills correcting, translating and editing different parts of the manuscript at various stages of its preparation.

We would like to express our sincere thanks to the authors for their commitment and readiness to accompany us throughout this editorial and intellectual enterprise. We appreciate their individual contributions as much as their willingness to engage in this conversation with us, thus linking their specific case studies to the questions we aimed to discuss herein.

Our gratitude goes also to the authors of the photographs, who have accorded the necessary publishing rights, and to Stefanie Schumacher, who diligently searched for and contacted those holding the copyright for the images. Every attempt has been made to contact the owners of property rights. If, however, any have inadvertently been overlooked, the editors and publishers will be more than willing to make the appropriate arrangements at the earliest opportunity.

The photograph illustrating the cover of this volume was taken by Esteban Luis Santamaría on the site of what was, under the Argentine military dictatorship in the 1970s, the clandestine detention centre El Campito, in the Province of Buenos Aires. This land still belongs to Campo de Mayo, where Argentina's main military corps continues to operate its headquarters today. The former detention facilities have, however, been demolished in order to erase all traces of the kidnapping and murder of thousands of people. Meanwhile, the place has been expropriated from the military to search for remnants of the disappeared, and trials to judge the crimes committed there are being carried out in Argentine courts. The picture was taken in September 1999 – a time when impunity laws still prevailed in the country – during a commemoration organized by relatives and friends of the disappeared, in order to draw attention to the place. The act involved placing the silhouettes that have become characteristic of actions carried out by Argentine human rights movements in memory of the *desaparecidos*. When Esteban Santamaría – himself a son of disappeared – gave his permission to use the picture, he wrote the following words about the moment the photograph was taken: 'When they installed the silhouettes, the wind was buffeting against them, the landscape behind them was infinite, the trees had no leaves, everything seemed so solitary. As we were leaving, I looked at everybody and noticed how sad we were to leave those silhouettes of the detainee-disappeared there alone.' The editors wish that this book may help the memories of the disappeared and murdered not to remain alone, with the wind and a desolate landscape as sole witnesses.

Estela Schindel dedicates her work in this book in memory of Leib and Ester Malka Ortner Z'L and their children and grandchildren murdered in Belzec in 1942.

Pamela Colombo wishes to dedicate this book to her niece, Anita, and nephew, Benicio, hoping that they can grow up imagining new spaces of hope.

Contributors

Meltem Ahıska is Professor of Sociology at Boğaziçi University, Istanbul. She graduated in Sociology in Istanbul and, after receiving her MA in Communications from the University of Westminster, completed her PhD in Sociology at Goldsmiths College, University of London, in 2000. She has written and edited a number of books among which *Occidentalism in Turkey: Questions of Modernity and National Identity in Turkish Radio Broadcasting* (2010) is the most recent. Her articles and essays on Occidentalism, social memory, national identity and gender have appeared in various journals and edited volumes. She has published a book of poems, *Havalandırma* (2002), and curated exhibitions, the most recent being *The Person You Have Called Cannot Be Reached at the Moment: Representations of Lifestyles in Turkey, 1980–2005*. Ahıska's current research focuses on monumentalization and counter-monumentalization in Turkey. She is a member of the editorial board of the e-journal *Red Thread*.

Aleida Assmann is one of the most renowned scholars in British and American Studies, Egyptology, and Literary and Cultural Studies. She has dealt extensively with the history of memory in Germany after the Second World War as well as with cultural academic research into, and theories of, memory. Her works on the cultural transmission of memory had a broad reception in the German and Anglo-saxon debate and have become canonical in the study of social and cultural memory. Her recent publications in English are *Cultural Memory and Western Civilization: Functions, Media, Archives* (2012), and the co-edition of *Memory and Political Change* (Palgrave 2011) and *Memory in a Global Age: Discourses, Practices and Trajectories* (Palgrave 2010). Professor Assmann was a fellow at the universities of Rice, Princeton, Yale, Chicago and Vienna and is affiliated with the Center of Excellence Cultural Foundations of Social Integration at the University of Konstanz. She was presented the Paul Watzlawick Ehrenring Award (2009), the Ernst Robert Curtius Prize (2011), the Max Planck Research Award (2009) and an honorary doctorate by the University of Oslo.

Pilar Calveiro received her PhD from the Universidad Nacional Autónoma de México and is currently a Professor and Researcher at the Benemérita Universidad Autónoma de Puebla, as well as a member of the Mexican National Researchers System. In her several works about violence, politics and memory, Calveiro sharply analyses the dynamics of power relations and their effects of resistance as well as the social context, where such disputes take place. Her book *Poder y desaparición, los campos de concentración* *en Argentina* (1998) has since been an ineludible reference for the study of the phenomenon of enforced disappearances in Argentina. She is also the author of *Política y/o Violencia* (2005) and *Violencias de Estado* (2012). Pilar Calveiro was kidnapped by military forces during the Argentinean dictatorship in 1977 and spent a year and a half in several clandestine detention centres as a detainee-disappeared. After a short exile in Spain, she established herself in Mexico, where she lives since 1979.

Pamela Colombo studied Sociology at the University of Buenos Aires and holds a PhD in Sociology from the University of the Basque Country (UPV). She is currently a post-doctoral fellow from the Fondation Fyssen (2014–16) at the EHESS-IRIS and a researcher at the ERC project 'Corpses of Mass Violence and Genocide'. Her research focuses on the social production of space, particularly on the constitution of imaginary geographies in contexts of political violence. She was a doctoral researcher at the Spanish National Research Council (CSIC, 2009–13) and a visiting researcher at the Center for Place, Culture and Politics (CUNY, New York), the Centre for Research Architecture (Goldsmiths College, London), the Freie Universität Berlin (FU, Berlin) and the University of Konstanz (Germany). She co-organized the International Conferences 'Spatialities of Exception, Violence, and Memory' (Madrid, February 2012) and 'Thinking Memory through Space: Materiality, Representation and Imagination' (London, 2013). Her current research deals with the spatiality of mass graves in post-dictatorship Argentina.

Zuzanna Dziuban holds a PhD in Cultural Studies from the Adam Mickiewicz University in Poznań, Poland, where she also completed a Master in Cultural Studies and studied Philosophy. She has been a researcher and teaching assistant at the Adam Mickiewicz University (2009–11) and a lecturer at the School of Humanities and Journalism in Poznań. She has been a fellow at the University of Siegen (2004/2005), at the University of Konstanz (2011–12 DAAD Post-doctoral Research Fellow), and at the Humboldt University of Berlin (Fritz-Thyssen Stiftung fellowship, 2012). Since December 2012, she has been an Alexander von Humboldt-Foundation fellow at the University of Konstanz (Research Group 'Geschichte + Gedächtnis') and the Humboldt University. Her current research interests focus on the relation between trauma, memory and space, and Polish post-war politics of memory. She published the monograph *Foreignness, Homelessness, Loss: Dimensions of Atopia of the Contemporary Cultural Experience* (*Obcość, bezdomność, utrata. Wymiary atopii współczesnego doświadczenia kulturowego*, 2009) and wrote the articles 'Architecture as a Medium of Transnational Postmemory' (2012) and 'Spatialized Trauma: The Holocaust and the Architecture of Postmemory' (2013).

Francisco Ferrándiz is tenured researcher at the Instituto de Lengua, Literatura y Antropología (ILLA), Spanish National Research Council (CSIC).

He studied Anthropology and History at the universities of Madrid and Berkeley and wrote his PhD at the Department of Anthropology at the University of California, Berkeley. His areas of interest include anthropology of the body, anthropology of violence and social memory and trauma. His largest ethnographical projects have dealt with the spiritist cult of Maria Lionza in Venezuela and, since 2003, the politics of memory in contemporary Spain through the analysis of the exhumations of mass graves from the Civil War (1936–39). He is the author of *Escenarios del cuerpo: Espiritismo y sociedad en Venezuela* (2004), *Etnografías contemporaneas* (2011) and *El pasado bajo tierra* (Anthropos/Siglo XXI, 2014), and the co-editor of *Down to Earth: Mass Graves and Exhumations in the Contemporary World* (forthcoming).

Gabriel Gatti is Professor of Contemporary Sociological Theory and Sociology of Identity at UPV. He is the co-ordinator of the Centre for Collective Identity Studies (CEIC), where he directs the project 'Mundo(s) de víctimas'. He was a guest researcher at the École des Hautes Études en Sciences Sociales (Paris), CERI-Sciences Po (Paris), Nevada University (Reno), IDES – Economic and Social Development Institute (Buenos Aires) and a guest lecturer at Paris 3-Sorbonne Nouvelle (chaire 'Pablo Neruda', Paris), University of the Republic – UdelaR (Montevideo), the University of Buenos Aires, the Universidad Autónoma de Barcelona and the Universidad de Coimbra. His current research interests include sociology theory, identity sociology (including their intersections) and human rights sociology. He is the author, among other titles, of *Identidades desaparecidas* (2011), *El detenido-desaparecido* (2008), *Identidades débiles* (2007) *and Surviving Forced Disappearing in Argentina and Uruguay* (Palgrave 2014).

David Harvey is Distinguished Professor of Anthropology and Geography at the Graduate Center of the City University of New York (CUNY) and the Director of the Center for Place, Culture and Politics. His theoretical developments in the field of human geography and social theory turned David Harvey to be one of the most influential Marxist theorists and the most quoted living geographer. Among his many books are *The Condition of Postmodernity* (1989), *Justice, Nature and the Geography of Difference* (1996), *Spaces of Hope* (2000), *Spaces of Capital: Towards a Critical Geography* (2001) and *Spaces of Global Capitalism: Towards a Theory of Uneven Geographical Development* (2005). In recent years, his work has reached far beyond the academic field and has increasingly become a reference for several political and social movements around the world. David Harvey has been granted many distinctions and awards of geographical societies and is an honorary doctor of the universities of Buenos Aires, Roskilde, Uppsala, Ohio State and Lund.

Kirsten Mahlke studied Romance and Slavic Languages and Cultures, and Anthropology at the Johann Wolfgang Goethe University in Frankfurt, where she also received her PhD (*Revelations in the West: Early Reports from the New World*, 2005). Her second book is a study of Argentina's literature and its reception and assimilation of Physics' quantic theory. Kirsten Mahlke was awarded scholarships from the Studienstiftung des deutschen Volk and was a fellow at the University of Konstanz and at the Heidelberg Academy of Sciences. She was Professor of Romance Literature at the University of Heidelberg (2009–10) and is currently tenured Professor of Cultural Theory and Methodology at the University of Konstanz. In 2009, she was awarded a Starting Grant from the European Research Council to direct the research project 'Narratives of Terror and Disappearance: Fantastic Dimensions of Collective Memory of the Last Military Dictatorship in Argentina' (2010–15), which explores the narrative and social elaboration of violence and trauma from an interdisciplinary perspective.

Silvana Mandolessi is a post-doctoral fellow of the European Research Council at the University of Konstanz and an Assistant Professor at the KU Leuven. She has published articles in, among other journals, *Russian Literature*, *Chasqui*, *Revista Canadiense de Estudios Hispánicos* and *Confluencia* and *América: Cahiers du Criccal*. She is the author of *Una literatura abyecta. Gombrowicz en la tradición argentina* (2012) and co-editor of *El juego con los estereotipos. La redefinición de la identidad hispánica en la literatura y el cine posnacionales* (2012) and co-editor of the special issue 'Transnational Memory in the Hispanic World' (2014), *European Review*. She is the project manager of the project 'Transit: Transnationality at Large', supported by the European Commission, and director of the organization CONEXX-Europe, which specializes in scientific and technical cooperation between Europe and Latin America. Her research areas include migrant literature – post/transnational identity, contemporary Argentine literature and the theory and politics of abjection.

Juan Mayorga is one of the most important Spanish playwrights of his generation. Among many others, Mayorga wrote *El jardín quemado, Cartas de amor a Stalin, Himmelweg, El cartógrafo, Los yugoslavos* and *Reikiavik*. He was awarded several national awards, among them are the Spain's National Theatre Prize (2007) and the Spain's National Dramatic Literature Prize (2013). Mayorga's work has been translated into many languages and performed widely throughout the world. He has also adapted versions of classical dramas for the Spanish stage and was a founding member of the El Astillero theatre company in 1993. In 1998, he began teaching Dramaturgy, History of Thought and Sociology at the Real Escuela Superior de Arte Dramático in Madrid. Mayorga graduated in Mathematics and Philosophy, completed his studies in Münster, Berlin and Paris and received his PhD in Philosophy in 1997. His most important philosophical work is *Revolución conservadora y conservación revolucionaria. Política y memoria en Walter Benjamin* (2003).

Mariana Eva Perez graduated in Political Science from the University of Buenos Aires. She was granted several research scholarships of this school and of the Antorchas Foundation to develop her studies on memory and identity. She received her training as a playwright from Patricia Zangaro (2002–07) and participated with her own work in the initial phase of *Teatroxlaidentidad*. Her plays have been published in several anthologies and shown in Spain, Belgium, France, Bolivia, Venezuela and Scotland. Her work *Peaje* was distinguished with the Fourth German Rozenmacher Prize for New Dramaturgy at the International Festival of Buenos Aires. She is also the author of the plays *Ábaco, La Muñeca, Sin voz* and *Instrucciones para un coleccionista de mariposas*, and of the book *Diario de una princesa montonera* (2012), based on a fictionalized blog-autobiography. Perez is doing her PhD about post-dictatorship Argentine theatre in the project 'Narratives of Terror and Disappearance' at the University of Konstanz.

Gudrun Rath studied Romanic and German Literature and Culture at the Universidad Complutense de Madrid and the University of Vienna, where she also took part in the EU project 'Biennale Est – Europe as a Space of Translation' and served as a teacher. She held research positions at the universities of Heidelberg and Konstanz and is now a full-time post-doctoral researcher at the Chair of Literature and Cultural Theory and Methodology as well as a member of the Center of Excellence Cultural Foundations of Social Integration at the University of Konstanz. She received her PhD from the University of Vienna. Gudrun Rath focuses on Postcolonial Studies, Translation Studies, Latin American Literatures and Francophone Literatures and Film. She has published articles on literature, migration, urban cultures and translation theory and is the author of *Zwischenzonen. Theorien und Fiktionen des Übersetzens* (2013).

Estela Schindel studied Communications at the University of Buenos Aires and received a PhD in Sociology from the Free University Berlin. She has taught graduate courses at German and Argentinean universities and published extensively on the relation between art, memory and the urban space and on the social construction of exclusion. She was a guest researcher at the Center for the Study of Anti-Semitism of the Technical University Berlin and at the Ibero-American Institute, where she studied the Holocaust Reception in Latin American intellectual field. She conceived and co-organized the international symposium 'Urban Memory Cultures: Berlin and Buenos Aires' (Berlin, 2005) and co-edited the German and Spanish language volumes based on that encounter (2009, 2010). Estela Schindel was a founding member of the artistic collective migrantas, an independent consultant in projects about historical memory for the German international cooperation (InWEnt/GIZ) and a post-doctoral researcher with the ERC Research Group 'Narratives of Terror and Disappearance'. She is currently a researcher and scientific coordinator of the PhD Program 'Europe in the Globalized World' at the Center of Excellence Cultural Foundations of Social Integration at the University of Konstanz. Her current research project deals with the social and cultural manifestations of violence at the EU border regime.

Stavros Stavrides is Associate Professor at the School of Architecture, National Technical University of Athens, Greece, where he teaches the graduate courses on social housing and house design, as well as a postgraduate course on the meaning of metropolitan experience. His areas of research are Architecture, Sociology, Space Theory, Urban Anthropology and Urban Geography. He has published six books (as well as numerous articles and contributions to essay collections) on spatial theory: *The Symbolic Relation to Space* (1990), *Advertising and the Meaning of Space* (1996), *The Texture of Things* (1996), *From the City-as-Screen to the City-as-Stage* (2002), *Suspended Spaces of Alterity* (2010) and *Towards the City of Thresholds* (in English, 2010). His research is currently focused on forms of emancipating spatial practices and urban communing.

James A. Tyner completed his PhD in Geography at the University of Southern California in 1995. He is currently a professor at Kent University in Ohio. His most recent work has addressed war, violence and genocide, where he made important contributions to the comprehension of the spatial dimensions of mass violence and genocide. He is the author of 13 books, including *War, Violence, and Population: Making the Body Count* (2009), *Genocide and the Geographic Imagination: Life and Death in Germany, China, and Cambodia* (2012), *Space, Place, and Violence: Violence and the Embodied Geographies of Race, Sex, and Gender* (2011) and *The Killing of Cambodia: Geography, Genocide and the Unmaking of Space* (2008).

Jay Winter, the Charles J. Stille Professor of History at Yale University, is a specialist on the First World War and its impact on the twentieth century. His other interests include remembrance of war in the twentieth century, such as memorial and mourning sites, European population decline, the causes and institutions of war, British popular culture in the era of the Great War and the Armenian genocide of 1915. He is the author or co-author of a dozen books, including *Socialism and the Challenge of War, Ideas and Politics in Britain, 1912–1918* (1993), *Sites of Memory, Sites of Mourning: The Great War in European Cultural History* (1994), *Remembering War: The Great War Between History and Memory in the 20th Century* (2006) and *Dreams of Peace and Freedom: Utopian Moments in the 20th Century* (2006). He was co-producer, co-writer and chief historian for the PBS series *The Great War and the Shaping of the 20th Century*.

Introduction: The Multi-Layered Memories of Space

Pamela Colombo and Estela Schindel

At the origin of this book is a salon, and a piano on which Federico García Lorca used to play. The inaugural session of the symposium 'Spatialities of Exception, Violence, and Memory', for which the contributions gathered in this volume were originally written, took place in February 2012 at the Residencia de Estudiantes (Students' Residency) in Madrid. This institution has a legendary place in the intellectual history of Spain, having served as an active cultural centre in the interwar period. Before Franco's dictatorship put an end to it, the building had offered a fertile space for creation, thought and interdisciplinary dialogue and had housed many prominent avant-garde artists and scientists, like Lorca himself. Sitting in that salon and with the piano still standing there as a silent witness, the research topics that had gathered us there became particularly tangible. How is memory inscribed in space? Do the places themselves bear and transmit the remembrance or is it that our knowledge and affect attach meaning to them? Evoking the figure of García Lorca – who was executed by the Francoist regime but whose corpse has never been found – the question about the entanglement of places and memory became palpable in this room. The greatest Spanish-language poet of the twentieth century is a 'desaparecido' (disappeared), since his remains have never been found. What happens when state crimes do not leave traces and when there are no recognizable graves? How can the absence be made visible?

This book aims to contribute to the broader discussion of these questions from a variety of disciplinary perspectives and based on a diversity of historical cases from multiple geographical contexts. The contributions gathered here grant new insights into social memory by analysing how violent processes unfold in space and reconfigure it in the long term; how past atrocities continue to haunt the present; and how policies, practices and subjectivities are determined by, and simultaneously shape, the social production of space. The aim of this volume is to provide a wider framework for the inquiry into the relation between memory and space, taking it beyond the debates about memorialization in former sites of terror, on which much scholarly production focuses its attention. The creation and management of sites dedicated to remembrance is indeed politically crucial, and some chapters in this book engage critically with a number of these. Our emphasis though lies on the ways in which violence and the social production of space are inextricably linked and thus influence social memories, imaginaries and practices. This influence extends beyond the places that would be obviously related to state violence, and hence beyond their material remains. This volume thus seeks to expand the scope of studies on collective memories incorporating a complex definition of space. At the same time, these articles contribute to the discussion about the legacies of state violence by inquiring into their inscription and unfolding in space.

Since the coming of the 'spatial turn' in the social sciences and the humanities, the notion of space as something fixed, immobile or naturally given has been definitively challenged (Lefebvre, 1991; Soja, 1989; Harvey, 1990; Massey, 1994; Schlögel, 2003). In the context of a growing awareness of the spatial dimension as a constitutive element of social life, and under the major influence of the writings of Henri Lefebvre, space is no longer regarded as a mere stage upon which history unfolds or into which social actors intervene. Rather, space is increasingly held to be both produced by, and productive of, the social. However, this approach has only begun to be acknowledged and integrated into the studies that deal with state-sponsored violence and their memories. Much important scholarly work devoted to this subject still fails at acknowledging the productive and social dimension of space, which is rather regarded as a more or less neutral background. Geographers, space theorists and architects are for their part becoming more and more concerned with the study of contemporary cartographies and topographies of exclusion, exception and state violence, and are at the same time paying more attention to the spatial manifestations of trauma and memory. However, the study of the specific traits of the geographies of violence, like the particular spatiality of the concentrationary apparatus, still deserves further academic attention.

One of the queries that motivated us when conceiving this book was whether and why important work on social theory leaves a void when it comes to incorporating extreme state violence and regimes of exception into the study of space. Even influential authors who have dealt extensively with the spatial manifestations of oppression and injustice in their work did not seem to us to have paid enough attention to the most specific space of domination brought about by the twentieth century, namely the concentration and extermination camps. Henri Lefebvre's seminal book *The Production of Space* (1991), first published in 1974, dedicates many pages to unravelling the ways in which domination and violence are imbricated in space but does not devote one word to the concentrationary universe of the totalitarian regimes. The work of the eminent Marxist geographer David Harvey, whose interpretation of space as relational attributes an important role to memory, puzzled us for revealing a similar omission. Harvey has made a thorough study of the origins and development of the spatial inequalities produced by capitalism but does not engage with the particular spatiality of the concentrationary sites or the spaces of exception, a term which, as shown in the interview given especially for this volume, he regards rather sceptically. Harvey's privileged focus on class conflict as the main factor for the interpretation of spatial injustice leaves unanswered the question of whether and how urban capitalism makes possible, fosters, relies on or even requires the existence of specific spaces of violence, disappearance and exception. However, his analysis reminds us that even while violence and oppression might find their most virulent expression in mass murder they also exist and reproduce themselves through class domination and the spatial inequality that accompanies it.

In recent decades geographers and architects have started to recognize and consider the places of exception and the location of extreme violence as worthy of study along with the ordinary, 'normal' spaces. At the same time, memory studies are paying greater attention to the ways in which space shapes and reflects the collective memories. However, we believe that the broad field opened by these interconnected perspectives deserves further mapping and exploration. This book aims to make a contribution to bridging the gap between these perspectives, bringing together studies on the spatial dimension of social life with findings of the research on violence, memory and trauma. In our own previous individual work, we have pointed out this need to integrate these complementary approaches and attempted to include a more complex understanding and definition of space into our study of the memories of state violence. This has also included the analysis of past violence and the ways in which victims continue to live and imagine space in the aftermath of conflict (an approach enabled by the comprehension of space in relational terms), a study which helps to understand how these violent spaces still produce effects today (Colombo, 2013). The analysis of policies and practices of memory, on the other hand, could and should consider the question of how state-sponsored violence militates against certain uses of space and promotes others, and thus reflect on how collective memory may contribute to a strengthening of the social networks and even the reversal of the disintegrating effects of genocidal and annihilatory practices (Schindel, 2012). The plurality of approaches and historical experiences reflected in this collective volume, we expect, will provide further evidence of the complex and inextricable links between the memory of violent pasts and the perception, uses and imagination of space today. The study of space was largely believed to be a tool of the powerful, an instrument at the service of domination and allied to the military imaginary (Schlögel, 2003). In this new awareness of space by the social sciences and humanities, the spatial dimension is rather apprehended as a product of people's perceptions, practices and imagination (De

Certeau, 2011), opening up new possibilities of emancipation that are rooted in space.

Spatial violence, violence in space

The majority of the historical cases studied in this volume refer to forms of state violence such as genocide and political persecution that are targeted at a long-term reconfiguration of society. Some of those violent practices, like enforced disappearances, are characterized by being clandestine and leaving no visible traces: they do not modify space in a manifest way. In other cases, the erasure of a determinate topography is intentional and evident. However, spatial reconfigurations brought about by state-sponsored violence concern not only the destruction or disappearance of certain spaces but also the emergence and transformation of others. Moreover, inquiring into the spatialities of state violence, disappearance and exception implies the consideration of what kind of subjectivity is promoted by such violent processes. The ways in which subjects remember and dispute meanings about what happened, the haunting effects emanating from the buildings and the practices of living and using the spaces in the aftermath of conflict are equally part of these mutated landscapes even if the material remnants seemingly remain untouched. For this reason, the spatial reconfigurations analysed in this book focus not only on the moment when the violent event took place but also consider the ways in which those spaces are evoked today, whether individually or collectively, whether by deliberate remembrance or by involuntary recall. This afterlife of violence similarly influences the possibility and capacity of the subjects to imagine certain actions as possible in the space.

Space is assumed here not to be a static and fixed support of the historical events, nor a naturally given, neutral dimension but a social product and a productive force. Therefore, the process by which violence reconfigures space cannot be considered in a unidirectional way. Scholars have analysed the material expression of armed conflicts in space, mainly paying attention to their effects on the built environment (Coward, 2009; Elden, 2009; Graham, 2004; Graham et al., 2008; Thrift, 2007). Several authors have dealt with the traces of violence from the specific perspective of material culture, the archaeology of recent conflict or forensic architecture and urbanism (like González-Ruibal, 2007; Myers and Moshenska, 2011; Schofield et al., 2002; Sturdy Colls, 2012; Weizman, 2010; Zarankin and Salerno, 2011). The very spatial configuration of space can be used as a tool in order to disarticulate or annihilate populations, as it has been the case in the process of deterritorialization and reterritorialization produced in the context of Colombia's long armed conflict (Blair, 2005; Oslender, 2007; Pécaut, 2000). By considering the material, symbolic and imaginary dimensions of space as mutually related spheres, some authors have shown the importance of paying attention to the affective and subjective influences on space (Kohn,

2003; Navaro-Yashin, 2012). The interest in the present volume thus lies not only in giving an account of the ways in which space can be manipulated or constructed in contexts of violent processes, but also of how subjectivities, practices and discourses involved in the production of space are modified as well.

Michel Foucault (1975) has shown how space was conceived and used as an apparatus for domination in the hands of the dominant elites, scientists or the military who relied on hierarchical spatial dispositions based on expert knowledge. By means of a spatial metaphor, that of the garden, Zygmunt Bauman (1989) explains modern genocide as also an element of social engineering meant to create a certain social order. Modernity's typical principle of 'gardening' separates and sets apart elements with the aim of creating an ideal society. In these interpretations, therefore, space is much more than scenery or setting to the state-sponsored violence, and it becomes the very matter of social transformation and domination. In the cases analysed in this book, state violence aims not only at concealing persons and places (Tyner, Ferrándiz) together with the mechanisms of destruction themselves (Dziuban, Schindel) but also defies realistic and figurative ways of representation (Winter, Mahlke, Mandolessi) and the capacity of the subjects to imagine certain actions as possible in the space (Colombo, Mayorga, Rath). Authors' contributions analyse the 'productive' dimension of violence that manifests itself when states not only kidnap and murder but simultaneously found towns and roads or provide for children (Pérez). They also explore the possibilities for creatively inhabiting the ruins (Gatti), for resisting the spaces of oppression (Calveiro) or for promoting transformative memories (Assmann, Ahıska, Stavrides, Harvey).

Concentrationary spaces and regimes of exception

The utilization of space as an instrument in the deployment of state violence finds its supreme expression in the creation of spaces of exception and, particularly, of concentration and extermination camps (Agamben, 1998; Diken and Bagge Laustsen, 2005; Ek, 2006; Sofsky, 1997; Tyner, 2008 and 2012). The state of exception begins where the rule of law is suspended and embodies the paramount expression of sovereign power: *'the camp is the space that opens up when the state of exception starts to become the rule'* (Agamben, 2000, p.39, emphasis in original). The proliferation of such spaces excepted from the law (not only prison camps but also enclaves, occupied territories and militarized areas) has led to the notion of 'archipelago of exceptions', meant to refer the multiplicity of extraterritorial zones that emerge either through legal procedures or as matters of fact (Weizman, 2007). These extraterritorial spaces, where sovereign power is contested or removed altogether, do not need to be topographies isolated from ordinary geographies. On the contrary, they can exist side by side with everyday spaces, interact and even overlap temporally with them. That is the case of the clandestine detention centres of the Argentine dictatorship, that were contiguous to the 'normal' city and separated from it only by 'porous' borders (Calveiro, 1998; Colombo, 2011). Thus, the effects of terror could spread through a reticular network permeating all of society (Feierstein, 2007; Schindel, 2012).

The authors gathered in this volume inquire about the ways in which exceptionalities and concentrationary structures are deployed on a diversity of territories. The 'camp', understood with Agamben as a juridical-political structure rather than as a particular historical phenomenon, can be found every time that a state of exception is created (Agamben, 1998, p.174). It can thus emerge in the most diverse situations and can either expand, becoming a global network, or shrink to the most intimate space. In the cases studies here, violent, exceptional spaces can exceed the confines of the nation and extend to the worldwide system of the CIA's illegal detention centres (Calveiro). In other cases, they are superimposed on the everyday, recognizable architectures as in the enforced confinement of the ghetto (Mayorga) or persist by haunting the urban spaces of cities where disappearances took place (Mandolessi). For the children of the disappeared who were illegally appropriated, the concentrationary structure reaches into the home where they were raised by their appropriators (Pérez), thus challenging the largely cherished bourgeois assumption of the private realm as separate and protected from the threats and dangers of the public sphere. At the limit, these methods of torture aimed at destroying the individual subjectivity concentrate all the suffering in the minimal space of the person's consciousness (Mahlke). The manipulation of spatial perception to destroy the subject, as revealed by Calveiro and Mahlke, turns space itself into an instrument of torture. These authors reveal how expert knowledge on torture methods has circulated and been reused in successive historical moments by different power regimes in the course of the twentieth century.

Another kind of knowledge is involved when it comes to converting former concentration camps and detention centres into sites of memory, managing them and defining their social uses and discourse, in alliance, tension or confrontation with sectors of civil society (Ferrándiz, Dziuban, Assmann). The 'authentic' spaces are then occupied, modified, qualified and re-signified in a permanent dialogue between the infrastructure and the discourses that aim at interpreting or translating that materiality. These operations may involve political uses (Tyner) and often incorporate the work of 'professionals' in the construction of meaning, who arrogate to themselves the role of translators of the materiality of space (Keenan and Weizman, 2012), set certain discourses in movement and trace cartographies of remembrance (Till, 2010). This 'expert' knowledge not only creates the scripts deployed by museums (Gatti) but also selects and hides certain parts of the history by deciding which contents to highlight (Tyner). An invisible map is then created, by omission, one where places are relegated and forgotten in official policies of memory (Dziuban). Maps, however, can also be used to subvert the system of oppression or to register things before they vanish forever (Mayorga). And as Harvey and Stavrides claim in their contributions, the exception emerges not only where sovereign power suspends the rule of law, but it can also arise through the spatial practices of rebellious or contestatory individuals and groups. Occupations, revolutions, resistance movements propelled by 'exceptional' subjects (Harvey) can alter and defy the spatialities of power and subvert the given order, even if by ephemeral actions in the compact space of a square (Stavrides).

The memories of space

Space contains and accumulates several layers of memories proceeding from different historical times. As pointed out by Lefebvre (1991), the experiences that subjects have of space and the ways in which they activate those different memories are never linear. Even if there is a considerable amount of research on the processes of memorialization and issues related to the uses and problems of former massacre sites, it has rarely articulated these questions with the fact that spaces are also socially produced and therefore require a critical approach. Pierre Nora's notion of 'lieux de mémoire' (1986) – which tends towards an essentialist approach to emblematic national places, and is difficult to extrapolate to extra-European contexts, as the author himself recognized (Nora, 1998) – offered the main interpretative framework for much research on spaces of memory around the globe (for the Latin American case see, for instance, Jelin and Langland, 2003). An abundant scholarly corpus has studied the particularities, timings and political disputes around memorial sites and has reflected on the ethical and aesthetic problems they pose (as in the case of Ashworth and Hartmann, 2005; Barsalou and Baxter, 2007; Fleury and Walter, 2008; Williams, 2007; Winter, 1995). However, the relation between remnants and memory is not evident, and it must always be thought of in the context of how spaces are socially produced.

Memory is a complex process that carries and hides parts of the past while simultaneously modifying the content of what is being remembered (Benjamin, 1991). There is no transparent access to the past, which is irrecoverable, and can only persist in a different space and time. For this reason, the narratives of memory are central to the construction of 'imaginary geographies' (Gregory, 1994) that exceed the mere materiality of space. Memories are internalized in the body, modifying how the subjects inhabit space but also how they imagine it in the aftermath of violence (Colombo). Memories can not only reproduce and diffuse the effects of terror but can also bear traditions of emancipation that can be shared in, and joined to, contemporary spatial practices (Ahıska, Harvey).

Memory can grasp and retain what is gone, but sometimes the past assaults the present in ways that dislocate the chronological understanding of historical time. Following Derrida's conceptualization of 'hauntology' (Derrida, 1994), a number of scholars have drawn on the concept of haunting as a way to account for those pasts that continue to affect the present of the living (Buse and Stott, 1999; Davis, 2007) and for the unaccounted effects of mass murder, genocide, slavery and colonial oppression through generations (Etkind, 2009; Kwon, 2008; Jonker and Till, 2009; Schwab, 2010). Echoes of the past, spectres, ghostly appearances account for an unresolved past haunting the spaces of the present (Hockey et al., 2005; Pile, 2005; Schindel, 2014; Trigg, 2012) and transfigure familiar places, turning them into 'uncanny environments' (Rose, 2009). Avery Gordon (2008) has emphasized the particular affinity that links the figure of the ghost with the disappeared, an argument used in the analysis of the haunted spaces of post-dictatorship Argentina in this volume (Mandolessi). What cannot be accounted for through rational or scientific approaches, like haunting, can yet be named and imaged through the languages of art. The sphere of artistic representation is crucial for understanding how violent spaces are socially constructed and for observing their relation to subjectivity and the imagination (Das et al., 2000; Burgin, 1995). It is precisely in the field of the arts that the abstract conceptualization of space, traditionally associated with Euclidian geometry, was first questioned (Kern, 1983). Responses and approaches from the arts, literature and theatre are therefore given appropriate attention in this volume. Artistic approaches have the ability to reach those zones where intellectual and representational strategies fail. Art not only represents but also constructs spaces, and opens spaces of experience where academic reflection becomes dumb. In the renderings of the horrors of war through art, it is possible to trace a line from a figurative approach to the face to the intimacy of voice (Winter). The languages of art permit the creation of imaginary cities for resistance (Rath), articulating a mourning that cannot be elaborated in a merely realistic way (Mandolessi) and remembering places where one has never been (Mayorga). Artistic approaches to the spaces of violence might offer the only possible response to the dissolution of material remains (Dziuban, Schindel). The inclusion in this book of the fragments of Juan Mayorga's theatre piece about the multi-layered memories of Warsaw is meant to acknowledge the capacity of artistic language to reflect on historical matters in its own right.

Disappearance, memory and space: An international conversation

The idea for this book originated several years ago when we began to think about what concepts and theories could help us to grasp the problem of space in relation to enforced disappearances during the Argentine dictatorship (1976–83), which was at the centre of our research interests at that point. The regime that seized power there in 1976 aimed at putting an end to the intense political mobilization within the country. In the twentieth century five military coups had already interrupted the constitutional system and subsequently applied repressive policies, which included the persecution of political opponents. Convinced that repressive measures such as the prolonged imprisonment of dissidents did not interrupt the transmission of collective memories and fearing that open executions could provoke severe international condemnation, as had happened already with Pinochet's Chile after 1973, the armed forces opted to have their political enemies 'disappear'. A series of questions related to this specific form of violence concerned us then. How is a repressive method aimed at erasing all traces of the crime to be located and re-inscribed in space? Why does a crime that leaves no apparent material residue still reconfigure the social production and practice of space? How does it haunt places and individuals subsequently?

In tackling these questions and coming into contact with scholarly production on the spatial configurations and memories of other past massacres, we started a dialogue with colleagues of various national and disciplinary backgrounds. This exchange led us to a fruitful conversation that resulted in the organization of the Madrid symposium and the publication of this volume. The presence of several chapters committed to analysing enforced disappearance as a specific form of violence – of which the Argentine case became a paradigm – is, in part, a consequence of the above described process. It also bears testimony to the growing research interest in the issue of enforced disappearance worldwide, which attracted particular attention after the revelation of the existence of new forms of disappearances under the CIA's 'extraordinary renditions'. Furthermore, the practices and discourses of memory developed in relation to the figure of the disappeared in Latin America had a strong reception in other contexts, such as Spain in recent years (Capdepón, 2011; Elsemann, 2011; Ferrándiz, 2010) and even Turkey, as Ahıska discusses in her contribution to this volume. However, our goal is not to single out this particular form of state violence but, on the contrary, to compare and contrast its features with those of other repressive or genocidal practices, past and present. This book thus tells, among other things, a success story in the practice of transnational circulation of concepts and ideas beyond the North–South divide. It also represents an acknowledgement of the fact that, in times of multidirectional, transnational and transcultural memories (Rothberg, 2009; Assmann and Conrad, 2010; Radstone, 2011), contrasting past traumas and memories proceeding from diverse historical experiences can illuminate each other, provide a space for fruitful mutual learning and even foster the construction of 'geographically flexible networks' of resistance (Bosco, 2006).

The contributions gathered here stem from areas as varied as history, geography, sociology, political science, literature, cultural studies, philosophy, architecture and theatre. They engage with a multiplicity of spaces ranging from the central squares of the city to the rural 'monte' (the tropical forest of North Western Argentina), from the cells of the detention centres to the home, from the human face as a surface for the inscription of violence to water and air themselves as spaces where all traces disappear. The empirical referents studied by the authors are likewise multiple and include art works, memorials, testimonial pieces, interviews and documents. Some elements resonate through several chapters, like the Baltimore of the TV series 'The Wire' that Harvey considers characteristic of a type of urban capitalist formation and Gatti contrasts with the New Orleans of 'Treme', both authors acknowledging the growing cultural relevance acquired by this current media format. The book is also traversed by events that were topical when the chapters were being written, such as the demonstrations in the squares in Athens and Istanbul discussed by Stavrides and Ahıska. These reveal affinities between peoples' spatial practices that bring them closer to each other than governmental policies and nationalist discourses in Greece or Turkey might claim.

The structure of the book

The first part of the book deals with the ways in which extermination processes are inscribed in space. This includes the physical modifications on the landscape or the built environment, the alterations to the spatial practices of the subjects who inhabit those spaces in the aftermath of conflict and the way in which the spatial representations of those spaces are contested and disputed today by the actors involved. Chapter 1 by James Tyner, 'Violent Erasures and Erasing Violence: Contesting Cambodia's Landscapes of Violence' contrasts the violent erasure of space during the genocide in Cambodia with the repeated contemporary attempts to erase the traces of violence from the landscape. He argues that the social, spatial and temporal bounding of the remembrance of genocide serves to obfuscate our understanding of genocide and its legacy. Practices of annihilation are not spatially isolated but establish continuities and relations with (and within) social space at large. This is particularly striking in Chapter 2, 'Polish Landscapes of Memory at the Sites of Extermination: The Politics of Framing' by Zuzanna Dziuban. This chapter highlights the problem of the framing of Holocaust memory at the sites where it took place. While tracing the fate of two National Socialist extermination camps in Poland, Bełżec and Sobibór, Dziuban provides a critical contextualization of the commemorative efforts and interprets them through the prism of transformations of post-war Polish cultural politics of grief. That spaces of (past) violence can act as an arena for disputes in the present is also a central issue in Chapter 3, 'Spaces of Confrontation and Defeat: The Spatial Dispossession of the Revolution in Tucumán, Argentina', written by Pamela Colombo. The author of this chapter shows that the deterritorialization and reterritorialization carried out on the Tucumán's 'monte' – a territory in which direct confrontation between the military and guerrilla forces took place – have modified not only the material features but also the conditions which made it possible to imagine revolution as associated with that space. Using the concept of 'accumulation by dispossession' (Harvey, 2003), Colombo shows how the state can appropriate those spaces that challenge the established power, like the 'monte', not by occupation but by emptying them out. Spain is another case where spaces have been reconfigured by extreme state violence, for example in relation to the numerous – still largely undiscovered – mass graves dating back to the Civil War (1936–39). In Chapter 4, 'Subterranean Autopsies: Exhumations of Mass Graves in Contemporary Spain', Francisco Ferrándiz draws the possible political, judicial, scientific, media and associative maps of the post-mortem trajectories of the disappeared in Spain. According to his conceptual reading, the mass graves of Republican victims can be understood as a radical form of subterranean internal exile.

The second part of the book deals with spatial strategies that account for violence. How to represent spaces that were the object of violent policies of erasure? What responses can art offer to this problem? In Chapter 5, 'Faces, Voices, and the Shadow of Catastrophe', Jay Winter engages with a particular symbolic space, upon which the cultural elaboration of war and massacre is inscribed: the human face. According to Winter, representations of war in art are no longer configured through the face. He understands this shift in part as a reflection of the changing nature of war. In Chapter 6, the excerpts of the play *The Cartographer. Warsaw, 1:400,000* by Juan Mayorga, which is reproduced here in its first English translation by Sarah Maitland, offer a reflection on the connection between trauma, absence and space through the generations. This play shows how a city marked by extremely violent processes of exclusion and extermination acquires new meanings when examined in relation to the spaces lived and imagined there today. In Chapter 7, 'All Limits Were Exceeded Over There: The Chronotope of Terror in Modern Warfare and Testimony', Kirsten Mahlke analyses rhetorical manipulations of spatio-temporality by means of a theory and praxis of 'modern warfare' based on state terror. Drawing on Mikhail Bakhtin's concept of the chronotope, she addresses these distortions particularly in the representations of space–time perceptions of survivors of concentration camps and clandestine detention centres. The last chapter of this part leads us to the question of the possibilities and limits of representing what took place in concentrationary spaces. Art has played, and continues to play, a crucial role in attempting to represent such extreme spaces. In the case of Argentine concentrationary structures, in Chapter 8 Mariana Eva Perez shows how the space of the former clandestine detention centres exceeds the physicality of the camps and extends into the homes of the perpetrators who illegally appropriated the children of the disappeared. Based on post-dictatorship theatre in Argentina, this chapter addresses the disappearance of children in its paradoxical state/private configuration, as a biopolitical phenomenon that is still taking place within the uncanny space of the 'unhomely home'.

The third part of the book examines the ways in which the memories of traumatic pasts circulate and irrupt into the spaces of the present. What spaces are remembered and why? How is memory attached to concrete 'sites of horror' and how do state policies and social initiatives dispute the meaning of such sites? These questions inform Chapter 9, ' "The Whole Country Is a Monument": Framing Places of Terror in Post-War Germany', by Aleida Assmann. The author differentiates between places that are intentionally chosen and embraced for a memorial purpose and those that remain ignored and unmarked until they suddenly reappear and resurface unexpectedly, confronting the society with a history that it had preferred to forget. Assmann shows that sites of memory differ considerably from monuments, memorials and museums in that they are never congruent with the meaning given to them in retrospect: authentic historic sites can never be totally appropriated, nor made to disappear completely within a new geopolitical order. In other cases, the irruption of the past into the present takes the form of a haunting, as in the literature from post-dictatorship Argentina analysed by Silvana Mandolessi in Chapter 10, 'Haunted Houses, Horror Literature and the Space of Memory in Post-Dictatorship Argentine Literature'. Mandolessi analyses the category of space in some recent Argentine novels that draw on the literary tradition of the gothic and the fantastic. The author suggests that, on the one hand, the terror that dominates the social body finds a maximum concentration of space in the haunted house; on the other hand, she argues, the experience of the absence caused by disappearance manifests itself in haunted city landscapes. Chapter 11, 'Counter-Movement, Space and Politics: How the Saturday Mothers of Turkey Make Enforced Disappearances Visible' by Meltem Ahıska starts from an analysis of the Gezi square movement in 2013 in order to show how the histories repressed within the national frame were brought into a dialogue in the present through the prism of a particular place: Taksim Square. Ahıska examines how a counter-movement can play a vital role not only in producing a new space for politics but also in enacting political memory in the particular case of the Saturday Mothers – the mothers of the disappeared in Turkey. Chapter 12, 'An Orderly Landscape of Remnants: Notes for Reflecting on the Spatiality of the Disappeared' by Gabriel Gatti, analyses how the catastrophe of the forced disappearance of people redefined space by producing an orderly landscape of remains (above all of tangible remnants: bodily remains, remnants of spaces, scraps of files). The author proposes that the sphere of 'ordinary garbage' and that of 'extraordinary waste' are connected by the deployment of a similar expertise, based on techniques applied to the recovery of remnants. Irruptions and hauntings, albeit partially silenced, are part of the legacy left to Argentine society by the 'death flights' – the illegal method of killing used by the military which consisted of throwing political opponents alive from planes into the waters of the River Plate. Chapter 13, 'A Limitless Grave: Memory and Abjection of the Río de la Plata', by Estela Schindel, reflects on the legacy of the River Plate, a mass of water that has been historically charged with cultural and political associations in the Argentine imaginary, and on the artistic, forensic and judicial initiatives aimed at inscribing memory in this place-less territory. Despite these attempts, Schindel argues, there is an abject quality attached to the river that still pervades the everyday life in the city of Buenos Aires.

The last part of the book introduces the question of how spaces of domination can be disputed and resisted. This part also explores the uses and limitations of the concept of 'space of exception' on the one hand, analysing contemporary forms of state violence and, on the other, imagining emancipatory political practices. In Chapter 14, 'Spatialities of Exception', Pilar Calveiro shows that despite the changing regimes of power, the concentration camp continues to operate as an effective institution. Calveiro analyses the similarities and divergences of camp space configurations in three different repressive systems: the Nazi concentration camps, the clandestine detention centres in Argentina and the CIA 'black sites'. Her analysis reveals how each of these power regimes aims at different subjective effects and thus makes different uses of the space of confinement, constructing specific spatial configurations. What is the margin for resistance in each specific context? The question of resistance also informs Chapter 15, 'Imaginary Cities, Violence and Memory: A Literary Mapping', by Gudrun Rath. The capacity to imagine something different and to conceive of dystopian or emancipatory spaces has a long literary tradition, especially in Latin America. This chapter engages in the first place with the possible functions of the imaginary cities in contexts of violence and repression. Secondly, the author proposes that these spatial expressions can be understood not only as confined to the mimetic function of literature, but also as a way to regain 'the right to the city' (Harvey, 2012). An utopian spirit is present as well in Chapter 16, 'Occupied Squares and the Urban "State of Exception": In, Against and Beyond the City of Enclaves', written by Stavros Stavrides. 'Squares Movements' have emerged almost unexpectedly in many metropolises throughout the world. Stavrides argues that even though they were exceptional and short lived, the squares movements are urban experiments that have produced an interesting counterexample to the prevailing urban model of the 'city of enclaves'. In his view, dissident squares created glimpses of a possible 'city of thresholds' where, at the same time, a different form of urban exception could emerge.

The book concludes, as it started, under the sign of Federico García Lorca. The interview with David Harvey that is reproduced in Chapter 17 took place at the Hotel Castelar of Buenos Aires, where the Spanish poet lived during his visit to Argentina in 1933 and where his room is still kept exactly as it was, as a piece of historical testimony. In the conversation, Harvey highlights precisely the political potential of memory, by providing examples of its powerful transmission through epochs and regions. In doing so, Harvey revisits many of the questions analysed previously in the book, revealing them in a different light. Harvey addresses the ambiguity of memorials, the misuses and limitations of the notion of 'space of exception' for understanding oppression and the violence deployed in everyday 'living space' by neo-liberal state policies. In a passionate statement advocating the reintegration of historical memory and justice with an emancipated urban life, Harvey concludes by emphasizing the political force of memory for creating 'spaces of hope'.

Bibliography

Agamben, Giorgio. 1998. *Homo Sacer: Sovereign Power and Bare Life*. Stanford: Stanford University Press.
Agamben, Giorgio. 2000. *Means Without End. Notes on Politics*. Minneapolis: University of Minnesota Press.
Ashworth, Gregory and Rudi Hartmann, eds. 2005. *Horror and Human Tragedy Revisited: The Management of Sites of Atrocities for Tourism*. New York: Cognizant.
Assmann, Aleida and Sebastian Conrad, eds. 2010. *Memory in a Global Age. Discourses, Practices and Trajectories, Memory Studies*. Basingstoke: Palgrave Macmillan.
Barsalou, Judy and Victoria Baxter. 2007. *The Urge to Remember: The Role of Memorials in Social Reconstruction and Transitional Justice*. Washington: United States Institute of Peace.
Bauman, Zygmunt. 1989. *Modernity and the Holocaust*. Cambridge: Polity Press.
Benjamin, Walter. 1991. *Gesammelte Schriften*. Frankfurt: Suhrkamp.
Blair, Elsa. 2005. *Muertes violentas. La teatralización del exceso*. Medelllín: Editorial Universidad de Antioquia.
Bosco, Fernando. 2006. 'The Madres de Plaza de Mayo and Three Decades of Human Rights Activism: Embeddedness, Emotions and Social Movements'. *Annals of the Association of American Geographers*, 96/2: 342–365.
Burgin, Victor. 1995. *In/Different Spaces: Place and Memory in Visual Culture*. Berkeley: University of California Press.
Buse, Peter and Andrew Stott, eds. 1999. *Ghosts: Deconstruction, Psychoanalysis, History*. Basingstoke: Palgrave Macmillan.
Calveiro, Pilar. 1998. *Poder y desaparición. Los campos de concentración en Argentina*. Buenos Aires: Colihue.
Capdepón, Ulrike. 2011. 'The Influence of Human Rights Discourses and Practices from the Southern Cone on the Confrontation with the Franco Dictatorship in Spain'. *Human Security Perspectives*, 1: 84–90.
Colombo, Pamela. 2011. 'Espacio y desaparición: los campos de concentración en Argentina'. *Isegoría*, 45: 639–652.
Colombo, Pamela. 2013. *Espacios de desaparición. Espacios vividos e imaginarios tras la desaparición forzada de personas (1974–1983) en la provincia de Tucumán, Argentina*. Unpublished doctoral thesis in sociology, Universidad del País Vasco, Bilbao.

Coward, Martin. 2009. *Urbicide. The Politics of Urban Destruction*. New York: Routledge.
Das, Veena, Arthur Kleinman, Mamphela Ramphele and Pamela Reynolds, eds. 2000. *Violence and Subjectivity*. Berkeley: University of California Press.
Davis, Colin. 2007. *Haunted Subjects: Deconstruction, Psychoanalysis and the Return of the Dead*. Basingstoke: Palgrave Macmillan.
de Certeau, Michel. 2011. *The Practice of Everyday Life*. Berkeley: University of California Press.
Derrida, Jacques. 1994. *Specters of Marx: The State of the Debt, the Work of Mourning and the New International*. New York: Routledge.
Diken, Bülent and Carsten Bagge Laustsen. 2005. *The Culture of Exception. Sociology Facing the Camp*. London and New York: Routledge.
Ek, Richard. 2006. 'Giorgio Agamben and the Spatialitites of the Camp: An Introduction'. *Geografikka Annualer*, no. 88 B/4: 363–386.
Elden, Stuart. 2009. *Terror and Territory: The Spatial Extent of Sovereignty*. Minneapolis: University of Minnesota Press.
Elsemann, Nina. 2011. *Umkämpfte Erinnerungen. Die Bedeutung lateinamerikanischer Erfahrungen für die spanische Geschichtspolitik nach Franco*. Frankfurt: Campus.
Etkind, Alexander. 2009. 'Post-Soviet Hauntology: Cultural Memory of the Soviet Terror'. *Constellations*, 16/1: 182–200.
Feierstein, Daniel. 2007. *El genocidio como práctica social. Entre el nazismo y la experiencia argentina*. Buenos Aires: Fondo de Cultura Económica.
Ferrándiz, Francisco. 2010. 'De las fosas comunes a los derechos humanos: El descubrimiento de las desapariciones forzadas en la España contemporánea'. *Revista de Antropología Social*, 19: 161–189.
Fleury, Béatrice and Jacques Walter, eds. 2008. *Memoires des Lieux de detention et de massacre*. Nancy: Presses universitaires de Nancy.
Foucault, Michael. 1975. *Surveiller et punir. Naissace de la prison*. Paris: Gallimard.
Gillis, John R., ed. 1996. *Commemorations. The Politics of National Identity*. Princeton: Princeton University Press.
González-Ruibal, Alfredo. 2007. 'Making Things Public. Archaeologies of the Spanish Civil War'. *Public Archaeology*, 6/4: 203–226.
Gordon, Avery. 2008. *Ghostly Matters. Haunting and the Sociological Imagination*. Minneapolis: University of Minnesota Press.
Graham, Stephen, ed. 2004. *Cities, War, and Terrorism. Towards an Urban Geopolitics*. Oxford: Wiley-Blackwell.
Graham, Stephen et al. 2008. *Architectures of Fear. Terrorism and the Future of Urbanism in the West*, Barcelona: Centre de Cultura Contemporània de Barcelona.
Gregory, Derek. 1994. *Geographical Imaginations*. Massachusetts: Blackwell Publishers.
Harvey, David. 1990. *The Condition of Postmodernity. An Enquire into the Originis of Cultural Change*. London: Basil Blackwell.
Harvey, David. 2003. *The New Imperialism*. Oxford: Oxford University Press.
Harvey, David. 2006. 'Space as a Keyword'. In *David Harvey. Critical Reader*, edited by N. Castree and D. Gregory. Oxford: Blackwell Publishing.
Harvey, David. 2012. *Rebel Cities: From the Right to the City to the Urban Revolution*. London: Verso.
Hockey, Jenny, Bridget Penhale and David Sibley. 2005. 'Environments of Memory: Home Space, Later Life and Grief'. In *Emotional Geographies*, edited by Joyce Davidson et al. Burlington: Ashgate.
Jelin, Elizabeth and Victoria Langland, eds. 2003. *Monumentos, memoriales y marcas territoriales*. Madrid: Siglo Veintiuno Editores.

Jonker, Julian and Karen Till. 2009. 'Mapping and Excavating Spectral Traces in Post-Apartheid Cape Town'. *Memory Studies*, 2/3: 303–335.
Keenan, Thomas and Eyal Weizman. 2012. *Mengele's Skull: The Advent of a Forensic Aesthetics*. Berlin: Sternberg Press.
Kern, Stephen. 1983. *The Culture of Time and Space 1880–1918*. Massachusetts: Harvard University Press.
Kohn, Margaret. 2003. *Radical Space. Building the House of the People*. Ithaca and London: Cornell University Press.
Kwon, Heonik. 2008. *Ghosts of War in Vietnam*. Cambridge: Cambridge University Press.
Lefebvre, Henri. 1991. *The Production of Space*. Oxford: Blackwell Publishing.
Massey, Doreen. 1994. *Space, Place, and Gender*. Minneapolis: University of Minnesota Press.
Myers, Adrian and Gabriel Moshenska, eds. 2011. *Archaeologies of Internment*. New York: Springer.
Navaro-Yashin, Yael. 2012. *The Make-Believe Space. Affective Geography in a Postwar Polity*. Durham: Duke University Press.
Nora, Pierre. 1986. *Les lieux de mémoire: La République*. Paris: Gallimard.
Nora, Pierre. 1998. 'La aventura de *Les Lieux de mémoire*', *Memoria e Historia*, edited by Josefina Cuesta Bustillo. Madrid: Marcial Pons.
Oslender, Ulrich. 2007. 'Spaces of Terror and Fear on Colombia's Pacific Coast'. In *Violent Geographies. Fear, Terror, and Political Violence*, edited by Derek Gregory and Allan Pred. New York: Routledge.
Pécaut, Daniel. 2000. 'Configuration of Space, Time, and Subjectivity in a Context of Terror: The Colombian Example'. *International Journal of Politics, Culture and Society*, 14/1.
Pile, Steve. 2005. *Real Cities. Modernity, Spaces and the Phantasmagorias of City Life*. Londres: SAGE Publications.
Radstone, Susannah. 2011. 'What Place Is This? Transcultural Memory and the Locations of Memory Studies'. *Parallax*, 17/4: 109–123.
Rose, Gillian. 2009. 'Who Cares for Which Dead and How? British Newspaper Reporting of the Bombings in London, July 2005'. *Geoforum*, 40: 46–54.
Rothberg, Michael. 2009. *Multidirectional Memory. Remembering the Holocaust in the Age of Decolonization*. Stanford: Stanford University Press.
Schindel, Estela. 2012. ' "Now the Neighbors Lose Their Fear": Restoring the Social Network Around Former Sites of Terror in Argentina'. *The International Journal of Transitional Justice*, 6: 467–485.
Schindel, Estela. 2014. 'Ghosts and *Compañeros*: Haunting Stories and the Quest for Justice around Argentina's Former Terror Sites'. *Rethinking History*, 18/2: 244–264.
Schlögel, Karl. 2003. *Im Räume lesen wir die Zeit*. Munich: Carl Hanser Verlag.
Schofield, John, William Gray Johnson and Colleen M. Beck, eds. 2002. *Matériel Culture. The Archaeology of Twentieth-Century Conflict*. London: Routledge.
Schwab, Gabriele. 2010. *Haunting Legacies: Violent Histories and Transgenerational Trauma*. New York: Columbia University Press.
Sofsky, Wolfgang. 1997. *The Order of Terror: The Concentration Camp*. Princeton: Princeton University Press.
Soja, Edward. 1989. *Postmodern Geographies. The Reassertion of Space in Critical Theory*. London: Verso.
Sturdy Colls, Caroline. 2012. 'Holocaust Archaeology: Archaeological Approaches to Landscapes of Nazi Genocide and Persecution'. *Journal of Conflict Archaeology*, 7/2: 70–104.

Thrift, Nigel. 2007. 'Immaculate Warfare: The Spatial Politics of Extreme Violence'. In *Violent Geographies: Fear, Terror and Political Violence*, edited by Derek Gregory and Allan Pred. New York: Routledge.
Till, Karen, ed. 2010. *Mapping Spectral Traces*. Blacksburg: Virginia Tech College of Architecture and Urban Affairs.
Trigg, Dylan. 2012. *The Memory of Place. A Phenomenology of the Uncanny*. Ohio: Ohio University Press.
Tyner, James. 2008. *The Killing of Cambodia: Geography, Genocide, and the Unmaking of Space*. Hampshire: Ashgate.
Tyner, James. 2012. *Genocide and the Geographical Imagination: Life and Death in Germany, China, and Cambodia*. Plymouth: Rowman & Littlefield Publishers.
Weizman, Eyal. 2007. 'On extraterritoriality'. In *Arxipèlag d'excepcions*, edited by Ramoneda et al. Barcelona: Centre de Cultura Contemporània de Barcelona, 13–20.
Weizman, Eyal. 2010. 'Forensic Architecture: Only the Criminal Can Solve the Crime'. *Radical Philosophy. Journal of Socialist and Feminist Philosophy*, 164: 9–24.
Williams, Paul. 2007. *The Global Rush to Commemorate Atrocities*. Oxford: Berg.
Winter, Jay. 1995. *Sites of Memory, Sites of Mourning. The Great War in European Cultural History*. London: Canton.
Zarankin, Andrés and Melisa Salerno. 2011. 'The Engineering of Genocide: An Archaeology of Dictatorship in Argentina'. In *Archeologies of Internment*, edited by Adrian Myers and Gabriel Moshenska. New York: Springer.

Part I
Spatial Inscriptions of Annihilation

1
Violent Erasures and Erasing Violence: Contesting Cambodia's Landscapes of Violence

James A. Tyner

All that remains of Keat Sophal is a photograph (Figure 1.1). We know little about her death, and even less about her life. Documentary evidence indicates that she was arrested on 13 April 1977. She was detained at Tuol Sleng, the infamous 'security center' code-named 'S-21', for 99 days until the day of her 'termination' on 22 July 1977. Her remains have never been identified; it is not known if anyone remembers her in life.

We know that she was Khmer Rouge cadre; her job was to take care of children. No information has been forthcoming about her family or what she did prior to the time of the genocide. Nor do we know why she was arrested or killed or what she experienced while detained at Tuol Sleng. In all likelihood, she was interrogated and tortured; perhaps she was raped. No confession or record of her 'crimes' remain. Was she found 'guilty' of traitorous activities to the state? Was she found 'delinquent' in her patriotic duties? Or was Sophal simply arrested because she was associated with someone else charged of a crime? It is not known. It is also not known whether she died at S-21, or was taken to the nearby killing fields, Choeung Ek, to be killed.

Two dates – a date of arrest and a date of termination – and a photograph. This is all that remains of the life and death of Keat Sophal. Her facial expression suggests resignation. As a Khmer Rouge cadre, Sophal most likely knew of her eventual fate. By the summer of 1977, she had probably witnessed many deaths and was well aware that once accused by Angkar her fate was sealed. In Cambodia, during the time of the genocide, to be accused was to be guilty; to be guilty was to be sentenced to death. Keat Sophal was one of approximately two million people who died throughout the Cambodian genocide. And in certain respects, her legacy – and photograph – raises a disturbing question for our subsequent remembrance and memorialization of

22 *Spatial Inscriptions of Annihilation*

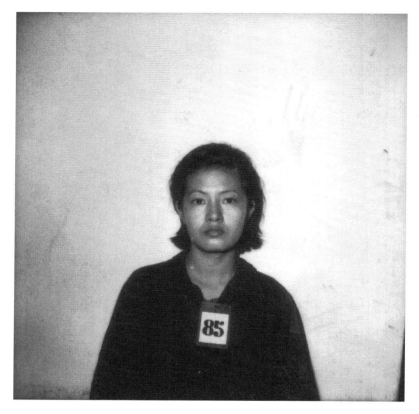

Figure 1.1 Mugshot of Keat Sophal, arrested on 13 April 1977. She was detained for 99 days until she was executed on 22 July
Courtesy of Documentation Center of Cambodia.

genocide. As Bronfen asks, 'Do we see the real, while denying the representation or do we see the representation, thus putting the real under erasure?' (Bronfen, 1990, p.304).

In Cambodia, we see clearly that how we understand the past – and how the past is spatially inscribed – matters. It matters, as Elizabeth Lunstrum writes, 'for who has access to and who can legitimately claim ownership of certain spaces; it matters for whether and how certain spaces can be transformed and reinvented; and it matters for who can reap the benefits of these transformations and equally who must make sacrifices to enable them' (Lunstrum, 2010, pp.131–132). During the Cambodian genocide, the Khmer Rouge sought to erase space in an attempt to construct a communal utopia. In the process, however, the Khmer Rouge produced a 'non-place', an alienated and inauthentic place. Forty years later the coordinates of this place are barely legible, hidden from view, ironically, by the ongoing attempts to bring those responsible to justice. In this chapter I contrast the violent erasure of space during the genocide with the repeated attempts to (selectively) erase violence from the contemporary landscape. Situating the ongoing memorialization of Cambodia's recent genocidal violence within the context of a spatially informed 'politics of memory', I highlight that current efforts to *remember* the genocide are spatially, temporally and socially bounded; and that this bounding serves to construct a particular, officially sanctioned narrative while simultaneously limiting the emergence of counter-narratives.

Cambodia and the politics of memory

Memory is spatially constituted; it is 'attached to "sites" that are concrete and physical – the burial places, cathedrals, battlefields, prisons that embody tangible notions of the past – as well as to "sites" that are non-material – the celebrations, spectacles and rituals that provide an aura of the past' (Hoelscher and Alderman, 2004, p.349). However, memorials and monuments are also political. As Dwyer explains, memorials and monuments 'are inextricably entwined in the production of the past'; however, these 'landscapes seek to present in tangible form the past itself, not the processes through which the "past" is produced' (Dwyer, 2004, p.425). In short, landscapes represent, and are represented by, political processes: a politics of memory. A politics of memory thus highlights the observation that what is commemorated is not synonymous with what has happened in the past (Dwyer and Alderman, 2008, p.167). Rather, the past – that which is potentially remembered – becomes subject to dominant power relations that determine what, if anything, is memorialized.

A politics of memory is intimately connected to the 'production of space'. Following Henri Lefebvre, every society produces its own space. He argued that every system of economic organization, whether feudalism or slavery, mercantilism or industrial capitalism, is manifest on the landscape. However, space is neither an '*a priori* condition' of institutions or structures, nor is it 'an aggregate of the places of locations' of phenomena or products. Space, according to Lefebvre, is *produced* via competing discursive claims and material practices. However, since each mode of production has its own particular space, the shift from one mode to another must entail the production of new space. Landscapes of feudalism give way to landscapes of merchant capitalism; landscapes of merchant capitalism are refashioned into landscapes of industrial capitalism. In an ongoing process of dialectical materialism, as revolutions transform one economic system into another, the landscape reflects the accumulated sedimentation of previous economic systems. Lefebvre also theorized that as social space is produced and reproduced in connection with the forces of production, these forces, as they develop, do not take over pre-existing, empty or neutral space. Rather, dialectically, new forms of socio-economic organization are secreted onto the remnants of earlier forms.

In 1975 the material landscape of Cambodia would have revealed vestiges of its past histories and geographies. It would have reflected an 'indigenous' pre-colonial Khmer society; but also present, unevenly, would have been the trappings of French colonialism and, to a lesser extent, an American presence. For the Khmer Rouge, however, in accordance with their understanding of 'total revolution', it was not acceptable to simply build on earlier foundations. For the Khmer Rouge, the planned and organized spaces of Democratic Kampuchea were not to be tainted by any association with Cambodia's pre-existing spaces. Instead, the Khmer Rouge explicitly sought to erase time and space to create (in their minds) a pure utopian society. This is seen in the Khmer Rouge's decision to evacuate Phnom Penh and other urban areas; it is seen also in the elimination of those people who were previously associated with Western society: doctors, nurses and teachers. The intent of the Khmer Rouge leadership was not to re-create the indigenous spaces of the Angkorian Kingdom (approximately the ninth to the fourteenth centuries) but instead to make an entirely new, modern, productive communal society. This transformation entailed wiping clean the slate that was Cambodia. Not only did 17 April 1975 mark, in the words of the Khmer Rouge, 'Year Zero'; it also marked 'Ground Zero'. Both time and space were to begin anew.

But what 'place' emerged as a result of Khmer Rouge practice? I suggest that Democratic Kampuchea became a site of placelessness. Following Edward Relph, it is not just the identity of a place that is important, but also the identity that a person or group has with that place, in particular whether they are experiencing it as an insider or an outsider (Relph, 1976). Relph's argument conforms to existing literature on genocide, and specifically how different groups are considered to be 'outsiders' and thus socially excluded. Relph, however, expands our understanding through a discussion of various levels of intensity of the experience of outsideness and insideness in places. Specifically, he develops a seven-fold typology in an attempt to flesh out the various 'experiences' of being an outsider or an insider in any given place. Here, I draw on two of these relationships: 'objective outsideness' and 'existential insideness'. According to Relph, objective outsideness is a perspective whereby all places are viewed scientifically and passively; accordingly, it dovetails readily with Lefebvre's theorization of representations of space. Objective outsideness involves a deep separation of person and place, and has a long tradition in both military and urban planning. Such a perspective reduces places either to the single dimension of location, or to a space of located objects and activities. Conversely, existential insideness constitutes the most fundamental and 'intense' relationship of experience to place. To experience a place as an existential insider, one experiences place without deliberate or self-conscious reflection, yet all the while knowing that the place is full of significance. For Relph, this is an insideness that most people experience when 'at home': places 'are lived and dynamic, full with meanings...that are known and experienced without reflection' (1976, p.61).

The Khmer Rouge leadership approached the revolution from the standpoint of 'objective outsiders'. This may strike some as odd, given that the Khmer Rouge must certainly be seen as 'insiders' to Cambodia; indeed, the genocide of Cambodia has repeatedly been re-presented as an 'auto-genocide'. The Khmer Rouge were not 'foreigners' who came to Cambodia; they did not consider themselves as a separate people – as was the case in the Holocaust, Rwanda or the former Yugoslavia. However, many of the CPK leadership came from Cambodia's elite. They had little or no exposure to the day-to-day lives of the peasantry. They did not experience Cambodia as 'existential insiders'; they were not necessarily privy to the deeply felt emotional bonds between the people and their lands. Furthermore, many of the CPK leaders were schooled in French institutions. On the one hand, this further instilled a separation between the revolutionaries and the people of Cambodia. On the other hand, much of their French-based education – including their schooling in Marxism – was positivist in orientation. Marx, of course, proposed a scientific and objective interpretation of revolution. I argue that the Khmer Rouge looked upon Cambodia as detached observers; they were the planners and designers of a revolution and of a place. Such a perspective is evident in the various policies and practices produced by the Khmer Rouge (for example, the Party's Four-Year Plan), whereby they provided a pragmatic understanding of the revolution. The Khmer Rouge behaved much as 'scientists' or 'regional planners' might approach their tasks, delimiting the problem, establishing parameters and identifying solutions. Khmer Rouge documents are devoid of any qualities that might be considered as displaying an existential (or even empathetic) insideness. The Khmer Rouge who prepared these documents – notably Pol Pot, Nuon Chea and Ieng Sary – were not interested in how places were to be experienced emotionally, of how different regions might exhibit different meanings and experiences. Rather, in their violent pursuit of conformity, the Khmer Rouge deliberately sought to eliminate the 'individualized' or 'personalized' attachment to place.

The conformity sought by the Khmer Rouge is well-established. They attempted to promote a singular sameness of people, one based on an idealized imaginary of the peasantry. All people were to dress and groom alike. Men and women were to wear black peasant garb; colourful clothing was banned. Hairstyles were regulated, with short hair imposed on all. People were to eat collectively, in communal dining halls. Marriages, likewise, were to be arranged by the Party, for the collective utility of the state. Such conformity, I argue, relates directly to Relph's thesis of 'placelessness'. Relph suggested that a 'sense of place' may be authentic and genuine, or inauthentic and artificial. An authentic sense of place suggests a belonging to a place and of knowing this without having to reflect on it. Such an authentic and unselfconscious sense of place remains important, for it provides a significant source of identity to individuals and communities. Conversely, an 'inauthentic' sense of place entails a weakening of the identity of places. The Khmer Rouge, in their attempts to promote uniformity and conformity, produced a landscape of placelessness and inauthenticity. The Khmer Rouge sought to impose a radical and utopian geographical imaginary. The Khmer Rouge, through their annihilation of space, their destruction of cities, their severing of social relations, their violent enforcement of conformity and obedience, attempted to obliterate all that was known, felt and lived. Consequently, just as the Khmer Rouge sought to erase the previous spatial practices embedded within the landscapes of Cambodia, so too did they attempt to produce a new place that was conceived and designed to serve the revolution. Just as people were expected to serve the revolution – with a rifle in one hand and a hoe in the other – so too were places to serve the revolution.

The politics of memory in post-democratic Kampuchea

On 25 December 1978 Vietnamese forces totalling over 100,000 surged into Democratic Kampuchea. They were joined by approximately 20,000 Cambodians, many of whom were former Khmer Rouge cadre who had established a government-in-exile known as the National Salvation Front. After years of escalating tension and sporadic fighting, the move by Vietnam was portrayed as an act of liberation: to bring an end to nearly four years of genocide. For many other states – including both Democratic Kampuchea and the United States, Vietnam's intervention was portrayed as an invasion.

The disorganized forces of the Khmer Rouge were ill prepared to withstand the Vietnamese onslaught and, on 7 January, Phnom Penh fell. Soon thereafter, the leaders of the Hanoi-backed National Salvation Front declared the People's Republic of Kampuchea (PRK). Just as Cambodia ceased to exist, so too did Democratic Kampuchea. However, unlike Cambodia, which was *erased* by the Khmer Rouge, Democratic Kampuchea was not to be erased, but rather re-presented as one might alter a photograph. Such a production was necessary, in part, because of the broader geopolitical context. The PRK was viewed by the international community as a Vietnamese-puppet government; it was thus denied recognition – and aid – from most other governments. In particular, the United States, China and ASEAN refused recognize the PRK. As Tully writes, the 'very countries that had conspired to drag Cambodia to its ruin were now set on blocking its recovery' (Tully, 2005, p.203). Indeed, largely through the efforts of both China and the United States, the Khmer Rouge continued to occupy Cambodia's seat at the United Nations General Assembly. Faced with intense geopolitical opposition, the

PRK (and its Vietnamese backers) was impelled to re-present their actions – as well as those of the Khmer Rouge – through a politics of memory.

In Cambodia today there are over 300 documented 'killing fields'; approximately 200 former prison/torture sites; and more than 100 memorials related to the genocide. However, for many visitors to the country, Cambodia's genocidal past is circumscribed to two sites: the Tuol Sleng Museum of Genocide Crimes and the Choeung Ek Center for Genocide Crimes (Hughes, 2008; Sion, 2011; Tyner et al., 2012). These two sites have become internationally (in)famous in their representation of mass violence and tragedy. However, as Dwyer and Alderman (Dwyer and Alderman, 2008, p.168) remind us, memorials 'narrate history in selective and controlled ways – hiding as much as they reveal'. There is always and already a 'politics of memory' associated with the commemoration of the past.

In the days following the collapse of Phnom Penh, two Vietnamese photojournalists were drawn towards a particular compound by the smell of decomposing bodies (Chandler, 1999, p.2). Within the compound, as Chandler describes, the two men came across the corpses of several recently murdered men; some were chained to iron beds in rooms that once had been classrooms (Chandler, 1999, p.3). Over the next several days the Vietnamese and their Cambodian assistants discovered thousands of documents: mugshot photographs (including that of Keat Sophal) and undeveloped negatives, hundreds of cadre notebooks, numerous DK publications and myriad instruments of torture and detainment (Chandler, 1999, p.3).

What the photojournalists had uncovered was the former security centre known as S-21. Located in the southern part of Phnom Penh, S-21 was a former high school that had been converted in 1976 into a primary facility for the detention, torture and execution of suspected enemies of the Khmer Rouge. Throughout its brief existence, S-21 received more than 12,000 prisoners; less than 300 detainees are known to have survived. And while S-21 was but one of the approximately 200 'security centres' established throughout Democratic Kampuchea, it was significant in that most of the prisoners at S-21 were former Khmer Rouge cadres and soldiers accused of betraying the revolution (Dy, 2007, p.42).

Leadership of the PRK saw a political opportunity at S-21. According to Hughes (Hughes, 2003, p.26), the long-term 'national and international legitimacy of the People's Republic of Kampuchea hinged on the exposure of the violent excesses of Pol Pot...and the continued production of a coherent memory of the past, that is, of liberation and reconstruction at the hands of a benevolent fraternal state'. Under the guidance of Mai Lam, a Vietnamese colonel who was fluent in Khmer and had extensive experience in legal studies and museology, the site was rapidly transformed into an internationally known 'museum of genocide' (Chandler, 1999, p.4). Indeed, by 25 January 1979 – a mere two weeks since the 'discovery' of Tuol Sleng – a group of journalists from socialist countries was invited; these were the

28 *Spatial Inscriptions of Annihilation*

Figure 1.2 Tuol Sleng Security-Center, Phnom Penh, Cambodia
Photograph by James Tyner.

first official visitors to Tuol Sleng (Chandler, 1999, p.4). The Museum was officially opened to the public in July 1980.

As a museum, S-21 was kept largely intact with only minor modifications to the compound made (Figure 1.2). Surrounded by a corrugated tin fence topped with coils of barbed wire, Tuol Sleng consists of four three-storey concrete buildings arranged in a U-shape pattern around a grassy courtyard dotted with palm trees. In the middle is the former administrative building and current site of the museum's archives. To the left of the courtyard are 14 tombstones and hanging poles. Visitors, upon their entrance, are directed first to Building A, located at the southern end of the compound.[1] This building includes the torture rooms. All are empty save for the rusty metal beds and shackles and various torture instruments. The corpses have been removed, replaced by grainy photographs of the dead bodies discovered in January 1979. Even the blood was left on the floor – until finally cleansed in 2010.

Adjoining Building A are two buildings that were used to detain prisoners. Building B consists of large classrooms that were converted into communal holding cells. Now, these vacuous rooms are filled with thousands of black-and-white photographs taken of the prisoners upon their entry to Tuol Sleng. Keat Sophal's photograph is displayed in this room; her image, like all others, remains nameless. Building C was likewise used to detain prisoners. However, in this building the former classrooms were subdivided with brick walls to create individual 'private' cells for important prisoners. Inside the smaller cells are shackles and chains. Directly opposite Building A, on the northern end of the compound, is Building D. Under the Khmer Rouge, this building was also used to detain prisoners. It now houses various instruments of torture, thousands of shackles and disinterred skulls.

As a museum, Toul Sleng is remarkable for its literal and metaphoric silences. There is little textual material; most photographs and exhibits are unmarked. Such a minimalist approach was (and is) deliberate. At one level, the museum seemingly provides an 'authentic' experience, one where visitors can enter into cells or interrogation rooms 'just as the rooms were' when prisoners were actually detained and tortured. The intent is clear: to signify that these crimes took place. But the attendant question of why these crimes took place remains largely unasked and unanswered. And thus, at another level, we unconsciously experience the museum as a political lesson – as a circumscribed narrative of genocidal violence that is both universal and particular. For it was the intent of Mai Lam, and the PRK more generally, to provide not a conceptual or contextual understanding of S-21, or the Khmer Rouge, or even of the genocide, but rather to affect a separation between the crimes of the Khmer Rouge and the newly-installed government of the People's Republic of Kampuchea – itself dominated by former Khmer Rouge members. In other words, the physical presence of actual artefacts represents, paradoxically, a more generic experience of mass violence and torture.

The display of 'physical horrors' – the shackles, instruments of torture and skulls – serves political goals: the legitimacy of political rule in the country (Sion, 2011, p.3). As Chandler explains, 'Mai Lam wanted to arrange Cambodia's recent past to fit the requirements of the PRK and its Vietnamese mentors as well as the long-term needs, as he saw them, of the Cambodian people' (Chandler, 1999, p.5). The former would take precedence over the latter. Indeed, as Sion argues, the 'rush to turn a death site into a gallery for visitors is [an] indication that the new leadership had less concern about the memory of victims than about using the site for immediate political purposes' (Sion, 2011, p.5).

Memorial exhibits at S-21 are graphic and poignant, yet devoid of 'history' and 'geography'. While visitors experience the photographic stares of people long since dead, there is little to indicate who they were, where they died, or (most importantly) why they died. Only a select few 'faces' are named, as the genocide was to be re-presented as the product of a small clique of Khmer Rouge cadre, notably Pol Pot, Ieng Sary, Nuon Chea and Khieu Samphan. Moreover, the actions of these few people are portrayed as isolated events, devoid of any assistance from the Vietnamese Communist Party or the international community – including the People's Republic of China. These re-presentations are important, given that the PRK was both dominated by former Khmer Rouge cadre who either participated in, or witnessed, crimes (Sion, 2011, p.4). Thus, rather than directly addressing the violent past, the new regime promoted (and continues to promote) national 'reconciliation' through a selective erasure of the past.

The Tuol Sleng Museum of Genocide Crimes is linked – symbolically and in historical practice – to another memorial site: the killing fields of Choeung Ek. In the early 1980s, forensic teams of the PRK excavated a mass grave site located 15 kilometres south of Phnom Penh. Once an orchard and later a Chinese cemetery, the site was utilized by the Khmer Rouge for mass executions – most of whom were former detainees at Tuol Sleng. In total, an estimated 9,000 victims were killed and buried at the site. In 1989 however the site was opened to the public, dominated by the erection of a monumental stupa, filled with skulls and other bones visible through windows on all four sides. As both Hughes (2008) and Sion (2011) explain, the entire memorial is geared towards international tourists and, consequently, towards the promotion of both a political message and economic profit. As with Tuol Sleng, little historical background is given as to how the Khmer Rouge came to power, what drove their ideology, how they implemented their genocidal policy and how they were later defeated (Sion, 2011, p.8).

The killing fields of Choeung Ek have undergone significant, albeit superficial, renovations. Throughout the 1990s and into the twenty-first century, the site remained largely undisturbed after the initial excavations. A simple dirt road led to a simple entrance; a small 'gift' store sat forlornly to the side. In 2005, however, a Japanese corporation, JC Royal, obtained from the Cambodian government a 30-year license to operate the site. In return, JC Royal pays an annual fee of US$15,000 and awards an undisclosed number of scholarships to Cambodian students (Sion, 2011). Now, visitors to Choeung Ek – the overwhelming majority of whom are foreign – are confronted with an elaborate gated entrance, a ticket counter, public toilets, a renovated gift shop (where it is possible to buy a replica 'Khmer Rouge' uniform) and an air-conditioned screening room showing a brief documentary of the genocide. The once-dirt road has been replaced by tarmac, and a series of cafes and a miniature golf range dot the journey. The ongoing memorialization of Cheoung Ek, however, continues to provide little understanding for visitors. The site is more of a profit-making venture than it is a site to reflect upon genocide or to gain insight into the violence that gripped Cambodia during the 1970s.

Both Tuol Sleng and Cheoung Ek stand in marked contrast to other, less visible sites of mass violence (Tyner et al., 2012). For throughout Cambodia there are literally hundreds of unmarked sites of brutality that remain hidden in plain sight. One such place is the Koh Sla Dam. Some 60 kilometres south of Phnom Penh, nestled among the rolling hills of Kampot province, sits an altogether unremarkable earthen structure. Spanning nearly 12 kilometres in length, 15 metres high and 20 metres wide, what remains of the Koh Sla Dam seems at peace among the short grass and scrub, fish ponds and stilt houses. But the peacefulness of the location conceals a more violent past. For the dam itself was born of starvation, disease, exposure and execution. Nine thousand men, women and children perished here, killed or left to die at the hands of the Khmer Rouge. However, unlike Tuol Sleng and Cheoung Ek, the landscape of Koh Sla bears no memorial. There are no signs detailing the violence that formed the landscape; no monuments to the dead. The landscape of Koh Sla is remarkable precisely for being so *un-marked* (Tyner et al., 2012).

In 1973, Khmer Rouge cadre began work on the dam. Thousands of Cambodians were forcibly relocated to the site. Conditions were deplorable, with many people dying of starvation, exposure and disease. Construction was slow and, after 17 April 1975, local Khmer Rouge officials re-doubled their efforts. Additional work-brigades were deployed to the site and work continued through 1977. Labourers continued to suffer. Malaria and cholera was rampant, and many others died from injuries. Since its completion in 1977, however, the dam and abutting reservoir continue to be utilized. Long after the collapse of the Khmer Rouge, residents have moved to the site; many newcomers were (and remain) aware of the tragedy surrounding the dam. Yet decades later the site remains unmarked, overgrown with trees and bushes. The stories of forced work, malnutrition, starvation and executions are mute on the landscape – but remain vivid in the memories of those who continue to occupy and work the site. The ongoing significance of the site is that it reveals the everydayness of violence. Most deaths attributed to this site – and quite literally thousands of other work sites throughout the country – were not 'spectacular' in the sense of torture, forced confessions and mass executions. Rather, these deaths reflect, in Hannah Arendt's well-worn phrase, the 'banality of evil'. The physical and social erasure of Koh Sla is testimony to the contestation of memory within Cambodia and the ongoing spatial, temporal and social bounding of the memorialization of mass violence.

Conclusions

Within Democratic Kampuchea, the Khmer Rouge attempted to literally erase history and memory. In the People's Republic of Kampuchea, conversely, history and memory became political resources to affect legitimacy. Specifically, we witness the imposition of three forms of bounding: social, spatial and temporal. First, the genocide has been socially bounded to assign blame and culpability to only a few select individuals – notably those associated with the 'Pol Pot – Ieng Sary' clique. Second, there has been a continued spatial bounding of the genocide, one that has continued to spatially limit the memorialization of the genocide primarily to two sites: Tuol Sleng or Choeung Ek. Consequently, the international visibility of Tuol Sleng and Choeung Ek neutralize political discourse. Rather than allowing dialogue to take place, the minimalist displays at these two sites preclude any discussion about the broader geopolitical context of the genocide. More egregious, there is no opportunity for visitors to relate to those who suffered. Where Democratic Kampuchea was once a violent, placeless place, it has been reworked; it remains placeless, but now it is in danger of becoming a placeless site of mass atrocity, one stop of many within a global circuit of dark tourism. Third, there has been a temporal bounding. The Cambodian genocide is re-presented as a historical moment, with a distinct beginning (17 April 1975) and a distinct end (7 January 1979). And yet we know that the genocide did not end or begin on these dates; but events leading up to, and following, these book-ends are erased from the collective memory of Cambodia. These three forms of bounding have become the official narrative; in the process, this selective official commemoration serves to prevent any broader attempts at reconciliation or restorative/retributive justice.

Note

1. To facilitate the 'standard' tour of the site, in 2010 the main entrance gate to S-21 was relocated from the centre wall to the southeastern corner.

Bibliography

Bronfen, Elisabeth. 1990. 'Violence of Representation – Representation of Violence'. *LIT: Literature Interpretation Theory*, 1: 303–321.

Chandler, David P. 1999. *Voices from S-21: Terror and History in Pol Pot's Secret Prison*. Berkeley: University of California Press.

De Duve, Thierry. 2008. 'Art in the Face of Radical Evil'. *October*, 125: 3–23.

Dwyer, Owen J. 2004. 'Symbolic Accretion and Commemoration'. *Social & Cultural Geography*, 5: 419–435.

Dwyer, Owen J. and Alderman, D. H. 2008. 'Memorial Landscapes: Analytic Questions and Metaphors'. *GeoJournal*, 73: 165–178.

Dy, Khamboly. 2007. *A History of Democratic Kampuchea (1975–1979)*. Phnom Penh: Documentation Center of Cambodia.
Hoelscher, Steven and Alderman, D. H. 2004. 'Memory and Place: Geographies of a Critical Relationship'. *Social & Cultural Geography*, 5: 347–355.
Hughes, Rachel. 2003. 'The Abject Artefacts of Memory: Photographs from Cambodia's Genocide'. *Media, Culture & Society*, 25: 23–44.
Hughes, Rachel. 2008. 'Dutiful Tourism: Encountering the Cambodian Genocide'. *Asia Pacific Viewpoint*, 49: 318–330.
Lefebvre, Henri. 1991. *The Production of Space*, translated by D. Nicholson-Smith. Oxford: Blackwell.
Lunstrum, Elizabeth. 2010. 'Reconstructing History, Grounding Claims to Space: History, Memory, and Displacement in the Great Limpopo Transfrontier Park'. *South African Geographical Journal*, 92: 129–143.
Ly, Boreth. 2008. 'Of Performance and the Persistent Temporality of Trauma: Memory, Art, and Visions'. *Positions*, 16: 109–130.
Relph, Edward. 1976. *Place and Placelessness*. London: Pion.
Sion, Brigitte. 2011. 'Conflicting Sites of Memory in Post-Genocide Cambodia'. *Humanity*, 2: 1–21.
Tully, John. 2005. *A Short History of Cambodia: From Empire to Survival*. Sydney and Chiang Mai: Allen & Unwin.
Tyner, James. 2008. *The Killing of Cambodia: Geography, Genocide and the Unmaking of Space*. Aldershot: Ashgate.
Tyner, James, Gabriela Brindis Alvarez and Alex Colucci. 2012. 'Memory and the Everyday Landscape of Violence in Post-Genocide Cambodia'. *Social & Cultural Geography*, 13: 853–871.

2
Polish Landscapes of Memory at the Sites of Extermination: The Politics of Framing

Zuzanna Dziuban

Framing the frame

In *The Site, Despite Everything*, a short essay on Claude Lanzmann's *Shoah*, Georges Didi-Huberman describes the sites of the National Socialist death camps as *'real but impossible sites'* (Didi-Huberman, 2007, p.114, original emphasis). Impossible, because unreachable for us today in their actuality as extermination centres, the sites are nonetheless real due to their insistent presence as unsettling reminders of the Holocaust – as long as returned to and artistically framed. The fact that there is an irreducible interplay between the sites' inaccessible past as camps and their challenging present existence allows Didi-Huberman to recognize them as paradoxical 'sites, despite everything' (Didi-Huberman, 2007, p.115). Therefore, by addressing the aporia of the 'return to the sites' where the extermination took place, already non-existent but tenaciously 'still there', the author of *Images in Spite of All* points out both the unreachability of the extermination camps and the necessity or moral obligation to continuously revisit and interrogate those sites through the agency of art. Hence, acknowledging the importance of aesthetic framings for 'rendering visible' and, in fact, producing camp sites as carriers of Holocaust memory that is of importance today, Didi-Huberman asks 'what sorts of thoughts and what kinds of visualizations do the camp sites require of us?' (Didi-Huberman, 2007, p.114).

Insisting on the pertinence of Didi-Huberman's question, in what follows I would like to locate it in a more specific interpretive frame. By focusing on commemorative art and architectural interventions at the sites of two National Socialist extermination camps in Poland, Bełżec and Sobibór, I will attempt to investigate the parameters of the 'return to the sites' undertaken in Polish art. The critical analysis of architectural and sculptural projects aimed at transforming the camp sites into landscapes of memory will be guided by the basic assumption that they can and should be read as politically and ethically motivated attempts to work through the difficult legacy of the Holocaust in Poland – and, in fact, a lot more than that. Thus, the complex contexts in and by which the memory of the Holocaust in Poland has figured since the end of the Second World War is the prism through which the artistic framings of the camp sites will be analysed. Paradoxically, in order to reflect upon and elucidate this interpretive frame, I would like to take a closer look at a work in many respects different from the state-sponsored architectural and sculptural projects interpreted later on. A short detour to consider a photographic series *The Odd Place* (Miejsce Nieparzyste) created by Polish artist and scholar Elżbieta Janicka will function here as the starting point and occasion for a closer analysis of the politics of framing that underlie Polish artistic practices dealing with the Holocaust. There are at least two reasons for this. Not only does Janicka's work directly touch upon the two sites to which this chapter is devoted, namely, Bełżec and Sobibór, but *The Odd Place* also seeks to interrogate – in a particularly self-reflexive and critical way – the problem of the 'frame', conceived both as a horizon within which the meaning of the analysed artworks is constituted and as a signifying device through which the art operates – something that I, too, would like to focus upon.

First exhibited at the Atlas Sztuki gallery in Łódź in 2006, Janicka's work consists of six large square photographs (127 × 127 cm) taken in 2003 and 2004 at the sites of six former National Socialist extermination camps operating on the territory of Poland: Auschwitz II Birkenau, Majdanek, Treblinka II, Bełżec, Sobibór, and Kulmhof am Ner. The photographs are named after the extermination centres and supplemented with inscriptions stating the number of victims at each camp, as well as the exact date when the picture was taken. Each image shows a white surface framed within a black frame, upon which the name of the producer of photographic film, *Agfa*, is inscribed (Figure 2.1). The photographs, which 'represent' the air drifting above the grounds of the extermination sites where several hundred thousand people were gassed and burned, function as an artistic commentary on the persistent presence of the traces of the Holocaust – the ashes of the victims still circulating in the air – at the places where it took place.[1]

At the same time, the images capture the radical difference or imaginative incompatibility between the contemporary experience of those sites, totally emptied of all remains of the camps in the case of Bełżec, Sobibór, Treblinka II and Kulmhof am Ner, and the monstrous events that unfolded at them (Cichoń and Janicka, 2006). Thus, the temptation to locate *The Odd Place* – six perfectly white squares surrounded by imperfectly black frames – within the horizon of broader debates on the limits of representation in the face of the Holocaust is certainly hard to resist (Ankersmit, 2001; LaCapra, 1998; Rancière, 2006; Didi-Huberman, 2012). Yet, to see *The Odd Place* merely as an attempt to elaborate on the thesis, itself highly contested, of the unrepresentability of the Holocaust neither does justice to nor exhausts the

36 Spatial Inscriptions of Annihilation

Figure 2.1 Elżbieta Janicka, *Sobibór*, 250,000 (4 July 2003); from the cycle *The Odd Place*
Courtesy of Elżbieta Janicka

multitude of the meanings that Janicka's work evokes. In order to get closer to that goal one has to change the frame.

The need to focus on the variety of frames through and by which the meanings of Janicka's work are being constituted and produced is acknowledged by many interpreters of *The Odd Place*. According to Izabela Kowalczyk, the photographs' inscriptions, titles and (literal) frames, as well as authorial utterances and critical responses to the work, all contribute to a 'framing discourse' – the Derridean 'parergon'[2] – which is at the same time supplementary and constitutive of the work (Kowalczyk, 2010, p.175). In particular, the significance of the work's title, itself framed as an introductory *parergon* (Derrida, 1987, p.18), must be emphasized in the case of Janicka's photographic series. The 'odd place' – an abbreviation of the inscription 'the place on the odd bench' written in the record books of some students of Warsaw University from 1937 onwards – refers to the pre-war discriminatory policy of so-called ghetto benches assigned to representatives of the Jewish national minority. As a means of symbolic differentiation and spatial segregation of 'Jews' and 'Poles', the 'ghetto benches', introduced by the government at Polish universities on the initiative of the members of right-wing All-Polish Youth, academics and students, function here as a paradigmatic example of the operations of Polish anti-Semitism.

By referencing this in her title, Janicka's photographs imply a connection between their subject – the extermination camps – with one of the forms of discrimination exercised on Jews before the war. In this light, Bełżec, Sobibór, Treblinka II, Kulmhof am Ner, Auschwitz II Birkenau and Majdanek appear as the ultimate 'odd places' (Bojarska, 2009, p.20) – that is, as the places where anti-Semitic policy of differentiation and exclusion implemented by the Nazis took its most radical form. And yet, Janicka's decision to introduce the theme of anti-Semitism into her work by referring to specifically Polish anti-Jewish policies also unsettles, without negating, this particular interpretive frame. By forcing us to conceive of 'the odd place' as a Polish invention and as a consequence of Polish discriminatory politics, while at the same time pointing towards its disturbing connections with the crimes committed by the National Socialists, *The Odd Place* rephrases the question – not new, but since only very recently faced by Poles themselves – of the co-responsibility of Polish anti-Semitism for the 'efficiency' of the Nazi extermination policy (Rejak and Frister, 2012). A co-responsibility, one might add, which can be thematized in at least two different ways: in terms of an active participation in violence directed against the Jews before and during the war, and as a failure to properly address the Holocaust after the war. Thus, the problem of forgetting the Holocaust inscribed in Polish post-war politics of memory – based on a radical separation of the memory of Jewish suffering from both heroic and martyrological Polish narratives of war (Wóycicka, 2009; Steinlauf, 1997; Forecki, 2010) – can be seen as a subsequent (or parallel) frame through which the meaning of *The Odd Place* is produced. The 'white empty photographs' (Śmiechowska, 2013, p.32) act, therefore, as reminders of the concealment, repression and erasure that for many years characterized Polish responses to the Holocaust.

The problem of active forgetting as a form of complicity in a crime is not the only one posed by Janicka's work, which also seems to query the role of representation and memorialization as forms of entanglement or unintended involvement in the violence brought about by the Holocaust. This is suggested by the disturbing presence of the *Agfa* sign on the margins of the white surfaces of Janicka's photographs. The white inscription on the black frames of the photographs reminds us of the participation of AGFA in Nazi extermination machinery (as a part of IG Farben company, which not only utilized slave labour by concentration camp inmates but also provided the camps' administration with the Zyklon B used in Birkenau's and Majdanek's gas chambers), and therefore impugns the innocence of the very photographic medium used to create this work (Jakubowicz, 2006). Consequently, the innocence of artistic representation is also being questioned. This shift of emphasis from thematic concerns towards a critique of the medium and frame within which the work is produced announces an important relocation of the centre of gravity of Janicka's work – a move from the impossibility of representation to the ethics of representation, from the problem of its limits to the problem of its frames. A deliberate focus on the frame exposes it again as a focal point of meaning production, but also, at the same time, as an agent of complicity. The question could be posed: is the framing of *Bełżec, Sobibór, Treblinka II, Kulmhof am Ner, Majdanek* and *Auschwitz II Birkenau* as 'odd places' not a repetition of the gesture of locating them outside of the 'frame'?

Spatializing grievability

The above-suggested understanding of aesthetic framing as a form of 'political practice – of exclusion' (Bal, 2002, p.145), as conceptualized by Mieke Bal in *Travelling Concepts in the Humanities*, allows us to introduce another dimension of the problem of the frame into the discursive game. Conceived as a 'structure made for admitting, enclosing, or supporting something' (Bal, 2002, p.132), the frame points towards the activity of showing, bringing into being or making visible. Based on a variety of mechanisms of exclusion and inclusion – locating inside or outside of the frame – the act of framing consists, therefore, primarily in creating aesthetic, cultural or social visibility. It is precisely this delimiting sense of framing understood as both opening and closing – making something visible while at the same time making something else invisible – that can be best translated into or, rather, articulated in political terms. 'As a complex system of permission and prohibition, of presence and absence' (Kipnis, 1988, p.158), visibility is, after all, not only politically saturated, but it also functions as the highest stake in the process of constituting the political field. According to Judith Butler, the power to frame is the power to establish 'the boundaries that constitute what will and will not appear within public life, the limits of a publicly acknowledged field of appearance' (Butler, 2006, p.xviii).

This conceptual link between aesthetic and political framing, exclusion and haunting invisibility, found in Janicka's work, provoked me to think about the politics of framing that underlie commemorative art in Bełżec and Sobibór in terms of 'spatialising grievability'. The latter term, borrowed from Judith Butler (Butler, 2006, 2010), refers to 'the differential distribution of public grieving [understood] as a political issue of enormous significance' (Butler, 2010, p.38). Naming the cultural politics of grief responsible for its uneven allocation between different social actors, populations and communities, the notion of grievability directs attention to discursively and visually established frames of recognition as a means of designating some lives as worth grieving and some as not. In *Frames of War*, where Butler exposes a variety of operations of exclusion and foreclosure that regulate whose lives and whose losses can appear as noteworthy and mournable in public life, grievability is conceived as a precondition of 'life's visibility as life' and, as a consequence, of an affective response to someone else's suffering and death (Butler, 2010, p.26).

In Butler's analysis, the discursive and visual fields appear as the privileged realms in and through which grievability is established and framed. In what follows, however, I would like to focus on the role of space, conceived in Lefebvrian terms as socially and culturally produced (Lefebvre, 2005), in the process of creating and stabilizing the politically saturated frames of grievability. Thus, while referring to architectural and sculptural forms, memorials and monuments erected at the sites of former extermination camps, I will treat these as elements of broader, encompassing spatial structures: landscapes of memory. The concept of a cultural landscape, as developed in the field of cultural geography, will function as my point of reference. Pointing towards the role of space as both a site of inscription of cultural and political representations and as a productive force in itself (Mitchell, 2000, p.102), the notion of a landscape allows space to be conceived not merely as a 'container', but also as an 'agent' actively participating in the processes that shape and maintain specific configurations of power and particular visions of reality. In this sense, the landscape can be defined as a double 'framing convention' (Hirsch, 1995, p.1); it is, on the one hand, a cultural product established through the processes of spatial and architectural framing, therefore mirroring dominant cultural politics, and, on the other, a frame which itself shapes and constitutes social and spatial practices – or, in the case of landscapes of memory, the cultural processes of remembering. Keeping that in mind, I want to consider the landscapes of memory created at the sites of former extermination camps – the largest Jewish cemeteries on Polish soil and ultimate symbols of Jewish suffering – both as the media of cultural memory of the Holocaust shaped by Polish official memory politics and as sites where public grievability of the people killed there could be best inscribed and framed.

The decision to pose Butler's question regarding 'how certain forms of grief become nationally recognized and amplified, whereas other losses become unthinkable and ungrievable' (Butler, 2006, p.xiv) in the context of commemorative practices undertaken in Bełżec and Sobibór, and not for instance Auschwitz-Birkenau or Majdanek, can easily be justified. Unlike Auschwitz-Birkenau and Majdanek, which also functioned as concentration camps where Poles were imprisoned and killed, Bełżec and Sobibór operated within the framework of *Aktion Reinhardt*, aimed exclusively at the extermination of the Jews, mostly from Poland (Musiał, 2004).[3] Thus, the distinction between extermination and concentration camps obviously played a very important role in the cultural politics of grief: the fact that death camps could not easily be inscribed into Polish official memory work as symbols of 'Polish suffering and martyrdom' had an immediate effect on their spatial character, and on their place on the symbolic map of the Second World War commemoration in Poland.

While Auschwitz-Birkenau and Majdanek were transformed into officially recognized 'monuments of martyrdom of Polish and other nations' as early as 1947 (the initial efforts to commemorate the victims of those two camps and initiatives aimed at creating memorial landscapes at the sites were undertaken right after the liberation of the camps), the first monuments were only erected at Bełżec and Sobibór, under the supervision and on the initiative of the governmental Council for the Protection of Memorials of Combat and Martyrdom, in 1963 and 1965 respectively. Before that, no real actions aimed at transforming those sites into landscapes of memory had been undertaken – despite the fact that the representatives of Jewish communities in Poland had made demands to secure the terrains of former extermination centres, and that the members of the Council for the Protection of Memorials of Combat and Martyrdom unceasingly debated the need to commemorate the camps (ROPWIM, 1/1–5). At the same time, the neglected sites became the object of so-called treasure hunting – the digging up of the grounds of the extermination camps by the local Polish population in search of gold and other valuables allegedly left there by Jews. The activity of the 'grave-robbers', sometimes travelling to Bełżec and Sobibór from cities as distant as Lublin, was reported up until the early 1960s (ROPWIM, 52/6). Could this horrifying practice of devastating the mass graves in which the Nazis buried the ashes of the hundreds of thousands of victims of the camps not be seen as a symptom of a failure to frame and conceive 'Jewish life' as grievable life?

Even when 'Polish signs of memory' (Taborska, 2010, p.15) were introduced at the sites of the former extermination camps in the 1960s – in the form of complexes of monuments, sculptures, obelisks, urns and mausoleums housing the ashes of victims of the camps – the grief they staged was a somewhat generalized grief. Dedicated to 'the victims of Nazi terror' (Bełżec) or 'those murdered by the Nazis in the years 1942–43' (Sobibór), the memorial landscapes at Bełżec and Sobibór, designed in rather traditional artistic means by Polish sculptors and architects, did not aim exclusively at honouring the memory of a particular group. In Sobibór, the inscription placed on one of the monuments even gave incorrect information about the actual nationality of the fatalities of the camp.[4] In accordance with the memory politics of that time, the main goal of memorial landscapes was, after all, to emphasize both the international character of the camps and the monstrosity of the crimes committed there by the Germans, who were still regarded as a threat. Thus, while the early memorial landscapes at the sites may have succeeded to a certain extent in spatializing grief, they failed to convincingly acknowledge or reframe the victims that were to be grieved in terms of their grievability. That is probably the reason why the two landscapes of memory, very rarely visited, began to deteriorate soon after being built.

To cut and re-link[5]

The decision to remove Bełżec's existing monuments and design its landscape of memory anew was made in the second half of the 1990s, as a result of an agreement reached by the Polish government, the US Holocaust Memorial Museum in Washington, and the American Jewish Committee. The agreement guaranteed that the new commemoration would be finalized in accordance with rabbinical law. The prohibition against disturbing or removing the graves, which were discovered and marked during the archaeological research conducted in Bełżec from 1997 to 2003,[6] was of fundamental importance for the authors of the new design. Selected in a closed national competition in 1997, the winning project by Polish sculptors Andrzej Sołyga, Zdzisław Pidek and Marcin Roszczyk opened to the public in the summer of 2004. The open international competition for a new landscape and architectural design for Sobibór, initiated by an International Steering Committee consisting of representatives of the Polish, Israeli, Slovak and Dutch governments and organized by the State Museum in Majdanek together with the Foundation 'Polish-German Reconciliation', was announced in January 2013.[7] From among 63 competing projects (three of which were submitted by citizens of countries other than Poland),[8] the jury selected a design proposed by architects Marcin Urbanek, Piotr Michalewicz and artist and historian Łukasz Mieszkowski. The final results and the decision to implement the project were made public in the autumn of the same year. As at Bełżec, the architectural project for Sobibór, which is expected to be completed by the end of 2015, is to be built in conformity with Jewish tradition and aims to protect the mass graves uncovered during archaeological research conducted at the site since 2000. While the two landscapes of memory were or will be erected thanks to international financial support and are aimed at international audiences, one could still argue that they can be conceived as Polish commemorative art mirroring important transformations of the cultural politics of grief.

The memorial landscape at Bełżec, separated from the surrounding area by a concrete wall and said to 'cover [almost] the entire area of the former death camp' (Bełżec, 2003), provides a symbolic and architectural framing of the cemetery, into which it is intentionally transformed. At the same time, it aims to represent the structure of the extermination centre by retracing the steps taken by the victims of the camp. The experience of the visitor of the memorial landscape is carefully orchestrated by the sculptors responsible for the spatial organization of the site. It begins with the entrance to the site via the symbolic ramp, marked by a museum building on one

Figure 2.2 Museum-Memorial Site in Bełżec
Photograph by Zuzanna Dziuban

side and by a monument representing a pile of scorched rails (on which the corpses of the gassed victims were burnt) on the other. Visitors are led from the ramp to the point of symbolic entrance into the cemetery, where they have to walk through a horizontal sculpture covered with a relief depicting a deconstructed Star of David – conceived as an emblem of the camp (Figure 2.2).

The actual burial grounds, rising in front of the ramp and covered with clinker, ash, and sterilized earth (darkened in the places where 33 mass graves were found), are fenced off by a cast-iron border and are inaccessible to the visitors. The cemetery is approachable only through a narrow interstice or tunnel leading the visitors through the burial grounds, from which the path is separated by massive walls; this is the only part of the cemetery that is free from human remains and is, most likely, also the camp's 'death road' (the route to the gas chambers). The interstice ends in a Niche framed by two stone walls, on which the names of the victims and a quote from the book of Job ('Earth do not cover my blood; let there be no resting place for my outcry') are inscribed. The steps leading out of the Niche and, thereby, out of the burial grounds, direct the visitor to a path surrounding the cemetery, which is marked by small plaques dedicated to the inhabitants of Polish (and other) towns and cities who were exterminated in the camp. Thus, the initial 'identification' of the visitor with the victims of the camp inaugurated by the architectural form of the memorial, and strengthened by the disturbing experience of crossing the tunnel between the graves is, in the end, problematized.

The insistence on a separation between the realm of the dead and the realm of the living, definitively at work in the memorial landscape designed for Bełżec, is stressed even more clearly in the much less invasive project for Sobibór.[9] The architectural framing of the camp, while marking its key elements, radically challenges the idea of a visitor taking the 'position' of a victim of the camp. The proposed Memory Trail, which will lead from the ramp to the burial grounds, acknowledges but does not repeat the trajectory of the 'death road' that was discovered during archaeological research. Distinctively marked by a high concrete wall, yet barely visible beyond the trees separating it from the visitors' path, the route to the gas chambers is incorporated within 'the space which belongs to the dead' (Sobibór, 2013) (Figure 2.3).

There are, however, two sites at which the concrete wall intersects with the visitors' path, 'gradually closing around the visitor' in the place where victims' hair was cut, and creating a small, enclosed area in the place where the gas chamber use to stand. Its exit – a narrow interstice fashioned by the separation of two walls – directs the visitor towards the square located in front of the burial grounds, again separating her experience from that of the victim of the camp. Inaccessible and, for the most part, walled, the mass graves are covered with white gravel, thus providing a sharp contrast to both the concrete wall and treetops behind it. A 32-metre wide opening in the wall allows visual contact with the cemetery, framed both as the climax and as the centre of the memorial landscape. Interestingly, the decision to broaden this aperture, initially planned as a narrow rupture in the wall allowing only one

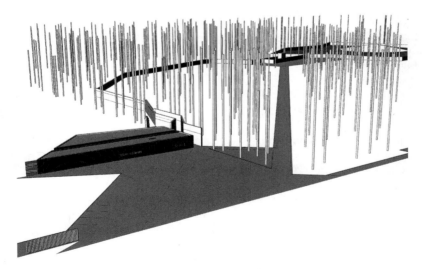

Figure 2.3 Sobibór Death Camp Memorial Site
Courtesy of Marcin Urbanek

person at a time to look at the burial grounds, was demanded by the organizers of the competition. Probably the most self-reflexive element of the project, the idea to radically limit the access to the mass graves and, thereby, direct attention to the violence of both the architectural intervention and the visitors' gaze, turned out to be impractical.[10]

Nonetheless, it is precisely this partially failed effort to foreground the frame and, in this way, to critically address the memorial landscape's 'very premises of (...) being' (Young, 2000, p.7),[11] which distinguishes the projects for Bełżec and Sobibór from one another. Providing an unambiguous and totalizing interpretive frame, presumptuously imposed on the visitors, the memorial project at Bełżec lacks the self-referentiality of the Sobibór proposal. Hence, the beautiful but overpowering landscape itself is paradoxically transformed into a 'cemetery memorial' (Bełżec, 2003), entombing the very possibility of 'poly-framing' and foreclosing its own productive ambiguity. What both projects have in common, however, is an endeavour to make 'visible' the suffering of the victims of the camps through which the meaning of the burial grounds is framed; an attempt that is restaged by the architectural organization of the memorial landscapes and that aims to generate an affective, empathetic response. In this way, a link between the visitors and the victims is built, in which the grievability of the latter can definitely be anchored.

Thus, the intentional effort to re-establish the meaning of the sites of former extermination centres as Jewish cemeteries, accomplished thanks to the foregrounding of the spatial difference between the burial grounds and the visitors' paths, allows the creation of the memorial complex at both Bełżec and Sobibór to be interpreted in terms of its enacting a second, proper burial for the victims of the camp. Aimed at honouring 'the Jews murdered here according to the tradition, culture and religion in which they and their ancestors lived' (Bełżec, 2003), the memorial landscapes set the stage for a symbolic commemorative reburial through which the space of the former camps is returned and awarded to the dead. In that way, the architectural and spatial framings at the sites, which signal and spatialize the separation between death and life, the sacred and secular realms, past and present, transform the mass graves – long neglected and devastated – into cemeteries into which both the 'identity' of the victims and their grievability can be inscribed (according to Butler, an ungrievable life is in principle 'unburiable' – Butler, 2006, p.34).

Nevertheless, there is, in my opinion, one important element missing in the projects for Bełżec and Sobibór, which I found so important in Elżbieta Janicka's work: a critical contextualization of the aesthetic framings and commemorative efforts undertaken at the camp sites aimed, for instance, at reworking the legacy of Polish anti-Semitism. The lack of a deliberate attempt to address and problematize the place of both sites on the map of Polish memory of the Holocaust[12] – and in that way to locate them within a broader debate on the problem of Polish–Jewish relations before, during, and after the war – makes the very politics of framing underlying both memorial landscapes somewhat invisible. Hence, a rather redemptive sense of closure is inscribed into the experience of memorial landscapes at Bełżec and Sobibór.[13] Consequently, the redefinition of the relations between the dead and the living in terms of grievability can also hardly be interpreted in political terms. This observation may lead us to pose the question once more: are these landscapes of memory really reframing the relationship between 'Poles' and 'Jews' or, are they, again, only repeating the difference?

Notes

1. 'The ashes flow in the air. We breathe this air. (...) The ashes are in the soil, in the rivers, on the meadows, and in the forests – subjected to constant recycling, in which we participate' (Cichoń and Janicka, 2006). Interpreting this unsettling recycling in terms of the impossibility of burial of the victims of the camps, the artist can be seen as critically addressing the problem of closure in the context of Holocaust memory. At the same time, the work symbolically designates those who breathe the 'contaminated' air, the Poles, to serve as the sarcophagi for the otherwise unburiable dead.
2. In *The Truth in Painting*, where Derrida seeks to deconstruct the logic of Kant's theory of beauty – based on a radical separation of the 'proper' work of art (*ergon*) and that which is outside of the work (a frame, *parergon*) – the focus on the frame as a constitutive and active component of the work calls into question the distinction between the inside and the outside of the work, that is, the work and the world, and exposes their interdependence in the processes of reading and meaning production (Derrida, 1987).
3. Among the victims of Bełżec and Sobibór were also Jews from Germany and Austria, the Protectorate of Bohemia and Moravia, Slovakia, former Soviet Union, France, and the Netherlands. It is assumed that a small number of representatives of Sinti and Roma were exterminated in Bełżec and Sobibór as well. The conviction that several thousand ethnic Poles were killed in the camps is nowadays questioned.
4. The plaque in Sobibór informed visitors that '250,000 Soviet prisoners of war, Jews, Poles, and Gypsies' were murdered in the camp. It was taken down in the second half of the 1980s.
5. That is, to reframe (Bal, 2002, p.140).
6. The aim of the archaeological research at both Bełżec and Sobibór, commissioned by the renamed Council for the Protection of the Memory of Combat and Martyrdom, was to survey the topography of the camps in order to locate the areas with the remains of the dead and, in that way, prepare the terrains of the former extermination centres for planned architectural interventions. An effort to prevent further devastation of the mass graves was of primary importance for the initiators of commemorative activities – 'so that we, in commemorating, do not violate the memory of those whom we want to commemorate' (Lerman, 2000, p.3).
7. The efforts to redesign the memorial landscape in Sobibór were already underway in the early 1990s. In 1993 the Museum of Former Nazi Death Camp in Sobibór

was opened to the public. Nevertheless, the commemorative project proposed in 2003 by its former director Marek Bem was never fully implemented (Bem, 2006).
8. The explanation for that is quite simple: all documents and project descriptions were to be submitted in Polish.
9. To see full presentation of the project visit: http://www.majdanek.eu/images/media/Prezentacja.Sobibor.pdf.
10. The objection that the implementation of the initial idea could be viewed as a repetition of the gesture to exclude and cut away the victims once more was also voiced.
11. An effort that, according to James Young, characterizes Holocaust counter-monuments.
12. Even though, in Sobibór, two monuments from the 1960s are incorporated into the new memorial landscape, their presence is not addressed critically.
13. Paradoxically, while performing the 'buriability' of the victims of the camps, the memorial landscapes at Bełżec and Sobibór symbolically block the unsettling circulation of the ashes in the air above the extermination sites interpreted in *The Odd Place* in terms of the impossibility of closure in the context of Holocaust memory in Poland.

Bibliography

Ankersmit, Frank. 2001. 'Remembering the Holocaust: Mourning and Melancholia'. In *Historical Representation*, edited by F. Ankersmit. Stanford: Stanford University Press.
Bal, Mieke. 2002. *Travelling Concepts in the Humanities: A Rough Guide*. Toronto, Buffalo, London: University of Toronto Press.
Bełżec. 2003. *The Project of the Cemetery Memorial to the Jewish Victims of the Nazi Death Camp in Bełżec*. Warszawa: ROPWIM, The American Jewish Committee.
Bem, Marek. 2006. *Masterplan Sobibór*. Muzeum Pojezierza Łęczyńsko-Włodawskiego: Włodawa.
Bojarska, Katarzyna. 2009. 'Obecność Zagłady w twórczości Polskich artystów'. *Culture.pl*, Instytut Adama Mickiewicza. On-line at: http://www.culture.pl, date accessed 15 May 2013.
Butler, Judith. 2006. *Precarious Life: The Powers of Mourning and Violence*. New York, London: Verso.
Butler, Judith. 2010. *Frames of War: When Is Life Grievable?* New York, London: Verso.
Cichoń, Krzysztof and Elżbieta Janicka. 2006. 'Portrety Powietrza'. *Atlas Sztuki*, 21: unnumbered pages.
Derrida, Jacques. 1987. *The Truth in Painting*. Chicago and London: The University of Chicago Press.
Didi-Huberman, Georges. 2007. 'The Site, Despite Everything'. In *Claude Lanzmann's Shoah: Key Essays*, edited by S. Lieberman. Oxford: Oxford University Press.
Didi-Huberman, Georges. 2012. *Images in Spite of All: Four Photographs from Auschwitz*. Chicago: The University Press of Chicago.
Forecki, Piotr. 2010. *Od Shoah do Strachu. Spory o polsko-żydowską przeszłość i pamięć w debatach publicznych*. Poznań: Wydawnictwo Poznańskie.
Hirsch, Eric. 1995. 'Landscape Between Place and Space'. In *The Anthropology of Landscape: Perspectives on Place and Space*, edited by E. Hirsch and M. O'Hanlon. Oxford: Calderon Press.

Jakubowicz, Rafał. 2006. 'Kolory. Albo gdzie szukać prawdy?' *Atlas Sztuki*, 21: unnumbered pages.
Kipnis, Laura. 1988. 'Feminism: The Political Conscience of Postmodernism'. In *Universal Abandon? The Politics of Postmodernism*, edited by Andrew Ross. Minneapolis: University of Minnesota Press.
Kowalczyk, Izabela. 2010. *Podróż do przeszłości. Interpretacje najnowszej historii w polskiej sztuce krytycznej*. Warszawa: Wydawnictwo SWPS Academica.
LaCapra, Dominic. 1998. *History and Memory After Auschwitz*. Ithaca and London: Cornell University Press.
Lefebvre, Henri. 2005. *The Production of Space*. Oxford: Blackwell.
Lerman, Miles. 2000. 'Foreword'. In *Bełżec. The Nazi Camp for Jews in the Light of Archaeological Sources*, edited by A. Kola. Warsaw and Washington: The Council of Protection of Memory of Combat and Martyrdom, US Holocaust Memorial Museum.
Mitchell, Don. 2000. *Cultural Geography: A Critical Introduction*. Oxford: Blackwell.
Musiał, Bogdan. ed. 2004. *Aktion Reinhardt. Der Völkermord an den Juden im Generalgouvernement 1941–1944*. Osnabrück: Fibre Verlag.
Rancière, Jacques. 2006. *The Politics of Aesthetics*. London: Continuum.
Rejak, Sebastian and Elżbieta Frister. eds. 2012. *The Inferno of Choices: Poles and the Holocaust*. Warszawa: Oficyna Wydawnicza RYTM.
ROPWiM, The Archival Materials of The Council for the Protection of Memory of Combat and Martyrdom: Protokoły z posiedzeń Rady OPWiM, syg. 1/1–5; Opiniowanie spraw związanych z opieką nad byłymi hitlerowskimi obozoami w Bełżcu i Sobiborze 1962–1975, syg. 52/6.
Śmiechowska, Teresa. 2013. 'Attempts. Trying to Give Shape to Silence'. In *Sztuka Polska Wobec Holokaustu/ Polish Art and the Holocaust*. Warszawa: Żydowski Instytut Historyczny.
Sobibór. 2013. *The Project to Commemorate Victims of the Sobibór Death Camp*. Courtesy Marcin Urbanek, Piotr Michalewicz, and Łukasz Mieszkowski. Unpublished document, available in Polish in http://www.majdanek.eu/images/media/Prezentacja.Sobibor.pdf, date accessed 5 August 2014.
Steinlauf, Michael. 1997. *Bondage to the Dead: Poland and the Memory of the Holocaust*. Syracuse: Syracuse University Press.
Taborska, Halina. 2010. 'Polish Signs of Memory in the Nazi Death Camps'. In *Shoah. Cultural Representations and Commemorative Practices*, edited by T. Majewski and A. Zeidler-Janiszewska. Lodz: Officyna.
Wóycicka, Zofia. 2009. *Przerwana Żałoba. Polskie spory wokół pamięci nazistowskich obozów koncentracyjnych i zagłady 1944–1950*. Warszawa: TRIO.
Young, James. 2000. *At Memory's Edge: After-Images of the Holocaust in Contemporary Art and Architecture*. New Haven and London: Yale University Press.

3
Spaces of Confrontation and Defeat: The Spatial Dispossession of the Revolution in Tucumán, Argentina

Pamela Colombo

This is the story of a space that was lost; a space in rebellion that became a space of defeat. This story revolves around the space of the *monte*[1] of Tucumán situated in the north of Argentina. There, on 9 February 1975, the so-called *Operativo Independencia* (Operation Independence) was launched with the aim of undertaking 'all military operations deemed necessary in order to neutralize or annihilate any uprising of subversive elements operating in the province of Tucumán' (Decree N261/75).[2] The objective was, more specifically, to eliminate the rural guerrillas belonging to the armed wing of the *Partido Revolucionario de los Trabajadores* (Workers' Revolutionary Party, PRT) the *Ejército Revolucinario del Pueblo* (the People's Revolutionary Army – ERP) and break the ties that it had forged with workers' and peasants' movements.

Throughout the 1960s and 1970s there was an escalating process of confrontation between the state and leftist social forces. In the province of Tucumán, the level of direct confrontation was high, especially among those working class and farming sectors involved in the sugar industry. This situation of social conflict was the precursor to military intervention in Tucumán in 1975. The occupation involved the sudden arrival of a large number of military personnel who had moved into the area, the creation of military bases, firm control over the civilian population that lived there, forced displacement, the founding of new towns and even a census. Traffic controls likewise became systematic, as did curfews, 'controls' inside homes, the presence of military vehicles and the sounds of bombs being dropped in the distance. The military occupation resulted in a disciplined use of time and space – both social and private.

In the rest of Argentina during the military dictatorship (1976–83), military forces used space in a way that was fleeting, in the form of kidnappings, and furtive, in the form of clandestine detention centres. Although this also took place in Tucumán, what was distinctive in the southern zone of this province was the fact that this situation was superimposed onto the stationing of occupying forces. The systematic and clandestine plan to carry out the forced disappearance of people took place alongside the presence of occupying forces, which was more akin to the logic of conventional warfare. Space is an element of power which subjects dispute, look for and need in order to exist and constitute their own sense of self. The effects of de-figuration and reconfiguration of a rebellious space, as was the case in the Tucumán *monte*, will be the focus of this investigation. My analysis of the link between confrontation and space is not confined to 'physical' space, but includes the manner in which this space is remembered from the present. In order to do this, I will try to understand how the space of confrontation in the *monte* is talked about, once traversed by strong processes of state violence; or, to put it in other words, the forest as a space of confrontation recounted from the point of view of defeat. The analysis is based on a series of interviews carried out in Tucumán (between 2007 and 2012) with those who were most affected by the process of forced disappearance: the families of the disappeared, survivors of the clandestine detention centres and militants belonging to left-wing parties.[3] The act of investigating the spaces that are imagined by subjects, and under what conditions these spaces emerge, is crucial to being able to think about politics in societies that have undergone processes of state violence.

In the first section of the chapter, the term 'space of confrontation' will be posited alongside the reasons why the Tucumán *monte* is a paradigm of this kind of space. What will then be examined is how the forest served to territorialize the enemy in order to subsequently carry out a process of deterritorialization. Hence, I will analyse the manner in which defeat becomes spatial at the moment the forest is de-figured as a space of rebellion, analysing primarily the displacement of the population and the founding of new towns. Finally, I will set out the central idea of this text which argues that this process should be thought of in terms of the spatial dispossession of the revolutionary project.

Spaces of confrontation

At the beginning of 1974, the establishment of a rural guerrilla by the PRT-ERP in the Tucumán *monte* was made public (Carnovale, 2010). This is a story that takes place in the *monte*, one of open confrontation, of a guerrilla force that appears and then becomes hidden. It is one of the army occupying a territory, appropriating and modifying it. It is also a story of citizens who get caught in the middle and join one front or the other; of citizens who are placed under census, displaced and relocated. This confrontation is told with spatial metaphors: those who are above (the guerrillas); those who are below (the army); and those who are in the middle (the citizens). But there is also the *monte* itself, which at times takes on anthropomorphic characteristics and is feared and respected like any other actor in the conflict. The forest appears like a mirror that returns confusing images; images of heroes and villains, of citizens who are suppressed and those who take part. What takes place in the *monte* is the 'mise-en-scène' (Garaño, 2012) of what cannot be seen and, for precisely this reason, has to be imagined. On this same stage, what is also being constructed is the forest as a space of confrontation.

A space of confrontation is constituted by at least two dimensions. The first refers to a struggle within the space in which the protagonists confront one another and in this same process, as they position themselves face-to-face, build and affirm the traits that identify them both to themselves and everyone else. Second, space of confrontation refers to the fact that what also happens therein is a struggle for control over the representations of this space, in which the aforementioned confrontation occurs.

The first dimension enables us to understand the *monte* as a space in which subjects face the 'other' in opposition, or in which the confrontation is imagined as taking place. It is a space in which at least two different social actors – the armed forces and the guerrilla force – meet and confront one another, recognizing the other as an enemy and engaging in open confrontation. The act of mutual confrontation in space forges the link between subjects and the space in which the confrontation occurs. The fact that the subjects situate themselves and confront one another in a specific site modifies and alters this space. It is important to stress that space is also part of the dispute. Moreover, this confrontation in space enables subjects to acquire different qualities (courage, bravery, heroism, manliness and so on).

Henri Lefebvre states that 'groups, classes or fractions of classes cannot constitute themselves, or recognize one another, as "subjects" unless they generate (or produce) a space' (Lefebvre, 1991, p.416). His words are clear when they indicate the importance that exists between the construction of a rebel subjectivity and the space which is formed in parallel and which serves as a frame of reference and/or mirror. In the case dealt with here, the space that acts as a framework in the construction of identity is the same space that is disputed by various social actors. The identities of these subjects are built in the *monte*, and it is the specificity of this space- which is bestowed upon them because they exist within it- that makes them singular. It is in the confrontation with the other, who is different, where self-recognition occurs, and this act of distinguishing self and other as different subjects can be read in the disputes over space.

The second dimension that I consider to be constitutive of a space of confrontation has to do with the fact that what will take place therein is not only a fight to determine who will control the space in physical terms, but also a struggle for symbolic domination. David Harvey stresses the fact that 'those who command space can always control the politics of place even though, and this is a vital corollary, it takes control of some place to command space in the first instance' (Harvey, 1990, pp.233–234). If, therefore, the way in which the space is represented is under dispute, the space of confrontation should also be understood in terms of a struggle for what is imagined to be possible within that space. Hence, the construction (and imposition) of one representation of the space over and above other representations, as part and parcel of the result of the confrontation, either sets up or restricts the potential for action on the part of the subjects. The space of the *monte* is significant given that, at the time of the confrontation, this place was presented as a space in which revolution was possible, or at the very least in which it seemed closer.

The rebel territories wanted by the enemy

Within the framework of a growing process of social conflict and wide social mobilization throughout Argentina, the Marxist-Leninist leaning PRT was founded in 1965. In 1970, opting for armed struggle, the PRT set up the ERP. In the face of both state and para-state harassment, the majority of left-wing parties, including the PRT-ERP, started to operate in secret. In 1974, the PRT-ERP founded the rural guerrilla front, the 'Compañía de Monte Ramón Rosa Jiménez', which located itself in the Tucumán *monte*. This place seemed to bear several exceptional features, such as a geographical terrain that was conducive to the training and settlement of the guerrillas, and nearby towns with a long history of worker and peasant mobilization linked to the sugar industry.

Previous research has pointed to the fact that the space of the *monte* was the site that enabled the 'confrontation' to be staged, both for the military and the PRT-ERP militants (Garaño, 2012; Isla, 2007). Developing this idea, what I maintain in this chapter is that the *monte* was not only a stage on which to represent the confrontation, but was principally the space–time that meant the enemy could be territorialized, and thus rendered visible and tangible, so making it possible for it to be annihilated. The state used the rural guerrilla force in order to imagine and expose an enemy which, in the rest of the country seemed 'elusive and extremely mobile' (Vilas, 1977), but here could be tied to a fixed location. The interpretation that I propose is influenced by the work of Derek Gregory (2004) and Stuart Elden (2009), both of whom account for the way in which cartographic performances are staged within the War on Terror in order to fix the elusive al-Qaeda terrorist network in space. Gregory argues that the spatialization of the enemy produces a reinforcement of the state itself in spatial terms: its borders are secured and discourses on national security emerge therefrom (Gregory, 2004, pp.49–50). In more general terms, they indicate that the moment in which the enemy is territorialized is followed by a subsequent process of deterritorialization and reterritorialization. Elden – in line with Deleuze and Guattari – explains this process as

> an ongoing and complicated reconfiguration of spatial relation rather than their end. (...) and that deterritorialisation 'always occurs in

> relation to a complementary reterritorialization'. Indeed, they [Deleuze and Guattari] make this point more forcefully when they stress that territoriality itself is the condition for change. (...) [T]erritory is both its condition of possibility and, in some newly configured form, its necessary outcome.
>
> (Elden, 2009, p.xxvii)

As previously mentioned, the majority of the left-wing parties in Argentina had moved underground by the early 1970. The clandestine manner in which these parties were operating meant that the way in which they existed within space and occupied it, above all in the city, was transitory and floating. The dimensions of the big city granted them anonymity and the possibility of quickly going into hiding, thus evading the control of the state. In contrast, the sustained presence of the guerrillas in the montane forest offered a concrete time and space on the basis of which the confrontation could be located and temporalized. Furthermore, the act of giving the 'enemy', a fixed territory facilitated the process of its destruction. Even though this process of destruction relied on multiple factors (the outlawing and persecution of its members, the forced disappearance of many, and the dismantling of its support bases), space in particular played a pivotal role, not only in making such destruction possible, but also in creating the conditions that would prevent this type of movement re-emerging in the future.

The term 'deterritorialization' is used here to refer to the dismantling of the space of rebellion in the forest area together with the disappearance of subjects who embodied it and made it possible. It was not only the militants who were gestating an alternative use of space in the *monte*, but also the civilian population which supported that struggle. The *monte* thus gave rise to an accumulation of symbolic capital enabling this space to be associated with revolutionary processes that had previously taken place in Latin America. It could be argued that, at the time, a link existed between different spaces of a sort of pan-Latin American rebellion, which took as their most iconic points of reference the experience of the rural guerrillas in Cuba and Bolivia.

In order to break up and annihilate this space, in which something new was gestating, a radical reordering of space and time needed to be imprinted on both a physical and symbolic level. In other words, it was necessary to deterritorialize the idea of revolution. The process of deterritorialization and reterritorialization was, therefore, exacerbated in a place which had not only begun to mobilise other modes of socialization, but was also acquiring new definitions and meanings. Once the idea that the Tucumán *monte* was a breeding ground for revolution had been constructed and consolidated, it would be there that the state would deploy its power in excess and produce very particular spatial reconfigurations, including displacement of the population and the founding of new villages.

Pamela Colombo 53

Spatialization of defeat: Displacement of the population and the founding of new villages

The *Operativo Independencia* unfolded in the south of Tucumán province in February 1975, and by the end of 1976 the rural guerrillas had already been completely taken out (Carnovale, 2010). Law 4.530 (16 August 1976) explicitly set out two milestones in terms of spatial reconfiguration that were established during this period and which were crucial in the spatialization of defeat: namely relocating the population and creating four villages, which constitute two forms of spatial expression that, on the one hand, empty out the space of the montane forest region and, on the other, create new places (Figure 3.1).

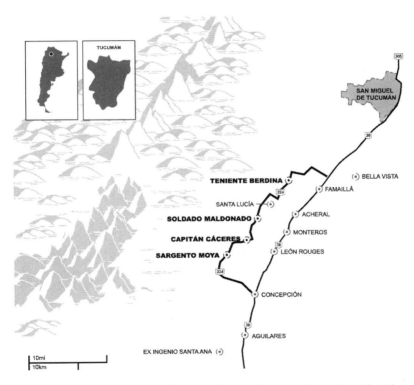

Figure 3.1 First, the map shows the four villages (Sargento Moya, Capitán Cáceres, Soldado Maldonado and Teniente Berdina) and the route 324 founded by the military during the dictatorship. Second, it exhibits the towns which were occupied during the *Operativo Independencia*, in which the author of this chapter conducted interviews: ex Ingenio Santa Ana, Aguilares, Concepción, León Rouge, Monteros, Acherál, Bella Vista, Famaillá, Santa Lucía
Drawn by Julián Colombo.

The process of emptying out the forest area involved different features, such as the forced disappearance of people, the dismantling of the rural guerrilla force, or population displacement. My analysis here focuses in detail on the latter. The people who lived in the area, in which the army was operating, associate these population displacements with the people who lived scattered across the *monte*. They also talk about the fact that inhabitants were displaced from villages that the military made 'disappear' (such as Yacuchina or Caspinchango): villages that had effectively been 'bulldozed' (E28).[4] The same Law 4.530 indicates 'that, moreover, the current dispersion of rural inhabitants across the affected area renders its control by the security forces difficult'. It was precisely this dispersion in the territory, this practice of being located outside the gridlines of a map, or this lack of 'accessibility', that these population movements aimed to counteract. The displacements created another map in parallel, which not only included ghost towns or 'emptied spaces' (Oslender, 2006, p.161), but also a map that included no-go-zones, places that were forbidden: the *monte* would gradually become transformed into a place that was feared and where one was not supposed to go. In contrast, other places that had been isolated suddenly become accessible. This occurred principally due to the construction of new roads which included these isolated places within a rational grid that enabled them to be reached.

Adel Vilas – commander of the first phase of the *Operativo Independencia* – wrote in his campaign diary that 'where the *monte* ends, the sugar cane fields begin immediately' (1977, my translation). This physical description of the territory laid out in this statement exposes the close and dangerous link, feared by the military, between the space of the guerrillas (in the montane forest) and the area occupied by the sugar industry (on the plain). As the military action in this territory unfolded, the separation between the montane forest and the plain became apparent. The new villages were connected physically by road 324, known as the inter-village route, consisting of 42km running parallel to national highway number 38 (Garaño, 2012, p.280). This small road that was built to connect four new villages to the rest of the territory can be interpreted as a frontier that marked out where the plain ended and the montane area began. This road meant that the space demarcating the limit between the *monte* and the plain could be traversed.

As one of my interviewees pointed out, the military was simultaneously

> creating the villages in order to encourage the rural population to retreat, bringing all the neighbors under their watch and control, rather than leaving them isolated out in the *monte*. (...) They built this whole structure, along with a road that linked the villages to the rest of the territory.
>
> (E39[5])

The simultaneous appearance of villages and roads meant the landscape changed. While one infrastructure was created, another was made to disappear: 'the landscape is different; many houses are derelict, abandoned, destroyed. Well, this is because no one was left (...) and everything has disappeared' (E28[6]). Those people who were scattered across a geography that was imagined to be uncontrollable – because it was located outside the control of the state – were reined in and relocated in spaces that rendered them visible, reordered them and made them accessible.

The four villages that were created in this period each took the name of a military figure who had fallen during the *Operativo Independencia*: Teniente Berdina, Capitán Cáceres, Sargento Moya and Soldado Maldonado. Those interviewed generally agree that one of the reasons for the displacements and the founding of new villages was the need to remove the civilian population from the *monte* and locate them in a place that was controllable: 'They did not want them there in the *monte*' (E23[7]); 'Those villages, (...) that were built at the foothills of the *monte* so that people could be taken, controlled and moved' (E28[8]).

Echoes of Vietnam reverberate around the Tucumán *monte*

The creation of strategic villages in the foothills of this area is frequently associated, both in interviews and in the trial of military personnel in Tucumán,[9] with the doctrine of 'strategic hamlets' developed by the government of the United States in Vietnam.[10] The 'strategic hamlets' project carried out in the south of Vietnam during the early part of the 1960s had the aim of displacing or regrouping the rural population in order to curb the influence of the Communist guerrillas and turn the population against them as it sought to isolate the guerrillas both physically and politically (Tenembaum, 2010). As part of the same process, the positioning of a 'development policy' took on an important role in the 'politics of counterinsurgency'.[11]

General Antonio Domingo Bussi, the de facto Governor of Tucumán during the dictatorship, had been trained in counterinsurgent warfare in the United States and had also been a military observer during the Vietnam War (Crenzel, 2001). It was indeed Bussi who was behind the idea of creating the new villages.

The design of these four villages was perfectly geometrical and almost identical: each of them constituted by approximately 20 rectangular blocks. In his analysis of the 'strategic hamlets' in Vietnam, James Tyner states that 'individual bodies were likewise observed, classified, and controlled. Similar to the asylums, prisons, schools, and factories of which Foucault writes, strategic hamlets permitted a discipline through surveillance' (Tyner, 2009, p.109). In the case of the villages in Tucumán, it could be argued that there was not only an attempt to discipline bodies in terms of space (Tyner, 2009, p.134), but at the same time create docile spaces, similar to the docile bodies described by Foucault (Foucault, 2013, p.160). By this I mean, submissive, usable, transformable and perfectible spaces. Therefore, forced displacement and relocalization do not only discipline displaced subjects, alongside those who observe these displacements, but also simultaneously discipline space itself. The villages are disciplined spaces that in turn discipline subjects who must get used to living under conditions that are completely new to them.

Although the project for strategic hamlets had the objective of causing a 'draining effect' (Tenembaum, 2010), the opposite happened in Tucumán. These villages today remain almost exactly the same, as if frozen at the moment of their creation, as if the fiction and violence of their origin had caused them to be static, disturbing and never growing in size:

> They built villages (...) but they have not grown (...). From the moment in which they were built to this very day, they remain the same (...). I am talking about '76, '77 when they were built and they are still the same. The same houses just as they were then and there they live, forgotten.
> (E30[12])

This process could be thought of as twofold: some villages became phantasmagorical as they were emptied out, and others were built by force, but are also phantasmagorical in that they became suspended in the time of their foundation and remain as such.

In Vietnam, the 'strategic hamlets' were created in the middle of the war with the clear purpose of serving as a tool for counterinsurgency. If we pay attention to the dates on which the villages in Tucumán were created, it becomes evident that the ultimate aim of these villages was altogether different, given that by the end of 1976 the rural guerrilla force had been almost entirely taken out. It was at this time that the new villages began to be built. One could therefore risk proffering the following hypothesis: that these villages were not so much created to halt or disrupt the guerrillas' advance, but rather to spatially reconfigure the area as a preventative and corrective measure with a view to the future. Infrastructure – roads and villages – was created for what was to come. More than simply serving as the basis on which members of the guerrilla forces were to be defeated, the setting up of the villages was above all a turning point in the process of confrontation.

Spatial disposession of the revolution

In this final section, I give an analysis of the possible implications these spatial reconfigurations might have on ways of inhabiting and imagining space, bearing in mind that my interest here centres on the way in which a space in rebellion is remembered once the confrontation and annihilation has already taken place. In this sense, rather than an analysis of the intentionality behind the dispute over the territory in question, this chapter focuses on the effects these spatial practices have had – and indeed continue to have – on the production of meaning.

The deterritorialization produced by the military in this area of Argentina not only reconfigured space in physical terms, but also operated at the level of meaning, principally by hampering the conditions that made it possible to imagine revolution as something that could happen in this space. Although the effects of reterritorialization can be multiple, what it achieved in this case was what I consider to be the spatial dispossession of the revolution. Taking as my point of reference the term 'accumulation by dispossession' devised by David Harvey (2003), I posit the concept of spatial dispossession in order to refer to the way in which dispossession is exercised over those spaces that question the established system. I understand that subjects were dispossessed of the space of rebellion, constituted by the *monte*, and that the state simultaneously reincorporated it into its territory, even if this reincorporation took a peculiar form. The state emptied out the *monte* and separated if from the rest of the region by establishing geometric and orderly spaces: the new villages and road.

The *monte* was enclosed but not occupied. I would even dare to say that this spatial dispossession operates retrospectively. What I mean is that this emptying out infiltrates many of the remembered accounts of what happened during the period of confrontation. It is unlikely that anyone who has lived in this region does not know about what happened in the *monte*, the stories about the guerrillas, the confrontations, and the reasons they were fighting. When I asked about what had happened in the *monte*, however, the most frequent response would suggest that there was no one there, that the guerrilla forces were only hiding there, and that the military was effectively bombing an empty forest. With the exception of the political militants whom I interviewed, very few people spoke openly about their disappeared relatives as linked to what had taken place in the *monte*, whether as collaborator or member of the guerrilla movement. Although this certainly has to do directly with the stigma that still weighs upon the stories of collaboration with members of the guerrilla force, I find this difficulty in speaking about this link between the space of the montane forest and the space of the plain significant. This difficulty refers to a process of spatial disarticulation worked at over time. Spatial dispossession operates, therefore, not only physically but also at the level of representation, and particularly in the way in which this cuts off the possibility of imagining revolution as taking place in this space.

Among the few references that I managed to collate in my fieldwork concerning instances of collaboration between the civilian population in the area and the guerrillas in the forest, one interviewee recounted that:

> yes, the people did in some way help the guerrilla forces with food. [...] And the people who were discovered by the military to be supplying them with food were killed. They killed them and brought them down. [...]

But I don't know what they [the guerrilla forces] were fighting for? No, no I don't know what their fight would have been about.

(E25[13])

The space of confrontation is recovered by the state, but in order to empty it out rather than occupy it. The state thus made this space governable on the basis of a latent, threatening emptiness. With the physical emptying out of the *monte*, its stories of struggle seem to have dissipated.

This reterritorialization that is produced on the basis of the emptying out is the state's way of creating a space that – albeit uninhabitable – becomes a constitutive part of its own spatiality. I do not consider the emptied forest to imply the absence of the state, but rather that the state regulates from this vacated place. The presence of the state can operate and exist on the basis of this emptiness. The state is also constructed in these spaces that it leaves unoccupied. In this sense, Brenner and Elden (2009) maintain that the state constantly produces its territory: 'the national territory results from a historically specific, mutually transformative articulation between the state, the continually contested processes within it, and the land or soil that it inhabits, owns, controls and exploits' (Brenner and Elden, 2009, p.362). My interpretation is that the creation of the villages alongside the emptying of the *monte* can be read as two exercises of territorial practice through which the state turned a rebel space into a deserted space and thus achieved a reconfiguration of the ways in which it can be both inhabited and imagined in rebellion.

However, spatial dispossession is not a fait accompli, but rather a constant process and, as a result, the spatial dispossession of the revolution is not a permanent condition. The confrontation over the definition of this space and over what can take place therein is a confrontation that is periodically revisited. It is in these confrontations that different ways of conceiving the world are settled, as well as divergent ways of being located and existing in space. The spatial dispossession of the revolution is not a condition that should forever remain associated with this particular territory.

Notes

The research leading to this chapter has received funding from the Spanish National Research Council (JAE Predoc scholarship CSIC, 2009–2013), the postdoctoral grant funded by the Fondation Fyssen (2014–2016) and the ERC funded research programme Corpses of Mass Violence and Genocide.

1. The *monte* is an elevated region, though not quite attaining the height of a mountain range. The Tucumán *monte* in particular has a thick, jungle like vegetation.
2. It is important to highlight that this military operation began under democracy, as the coup d'état in Argentina would not take place until a year later on 24 March 1976.

3. The analysis presented here is based on a total of 50 in-depth interviews, in which the confidentiality of interviewees was assured. The names of those interviewed will, therefore, not appear and will be referred to by the number given to their interview.
4. Militant belonging to the *Peronismo de Base* (Grassroots Peronism – PB) and subsequently for the *Fuerzas Armadas Peronistas* (Peronist Armed Forces – FAP) in the south of Tucumán. During the dictatorship he had to go into exile.
5. Militant belonging to the movement *Peronismo de Base* from the village of Monteros (a village situated within the Army's zone of operations). During the occupation, he gave up his militancy and continued living in the same village.
6. See footnote 4.
7. Originally from León Rouges (village located within the zone of operations), he was a worker in the sugar plantations. His father had disappeared and subsequent to this interview, his remains have been identified by the Argentine Team of Forensic Anthropology (Equipo Argentino de Antropología Forense – EAAF).
8. See footnote 4.
9. In the trial of Luciano Benjamín Menéndez (former Commander-in-Chief of the III Artillery of the Army) for the misappropriation of land in order to establish the village of Capitán Cáceres (*La Gaceta* 21 October 2010), District Attorney Emilio Ferrer made reference to the fact that these villages were built as if they were 'strategic hamlets'. Menéndez was sentenced to 12 years imprisonment for this crime in December 2013.
10. The 'strategic hamlets' project is not, however, limited to what took place in Vietnam. Tenembaum (2010) states that the origins of this idea go back to the technique employed in Malaysia by the British government. He adds furthermore that, if we were to shift our attention towards the contemporary theatre of conflict, continuities could also be detected with what was carried out by the 'Provincial Reconstruction Team' (PRT) of the United States in Afghanistan.
11. Since the 'Communist threat' was perceived to be as much a political and economic threat as much as a military threat, a major innovation of the Kennedy Administration was the coupling of civilian-led economic development programs to military counterinsurgency via the 'modernization theory' popularized by Walt Rostow, Lucien Pye and Alexis Johnson.

(Belcher, 2013, p.39)

12. Trade unionist and worker in the sugar factory in Aguilares (there was also a military base in the village of Aguilares). During the dictatorship, he disappeared in a clandestine detention centre in Tucumán.
13. The interviewee is a native of the village of Concepción (where there were also military bases) and has two brothers who have disappeared.

Bibliography

Belcher, Oliver. 2013. *The Afterlives of Counterinsurgency: Postcolonialism, Military Social Science and Afghanistan, 2006–2012*. Unpublished doctoral thesis in Geography, University of British Columbia.

Brenner, Neil and Stuart Elden. 2009. 'Henri Lefebvre on State, Space, Territory'. *International Political Sociology*, 3: 353–377.

Carnovale, Vera. 2010. 'La guerra revolucionaria del PRT-ERP'. *Sociohistórica*, 27: 41–75.

Crenzel, Emilio. 2001. 'Memorias enfrentadas. El voto a Bussi en Tucumán'. http://comisionporlamemoria.net/bibliografia2012/memorias/Crenzel.pdf, date accessed 15 January 2013.
De Santis, Daniel, ed. 2010. *La historia del PRT-ERP: por sus protagonistas*. Capital Federal: A FORMAR FILAS Editora Guevarista.
Deleuze, Gilles and Félix Guattari. 2012. *Mil Mesetas. Capitalismo y esquizofrenia*. Valencia: Pre-Textos.
Elden, Stuart. 2009. *Terror and Territory: The Spatial Extent of Sovereignty*. Minneapolis: University of Minnesota Press.
Foucault, Michel. 2013. *Surveiller et punir. Naissance de la prison*. Paris: Gallimard.
Garaño, Santiago. 2012. *Entre el cuartel y el monte. Soldados, militantes y militares durante el Operativo Independencia (Tucumán, 1975–1977)*. Unpublished doctoral thesis in Anthropology, Universidad de Buenos Aires, Buenos Aires.
Gregory, Derek. 2004. *The Colonial Present: Afghanistan, Palestine, Iraq*. Oxford: Wiley-Blackwell Publishing.
Harvey, David. 1990. *The Condition of Postmodernity: An Enquiry into the Origins of Cultural Change*. Malden: Blackwell.
Harvey, David. 2003. 'Accumulation by Dispossession'. In *The New Imperialism*, edited by David Harvey. Oxford: Oxford University Press, 137–182.
Isla, Alejandro. 2007. 'Disyuntivas de las memorias en el recuerdo y en las prácticas de la vida corriente'. *El Cotidiano*, 22 (145): 97–104.
La Gaceta. 2010. 'Una mujer de 86 años exige restitución de la sede la Municipalidad de Ganeros'. 21 October 2010. http://www.lagaceta.com.ar/nota/404470/mujer-86-anos-exige-restitucion-sede-municipalidad-graneros.html?origen=mlt, date accessed 15 March 2014.
Lefebvre, Henri. 1991. *The Production of Space*, translated by Donald Nicholson-Smith. Oxford: Blackwell Publishing.
Oslender, Ulrich. 2006. 'Des-territorialización y desplazamiento forzado en el Pacífico colombiano: La construcción de "geografías de terror"'. In *(Des)territorialidades y (No)lugares: Procesos de configuración y transformación del espacio social*, edited by Diego Herrera Gómez and Carlo Emilio Piazzini Suárez. Medellín: La Carreta Editores.
Said, Edward. 1979. *Orientalism*. New York: Random House.
Tenenbaum, Élie. 2010. 'Les déplacements de populations comme outil de contre-insurrection: l'exemple du programme des hameaux stratégiques au sud-vietnam'. *Guerres Mondiales et conflits contemporains*, 3 (239): 119–41.
Tyner, James A. 2009. *War, Violence, and Population: Making the Body Count*. New York: The Guilford Press.
Vilas, Adel. 1977. 'Diario de Campaña. Tucumán: Enero a Diciembre de 1975'. http://archive.is/JD6Gr, date accessed 15 January 2014.
Poder Ejecutivo. 1976. Ley N 4.530. 16 August 1976. San Miguel de Tucumán.

4
Subterranean Autopsies: Exhumations of Mass Graves in Contemporary Spain

Francisco Ferrándiz

Underground terror

The concept of 'subterranean' which I use in this text aims to extend the semantic field of the experience of defeat in the Spanish Civil War.[1] It tries to contribute to the deciphering of the historical, social, political and symbolic profile of the tens of thousands of people executed by the insurgent army and associated paramilitaries in the rearguard of the Spanish Civil War (1936–39) and subsequently in Francoist post-war Spain, and whose lives ended with their bodies heaped up in mass graves all over the country. In other words, 'subterranean' is a deeply spatial concept which refers to the historical translation and contemporary deciphering of a mapping of terror, whose efficacy has survived, albeit transformed, to the present day. In the year 2000, a process of unearthing this subterranean past began in Spain and, in the course of a decade, has affected some 300 mass graves and around 6,000 bodies (Etxeberria, 2012; Ferrándiz, 2013).

As a result of these contemporary exhumations, this specific group of war bodies, forgotten for decades, has gradually acquired visibility in public space in a series of different modalities which I will later analyse. This process has led to a profound and many-sided reterritorialization of these cadavers, radically transforming their social, historical and political profile. The contemporary opening of these mass graves – understood as memoryscapes (Cole, 2001, pp.289–293) – and the public exhibition of the cadavers they contain in the context of contemporary information and knowledge society (Castells, 1996), radically removed from the historical moment in which the executions occurred, have forced Spain into a painful confrontation with victims of repressive violence who were not only part of the justification shoring up the Francoist dictatorship, but were then deprived of legitimacy and recognition during the transition to democracy and the subsequent years.

The condition of being 'below ground' therefore refers to a kind of subterranean exodus, perhaps an extreme form of interior exile, which may share an historical origin with those who were exiled, banished or forced to abandon Spain after the war, but which occurred in circumstances, and entails a social, political, symbolic and judicial history, of its own. I refer, in particular, to its relationship with the experience of violent death in the context of a policy of extermination of the adversary, and to the successive diverse regimes of political and social amnesia suffered by the series of cadavers that were strewn, by way of example, in mass graves across the country.

The graves that have been opened in Spain since the year 2000 are, for the most part, the result of irregular burials derived from what prominent historians have dubbed the 'exterminating fury' of coordinated cleansing actions by the rearguard of the insurgent army, which then continued afterwards during the dictatorship (Juliá, 1999, p.19; Casanova, 1999, 2002). The historiography of recent years, written both in Spain and elsewhere, has taken major strides in documenting and analysing the multiplicity of forms of overlapping violence that took place during the Civil War and its aftermath, where there was less mortality on the battlefield than in the repressive actions taken away from the fronts (Rodrigo, 2008, p.25). More specifically, it has enabled a better mapping of the nature and scale of the rearguard exterminatory machinery on both sides, as well as their evolution, forms, regional variants and spatial characteristics.

According to this critical historiographical tendency, the mass graves that would later become those of the defeated side are a crucial part of an investment in terror associated with a planned 'pedagogy of blood' that had already been staged in the colonial wars in Morocco (Rodrigo, 2008; Preston, 2012), which was key to the insurgent army's military strategy in rearguard regions as they came under its control. As places of exemplifying memory or memorials of fear, the presence of the mass graves of the defeated on the national landscape contributed, not only physically, but also politically, symbolically and socially, to the shoring up of the dictatorial regime imposed on the country after the war, under the rule of General Francisco Franco.

Regarding the historical handling of the war cadavers, we can postulate the creation in Spain of two clearly differentiated 'spaces of death' (Taussig, 1987), in which the bodies accepted as 'belonging' to the victors received a privileged treatment that was radically distinct from that meted out to the cadavers of the vanquished. For the former, specific legislation was introduced after the end of the war, formal guidelines for retrieval and reburial were set out, municipal burial fees were eliminated or reduced, a heroic, martyrological account was constructed and diverse forms of visibilization, tribute and dignification were established. All the effort that went into this provision for funerary re-entry was expressed in a highly ideologized landscape commemorated by Francoist landmarks and memorials which have partially survived to the present day.

In contrast to this hegemonic and public reterritorialization of the 'martyrs' of the new 'motherland', the cadavers of the defeated were, on the one hand, held up as an example of the potential fate of those dissenting from the regime: execution and coup de grace. On the other, they were contemptuously abandoned to their fate in mass graves. This marked the start of a long subterranean odyssey lasting several decades. An analysis of postwar funerary legislation makes it clear that Francoist law applied only to the cadavers of the 'heroes', 'martyrs' and 'fallen' of the 'Crusade'; Republican corpses, and, by extension, the mass graves that contained them, were excluded from politically legitimate and socially prestigious sites of reburial, commemoration and dignification.

This legal and ideological discrimination against the Republican space of death is clearly expressed in the successive excavation and reburial guidelines drawn up after the war. In previous texts (Ferrándiz, 2009, 2013), I have highlighted the importance of understanding the twenty-first century exhumations in historical perspective: in other words, as the most recent episode in a series of different moments of dislocation and reterritorialization of war corpses across the country. To put it succinctly, the cycles of disinterment and reburial in Spain that have followed one after the other (at times overlapping) included, from the outset, a project for the generalized recovery and dignification – albeit in no way complete given the huge scale of the war, the high level of mortality and the state's organizational difficulties – of 'heroes' and 'martyrs' of the winning side in the post-war period, fully and officially endorsed by the dictatorship in ad hoc administrative procedures, ritualization and a legitimizing account within the political–religious framework known as 'National Catholicism' (Aguilar, 2008; Box, 2010). Subsequently, from the fifties onwards, more than 33,000 bodies from the Civil War were politically, administratively and symbolically hauled to the Valle de los Caídos, or Valley of the Fallen, as organized by the Francoist State, which entrusted their funerary and religious custody to the Benedictine order (Ferrándiz, 2011). In 1975, Francisco Franco was also buried in this monumental space of death, dissipating any doubt about its unmistakeable association with the military victory and the dictatorship.

In the twentieth century, underground Republican graves were also excavated. During the Francoist period, this was generally done in a piecemeal and clandestine way. During the transition to democracy and subsequently, a large number of excavations were conducted. These were still not part of a state public policy, but rather were carried out primarily on the initiative of local relatives' groups, devoid of any technical support and with little repercussion in the media. The mass graves that have been opened since the year 2000 are now adding a new stratum of exhumation, reburial and, in general, spatial relocation of war cadavers.

Bodies *unveiled*: Social autopsy

The work of Walter Benjamin represents a crucial vanishing point in understanding the dialectical relationship between past and present in the modern day and can help us conceptualize the condition I am calling 'subterranean'. For him, the historical knowledge required to produce critical awareness of the present comes, not from major milestones in the history of the victors, but from ruins and fragments, from remains that can be found buried, hidden or half-forgotten in the interstices of culture (Buck-Morss, 1991, pp.x–xi; Zamora, 2008, pp.110–11). For Benjamin, it is precisely the vestiges of the oppressed or the vanquished which demonstrate that the 'state of emergency' is not the exception but the rule, in industrial society and culture and, by extension, in the information society (Benjamin, 2005, Thesis VIII; Agamben, 2004).

In this context, those underground irrupt unexpectedly into contemporary life as the remains of the stories told and hegemonic funerary spatialities, as part of the ruins which progress has left in its wake, as fragments of a memory that flashes suddenly, like lightning, at a moment of danger, as part of the doom-laden vision of Benjamin's angel of history.[2] And this irruption turns wounded skeletons and the graves containing them into a basic enzyme, kickstarting the critical reinterpretation of the historical process of the past century in Spain, and in particular its complicity, silence and neglect. It does so, on the one hand, from the heart of a repression deeply branded into the landscape and a mapping of terror that has aged over the years. And it does so, on the other, from the edge of an historical awareness of the war, to which, for decades, they have been sidelined.

As has been documented in many other cases of mass burials derived from armed conflict and human rights violations, the deliberate mingling of unidentified bodies in unnamed graves and their funerary dislocation has great potential to inject disorder, anxiety and division into the social fabric for decades (Robben, 2000). The sudden reappearance of bodies violated and piled into mass graves, six or seven decades earlier, has triggered a parallel mapping of contemporary dangers which casts doubt upon the depth and quality of Spanish democracy (Benjamin, 2005; Mate, 2009; Buck-Morss, 1991, pp.253–262). I have argued that the distribution of mass graves all over the country stemmed from an attempt to inflict paralysis by provoking fear and spreading terror throughout social and political structures. The fact that these graves continue to generate tension and controversy in present-day Spanish society, and their entropic capacity, confirm that they are effective even in the long term. It would also be true to say, however, that their signification and the intensity of their effects on the social fabric, particularly in rural areas, have varied substantially over time.

Yet over and above the history of the exhumations resulting from the Civil War, the signification and status of the mass graves of defeat – which account for the majority of rearguard graves left disregarded across the state – were not arrested in time when the echoes of the shots died away and the perpetrators abandoned them. As a subterranean legacy – part of the 'shadow of the Republic' that has always loomed as a critique over Francoism (Mate, 2009, p.22) – the graves have never been lifeless objects, but are complex spatial processes which have gradually been 'impregnated' with 'successive presents' (Iniesta, 2009). They have thus been transformed, along with the country in which they were used, the regimes and political cultures that have followed and the criminal, between archaeological and patrimonial or funerary legislation which sidestepped them. As witnesses have died, as landscapes have been transformed, cemeteries moved or remodelled and infrastructures developed (especially roads, the extension of which has deleted a multitude of *cunetas* or roadside graves), those who were executed and thrown into mass graves have been left virtually defenceless in a cumulative series of abandonments of the same dead bodies, not only during the dictatorship, but also well into the democratic period.

In the last decade, there has been a radical change towards the death politics of the war and its aftermath. The stories of crime and execution revealed by these exhumations and their contemporary deployment from below ground into cyberspace, which I will outline later, has made them a focus of contemporary disputes about the memory of the Spanish Civil War, which can be perceived as a 'nervous system'. Taussig's metaphor (Taussig, 1992), derived in part from his interpretation of Benjamin's thought, understands the presence of a traumatic past in contemporary historical awareness as a network of highly sensitive synaptic terminals which encompasses, in the case of the Spanish Civil War, everything from historiographical accounts to places of memory, funerary spaces, museums, exhibitions, monuments, hymns, tributes, archives, works of art, albums and personal objects (Nora, 1989). When these synaptic terminals connect with mass graves and the space of death that they represent, the nerve impulse generated spreads throughout the social fabric, in its multiple ramifications and with differing degrees of acceleration, from the cruellest information about the repression (evidence of torture, malnutrition, bullet wounds) to the objects of deep personal significance which appear in them or the emotions that are still so hard to express.

But times have changed drastically between the moment of the executions and the contemporary reappearance of the bodies. Now children of the twenty-first century, these exceptional bodies, retrieved in extremis from the shadows and interstices of history, must confront a late modernity on a planetary scale, a globalized modernity, which many authors define in terms of interconnection, interdependence, collapse of time and space, cosmopolitanism, deterritorialization, acceleration, vertigo, simulation or saturation of experience (Harvey, 1989; Watts, 1992; Castells, 1996).

Their public revelation is therefore determined by a radical spatial and temporal disjunction between the conditions of life and death in the war and post-war period, and in a society profoundly transformed by globalizing processes and successive technological revolutions (Lyotard, 1984). The same transformation and acceleration or chronic emergency of experience which affects the inhabitants of this late-modern age, affects the dead bodies of the past irrupting into this same social fabric. Thus, the executed bodies make a dramatic and spectacular reappearance in the information and knowledge society, deeply conditioned in their appearance and diffusion – not just within the scope of a nation state but also, simultaneously, in a transnational context – through the viewing and dissemination capabilities of digital devices, and through proliferation in the media and social networks, particularly as of the second part of the decade. The bodies from the graves emerge from their underground context in a biopolitical regime which Mbembe – elaborating on Foucault's classic formulation for the analysis of the shadows which the exercise of power projects over death, war, wounded and executed bodies and so on – has called 'necropolitical' (Mbembe, 2003).

The executed bodies therefore emerge into the public space beneath the spotlight of the expansive transnational discourse on human rights and the growing prestige of mass grave exhumations, as a tool to right the wrongs of the past within a transnational justice paradigm. They are therefore bodies branded simultaneously with signification and violent death derived from two vast periods of time and two very different regimes of corporeal fragility. On the one hand there is the impunity of the arrests, abuses and executions carried out at the time the mass graves were made during the war and its aftermath. On the other there is the potential corporeal and iconographic precariousness derived from the fragmentation and loss of context of the cadavers when viewed under the magnifying glass or microscope of the information and knowledge society.

Having outlined the current context in which the unearthed bodies and the spaces of death containing them have been unveiled, we can go on to follow their escape routes from mass grave to public space in the social, political and technological context of contemporaneity. The underground bodies contained in the graves have become 'mute protagonists', albeit of extraordinary significance, in the process of the 'recovery of historical memory' in twenty-first century Spain (Ferrándiz, 2009, 2013). The monitoring and analysis of their deployment throughout diverse areas of contemporary experience, from more private spaces, including political, legal and symbolic practices, to the transnational sphere or cyberspace, allows us, to re-use a concept elaborated by Klinenberg (2002), to conduct a 'social autopsy' of their impact on contemporary Spain and, at the same time, indicate their trajectory beyond national boundaries, into the transnational catalogue of crimes against humanity.

Afterlives: New spatialities beyond the mass grave

The unexpected reappearance of these underground bodies in contemporary Spain has triggered very diverse and controversial processes. The unearthed bodies – radically eloquent but a necessarily awkward reality – are deeply intertwined with their new host society, one that is very different from the society that executed them and left them to their fate decades earlier. By putting dissimilar spaces and temporalities under strain in their emergence, they question everything from domestic silence to crucial political agreements. In this process of spatial and temporal collapse between the repressive policies of the past and public exposure in exhumations in the present, the executed bodies are subject to discourses and technological regimes of different kinds and varying social influence and, at the same time are turned into new places of memory, debate and controversy for the living (Crossland, 2009, p.147). This is therefore a process of simultaneous inscription or reciprocal impregnation between the exhumed bodies and the different contemporary spheres through which they are deployed.

I shall briefly outline this anachronistic irruption of corpses marked by the violence of seven decades ago in a series of lives beyond the mass grave after exhumation, or 'afterlives', expanding on Katherine Verdery's well-known notion of the 'political lives of dead bodies' (Verdery, 1999). Verdery acknowledges that studying the political dimensions of the post-mortem handling of dead bodies is a vast subject which has to be understood in a cross-cutting and interdisciplinary manner. In the Spanish case, the extension of analysis of the areas of impact and controversy regarding a series of dead bodies reterritorialized after decades in 'inappropriate' burial sites requires us to consider a conceptual framework that is even broader and more diverse than she suggests.

Just as in Pierre Nora's initial text around 'places of memory' (Nora, 1989), the claim that the bodies of these mass interments have a 'life beyond the grave' does not lead us to produce a finite catalogue, but rather to explore the itineraries and the effects of each individual life, and their totality, on the emergent bodies and vice versa. Out of the many ways in which the rediscovered bodies could be deployed, we shall briefly consider the following afterlives: associative, political, media, judicial and scientific. These lives beyond the grave add a radical new dimension to the space of death whose historical configuration I have described.

Firstly, the progression of the associative movement based on recovered bodies and their significant reterritorialization has resulted in the gradual development of a political culture which has a certain common consciousness towards the interpretation and ritual and political treatment of these cadavers, despite the differences in their discourses and the practices of some associations (Ferrándiz, 2013). In their diversity and with the uneven institutional support they have received, their activism has had a clear spatial component since the beginning of the twenty-first century: excavations and reburials, revitalization of forgotten or abandoned places of memory, or the drawing up of maps of graves on a provincial, regional or even national scale, using digital technology. In short, a repertoire of redress and reparation has been set in motion, with local and regional variations, but necessarily dependent on the retrieval and spatial relocation of the executed bodies.

This 'associative life' of the dead bodies is intertwined with a complex political life, in the more restricted sense proposed by Verdery. Although the interweaving of underground bodies with political actions occurs at different levels and there are many stakeholders, I shall refer briefly to the main nationwide political initiative directly related to the reappearance of the dead bodies of the defeated. The Law on Historical Memory passed by the Socialist government of José Luis Rodríguez Zapatero at the end of December 2007 included specific sections on exhumations. In particular, Articles 11–14 established that the state would facilitate 'activities investigating, locating and identifying persons who violently disappeared during the Civil War or subsequent political repression and whose whereabouts are unknown'.[3] Although insufficient for many associations, this was the first time that direct, wholesale legislation had been passed on this space of death. The creation of an 'Office of Victims of the Civil War and Dictatorship' in December 2008 and the institutional expression of the process of historical memory in cyberspace through a Government website in 2011 (which included a much-disputed interactive map of graves nationwide) are some of the most tangible results of this law with regard to mass graves, exhumations and reburials.

The judicial afterlives of the people inhabiting this subterranean space of death are also proving both complex and controversial. This is related to the way in which the bodies were and still are ignored, judicialized or avoided by judicial logic and practice, both at the moment of their arrest and execution, and from the moment at which the twenty first century movement for the recovery of historical memory, and more specifically the exhumation process, was set in motion. There is a tense and contradictory relationship between the two periods and legal regimes affecting the cadavers – (a) the war in the rebel area and the Francoist post-war period and (b) the contemporary period – regarding both the excavation itself and the process of returning the dead bodies to politics and society.

This judicial afterlife reached a decisive point with the proposition put forward in October 2008 by Judge Baltasar Garzón to seek a transnational route to provide legal support for the executed in mass graves. His attempt was paralysed, first in Spain's High Court, the *Audiencia Nacional*, and subsequently in the Spanish Supreme Court. Nevertheless, the process set in motion by the reappearance of these exhumed cadavers was to make them a presence in seats of national judicial power, like those mentioned above, and even, at the international level, in the European Court of Human Rights in Strasbourg and at the United Nations.

The media are a crucial space for the projection of exhumed bodies in the contemporary age. Here, reterritorialization beyond the original grave tends, to a greater or lesser extent, to be sensationalized in the information and knowledge society, both by the more traditional media and by the new digital technologies of communication and cyberspace. As befits the vertigo and volatility of such a society of spectacle, the voyage of the exhumed bodies' through the media and the new digital technologies has had its ups and downs, its moments of greater intensity and lesser visibility, periods of new developments and even surprise, alongside others of visual, communicative and empathetic saturation or even overload (Ignatieff, 1998).

As an example of the contemporary process of entanglement of those underground – executed largely in very local contexts – with the circuits of transnational human rights, I shall mention very briefly the iconographic significance of their transformation from persons who have been executed to persons who have disappeared, as derived from Garzón's court order of 2008 which I have already discussed (Ferrándiz, 2010). As the Chilean writer and playwright Ariel Dorfman has stated, the images of the missing or disappeared are already 'a widespread, almost epidemic, image of tragedy and defiance that is just as much a part of our planetary imagination as the brands and logos that pervade us with an opposite sort of message' (Dorfman, 2006, p.255). In view of their iconographic strength and their potential for visual transgression, as this author indicates, they represent the most appropriate response to the disappearances, to the extent that they subvert the policies of making victims invisible. At the same time, they satisfy the needs of contemporary media 'with extreme efficiency and extraordinary poetry' (Dorfman, 2006, p.256; Ferrándiz and Baer, 2008). The arrival in Spain of what have since become prestigious iconographies are crucial in the new ways of making those below ground visible and part of a common space in the exhumations, ceremonies of dignification and handing over of mortal remains that have taken place in many parts of the country, giving them an extraordinary communicative efficacy and symbolic anchorage which no one could have anticipated a few years ago.

Finally, with regard to the technical profile of contemporary exhumations, particularly important is their scientific afterlife, which occurs across multiple dimensions. These include excavation protocols and the documentation which registers the cadavers in the present-day period, as well as their transit through laboratories, their representation in forensic reports, their mention in research projects, books and articles or at academic conferences and seminars, which includes everything from historiographical approaches to others that are philosophical, sociological, psychological or anthropological, as in the case of this chapter. Within this process of biopolitical inscription of the cadavers – in its necropolitical variant (Foucault, 1978; Hardt and Negri, 2000; Mbembe, 2003), the forensic manifestation of the scientific lives of underground bodies is particularly relevant because it generates new spatialities and subjectivities that are closely linked to the growing predominance of a new 'body-centred regime' of evidence and truth (Klinenberg, 2002).

The excavation of mass graves is coordinated by archaeologists and forensic scientists – in the presence of anthropologists, psychologists and other excavation specialists – and, in the absence of judicial guardianship, is geared towards the establishing of chains of custody and to the recovery and documentation of evidence. This is gleaned from the layout of the bodies, from each of the cadavers and objects accompanying it, whether personal items or bullet shells (Crossland, 2009). It is also ascertained from the events leading up to the burials, in particular the moment of death, as well as from other aspects such as social class, gender, age or the sequelae of peri-mortem abuse or torture. The slow, systematic unveiling of the graves occurs at the pace defined by scientific guidelines set out for the excavation. The staging of the viewing of the cadavers, the interpretation of ossuaries and the forms of redress and family and political mourning take place under the auspices of these same knowledge technologies.

Between 2006 and 2012, individualized identification by means of DNA profiling became possible. This has drastically transformed the expectations of many relatives of executed persons, so that they hope to recover specific bodies. There is thus a move away from the initial prestige of the communities of death – if they died together and were thrown together into the same grave, they should be buried together – which had governed sensitivities in the victims' associations of the early years. This process of individual identification of exhumed corpses, together with the growing contemporary prestige of the forensic sciences as a basic tool of redress in cases of human rights violations, is leading to the deployment of an incipient form of 'biological transnational citizenship' for the bodies. This new citizenship for those underground, connected with genetically determined forms of victimization, linked in turn to the spread of certain kinds of human rights discourse and practice, allows us to construct analogies and define differences with other historical experiences of crimes against humanity with the same symbolic and legal weight in other countries (Rose, 2007; Fox, 2005, pp.191–194).

With this social autopsy of some of the contemporary spatial and corporeal itineraries of the executed bodies that have come to light in the last decade, I would like to underline the profound and diverse impact which the exhumation of the mass graves derived from Francoist rearguard repression is having on current Spanish society and even beyond national borders. After this journey, it could be argued that the exhumation of graves and the processes of reterritorialization they set in motion are proving highly relevant in the process of unlearning Francoism and its militaristic legacy. This process of significative disarmament or dismantling of the repressive structure of Francoism and its propagandistic architecture, which, as I have indicated, has a crucial spatial component, is forcing Spain to descend into the almost microscopic details of the injuries by which such repression was branded on to the executed bodies. Thence, contemporary Spanish society must critically confront a diagnostic journey, which takes it from the repertoire of media appearances to laws and judicial proceedings, both present and absent, from the silence of decades to cyberspace, from political controversy and debate to popular commemorations, from books or academic articles to conceptual art, and from genetic profiling to digital representation.

Notes

This chapter is part of the I+D+i project *El pasado bajo tierra* (MINECO CSO2012-32709), and ISCH COST Action IS1203, *In Search of Transcultural Memory*. This is an abridged, adapted version of an article first published in Spanish as 'Autopsia social de un subtierro' (Ferrándiz, 2011).

1. In this text, I will use 'subterranean' and 'below ground' as synonyms, to translate the term 'subtierro' in Spanish, which has no easy equivalent in English. In both cases, they refer to the abandoned mass graves of the defeated in the Civil War which are being exhumed in the twenty-first century.
2. Thesis IX (Benjamin, 2005; Mate, 2009, pp.155–167).
3. Ley 52/2007, 26 December 2007: Law for the recognition and widening of rights and compensation for those who suffered persecution and violence during the Civil War and Dictatorship. *Boletín Oficial del Estado* n° 310 of 27 December 2007: 53410–53416.

Bibliography

Agamben, Giorgio. 2004. *Estado de excepción. Homo Sacer II, 1*. Valencia: Pre-Textos.
Aguilar, Paloma. 2008. *Políticas de la memoria y memorias de la política*. Madrid: Alianza.
Benjamin, Walter. 2005. *Tesis sobre la historia y otros fragmentos*. México: Contrahistorias.
Boletín Oficial del Estado. 27 December 2007. Number 310: 53410–53416. Madrid.
Box, Zira. 2010. *España, año cero*. Alianza: Madrid.
Buck-Morss, Susan. 1991. *The Dialectics of Seeing: Walter Benjamin and the Arcades Project*. Cambridge: MIT Press.
Casanova, Julián. 1999. 'Del terror "caliente" al terror "legal"'. In *Víctimas de la Guerra Civil*, edited by S. Juliá. Madrid: Temas de Hoy.
Casanova, Julián. 2002. 'Una dictadura de cuarenta años'. In *Morir, matar, sobrevivir: La violencia en la dictadura de Franco*, edited by J. Casanova et al. Barcelona: Crítica, 3–50.
Castells, Manuel. 1996. *The Rise of the Network Society, The Information Age: Economy, Society and Culture, Volume I*. Oxford: Blackwell.

Cole, Jennifer. 2001. *Forget Colonialism? Sacrifice and the Art of Memory in Madagascar*. Berkeley: University of California Press.
Crossland, Zoe. 2009. 'Acts of Estrangement: The Making of Self and Other Through Exhumation'. *Archaeological Dialogues*, 16/1: 102–25.
Dorfman, Ariel. 2006. 'The Missing and Photography: The Uses and Misuses of Globalization'. In *Spontaneous Shrines and the Public Memorialization of Death*, edited by J. Santino. New York: Palgrave Macmillan.
Etxeberria, Francisco. 2012. 'Exhumaciones contemporáneas en España: las fosas comunes de la Guerra Civil'. *Boletin Galego de Medicina Legal e Forense*, 18: 13–28.
Ferrándiz, Francisco. 2009. 'Fosas comunes, paisajes del terror'. *Revista de Dialectología y Tradiciones Populares*, LXIV/1: 61–94.
Ferrándiz, Francisco. 2010. 'De las fosas comunes a los derechos humanos: El descubrimiento de las desapariciones forzadas en la España contemporánea'. *Revista de Antropología Social*, 19: 161–189.
Ferrándiz, Francisco. 2011. 'Autopsia social de un subtierro'. *Isegoría*, 45: 524–544.
Ferrándiz, Francisco. 2013. 'Exhuming the Defeated: Civil War Mass Graves in 21st Century Spain'. *American Ethnologist*, 40/1: 38–54.
Ferrándiz, Francisco and Alejandro Baer. 2008. 'Digital Memory: The Visual Recording of Mass Grave Exhumations in Contemporary Spain'. *Forum Qualitative Sozialforschung/Forum: Qualitative Social Research*, 9/3, Article 35. http://www.qualitative-research.net/index.php/fqs/article/view/1152, date accessed 20 February 2014.
Foucault, Michel. 1978. *The Will to Knowledge: The History of Sexuality*, volume 1. New York: Penguin.
Fox, Jonathan. 2005. 'Unpacking "Transnational Citizenship"'. *Annual Review of Political Science*, 8: 171–201.
Hardt, Michael and Antonio Negri. 2000. *Empire*. Cambridge: Harvard University Press.
Harvey, David. 1989. *The Condition of Postmodernity*. Oxford: Blackwell.
Ignatieff, Michael. 1998. *The Warrior's Honor: Ethnic War and the Modern Conscience*. New York: Metropolitan Books.
Iniesta, Montserrat. 2009. 'Patrimonio, ágora, ciudadanía: Lugares para negociar memorias productivas'. In *El Estado y la memoria: Gobiernos y ciudadanos frente a los traumas de la historia*, edited by R. Vinyes. Barcelona: RBA.
Juliá, Santos. 1999. 'Prólogo: De "guerra contra el invasor" a "guerra fratricida"'. In *Víctimas de la Guerra Civil*, edited by S. Juliá. Madrid: Temas de Hoy.
Klinenberg, Eric. 2002. *Heat Wave: A Social Autopsy of Disaster in Chicago*. Chicago: University of Chicago Press.
Lyotard, Jean-François. 1984. *The Postmodern Condition: A Report on Knowledge*. Minneapolis: University of Minnesota Press.
Mate, Reyes. 2009. *Medianoche en la historia*. Madrid: Trotta.
Mbembe, Achille. 2003. 'Necropolitics'. *Public Culture*, 15/1: 11–40.
Nora, Pierre. 1989. 'Between Memory and History: Les Lieux de Memoire'. *Representations*, 26: 7–25.
Preston, Paul. 2012. *The Spanish Holocaust: Inquisition and Extermination in Twentieth-Century Spain*. London: Harper Press.
Robben, Antonius. 2000. 'State Terror in the Netherworld: Disappearance and Reburial in Argentina'. In *Death Squad: The Anthropology of State Terror*, edited by J.A. Sluka. Philadelphia: University of Pennsylvania Press.

Rodrigo, Javier. 2008. *Hasta la raíz: Violencia durante la Guerra Civil y la dictadura franquista*. Madrid: Alianza.
Rose, Nikolas. 2007. *The Politics of Life Itself: Biomedicine, Power, and Subjectivity in the Twenty-First Century*. Princeton: Princeton University Press.
Taussig, Michael. 1987. *Shamanism, Colonialism and the Wild Man: A Study in Terror and Healing*. Chicago: University of Chicago Press.
Taussig, Michael. 1992. *The Nervous System*. New York: Routledge.
Verdery, Katherine. 1999. *The Political Lives of Dead Bodies*. New York: Columbia University Press.
Watts, Michael. 1992. 'Capitalisms, Crisis and Cultures I. Notes Towards a Totality of Fragments'. In *Reworking Modernity: Capitalisms and Symbolic Discontent*, edited by A. Pred and M. Watts. New Brunswick: Rutgers University Press.
Zamora, José Antonio. 2008. 'Dialéctica mesiánica: Tiempo e interrupción en Walter Benjamin'. In *Ruptura de la tradición: estudios sobre Walter Benjamin y Martin Heidegger*, edited by G. Amengual i Coll, M. Cabot Ramis and J. L. Vermal Beretta. Madrid: Trotta.

Part II

The Representation of Violence: Spatial Strategies

5
Faces, Voices and the Shadow of Catastrophe

Jay Winter

The subject of this chapter is the effacement of war in the twentieth century. In painting, sculpture and installation art in many parts of the world today, war is no longer configured through the human face. In part this is a reflection of internal changes in the arts, but in part it is a reflection of the changing nature of war. In 1914, war had a human face – the face of the generation of soldiers who fought and died on the battlefields of the Great War. But over time, the faces of those who have fought war and at times of those who have become its victims have faded slowly from view. The way many of us see war today, I believe, is very different from the way the men and women of 1914–18 saw it. And since what we see matters much more than what we read, it is of some importance to trace the nature and consequences of this flight from figuration, this occlusion of the human face and form, in representations of war in the twentieth century and beyond.

To some extent what we have witnessed is the braiding together of war with terror over the past three generations. To be sure, this is in no sense a twentieth-century innovation. Goya's 'Disasters of War' left hardly anything about human cruelty to the imagination; and the art of photography accompanied both William Sherman's march to the sea in the American Civil War and the bloody suppression of the Boxer rebellion in China at the turn of the century.

What the visual arts were able to convey in the twentieth century were central shifts in the targets of war, and hence in its killing power. The terror in total war rests in part on the industrialization of violence, and in part on the fact that the reach of the state was greater than ever before; consequently, in wartime, no one was ever safe. After 1914, a new kind of assembly-line destruction emerged, mixing high explosive shells and poison gas, and by the 1930s air power as well as toxic forms of ideology in different deadly amalgams. As a result, war and mass terror became virtually synonymous.

The nature and rules of war itself shifted in significant ways too. In 1914–18, the rules of engagement on the battlefield changed; in the interwar years, the bombing of civilian targets became for the first time a centrepiece of armed conflict; after 1941, genocide became an integral part – some would say the defining part – of the war the Nazis waged. In each case, though in different ways, terror became the unavoidable face of war and artists were there to configure it, to give terror a face, a name and a place. This essay sketches some of the ways artists created enduring representations of the twentieth-century degeneration of warfare into inescapable terror. The individuals whose work I focus on are Otto Dix, Pablo Picasso and Anselm Kiefer, though I will refer to other individuals and forms of configuration of the victims of war as well.

All three artists are well known, but putting them together may help to see more clearly both the changing link between history and terror and the changing strategies of configuring war over the past century. The evolution of visual representations of war shows how images change when targets, or victims, change. In the Great War, terror had a face, and it was that of the soldier. There were tens of millions of victims, but the ones to receive iconic status, both during the conflict and in its aftermath, were the men at the front. There were other nominees we could name. The victims of the Armenian genocide were there, but the political conflict over their treatment went on and on and made their genocidal fate contested terrain. But no one doubted at the time that the enduring images of industrial killing in the 1914–18 returned again and again to the men in the trenches, the men we still call the 'lost generation'.

Aerial bombardment came to both Europe and the world with a vengeance in the 1930s. Both the Japanese and the Italians used poison gas in warfare in China and in Ethiopia, but it was aerial bombardment in Europe which presented another enduring set of images, this time of the plight of innocents in wartime. Here the iconic figures were civilians, townspeople, farmers and their animals, under indiscriminate and devastating bombardment from the air.

When we turn to the 1939–45 war, any interrogation of the linkage between war, terror and history must consider the Holocaust. And over time, the Holocaust has come to occupy a larger and larger place within the history of the Second World War. Still the Shoah was by no means the only wartime instance of mass murder and butchery of people not for what they did, but for who they were. The Rape of Nanjing in 1937, as well as the Ustasha-led genocide in Yugoslavia, both deserve our attention here, as does the terror induced by the 'conventional' fire-bombing of Tokyo or Dresden or the dropping of the two atomic bombs on Japan. These acts of war unleashed a debate about the use of terror, which echoes down to our own times.

This first point is a simple one: as war changed, so did its artistic configuration. The second point I present in this chapter is more formal in character. When one moves from the Great War to the interwar years and then to the Second World War, the partial occlusion of the human face in the configuration of terror is one of the most striking features of changing European representations of war. There are certainly exceptions, but on balance, the move I try to document here is one away from a naturalistic representation of the human face and figure. Thus the images in Otto Dix's Great War paintings, produced from 1914 to 1940, are still life-size and identifiably human, though the soldiers so represented faced monumental horror on the field of battle. The terror of the victims of the destruction of Guernica in Picasso's painting is inscribed in part in facial features, and in part in the cruciform and symbolic elements of the ensemble. In contrast, there is a much more complex set of choices in artistic representations of the Second World War in general and of the Holocaust in particular. There have been many non-figurative images used metonymically to stand for the monstrous whole. Many representations of the organized destruction of synagogues in Germany in November 1938 are void of figures; this was true of much, though not all, photography at the time. It remains true in later representations of this iconic act, as in the case of Kiefer's 'The Breaking of the Vessels', which will be examined later in this text.

A different set of problems emerged when artists approached the task of representing the emptying of a whole discrete world, the Jewish world of central and Eastern Europe, an entire population, its language, its culture, its presence, now almost entirely gone. The dimensions of this, the essential victory registered by Hitler, are in their magnitude, terrifying. And yet this terror has been made visceral first in art by portraiture, in prose, in poetry, and then later by the effacement of figuration itself. Consider first the face of Anne Frank on her published diary, or her conventional, and at times, sanitized, representation on the stage and in film as one end of the spectrum. Then consider the work of Anselm Kiefer or the architecture of Daniel Libeskind's Jewish Museum in Berlin as an alternative. To be sure, there is a vast array of configurations between the two, but my point is that this flight from figuration is not particularly evident in the case of the Great War or of warfare in the 1930s. Only after the Holocaust, and perhaps in part because of the Holocaust, has abstraction come into its own as an indispensable way of representing the links between war, terror and history.

Putting a human face on the Holocaust may be an impossibility, not because the crime was indescribable, but because its enormity seems to have undermined certain currents of humanistic thinking which return to the face as the source of our knowledge of ourselves and others. Rembrandt's self-portraits are eloquent of what I mean. Here is Emmanuel Levinas's phrasing of the issue: 'The face', he writes, 'a thing among other things, pierces' the fragility of our existence. 'The face speaks to me and thereby invites me into a relationship with another, a relationship without parallel, leading either to fulfillment or to recognition' (Levinas, 1961, p.172).[1] The Holocaust erased or blotted out that face, that relationship, that recognition. In that sense, it had no face, and thus no meaning. Facelessness is a language of post-Holocaust art.

In sum my claim is that over the past century war has had a history in the visual arts and in the arts of representation just as much as it does in the very material and lethal practices of war and mass murder. I suggest that, in contrast to the terror of trench warfare in 1914–18 or the destruction of towns and ordinary people under the bombers in the interwar years and after, there emerged a different kind of non-figurative configuration of war and terror after Auschwitz. And yet the human face, that profile about which Primo Levi asked us to consider 'if this be a man' (Levi, 1991), did not vanish completely. If conventional figuration seemed inadequate to the task at hand, many jurists, survivors, artists and healers turned to a different kind of portraiture, to a different field of force, this time one with voices attached to them. Conjuring up the Holocaust has turned to the human voice more and more, in an effort to capture the shape and sentiment of the six million who vanished during the Shoah, and of the men and women who survived the slaughter. Voices are speech acts to which we attach faces, as any radio listener can attest.

A more precise way of putting the point is to say that the Shoah made ambiguous a return to the human form as a metonym for mass suffering as occurred in the art dedicated to capturing some sense of the terror of war in 1914–18 or of warfare in the interwar years. Instead representations of the terror of the Holocaust describe a house of many mansions, most of them ruined. Some employ figuration – for example in Resnais's 1955 masterpiece *Nuit et Brouillard*, in the close-up photography and voices of Claude Lanzmann's *Shoah* (1985), and in the video portraits, preserved in Holocaust survivor archives around the world, to recapture the face of terror in the faces of those who survived it. At the same time, other artists have used more abstract metonyms, or gestures towards the terror in the art of ruins – here Kiefer is a central figure – or of what James Young has termed 'anti-monuments', those which disappear (Young, 2000). I want to discuss this shifting landscape of the representation of the terror of the Holocaust primarily through the installation art of Anselm Kiefer.

The distinction between privileging the voice and privileging the face in representations of terror and its victims is here a heuristic one. Both have had their place in the representation of war and terror. Still, I argue that there has been a change, in the sense that voices matter more now after the end of the twentieth century than at its beginning. The cry of wounded men in the battle of Somme in 1916 is something we can never hear; the drone of the bombers or the voices of those under the Condor legion's attack in Guernica are not available to us; but the voices of those who went through the camps and, in the words of Jeremiah (44:28), became *am s'ridai charev* ('the survivors of the sword'), those who came out of the slaughterhouse alive, those voices are with us: they are powerful and perhaps unique. I suggest that auditory commemoration is now an art form; it has now developed in museums, in archives, in film, on the Internet and in the court room, as a complex complement to the earlier facial and figurative representation of terror in wartime. We now hear what war and terror were and are, and perhaps through hearing it, in a way we can 'see' them or imagine them too.

What we hear, after all, when affect is attached to a voice, configures visual images in powerful ways. The great British journalist Alistair Cooke, whose 'Letter to America' was broadcast on BBC radio every Sunday morning for 40 years, was asked one day why he preferred to work in radio. His answer was: The pictures are better.

Mediations: Otto Dix and trench warfare

In Otto Dix's etchings of the Great War the range of horrors he configured was evident. He showed what it meant to live with the dead: indeed, the living begin to resemble the dead. He portrayed men descending a slope with machine gun equipment alongside what appears to be a landslide of corpses. Other times the living rest alongside and are braided together with the entrails of men and the roots of trees. Elsewhere he presents a crucifixion of living things and humans alike. He shows us the terror of combat, through the gas-mask covered faces of storm troopers, and the unmasked and unhinged face of a trench soldier. In one etching of this series entitled 'Transplantation' (Figure 5.1), the human face has been transformed in order to resemble something like a face, but in its very transformation, the horror of combat and injury take on new and terrifying forms.

Once more the notion of the human face as the measure of terror extends from the living to the dead, from the mad to the mutilated. If we do not look at the face of the warrior, Dix tells us, we do not know anything about war, nor do we know about the terror it spread among the millions of men who endured it.

Death descends from the skies

In the two decades after the 1914–18 conflict, war and terror again were redefined by technology; the emergence of bombers capable of reaching any city in Europe with a load of explosives made the terror of war move from trenches to cities. Stanley Baldwin, the British Prime Minister, famously asserted in 1932 that the bomber 'will always get through'. From 1936 on, the notion circulated very widely that the outbreak of war in Europe was bound to mean civilian deaths on a hitherto unknown scale. Even though this catastrophe did not happen in September 1939 when war broke out, its contours were already well known.

In part, that shift of the image of terror from trenches to cities was a function of newsreels. But while newsreels brought the facts of war to millions virtually at the same moment the violence happened, it was art mediated by newsreels, which provided us with iconic images of terror. I refer to Pablo

82 *The Representation of Violence: Spatial Strategies*

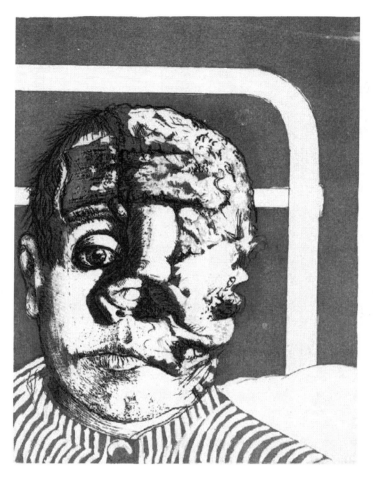

Figure 5.1 Dix, Otto. *Transplantation*
Copyright: VG Bild-Kunst, Bonn 2014.

Picasso's 'Guernica' (Figure 5.2), painted in a fever in the four weeks following the Condor Legion's attack on the Basque city on 26 April 1937. Here was what contemporaries termed 'terror bombing' the purpose of which was not to move the line to the advantage of one side in the war, but to destroy the lives of non-combatants behind the lines.

This obliteration of the distinction between civilian and military targets had begun in 1914, when Belgian and French civilians were targeted or executed by advancing German troops. This degeneration of the rules of warfare was evident in the case of Russian atrocities in Galicia in 1915, and in the expulsion and murder of nearly one million Armenians from Eastern Turkey,

Figure 5.2 Picasso, Pablo. *Guernica*
Copyright: Sucession Picasso/ VG Bild-Kunst, Bonn 2014.

begun in the same year. Civil wars throughout Eastern Europe and what was termed euphemistically by diplomats 'population exchange' in Greece and Turkey after the war made everyone the target of military or paramilitary violence. But it was air power that transformed the face of war, and began to change the way the human face itself was represented in the visual arts.

Picasso's 'Guernica' is probably the most celebrated and perhaps the most circulated image of war in our times or at any time. Attention to its structure can tell us much about configurations of terror in the time when death came from the skies. The composition is marked, even framed, by newsprint, and by the black and white of newsreels. There are two clusters of faces. Three on the right, terrified faces of people are moving to the centre of the scene; three on the left are victims; one man, probably a soldier, broken sword in hand, is prostrate, indeed cruciform in shape, with a frozen cry on his face; his eyes still see, but those of the child to his left do not. His dead body is cradled by his mother. In the centre are two animals: an immutable bull and a terrified horse above which an electric light shimmers.

It is precisely that, a light bulb, which draws ironic attention to the power of electricity to deliver terror from the air. Picasso painted the 'Guernica' canvas to be displayed in the Spanish pavilion within the *Exposition international des arts et métiers de la vie moderne*, which opened in May 1937. That expo was a celebration of science, and in particular, of electricity, which turned Paris into the city of lights, of illumination promising a cornucopia of benefits to mankind. Raoul Dufy, an artist whom Picasso detested, painted for the expo the biggest mural ever made. It was entitled 'La Fée Électricité', and expressed this bold and naïve view of science as beneficent. It was in gazing at this fair that Walter Benjamin began the meditations which arrived at his celebrated epigram that there is no document of civilization which is not at one and the same time a document of barbarism (Benjamin, 1991). Picasso, casting a jaundiced eye at Dufy's mural, painted that document of barbarism. Terror here had a human face, but it was one detached not only from platitudes about science, but also from prior representations of warfare. Picasso was the artist of angular planes, of body parts decomposed, or rather recomposed to express something figurative art could no longer embody (Winter, 2006).

I prefer to see Picasso as a liminal figure, in which configurations of terror are visible, but not in the kind of composition Otto Dix and his contemporaries knew. Both Dix and Picasso constructed images of terror mediated by prior visual images; photographs in the case of Dix, newsreels in the case of Picasso. The question posed in this chapter is how were the horrors of the Second World War, and the Holocaust, configured? My response is a mixed one. There were conventional and figurative images of war and genocide available at the time. But what we see in the art of terror, which followed the Holocaust is a set of images in which the human figure is either absent or marginal.

Empty spaces

Anselm Kiefer, like me, was a child of the last months of the war. He studied with Joseph Beuys in 1970, and developed some of Beuys's approaches to the use of natural materials – trees, glass, straw, wood – in painting and sculpture. But unlike Beuys, he was never accused of avoiding the Holocaust or his own past. These critiques – mostly without any foundation – surrounded Beuys in his later years, and it is important not to draw too direct a line between Beuys and Kiefer. Here there are clear affinities, but dissimilarities too. Both have mystical elements in their work, but in the case of Kiefer, it is Jewish mysticism, as well as numerous Biblical texts, both Old and New Testament in origin, which have been at the centre of his art in recent years.

Kiefer has addressed the Jewish-German embrace in a host of ways, but rarely through the human face. He uses some figurative elements in his work, but most of the time, the face is effaced. There are notable exceptions. In his early years, he used photography to attack the smugness of Germany after the economic miracle brought it back to the centre of European life and world affairs. He famously photographed himself giving the Nazi salute in front of a military sculpture or other site. In addition, on some rare occasions, he used portraits for ironic purposes. One of his early works is 'The Ways of Worldly Wisdom. Arminius's Battle'. This oil on woodcut mounted on paper is a collage of German romanticism, using the faces of notables in German cultural life to question the still-present danger of the national idea and the myths of Germanness surrounding it.

In his youth, when Kiefer photographed or painted the face and figure, it was in a savagely ironic manner. The face of war was the face of those giving the Nazi salute. He has reproduced a number of photographic images from 1969, which he has integrated in later work. They represent what was no longer possible to configure – the human form frozen in worship of the 'Führer'. The question he has posed ever since is: how to go beyond the figurative and the facial in artistic meditations on the catastrophic century in which he and I were born?

In Kiefer's later work, the human figure is by and large absent. Could it be, I wonder, that he has taken to heart the teachings of the Kabbalah, that we must never reproduce the human face, because that puts us at risk of reproducing the face of God, something entirely forbidden in orthodox Jewish tradition? This may be indirectly evident in a theme Kiefer has returned to time and again: the kabbalistic story of the breaking of the vessels.

In short, the kabbalistic answer to the question posed by theodicy – how can evil exist in a world created by an omnipotent and benevolent God? – is that when God created the universe, he withdrew in space in order to create the void in which the universe was born. The creative material out of which the world came was contained in vessels, which broke into shards through the force of divine creation itself. Those shards fell to earth, and jagged and dangerous, they remained here, as evil in the world. In Kiefer's installation in the St Louis Museum of Art, entitled 'The Breaking of the Vessels' (Figure 5.3), what we see is the *Kristallnacht* or 'Night of Broken Glass', the Nazi driven pogrom of 8 November 1938: the shards of glass, the

Figure 5.3 Kiefer, Anselm. 'Breaking of the Vessels' in the collection of the Saint Louis Art Museum
Courtesy of Anselm Kiefer.

86 *The Representation of Violence: Spatial Strategies*

burnt library of a destroyed synagogue, framed by the kabbalistic signs of the zodiac as a kind of rainbow after the flood.

The photograph 'Holland House Library View after September 1940 Air Raid in London' (Figure 5.4) offers an unusual source for another visualization of the Holocaust, which has dispensed entirely with the human figure: the design of the Jewish Museum in Berlin by Daniel Libeskind. A comparison of installation art and of architecture is certainly difficult to justify. Architecture has abstract elements in it by definition. What is interesting in Libeskind's work is precisely the transformation of photography into architecture (Figure 5.5). The internal design of the museum presents visitors with the crossing lines of the broken and burnt beams of library destroyed by bombing. And it has a sense of an absence, a never to be filled void, which is both uncanny and very troubling. Each time I have visited the museum, I felt ill. It is partly due to the lack of straight lines; partly to the incline of all planes. In part it is due to the absence of the human face.

In recent years, the curators of the museum have filled it with faces. It contains a rich and varied collection of the history of German Jewry over 1000 years. I must admit that this collection, admirable though it is, leaves me cold. This is not because of its design or its meticulous presentation of a world that has vanished. It is because the building overwhelms its contents.

Figure 5.4 BB83_04456 – Holland House library after an air raid, 1940
Copyright: English Heritage.

Figure 5.5 Jewish Museum in Berlin
Photograph by Thomas Bruns. Courtesy of Jewish Museum Berlin.

The void sucks into it whatever objects come to fill it. It is its lack of representational elements, which gives the building its force to act as a work of art.

The external design of the building deploys the same mixture of art and architecture which Kiefer's installations have. It resembles a disassembled Star of David, or a bolt of lightning, which in a flash removed the Jews of Berlin from a city, which had hosted a Jewish community for centuries. Its polished titanium surface forces us to look at it, dazzling in the sun. It points towards Friedrichstrasse, a street where many of the decisions concerning the murder the Jews of Europe were taken. This design tells us much about the absence of human faces, the void at the heart of the Holocaust.

En Guise de conclusion

Terror has a history. It is a history filtered through images, which changed over time. In the Great War, terror took on the face of the *Frontsoldaten*, the *poilu*, Tommy Atkins, those unfortunate men who lived and died in a trench system stretching with various intervals across Europe, from Calais to Caporetto and beyond. Those who withstood the terror, who stood their moral ground, as it were, and remained recognizable human beings, like many of the Anzacs, these men could indeed be seen as heroes. And yet over time, when war lost its human face, so too did the hero. The cult of the military hero is one of the casualties of the changing face of warfare over the past century. This does not mean to diminish the extraordinary bravery of men and women in the Resistance or in later conflicts; it is simply to register a change in both the way war has been waged and how it has been represented.

In the interwar years, the killing power of the bomber separated those who killed from those who were killed, at least in Europe. Slaughter in China after the Japanese invasion of 1931 and the murderous campaigns of 1937 and after took on older forms. But the bomber changed perceptions of war and broadened the pool of victims trapped by the new technology of destruction.

In the Second World War, the face of victimhood changed again. This time there were millions of foot soldiers who died in combat, and millions more civilians who died either under aerial bombardment or in extermination camps. Those who vanished in the Shoah, those who were fed into the machines of assembly-line murder, were the victims of a technology of killing if not new, then one refined and perfected by a kind of demonic Taylorism, to an end almost beyond our imagination. When the liberators of the camps disclosed the remains of those trapped in the terror we now call the Holocaust, there were photographs and newsreels to record the moment. We have film and photos of this encounter between Allied soldiers and the strange, unearthly creatures who emerged from the camps. But over time, the visual record of what Primo Levi termed the actual injury, the insult to humanity, began to fade.

There followed a period when the victims of the camps went into the shadows. As Pieter Lagrou has shown, their face was occluded by the face of the Resistance, whose bravery was undoubted, but whose story of active defiance and struggle contrasted with and superseded that of the survivors of the Holocaust. Only by the late 1960s and early 1970s, when the political reconstruction of Europe was complete, was it possible for there to emerge an audience to hear and to see the survivors of the camps (Lagrou, 1999). This is when voices began to complement (and at times to displace) faces as traces of the catastrophe of Hitler's successful war against the Jews.

In this chapter, I have tried to establish three claims. The first claim is essentially a simple one: as war changed, so did artistic configurations of terror and the victims of terror in wartime. The second point is more formal in character. When we move from the Great War to the interwar years, and then to the Second World War and beyond, we can see that the partial occlusion of the human face is one of the most striking features of changing Western representations of war and terror. There are major exceptions here, to be sure, but on balance, the move is one initially away from a naturalistic or expressionistic representation of the human face and figure in artistic meditations on war and terror.

This turn is not universal. In the history of the Vietnam War, Americans retained many iconic images of a figurative kind, like the photograph of a young girl, her skin flayed by napalm, running in terror towards us or the one of the execution of a prisoner of war during the Tet offensive. Then there is another American icon of the 1960s: the Christ-like face of Che Guevara decked out to show that the CIA got him in the Bolivian jungle. That image has endured, in part because the war against communism endured, lasting throughout the Cold War. My suggestion is that European and American notions of war have diverged over time, and so have the images and forms artists in Europe and America have used to configure it.

My third claim is more speculative. It is not only abstraction which frames this shift; it is also a change in the stance of the victims of terror. From the 1970s on, the voices as well as the faces of the victims became central to their representation. This is in part due to the judicialization of memory, and in part it is a function of the appearance of forms of cheap and reliable technology enabling the capturing and preservation of both the voice and the face of the witness. We may not be able 'to see' the Holocaust, but we can hear the stories of those who saw it from within.

The circle comes full. The construction of dozens of Holocaust archives, starting with the first in 1982 at Yale University, has made a difference in the human cartography of terror. I would like to finish with this thought: the face of suffering in times of terror has faded from artistic representations in the century since 1914. But in recent times, the voices recording terror, and the faces of the men and women who recall it, have been preserved. These voices penetrate the void, people it, and give us some elements of the story and some ways to tell it. Perhaps we can hear what we cannot see; perhaps spoken words or voices convey images unavailable to us in other ways. If so, then the history of terror needs to be traced not only through the faces but also through the voices of those who knew it from within.

Note

1. I owe this reference to Paul Gradvohl.

Bibliography

Benjamin, Walter. 1991. *Gesammelte Schriften*. Berlin: Suhrkamp.
Lagrou, Pieter. 1999. *The Legacy of Nazi Occupation: Patriotic Memory and National Recovery in Western Europe, 1945–1965*. Cambridge: Cambridge University Press.
Levi, Primo. 1991. *If This Is a Man* and *The Truce*, translated by Stuart Woolf. London: Abacus.
Levinas, Emmanuel. 1961. *Totalité et infini*. Paris: Martinus Nijhoff.
Winter, Jay. 2006. '1937: Illumination'. In *Dreams of Peace and Freedom: Utopian Moments in the Twentieth Century*. New Haven: Yale University.
Young, James. 2000. *The Texture of Memory*. New Haven: Yale University Press.

6
The Cartographer. Warsaw, 1: 400,000

Juan Mayorga
In its first English translation by Sarah Maitland[1]

Introduction: Theatrical cartography of a space of exception

In January 2008, theatre took me to the city of Warsaw for the very first time. One morning, free of any prior engagement, I set out on a walk and allowed myself be guided by the map which had been given to me by the hotel reception. I was returning to the hotel for a bite to eat, having visited the now restored old quarter, when I happened upon what seemed to be an old church. But as I came closer I saw that the building, in front of which stood a police car, was in fact not a church but rather a synagogue. I had never been inside a synagogue, although I did at that moment recall how, as a child in Madrid, I had walked many a time past a building, which I remember hearing was a synagogue, on my way to the public library in the street named after Philip the Fair. There was always, as indeed in the case here, a police car parked outside the front door.

The synagogue in front of which I now found myself was open to visitors outside times of worship, so I went inside. After I had attentively looked around the temple – so familiar and yet so different from Christian churches – I discovered a staircase leading to an upper floor. There, in a small room, a woman was busy setting up an exhibition. The exhibition, she explained, was of recently discovered photos of the ghetto. Next to each photograph the woman hung a label, indicating in Polish and English the probable location in which the snapshot had been taken some sixty years before. It then occurred to me, at that point, to take out my map and mark these places with a cross. When I left the temple, instead of carrying on back to the hotel, I looked for the nearest of those crosses I had now marked on my map. When I arrived at the place, I did not find anything akin to what I had just seen in the photo. The people were of course missing, but so was everything else that surrounded them in the photo. I walked towards the second cross and once again found that everything – people and landscape alike – had disappeared. I carried on walking, guided by the crosses on my map, until I reached a small park. There, I halted in front of a black stone onto which the names of those who had risen up in April 1943 and fallen there were inscribed. It was at that instant, in front of this black stone, that I realized that night had descended around me.

Sometime later, I began to write *The Cartographer*, the subtitle of which is *Warsaw, 1:400,000*. In this play, the character Blanca – wife of a Spanish diplomat stationed in Warsaw – goes through a similar experience to the one I have just recounted. She goes into the same synagogue that I had been into and, when it is her turn to see the old photographs of the ghetto, she encounters a man who tells her the legend of the cartographer. According to this legend, during the German occupation an old invalid cartographer set about making a map of the ghetto; by this, I mean a place in which everything – starting with the 400,000 people incarcerated therein – was in danger. Unable to go out onto the streets, the success of his task depended on his granddaughter, a little girl who went wherever she was instructed to go in order to collect information with which to draft and re-draft the map. The legend of the cartographer, which I believe I invented, inspires the two plot lines developed in the work: of Blanca searching for this same map in Warsaw today and that of the old man and the little girl drawing it 60 years earlier. These two threads finally seem to converge when Blanca meets an old woman named Deborah in contemporary Warsaw. Blanca wants to see in her the infant cartographer, but Deborah denies being that same little girl and claims not to believe in the legend. Deborah does, however, admit that she would like the legend to be passed on, preferably as a play because, according to her, 'in theatre everything answers a question that someone has posed, just like maps do'.

I rarely share the opinions of my characters, but I do believe that Deborah is right in comparing the art of theatre with that of cartography. Maps, as the old cartographer explains to his granddaughter in one of the play's earlier scenes, are never neutral in that they are made on the basis of a decisive question: what should be included and what should be left out? This is precisely the first question that any thespian – whether a playwright, director or actor – begs and it is never neutral.

Those citizens who are actors call upon the city to examine the possibilities of human life: that is what theatre is, born out of the act of listening to the city, yet it cannot simply content itself with returning a mere echo of that noise to the city. A poetic experience also has to be properly tendered; not as a duplicate, but rather a map. It is political art insofar as it takes place before an assembly, more so if the actors convert the stage into a space of utopia and critique; a place in which *this* world can be examined and others imagined – if such actors face up to this world, that is. It may often be stated that theatre is the art of conflict, but what should be added to this is that there is no conflict more important than that which is created between actor and spectator. Theatre calls forth the city in order to lay down a challenge. Therefore, much like a map, theatre that does not incite controversy is theatre that is irrelevant. The best theatre divides the city. It sets before the city what the city does not wish to see. Instead of what is general, usual or agreed, it deals with what is singular, anomalous or uncertain; what the city would rather expel from both its territory and the map. Theatre that is of value positions us, as indeed does a valuable map, on the original stage on which the limits of the city are established.

I had all of this in mind when writing *The Cartographer*. Many doubts as well. I was afraid of becoming just another of those who approach spaces of suffering on account of their sinister glamour; for the paradoxical aura that emanates from them and attracts the creator of fictions as if locating stories in such spaces would somehow endow them with additional prestige, of supplementary value. I was afraid of giving naïve answers to problems that exceed the ethics of representation: How to represent what seems to be insuperably abstruse? How to communicate what seems to be incomprehensible? How to recuperate what should be unrepeatable? I was afraid of avoiding *the* question that every thespian should ask him or herself: What right do I have to attribute a body and a face to the victim? But alongside those doubts, I also know that I was compelled by particularly strong reasons – of a moral order over and above an aesthetical one – to write *The Cartographer*.

I am among those who believe we cannot relinquish the stage to revisionists or those in denial. Neither can we leave the representation of suffering in the hands of those who trivialize pain, look down on victims, or make allowances for torturers. I am also among those who believe that the memory of injustice is our strongest weapon of resistance against both old and new forms of domination over and by humankind. Creating theatre that can shed light on these places of suffering is part of our responsibility towards the dead *and* the living.

Theatre cannot turn the spectator into a witness, but it can turn him or her into a bearer of testimony. It cannot resuscitate the dead, yet it can construct an experience of loss. It may not be able to speak *for* the victims, but it can ensure that their silence is heard. As an art of the spoken word, theatre can make us listen to this silence. As an art of the body, theatre has the ability to make absence visible. In this way, it helps us be more critical, combative, vigilant and valiant against man's domination over man. The torturer's project of oblivion, subsequently inherited, must be opposed by a theatre of memory that partakes in the combat against docility and authoritarianism.

In *The Cartographer*, a wounded woman roams the streets of Warsaw in search of a map which, unknowingly, she is sketching out with her footsteps. My dream is that just one spectator, at the moment he or she watches the play on stage, may find the map that I did not know how to trace.

The Cartographer. Warsaw, 1: 400,000

1.
Warsaw, somewhere between 1940 and the present day.

RAÚL: You alright? Everything ok?
BLANCA: I'm fine.
RAÚL: What happened? Where were you? I didn't know what to do. I rang the police, fire brigade... I must've phoned every hospital in Warsaw.
BLANCA: I'm sorry. I lost track of time.
RAÚL: 'I lost track of time'. What does that even mean? I phoned you a hundred times. Did you lose track of your phone too?
BLANCA: I must've left it here.
RAÚL: We were supposed to have lunch at the ambassador's, remember? We were meeting there at two. I haven't heard from you all day.
BLANCA: I was going to the address you gave me. I was out walking... I had the map you gave me. There was plenty of time... There was this handball court, made of concrete... and beside it I saw this old church. I thought it was a church, but when I got closer it wasn't. There was a police car outside, but I went in and no one said a word. They just signalled for me to cover my hair. You can go in when it's not being used... they just ask for a donation to the building fund. I've never been to a synagogue before. Have you?
RAÚL: What are you talking about? The whole embassy was out looking for you.
BLANCA: Very different to our churches, inside. The way the pews are, all these shelves of books... There were two men talking in English. One was saying it's a miracle it's still standing. He said it was only spared because the Germans used it as a stable... When they saw me, they pointed to a small staircase. A sign said the women's section was upstairs... During the service they sit up there. It's this big balcony that wraps around the inside of the building. I don't know if all synagogues are like that. They were putting up an exhibition. Pictures they'd found... from back then.

RAÚL: Back when?

BLANCA: The ghetto. They were putting little placards under each photo. In Polish and English, all the places in the photos. Cars were banned, so they had to find other transport. Trams... pedal-taxis... There had a whole system of trade... police... they had their own police force.

RAÚL: I know. I've seen it in films.

BLANCA: So many people. Hairdressers, boxers, prostitutes... A wedding... Children... I started marking places on the map... I thought the street names would've changed or might've gone completely... but, there's lots still there. Look. Every photo has a mark. 35 Nowolipie Street. The crossroads at Zelazna and Chlodna... there were lots of Chlodna Street. Bonifraterska Street, at the top of Krasinski square. The corner of Dzika and Geisas Street. I went out of the synagogue and started walking here... to the crossroads at Zelazna and Ogrodowa. According to the map, it was the closest. It's all communist apartment blocks now... you can't see anything from the photo. Then I went to the junction between Zelazna and Chlodna. Nothing. But on Chlodna Street I did see this house that could've been from then...

RAÚL: You might want to re-think your story a little bit... I have to phone the ambassador in a minute and I can't tell him some shaggy dog's tale about old photos...

BLANCA: Forget it, then. Forget everything I said. How about this? I was leaving the house this morning and suddenly I felt a sharp pain at the back of my head. I think I was bundled into a car. When I woke up, I was in the middle of the countryside. Would that suit the ambassador better? Or how about this. I went to a bar, met a man, had some drinks...

RAÚL: You're right... I'm sorry... You said you'd found a house from the time of the ghetto. Please... Go on...

BLANCA: At the top of this street here... It was two storeys, with a gate leading onto a patio. I stood there, looking through the gate, until I saw a girl watching me from a window, almost hidden by a curtain. I thought she might be frightened, so I left. I kept going, along Nowolipie Street... until just here... where it crosses Karmelicka. One of the photos says that's where the uprising started... but there's no sign of it today... not that I could see, anyway. But this park here... there's a huge memorial. It's got a pedestal full of flowers, and wreaths and candles. The whole memorial... it's this huge mass of people. They're like shipwrecked sailors reaching dry land. What really gets you, more than the statues, is the emptiness all around them. A few yards away a sign says there's going to be a museum there... Some boys were leaning on it, smoking. I kept going along Zamenhofa Street, here, and then just after here, at the junction with Mila Street, I saw another memorial. There's no people on that one, just a big black stone... It's all charred... from the ruins of the ghetto. They've engraved hundreds and hundreds of names on it... it's the final resting place of the last ones to resist. They're buried right where they fell. But you can hardly see it with all the apartments. It's totally lost in a sea of concrete. In one of the photos, Mila Street looks like the happiest street in the world... full of children. There's nothing now... That's when I realised it was night... I'd been walking the whole day.

RAÚL: Have you had anything to eat? You should eat something.

BLANCA: It's not just people it's missing. It's like the whole thing vanished into thin air.

RAÚL: You should lie down. We can talk tomorrow. I'll phone and say you're back.

BLANCA: Our house... here... look at the map. Did you know our house is inside the ghetto?

5.

(...) OLD MAN: A map makes some things visible... and others invisible. If a cartographer ever tells you he's neutral don't you trust him. If he tells you he's neutral, you already know what side he's on. A map always takes sides. Maps cover and discover... they give form and deform. In Versailles, why was the cartographer the second-most important man after the king? Why was Servetus burned as a heretic? Ortelius of Antwerp... Mercator of Rupelmonde... They were all dangerous, and they all lived in danger too. In this map, the centre of the world is Athens... in this one, it's Jerusalem. These two here, are both of the same place but look... the Czechs call it Terezín; the Germans call it Theresienstadt. This one's Mexico... the way the indigenous people saw it... this one's the way the Spanish saw it, when Cortés landed. This is the very first map of India. The English made it so they could conquer it. The whole idea of India is an invention of English cartographers. And the Indian resistance made it their own. What you're really looking at, is a military map. What matters to the cartographer are strategic locations to control a stretch of land. Mountains... plains... In this old map of America, the whole continent looks unpopulated... as if it's just asking to be occupied... Where are the native tribes? Look at this one of Africa... Lions, chimpanzees... What about the people? This one of languages... this one of beliefs... this one of races... all weapons against other maps. They all help their owners prepare attacks... to erase borders and replace them with others. That's why there's always maps on powerful men's tables. Maps to scare their visitors... and secret maps no one ever gets to see but them. New maps, full of delights... and old maps they'll stick a knife in one day and signal the start of war. So many catastrophes... and all of them started by a map! Good for cartographers... bad for humanity.

GIRL: Four hundred triangles. They didn't even have machines!

OLD MAN: Machines help... but nothing beats an eye that knows how to see. The greatest virtue of the Cassini family... and the greatest strength of a cartographer... is knowing how to observe and select the essence of what he sees... and reflecting it in his work. Seeing, selecting, representing... that's the secret of a good cartographer. Hundreds of details in just a few strokes... how to make connections, show fronts... splits... With just a handful of symbols, the cartographer shows migrations... armies colliding... one world dying and another being born.

GIRL: Map of the retreat at Rawshire forest!

OLD MAN: There were actually three maps in all: 1800, 1850 and 1900. Three maps in one. That's the hardest thing to show of all... time. The most important aspect of all space is time. Look. Europe in 1914. Europe in 1918. Time!

GIRL: What about this one?

OLD MAN: The first map your father drew.

GIRL: These ones are so strange.

OLD MAN: Those are by Francis Galton. He made maps of smells and sounds.

GIRL: Smells. Sounds...

OLD MAN: You can make maps about anything. Joy. Pain.

(Silence)

OLD MAN: Put it back where you found it. On top of the white one.

(Silence)

OLD MAN: The key?

(Silence)

OLD MAN: Now you know where everything is... if something happens. They'll be yours... I've already talked to your father. And the ones on the walls... Your grandmother didn't like them there... in between the family portraits... But they're part of the family. Warsaw. 1874. When they started numbering the houses. Don't think it was to help the postman, either. It was so they knew the precise location of every single person. Map of the first partition of Poland, 1772. Map of the partitions of 1793 and 1795. Map in German, 1932. Map of the German-Soviet Boundary and Friendship Treaty, twenty-eighth of September, 1939. When you look at them, suddenly it all makes sense. How could anyone be surprised what's happening out there? Everything that's going on right now... was forecast in those maps. When you look at them... you feel the danger? You can almost see it, can't you?

GIRL: Yes.

OLD MAN: But we didn't learn how to read them in time. How could we be so blind?

(Silence)

OLD MAN: Now I know... all those them... all the maps I ever drew in my life... They were just a prelude... just a forerunner for what I have to draw today. One last map... but I can't do it alone anymore... If God would even grant me just an ounce of strength, should I have to drag myself... I'd go out there and make a map of the streets where men hunt men... But I can't even hold a pencil in my hand any more.

GIRL: ... I'll do it. I'll do it for you.

OLD MAN: ... Go and stand over there in the corner... and take a step forward. A normal step, like when you're walking down the street. Now... take the ruler and measure the distance between the corner and your mark. That's one of your steps... note it down over there. The first thing we have to measure is the perimeter. You'll count the number of steps along each side of the wall. Then we'll divide the space into grid squares... And then... we'll think about scale.

6. *The GIRL measures distances with her steps. BLANCA walks, following a map.*

10.

GIRL: Post office. Office of exchange with the Aryan sector. Office to Combat Usury. It's all a trading zone with the Germans. Office of Employment. Shoe factory. 'F' is for 'Factory'. The picture beside it's what they make inside. Shoes. Uniforms. Munitions. Every stripe means a hundred workers. The uniform factor has twelve thousand workers. The shoe factory has ten thousand. 'H' means hospitals, with the number of doctors and beds. 'S' for schools, 'O' for orphanages and 'C' for cafes. 'P' for police, divided into groups... Jewish, Polish, Ukrainian, Lithuanian...

OLD MAN: Alright. That's enough. Just forget it. This was a bad idea.

(Silence)

OLD MAN: It's not your fault. I was a fool to think you could do this by yourself. Go and play with your friends. And take that with you.

GIRL: But... what did I do wrong?

OLD MAN: The cartographer's worst vice is trying to cram everything in. If you try to put everything in, no one sees anything. I've told you a hundred times: *Definitio...*

GIRL: *Definitio est negatio*

OLD MAN: The most important thing... is deciding what to leave out. What do I want to show? What do I want to make visible? Once I know that... I know what to include... and what to exclude. Sacrifice... that's the most important thing when making a map. *Definitio est negatio.*

GIRL: I'm sorry.

OLD MAN: A map isn't a photograph. A map is far superior to any photograph. In a photograph, there's always answers to questions no one ever asked. In a map, there's only answers to the questions of the cartographer. What are your questions?

(Silence)

OLD MAN: Asking questions is harder than measuring or drawing. Those men who make bullets for the Germans... what do they think of their work? The Jewish policemen... how were they recruited? Who selected them?
(Silence)
OLD MAN: This isn't just any old map. It can't be like anything you've ever seen before. This is the map of a world in peril. It's an Ark.
GIRL: An ark. Like Noah's Ark?
OLD MAN: Go and open the cupboard, you know where the key is. Bring me the other folder... the white one.
(Silence)
OLD MAN: You're going to see something I've never shown another living soul, not even your grandmother. You know what this is?
GIRL: Warsaw. But it's very strange.
OLD MAN: It's the life of my mother. She never left the city. This is where she'd buy her bread... in this shop right here... they sold a hundred different kinds. This star here... that's where she died.
(Silence)
OLD MAN: This other one... this is the map of my father. Every day for forty years... he'd take this route to work. My parents were born a nearly thousand miles apart, but their maps crossed... at just the right time. This one here... this is his brother Stefan... He emigrated to Argentina. Compare that to my father's map... At the beginning... they're almost identical... but little by little... they get further and further apart... until their lines never meet again. And this one here... do you know whose map this one is?
GIRL: I don't know.
OLD MAN: Don't you recognise your father? This is his map. There you are... when you were born.
GIRL: ... What about that one?
OLD MAN: That map... is a failure. The map of my life. I spent years designing that system of symbols.... The road to school... where I saw a map for the very first time... The home of the man who taught me to draw. My best friend's house... The home of the first woman I ever kissed... Squares I danced in... bars I laughed in... or cried in... The park where I met your grandmother... The hospital where she died... Graves of men whose name no one remembers. Where I was loved... where I was humbled. The blue shows my dreams... and the black shows my nightmares. A map with lines of happiness and lines of misfortune... lines of fear and lines of hope. My greatest wish, was that whoever saw it would say: 'I know this man'. A complete picture of my life, that's what I wanted to draw. I'll never finish it now... Who can think of himself at times like this? I want you to keep this folder... please.

GIRL: Let me try again. Let me have another go.
OLD MAN: Ask yourself, what's more important: the police station or the brothel? The post office or the yard where Master Berman, in spite of everything that's happening, teaches children violin? There's four hundred thousand human beings in danger here...ask yourself what's most important. Go back outside and open your eyes. Ask yourself...what's essential...what must be protected? It's for you to save or condemn. I'm not going to help you with that.

18.

OLD MAN: What are you doing here? I thought I made myself clear.
GIRL: The *Umschlagplatz*. They've been rounding people up there since the twenty-third. Six thousand a day. They call it the *Umschlagplatz*, the 'concentration point'. They bring them on foot...and the trains are waiting. They say it's for work camps in the East...They took the prisoners from Pawiak...but they're also taking old people...and children, too. They took the children from Doctor Korczak's orphanage. The doctor got on the train with the children. I saw them...I went out through the sewers, and...
OLD MAN: You went outside? Outside the ghetto!
GIRL: They're putting a hundred in every car. Sixty cars.
OLD MAN: You shouldn't have come back. You should have stayed over there. You have to go back.
GIRL: Six thousand a day.
OLD MAN: What's the Jewish Council doing about it? What's Czerniakow doing?
GIRL: The Germans wanted him to sign a document. So they could take the ones the Council can't feed. Czerniakow said he needed time to think it over. He took cyanide. A lot of people take cyanide.
OLD: You know a way out. You can get people out. Use what you know to save lives. A life is far more important than all the maps in the world.
GIRL: Six thousand a day.

35.

OLD MAN: Where've you been? I haven't heard from you in two days. I've been hearing explosions all night. Sounded like they were coming from the north.
GIRL: The ghetto's rising up. The trains are back at the Umschlagplatz. The Germans came in to look for people in the brush factory, but our side rigged the door...they're saying they managed to get a hundred Germans. We've people here, here and here. We've guns, grenades, gasoline...Stones, sticks...anything we can find. They've gone...we've forced them to retreat. But they'll be back...I've come to bring you

this... I couldn't get any more. And this... There's two bullets in it. We couldn't spare any more.
OLD MAN: How many of you are there?
GIRL: Over a hundred.
OLD MAN: What about your father? Is he there?
GIRL: No.
OLD MAN: Tell me. Do you think the Germans can be beaten?
GIRL: No.
OLD MAN: It's still important to fight, though... of course it is... But... so is completing your mission... only you can do it.
GIRL: There's no more map to make. If you went outside you wouldn't recognise a thing... Fire... and ruins, that's what the ghetto is now.
OLD MAN: If there's still an escape, you're the only one who knows the way... you have to get out. Not for you. For the people no longer here, for every one of them. No one knows as well as you what's happened here. If you know an escape, it's your duty to tell the world what you've seen.

37.
(...) **DEBORAH:** So I researched it. But the house was built after the war. I'm really sorry... believe me... I like the story of the child cartographer. I'm just not her... I don't think she ever existed. I always thought it was too unlikely... an urban legend, an old wives' tale. But I've nothing against legends if they keep memory alive. What does it matter if she existed or not? She could have existed. But you want something more. You want to save her. Or the map, at least... to reassure yourself it wasn't all in vain. I don't think you'll ever find it. And even if you do, even if it's right in front of your very eyes... you wouldn't recognise it. They'd have made sure no one else would be able to use it. I'd like them to do that film... it'd be a way of talking indirectly about it all... it wouldn't be 'just another Holocaust film'. But the map shouldn't be in it... it would always disappoint. The film itself should be the map. But I don't think they'll ever make it... the idea of it... the cartographer of a world in peril... it's too difficult. I don't think people would see how important it was. I'd prefer them to make a play about it. Theatre's far superior to the cinema. Films are full of answers to questions no one ever asked. In the theatre, there's only answers to the questions of the playwright. Like maps. What a cruel story... the one about the Piper. He takes away all the children! This is the map of Europe they taught us in school. One day they took the map away and hung this one up instead, and I knew my life had changed. You'll find that too, one day. Suddenly, streets change name, some borders vanish and others take their place. Look at the wall over there. See how Europe's borders change? 1938, 1939, 1945, 1989... See how this tiny little place

changes name? Czernowitz, Cekanti, Chernovstsi... European train network, 1939. Whoever did that one had no idea what they were drawing. This is the extermination camp at Treblinka, one to one thousand scale. The Fietkau route. With that map in their hands... a precious few managed to cross the Pyrenees in time to save their lives. There are maps that kill and maps that save. Look at these two.

BLANCA: Sarajevo. And Sarajevo!

DEBORAH: This was the one the snipers used to hold a city to ransom. Fortunately... someone drew another one... a map of the underground city.

BLANCA: Two mapmakers: one a demon and the other an angel... What about this one?

DEBORAH: Map of Europe for Africans. Since I retired, I only make useful maps. How to get in, how to get help... Maps for people on the run. I see the world from the ghetto outwards.

BLANCA: What about this one? Warsaw, 2008?

DEBORAH: Warsaw... 2008... as if none of it ever happened. It's time to take my walk now, would you like to come with me?

BLANCA: I'd love to.

DEBORAH: Can you pass me those slippers? I usually go barefoot in the house. The doctor makes me walk an hour a day. I never feel like it now, my legs are heavier every day. He says, 'Let's go to such-and-such a place, Deborah, to see if it's still there'. So I go to see if things are still there or what they've been turned it into. But as soon as I'm outside, all I can think about is a new sign I hadn't noticed before, or a shop, or the hubbub of a street or its silence. Every day I find somewhere I've never been before... Every day I lose myself in Warsaw. If you really want to know a place, you have to lose yourself in it. If you want to know how it works, who makes the decisions and who obeys... If you want to see the border between the head of the city and the rest of the body, you have to lose yourself. I never take notes, but when I get back to the house I could retrace every single one of my steps. I walk slowly... committing everything to memory... as if someone was waiting for me to tell them everything I'd seen. I feel like people look at me strangely... walking so slowly, looking around... it arouses suspicion. I have time... all the time in the world... I could have died when I was ten. I never go directly to what I'm looking for... I get up close and then I step back again... I walk around and around it... at different times of day... and I try to remember what was there before. Don't trust your eyes. Your eyes hide many things. Let yourself stay still... while everything else moves, walk forward and then walk back. It's not enough to look, you have to commit it all to memory. The most difficult thing to see of all is time. The decoration over a door, a picture on the tiles of a floor. They're all signs on the verge of being lost forever. Chopin used to like walking through this park. The old ghetto prostitutes used to meet at this gate. Over there was a boxing club. The ring was over there. The boxers would come through here. My father liked boxing. I think he liked boxing. All of it...all of it will be wiped away...like a map surrounded by water...a piece of paper that wants to fall apart. But the one thing that can never be wiped away is that which no one can draw. The way their boots used to shine...our bare feet. The sound of the ghetto...the constant whine that never stopped, day or night. Also the silence of the ghetto. From here, it was two thousand steps to the school. Over there we'd queue for soup. My house was here, facing south. In winter we had the light until five. Here was my father's room...here was my room...In the attic we had the map table. The wall came through here. Just a few centimetres, that was all. Here it is, the Umschlagplatz...where the trains started. Here I saw my grandfather for the very last time.

39.

The GIRL enters. She selects a floor tile and pulls it up; marks can be seen on the reverse of the tile. The GIRL takes out a wood-working bradawl and makes another mark. Should every tile be pulled up and turned upside down, a grid map of Warsaw would be revealed.

Note

1. Please note that this translation is reproduced here in draft form.

7
'All Limits Were Exceeded Over There': The Chronotope of Terror in Modern Warfare and Testimony

Kirsten Mahlke

Traumatization has become a key term for understanding the collective experience of mass violence in the twentieth century. Scholarship on the representation of experiences of state terror since the Shoah conceives the effects of war against civil populations ex post in terms of psychological pathology (see Felman and Laub, 1992; LaCapra, 1994; Caruth, 1995; Rothberg, 2000). Much of what has been conceptualized with reference to the concept of traumatization, however, applies to the psychopolitical goals of regimes, which manipulate masses by means of terror. In this chapter 'trauma' can thus be seen as a politically intended, morbidly useful state of mind of populations. Instead of looking exclusively at the psychopathological effects in the form of trauma, I will focus on the spatio-temporal structure of these manipulations and their correlates on the level of narrative representation in testimonial literature. Psychological warfare continues to shape the individual and social imaginary after the actual cessation of state terror: (1) directly through massive distortions of space–time perception, which are not easily overcome but persist for a long time afterwards and (2) indirectly, through the seemingly incredible narrative representations of space-time in testimonies. The mechanism underlying this manipulation of spatio-temporality which deeply infects both perception and representation is thus followed by a loss of subsequent narrative credibility, a core characteristic of witnesses' experiences after mass violence. It is as if speaker and listener, although co-present in time and space, no longer share the same semiotic system. The aesthetic particularity of space–time representations will be considered in what follows as an element of the crimes of regimes of state terror. This essay analyses, in a first step, rhetorical manipulations of spatio-temporality by means of a theory and praxis of 'modern warfare' based on state terror (Trinquier, 2009). Are these manipulations operative with respect to the destruction of the classic notions of spatio-temporality which are so necessary for subjective integrity? To answer this question, the chapter will first theorize these spatio-temporal distortions based on Mikhail Bakhtin's concept of the chronotope, and then analyse the representations of space–time perceptions in selected testimonies by survivors of secret detention centres in Argentina and concentration camps in Nazi Germany. I consider it not enough to speak of 'spaces' of terror, disappearance and death (Taussig, 1984; Colombo, 2013) alone. It is rather necessary to conceptualize a spatio-temporality proper to the workings of state terror and their consequences for the long-term difficulties of communicating, addressing an audience or even making-believe.

The chronotope model

Bakhtin introduced the chronotope to literary studies in 1975 (English translation by Holquist and Emerson, 1981), well before the so-called spatial turn in cultural studies, in order to present an alternative to the insufficiencies of classic concepts of space. By introducing this concept, he explicitly acknowledged the mathematical model of theoretical physics for which time constitutes the fourth dimension of space. 'Time, as it were, thickens, takes on flesh, becomes artistically visible; likewise space becomes charged and responsive to the movements of time, plot, and history' (Bakhtin, 1981, p.84). Conceptions of the world cannot be regarded either only spatially or temporally, but with an awareness of the constitutive interdependence of both categories. The chronotope, a 'travelling concept' (Bal, 2002), is not confined to the exclusive domain of literary works of art. Bakhtin's theory of the chronotope assumes an aesthetic representation of spatio-temporal configurations of 'actual reality' (Bakhtin, 1981, p.243) in order to make it productive as a category of the history of literary genre. The consistent expansion of the Bakhtinian chronotope as an 'ordering structure of knowledge manifest in all areas of culture' (Lay-Brander, 2011, p.14), or more precisely as 'instances of socially determining structurations of practices that set limits not only on what can possibly happen within their effective confines but also what can be perceived and even imagined by agents acting within their constraints' (White, 2010, p.240) has already been undertaken in different fields of historical cultural analysis (see Bemong et al., 2010). According to them, chronotopes are imaginary entities which are concretized materially and whose material dimension retroactively informs conceptions of spatio-temporality. They belong to the fields of the imaginary as well as to concrete materialization in history. Just how radical chronotopic reconfiguration can be under conditions of massive violence and terror attests to the real historical dimensions of the spatio-temporal imaginary. We are confronted with a manipulation that is at its core aesthetic in the strict sense of the term (affecting perception), which in a second step attempts to induce psychic and physical destruction. It tends, as Adorno has shown in his analysis of Beckett's *Endgame* (Adorno, 1991, p.246 and following), towards the total erasure of the power to remember, the end of history. The concept of the chronotope makes it possible to investigate discontinuities of spatio-temporal experiences which are particularly extreme in terror narratives. The juxtaposition of spatial experiences of terror and a subsequent memory of past experience is supplemented by an awareness of significant ruptures perceived and represented with the accustomed order (often referred to as 'natural law') at one and the same time and at one and the same place. Phenomena familiar to trauma research – for instance, that time appears to come to a standstill and those affected remain trapped in the space of the experience of horror, which appears repeatedly and uncontrollably in the minds of the affected (Caruth, 1995, p.4) – become thereby more accurately describable than in classically separated dimensions of temporal flow and spatial setting. The suggestion of 'normality' or 'neutrality' inherent in the latter disregards the fundamental interconnected dynamics of chronotopic constellations. The chronotope of terror invokes an epistemic category that conceptualizes such mentally destructive experiences as a structurally mimetic problem inherent in the genre of testimony. Michael Rothberg has coined the term 'traumatic realism' (Rothberg, 2000, p.27) which offers a 'nonreductive articulation of the extreme and the everyday' (Rothberg, 2000, p.118) in autobiographical writings of the Holocaust, where fragmented speech, strong emphasis on tiny details, repetitions of words, phrases, scenes are identified among the aesthetic characteristics. Instead of analysing the texts as acts of 'passive mimesis', Rothberg shows that they transform 'the traumatic event into an object of knowledge' (Rothberg, 2000, p.103). My study enters at a level beneath 'traumatic realism', insofar as it is concerned with the violently established spatio-temporal conditions of its production and communication.

In what follows, I would like to consider two violent contexts of spatio-temporal deformation in the twentieth century, which are conceptually related as 'spaces of terror'. In order to avoid confusions or incongruous comparisons, I focus on the situation of political imprisonment in concentration camps, which cannot be compared with death camps. I follow Bruno Bettelheim's definition of a 'concentration camp for political prisoners'. The latter can be found in the descriptions of spatio-temporal distortion in his own testimony and socio-psychological study of the concentration camps in Dachau and Buchenwald, 'Individual and Mass Behavior in Extreme Situations' (Bettelheim, 1947). His study and its results are primarily illuminating for the question of how professional observation (as a psychologist) is possible for a victim of extreme violence. Pilar Calveiro's *Poder y Desaparición* (Power and Disappearance) (Calveiro, 2008) provides another study based on 'forced participatory observation' that resulted in a sociological and political analysis of Argentine secret detention centres. Both reports testify and analyse explicitly the space–time of terror. I will also refer to additional Argentine testimonies from the collection *Nunca más* (Never Again) by CONADEP (Comisión nacional sobre la desaparición de personas, 1984), the sociological study *El detenido-desaparecido* (The Detained-Disappeared) by Gabriel Gatti (2008) and a representation of terror as experienced by female survivors of Argentine secret detention centres in *Ese infierno* (That Hell) (Actis et al., 2006) that takes the form of a dialogue.[1] I have selected these examples because their reports provide evidence of methods of modern warfare and exemplify the characteristic spatio-temporal problem for the narratability of experiences of terror. The analogies between the experiences of internment are not reduced to mere representational and aesthetic similarities in testimonial literature. Victims' and perpetrators' textual productions will thus both be taken into account for a complementary description of how the chronotope of terror is produced. It is highly disturbing that the making of the chronotope of terror can be told as an intertextual relationship between testimonies of survivors of Nazi concentration camps and a scientific corpus of tested and taught knowledge about manipulation of spatio-temporal perception.[2] This sinister intertextuality links the horrific experiments on human beings in Nazi Camps to the wars of independence in Indochina and Algeria, the Vietnam war and the South American military dictatorships of the 1970s and 1980s. We are faced with a professional continuity of psychopolitical techniques of terror towards the civil population since the German concentration camps which derives from the transnational training of several generations of military personnel of all ranks (Pérès, 2009, p.391).

The manipulation of space–time becomes systematized between the end of the Second World War and the dictatorships of the 1970s and 1980s in the canonical handbook of counterinsurgency, *La Guerre moderne* (Modern War) by Roger Trinquier (published in French in Paris in 1961, and in English in London in 1964), as well as in the declassified *CIA-Handbook of Torture*, that builds on Trinquier and draws its claims to legitimacy from the defence of liberal-democratic values. An investigation of the chronotope of terror in survivors' accounts has to be prefaced by a consideration of how space–time is represented in these seminal texts of modern warfare. They show how the perpetrators' minds themselves are trained into a specific spatio-temporal conception, a sine qua non for the manipulation of civil society. While Trinquier's book is a rather theoretical introduction to modern warfare strategies, the CIA manual gives concrete instructions for the practical application of these theoretical insights in the micro-political space–time of the torture chamber.

Modern warfare

Modern warfare, in the view of Roger Trinquier, whose maxims had such a vast impact, is not a matter of attack but of defence. This strategic legitimation relies on a number of linguistic constructions. The foundation of modern tactics of warfare is the mimetic adaptation to the presumed tactics of the opponent. It can be considered as a mirror projection based on a creative metaphorical imaginary of worst case scenarios. These fantastic creations are determined by and will further determine the way space–time is conceived and will thus shape thoughts and actions. The enemy is potentially everywhere, yet invisible, because 'the enemy' operates furtively and is highly structured. It also includes the civil population, which, as a mass subject to manipulation, replaces classic warring parties in modern war (Trinquier, 2009, p.31 and following). For instructors of modern warfare, the greatest danger appears to be the fiction of peace deployed by the enemy. In light of the doctrine that peace can be a maliciously erected illusion, and that peace must indeed be read as a metaphor of war, state operations targeting the civil population in an everyday setting present a hermeneutic tool. The most striking rhetorical devices applied to concepts of spatiotemporality are metaphorical and metonymic combinations that produce expansion and reduction simultaneously. This holds for the extension of the 'battlefield' to transnational spaces and to the microcosm of the individual in his or her private environment. The temporal dimension of 'war' is at once extended in its entirety for an indeterminate period of time and reduced as an act of war to punctual 'operations'. The conventional vocabulary of war (war, battlefield, enemy, ally, attack, defence, frontline) is not abandoned but henceforth used in a metonymic sense. Unlimited metonymization enables 'battlefields' to be concentrated semantically into single bodies and at the same time expanded transnationally to a vaguely defined territory: 'The battlefield today is no longer restricted. It is limitless; it can encompass entire nations. The inhabitant in his home is the center of the conflict' (Trinquier, 2009, p.16). Corresponding to this extended metonymy, the acts of violence towards prisoners are to be understood as acts of war against an entire group, in the extreme case the entire population.

As in Don Quixote's battles against imaginary enemies, like windmills and herds of sheep, metaphors attain a life of their own through their powers of cognitive transformation and instigate a real fight for life and death against imaginary and ubiquitous enemies. Delusion becomes systematic; it is not only a side-effect, but a tool within the mental education of modern warfare. According to this linguistically evoked view of the world, nothing is as it seems, danger is absolute, and the measures taken must be radical, deadly. By means of rhetorical devices, the status of the imaginary is inflated at the expense of the physical and visible: the result is great fear. One of the preferred ways to make this happen is through the production of indeterminacy. Trinquier suggests that 'in modern warfare the enemy is far more difficult to identify. No physical frontier separates the two camps. The line of demarcation between friend and foe passes through the very heart of the nation, through the same village and sometimes divides the same family' (Trinquier, 2009, p.15).

The territory of war, divided among single civilian bodies and extended over entire nations, is also temporally unbounded: 'Day and night, armed soldiers will make unexpected intrusions into the home of peaceful citizens to carry out necessary arrests' (Trinquier, 2009, p.23). The entire 'war' is determined temporally in accordance with the goals of total annihilation, because it will have to continue until the last rebel is destroyed: 'No time limit for the operation should be set ahead of time. It will end when the enemy combat organizations [...] are completely destroyed' (Trinquier, 2009, p.87). The more mundane the location, the more common the occupation of the citizen, all the greater must be the certainty of the guardians of the state under conditions of terror that places and times occupy the centre of subversive or terrorist events.

Mental manipulation of the military is the first important step to establish a regime of terror. The population or 'the public' are Trinquier's next targets: His handbook remarks laconically that covert police and military violence 'can easily pass for brutalities in the eyes of a sensitive public'. The systematic, half-covert/half-overt institutionalization of secret detention centres, torture and concentration camps is an essential factor in the production of the widest reception of the effects of terror from the narrowest space possible (Bettelheim, 1947, p.452; Calveiro, 2008, p.78). 'Breaking resistance' for the purpose of compliance was the comprehensive political goal, targeting perpetrators (their human feelings of empathy), victims (their resistance to the regime) and population (through joint knowledge of the consequences of resistance).

The smallest spatio-temporal unit in the regime of terror is the torture cellar. The Kubark manual refined the methods for producing terror and breaking resistance through spatio-temporal distortion that had remained vague and limited to theoretical principles of organization in Trinquier's introduction. It could not be stated more clearly: 'All coercive techniques are designed to induce regression' (Kubark, 1963, p.5). The goal of breaking resistance in order to attain information was to be pursued by inducing regression through terror methods. It is well proven that adults regress when they lose spatio-temporal orientation.[3] The manipulative disorientation begins with an 'arrest' that causes an initial shock due to the silence about its reasons as well as its illegal circumstances. At the same time, the stage on which torture is conducted under the metonymic sign of 'interrogation' is primarily the site where language gets re-signified for the perpetrators and learned by repeated naming and doing. After an 'initiation torture', described by Bettelheim for Dachau and Buchenwald as well, which introduces the prisoner temporally and spatially into the violent reality of the camp and social relationships in the form of 'interrogation techniques', more subtle methods of manipulation are soon applied. Nothing should be left to chance in this spatio-temporal order. Objects are tactically estranged from practical everyday-purposes to psychological ones. An office is no longer an office, a desk is no longer a desk. These objects are transformed into psychotechnical tools to trigger certain reactions to authority and bureaucracy (Kubark, 1963, p.30).

Temporal confusion is of at least equal importance. So-called uncooperative sources are exposed to irregular interrogation times or brought to their cells to sleep for a few minutes before being taken back for interrogation 'as if eight hours had transpired'. Mealtimes, interrogation times, daily and nightly rhythms and digestion cycles are systematically unsettled and removed from the control of the individual in order to make him or her regress and subject him or her to the complete control of the apparatus. 'The underlying principle of this type of schedule is to unhinge the subject's sense of chronological time' (Kubark, 1963, p.32). In addition to the withdrawal of biological, physiological and customary rhythms, prisoners are also subjected to the mental manipulation of their perception of reality. Referring to a classic of children's literature that combines the various spatio-temporal distortions of childlike fantasy, the CIA handbook formulates under the rubric 'Alice in Wonderland' (Kubark, 1963, p.48) a grotesque 'method of confusion'. The culturally accustomed world of the victim is systematically deprived of meaning. The known world is erased and replaced by another, 'completely insane' one. Meaningless, ambivalent, incoherent questions, and deviations from the rules of intonation, prosody, logic and conversation are the recommended modes for producing this 'crazy world' and force the mental energies of the interrogated to concentrate and despair of nonsense until he or she will 'probably make significant confessions' in order 'to stop the nonsensical babble' (Kubark, 1963, p.48). An almost exemplary manipulation of space–time by the use of the Alice-in-Wonderland method can be found in file Number 1277 of *Nunca Más* in the testimony of Héctor Mariano Ballent: 'Treatment in [torture center I Martinez] was brutal, not only physically but also psychologically. If someone asked the time, he would be asked if he had to go out: if they served soup it was in a flat plate with a fork'.

In an atmosphere of mental and physiological disorientation, adults regress to the physiological and psychological state of little children and thereby become 'traitors' or 'collaborators', when they cling to their torturers as their last human counterparts or imagined parental figures. Shame about the loss of control and feelings of guilt (which are permanently induced) charge the memories of the space–time of terror with self-destructive forces. In testimonies by survivors of German and Argentine torture and secret detention centres, we can discover significant evidence of such spatio-temporal manipulations.

'Unforgettable but Unreal': Distortions in the space–time of terror

This section deals with experienced and remembered forms of the space–time of terror in testimonies.[4] The psycho-physical nature of subjects is itself spatio-temporally defined. The initial shock of his internment in Dachau had just been overcome as Bettelheim began to notice changes in his psyche and that those around him also behaved strangely. As a trained psychologist, he was able to diagnose his own pathology of dissociation. He puts it in a third-person narrative: 'He observed, for instance, the split in his person into one who observes and one to whom things happen, a typical psychopathological phenomenon' (Bettelheim, 1947, p.421).

The splitting of the personality into subject and object by terror causes a doubling of space–times, which are constantly re-combined with one another in a feedback loop by the need to understand: no coherent relationship between experiences of the known world (subject) and the lived world (object) can be produced by the perceiving subject. With regard to the attempt to master its situation narratively, the dissociated personality is compelled to become the narrator and protagonist of a fantastic story: events and the familiar order of the world are incompatible.[5] The attempts to transpose the unreality of experience and the realism of conceptualization are 'never wholly successful' (Bettelheim, 1947, p.433). Efforts to re-establish coherence through social interaction and comparison with others are equally doomed to fail, because the dissociation affects all individuals. 'He also observed that his fellow prisoners, who had been normal persons, now behaved like pathological liars, were unable to restrain themselves and to make objective evaluations' (Bettelheim, 1947, p.421). Many of the reports by survivors represent the personality dissociation as paradoxical and fantastic: 'The transportation was only one of the experiences transcending the normal frame of reference and the reaction to it may be described as "unforgettable, but unreal"' (Bettelheim, 1947, p.433). Pilar Calveiro writes in a similarly oxymoronic fashion about the experiences in the camp: 'Compared with the values of the entering individual, the camp appears as an unreal reality' (Calveiro, 2008, p.63).

The perception of irregularity can even make the natural laws of classic Newtonian physics seem no longer valid: 'The law of gravity was invalid there.' A survivor (E 41 quoted in Gatti, 2008, p.58) reports that she experienced an unknown dimension: 'One has a very clear feeling of being in a completely different dimension', in which 'all limits have been exceeded'. The superimposition of contradictions, the perception that one 'is in a type of uterus beyond the laws, beyond space and time' generates the feeling that the camp is a 'detached and total reality' (Calveiro, 2008, p.51). Such a reality had been most impressively described by Yehiel De Nur during the Eichmann trial as a different planet, where

> time [...] was not like it is here on earth. Every fraction of a minute there passed on a different scale of time. And the inhabitants of this planet had no names [...]; they breathed according to different laws of nature; they did not live – nor did they die – according to the laws of this world.
> (Eichmann Trial, 1961, Session 68, De Nur)

The detachment of a person's own subject/object dimension, of the social relations outside and inside, the lack of markers of reality, causes at its inception an untranslatability of the experience of terror into the language of binary logic. Instead, the spatio-temporal distortions are coded in paradoxes and the language of the fantastic.

Dissociation as a structure of experience and narrative consorts with an additional experience of incoherence that is triggered by the continuous presence of violent death. The repressors' goal of annihilation, which embraces all mundane phenomena in the form of semantic proliferation, stands in stark contradiction to the experience of still being alive. This resignification of space–time as a 'space of death' (Taussig, 1984) creates the excessive spatial expansion at a temporal standstill that is so dominant in the testimonies. Adriana, a survivor of the ESMA in Argentina, remembers in conversation with other survivors how the microcosm of the camp affected her like a magnifying glass for all that happened there: 'Events were prolonged in the present, in a world that only consisted of the present tense, without the expectation of a future' (Actis et al., 2006, p.98). The 'mass of time', which piles up in the narrowest space and even becomes stationary in a historical sense, cannot be sorted by chronological or metrical order.

Temporal standstill with simultaneous magnification of space are the basic structural elements of the chronotope determining the genre of testimonies by concentration camp survivors. In a great part this distortion occurs in 'traumatic realism' as a construction of perceived dimensions in a state of forced regression. It prevents temporal and causal sequentialization in favour of the repetition of individual fragments of experience. The specific spatio-temporal distortion induced among direct and indirect addressees of terror results from a spiralling interplay of terror and effects of dissociation, which leads to a loss of the feeling for everyday reality and the continuity of the self. With the enlargement of space, a feeling of temporal deceleration increases to the point of standstill. The specific spatio-temporal distortion and simultaneous loss of a sense of reality and continuity of the self affects the efforts to construct consistent narratives in the naïve sense of realism. We can rather observe a recurrent set of spatio-temporal elements which seem to be characteristic for traumatic realism. While later visiting the former secret detention centre Automotores Orletti, a former detainee cannot believe that the horrific world experienced by her as so enormous and so immeasurably dense could be located in such a seemingly mundane site: 'It seemed so small to me. I could not believe that all that happened to me should fit in that space. As if it didn't fit in there. As if it were much bigger than the locality appeared' (Gatti, 2008, p.59). It is not what happened that confounds narration, but the irreconcilable difference between spatio-temporal dimensions of terror and the world which is perceived as 'customary' that makes what happened there so difficult to represent. Yet it is not as if this 'bridge' existed for the survivors while only the words were missing. The survivors themselves could not believe what was happening to them while they were experiencing what was happening, 'as if what happened really did not matter to oneself. It was strangely mixed with a conviction that "this cannot be true, such things do not happen"' (Bettelheim, 1947, p.443). The words of a survivor of ESMA concur: 'I felt like I was encapsulated, like these things were not happening to me' (Gatti, 2008, p.36).

Time can also be staged in the form of space–times of traumatizing scenes that seem to repeat in cycles. The effects of trauma seem to be anticipated and 'applied' systematically: a method used in the Argentine secret detention centres to torture Jewish detainees in particular consisted in the repeated display of symbols and references belonging to the Nazi regime. Jorge Reyes reports that whenever he and his fellow inmates were beaten by the guards, the guards claimed that they were the Gestapo: 'When they were beating us up they would say, "We're the Gestapo!"' (CONADEP, 1984, file 2563, Jorge Reyes). They threatened to make soap out of the Jewish detainees Nora Strejilevich and Alicia Partnoy (Strejilevich, 2002, p.19; Partnoy, 2013, p.61) and they promised better treatment for a prisoner of German descent by encouraging him to join the SS (CONADEP, 1984, file 2826, Rubén Schell). Under these circumstances the question 'where and when am I?' leads into the abyss of a scene produced by a recycling machine of historical terror in the here and now.

Another survivor refers to the weight of history, which was suspended beyond life and death and meant for her the end of history: 'I could not think about life or death. It was like a measure of time that had been suspended forever, the end of history, seriously. After this, never anything again' (Actis et al., 2006, p.36). Bettelheim described the experience of temporal standstill in the eternal present as a symptom of regression: 'The prisoners lived, like children, only in the immediate present; they lost the feeling for the sequence of time; they became unable to plan for the future or to give up immediate pleasure satisfactions to gain greater ones in the near future' (Bettelheim, 1947, p.445).

On the one hand, regression to the infantile represses the acquired concept of space–time and replaces it with the childlike perception of an eternal present and immediate experience, which on the other hand is shaped by an abundance not of life but of death. Death infiltrates subjective perception to such an extent that one is dominated by the sense that one embodies the paradox of the living dead. That one is nevertheless capable of human needs such as eating, drinking, moving and sleeping, 'has something fantastic, unbelievable' (Calveiro, 2008, p.63). The location transforms into a place with its own laws that is 'governed by an absurd logic according to which everyday occurrences are played out in the most subterranean realms of cruelty and insanity' (CONADEP, 1984, p.19). The chronotope of terror is most effective where space is completely filled with the possibility of death and time no longer elapses. This spatio-temporal disposition is achieved whenever all acts of violence are kept discursively indeterminate. At its culminating point we can discern the method of forced disappearance, a method introduced in the terror machinery of the Nazi regime by the decree *Nacht und Nebel* (Night and Fog) in 1941 and refined during the military operations in Algeria and South America. Its structure has neither beginning nor end, it is – even in its juridical form – a crime in perpetuity. In contrast to murder, an act of violence towards one or more persons, making someone disappear is an act of violence towards the possibility of subjectivization in general, for it systematically denies or erases all points of orientation in the form of causality, place, and time (for those directly affected and relatives, for all potential witnesses and addressees of rumours): the reason for the kidnapping, the names of the kidnappers, torturers and murderers, the way to the camp, the site of incarceration, the refusal to issue an official charge of a crime, the denial that an arrest has taken place, the exact time and location of the murder, the location of the burial. The lack of a grave is only the last gap in an entire series of manipulative indeterminations which have significant destructive effects (Colombo, 2013). Narratives can no longer be ordered individually, because the single narrative sequences are missing spatio-temporal determinations. Many survivors continue to experience the suspension of the border between life and death in an unclassifiable spatio-temporality as an enduring sensation long after their release, in which other former detainees are identified who have 'disappeared'. Even years after the dictatorship, Liliana Gardella insists in her testimony that her fellow inmates who disappeared are all still alive somewhere (Actis et al., 2006, p.253). One's own unidentifiable status between life and death distorts the spatio-temporal classification of forms of movement as well. Whereas time receives all importance, persons lose it. They drift emptily through this strange dimension, localization is impossible and leads to a diffusion. Munú Actis's definition of the 'disappeared' most hauntingly verbalizes this effect: the disappeared 'is nowhere. For me he hovers through space' (Actis et al., 2006, p.98). Narratives of disappearance are beset by a double paradox: they are evidential without evidence (as a spatio-temporal gap) of the psychosocial and physical crimes against subjectivity, individuals and groups. They tell about a death without a death that could be determined spatio-temporally.

Conclusion

Testimonies constitute the genre in which a significant part of the history of twentieth century's 'modern wars' have been and continue to be written. They belong to a genre which, owing to their original function as juridical reference, depends upon credibility and the plausibility of representation. Far beyond the well-established imponderables of testimony (incompleteness and unreliability of subjective memory, missing material evidence) discussed in debates among historians of the Shoah since the

1990s (Friedlander, 1992) these texts reveal that forms of state terror have fundamental effects on experience and narratability. One of the presuppositions of subjective perception, representation, and transmission of terror experiences is the coherent representation of spatio-temporal dimensions. The ability of subjects to experience the self as a continuum is tied to the possibility of a spatio-temporal dimensioning of this self. The history of modern warfare in the twentieth century cannot be told without the essential qualification that the possibility of realistic narrative has itself fallen victim to the arbitrary destruction of the dimensions of space–time. It has been shown that the effects of dissociation, regression and general disorientation create a chronotopic constellation which is incompatible with everyday life experiences of space and time. Not only can space–time dimensions be made untranslatable to audiences of testimony; as Bettelheim's and others' accounts have testified, they are not even credible for dissociated witnesses whose subjectivity is destroyed through the key dimensions of spatio-temporality. The psychological weapons of modern warfare, as displayed in the infamous torture manuals of the CIA, aim at a mental dis- and re-organization of individuals, which culminates in a loss of social communicability and collective memory. In this essay I have tried to show in what way the chronotopic effects of state terror affect the capability of resistance of individuals. Resistance encompasses the three dimensions of insubordination to another's power, psychological and physical survival of individual subjectivity and the human capacity for empathy. The production of a reality where time tends to a standstill and space becomes all-embracing took and still takes place in torture chambers and infiltrates the mental states and narrative representations of the destructive experiences in a past that does not pass. The across-the-board attack on the subjectivity of human beings by destroying their coherent perception of space–time has the effect that this attack can only be experienced, remembered, narrated, and received realistically, but incompatibly in the framework of 'traumatic realism'. At its core, I argue, the chronotope of terror remains virulent.

Notes

1. All translations from these sources from the Spanish original are mine.
2. It has been shown that testimonies by survivors have been co-opted for 'methodological refinement'. One example is provided by operation 'Artichoke', which conducted psychological experiments on concentration camp survivors after the Second World War for the CIA (Weiner, 2008, pp.73 and following).
3. The result of external pressure of sufficient intensity is the loss of those defences most recently acquired by civilized man: '...the capacity to carry out the highest creative activities, to meet new, challenging, and complex situations, to deal with trying interpersonal relations, and to cope with repeated frustrations. Relatively small degrees of homeostatic derangement, fatigue, pain, sleep loss or

anxiety may impair these functions.' As a result, most people who are exposed to coercive procedures will talk and usually reveal some information that they might not have revealed otherwise.
(Kubark, 1963, p.83. The internal quote is from Hinkle)
4. They do not reflect the experiences of agents, but the suffering of those who have been violently and illegally interned. Even assuming that subjects do not fully relinquish their creative abilities in extreme circumstances, it is clear that terror methods target the sense of the subject that is most intimately connected to spatio-temporal orientation. Representations can hence be investigated as effects of terror, but not as autonomous constructions of chronotopes of terror. It is over this point that my approach diverges from that of Pamela Colombo, who assumes that a construction of the spaces of terror by the prisoners is still possible (Colombo, 2013, p.170).
5. The term 'fantastic' is borrowed from Rosemary Jackson to refer to a problem of both psychology/psychoanalysis and narrative theory, in which the fantastic is a 'telling index of the limits of [the dominant cultural] order' (Jackson, 1981, p.4).

Bibliography

Actis, Múnu, Cristina Aldini, Liliana Gardella, Miriam Lewin and Elisa Tokar. 2006. *Ese infierno. Conversaciones de cinco mujeres sobrevivientes de la ESMA*. Buenos Aires: Altamira.
Adorno, Theodor 1991. *Notes to Literature*, volume 1, translated by Sherry Weber. Columbia: Columbia University Press.
Bakhtin, Mikhail 1981. 'Forms of Time and of the Chronotope in the Novel'. In *Mikhail Bakhtin. The Dialogic Imagination: Four Essays*, edited by Michael Holquist and translated by Carol Emerson and Michael Holquist. Austin: University of Texas Press, 84–258.
Bal, Mieke. 2002. *Travelling Concepts in the Humanities*. Toronto: University of Toronto Press.
Bemong, Nele, Pieter Borghart, Michel De Dobbeleer and Kristoffel Demoen, eds. 2010. *Bakhtin's Theory of the Literary Chronotope. Reflections, Applications, Perspectives*. Ghent: Academia Press.
Bettelheim, Bruno. 1947. 'Individual and Mass Behaviour in Extreme Situations'. *Journal of Abnormal and Social Psychology*, 38: 417–452.
Calveiro, Pilar. 2008 (1998). *Poder y Desaparición. Los campos de concentración en Argentina*. Buenos Aires: Colihue.
Caruth, Cathy. 1995. *Trauma. Explorations in Memory*. Baltimore: Johns Hopkins University Press.
Colombo, Pamela. 2013. *Espacios de desaparición. Espacios vividos e imaginarios tras la desaparición forzada de personas (1974–1983) en la provincia de Tucumán, Argentina*. Unpublished doctoral thesis in sociology, Universidad del País Vasco, Bilbao, España.
CONADEP. 1984. *Nunca Más. Informe de la Comisión Nacional sobre la Desaparición Forzada de Personas*. Buenos Aires: EUDEBA.
De Nur, Yehiel. 1961. The Trial of Adolf Eichmann, Session 68. http://www.nizkor.org/hweb/people/e/eichmann-adolf/transcripts/Sessions/Session-068-01.html, date accessed 13 March 2014.

Felman, Shoshana and Dori Laub. 1992. *Testimony: Crises of Witnessing in Literature, Psychoanalysis, and History*. New York and Abingdon: Routledge.
Friedlander, Saul. 1992. *Probing the Limits of Representatio: Nazism and the 'Final Solution'*. Cambridge: Harvard University Press.
Gatti, Gabriel. 2008. *El detenido-desaparecido. Narrativas posibles para una catástrofe de la identidad*. Montevideo: Trilce.
Hinkle, Lawrence. 1961. 'The Physiological State of the Interrogation Subject as It Affects Brain Function'. In *The Manipulation of Human Behaviour*, edited by Albert Bidermann and Herbert Zimmer. New York and London: Wiley and Sons, 19–50.
Jackson, Rosemary. 1981. *Fantasy: The Literature of Subversion*. London and New York: Routledge.
Kubark. 1963. *CIA-Counterintelligence Interrogation – July 1963*. http://www2.gwu.edu/~nsarchiv/NSAEBB/NSAEBB122/index.htm#kubark, date accessed 10 January 2014.
La Capra, Dominick. 1994. *Representing the Holocaust: History Theory, Trauma*. Ithaca, New York: Cornell University Press.
Lay-Brander, Miriam. 2011. *Raum-Zeiten im Umbruch. Erzählen und Zeigen im Sevilla der Frühen Neuzeit*. Bielefeld: Transcript.
Partnoy, Alicia. 1998. *The Little School: Tales of Disappearance and Survival*. San Francisco: Midnight Editions.
Pérès, Gabriel. 2009. 'De Argelia a la Argentina: estudio comparativo sobre la internacionalización de las doctrinas militares francesas en la lucha anti-subversiva. Enfoque institucional y discursivo'. In *Lucha de clases, guerra civil y genocidio en la Argentina 1973–1983. Antecedentes, desarrollo, complicidades*, edited by Inés Izaguirre. Buenos Aires: Eudeba, 391–422.
Rothberg, Michael. 2000. *Traumatic Realism: The Demands of Holocaust Representation* Minnesota: University of Minnesota Press.
Strejilevich, Nora. 1997. *Una sola muerte numerosa*. Miami: North-South Center Press. English translation by Cristina de la Torre (2002) *A Single Numberless Death*. Charlottesville: University of Virginia Press.
Taussig, Michael. 1984. 'Culture of Terror, Space of Death: Roger Casement's Putumayo Report and the Explanation of Terror'. *Comparative Studies in Society and History*, 26: 467–497.
Trinquier, Roger. 2009. *Modern Warfare: A French View of Counterinsurgency*, translated by D. Lee. Westport: Praeger Security International.
Weiner, Tim. 2008. *Legacy of Ashes: The History of CIA*. New York: Anchor Books.
White, Hayden. 2010. 'The Nineteenth Century as Chronotope'. In *The Fiction of Narrative. Essays on History, Literature, and Theory (1957–2007)*. Edited and with an introduction by Robert Doran. Baltimore: Johns Hopkins University Press, 237–246.

8
The Concentration Camp and the 'Unhomely Home': The Disappearance of Children in Post-Dictatorship Argentine Theatre

Mariana Eva Perez

Introduction

The disappearance of children in Argentina has been examined in-depth using both psychological and legal approaches that have focused on the 'private' dimensions of this practice. There are, however, no spatially oriented analyses to date that take into account the intrinsic relationship between the concentration camp (where most of those children were born) and the homes (to which most of them were transferred). This article will address the disappearance of children in its paradoxical state/private configuration, as a biopolitical phenomenon that is still taking place within the uncanny space of the 'unhomely home'.[1]

It is a challenge to grasp the meaning of a practice that has officially been denied, one which left no records or traces beyond the testimonies of those who survived the concentration camps and the stories of the hundred or so men and women (former disappeared children) who have since been found. In my attempt to put into words what the Argentine dictatorship kept quiet, I will turn to narratives other than these: the propaganda surrounding the segregation, re-socialization and repatriation of children of the Republican victims in Francoist Spain; the public discourse on the family and society propagated by Argentine military personnel; the once resistant, and now official, human rights narrative concerning so-called appropriation in Argentina; and of particular focus here, the theatre. In several of the plays written and staged about the disappearance of children, the 'unhomely home' is a predominant dramatic space which often recalls the concentration camps. But theatre offers more than a reflection of the concentrationary features of these homes: analysis of the spatial layout of these theatrical works also raises questions that other narratives have tended to disregard about the features of this particular space, its borders and the possibilities of escaping from it.

The disappearance of children in Argentina: Perpetrators' homes as spaces of exception

Under the state terror deployed in Argentina in the 1970s, at least 500 children were 'disappeared' among thousands of political dissidents. Most of them were born inside the concentration camps, taken away from their detained-disappeared mothers and illegally adopted or falsely registered by the perpetrators themselves – or indeed couples close to them – as their own children, despite the ongoing search carried out since then by their relatives.

There are no laws or archives that allow us to analyse accurately the state policy towards these babies or the wider population of children of those who either disappeared, were murdered at the time of their kidnapping or who became political prisoners. Recent research about orphans of those who were disappeared and murdered registered by the Department of Human Rights accounted for a total of approximately 14,000 cases.[2] Around 70 of the children who had already been born were also victims of enforced disappearance through alteration of their parentage (Abuelas, 2013). By contrast, almost all babies born in the concentration camps were disappeared. This shows that while disappearance was the rule in the case of babies delivered in captivity, it was the exception for children already born at the time of their parents' disappearance, even the youngest ones. Why then was such a distinction made? There are reasons that, at a first glance, might seem pragmatic: their relatives outside the camps had no certainty about their births and the babies did not legally exist, which made it difficult to demand their release. At the same time, their appearance would have served as proof of the disappearance of their mothers, a fact that was denied by the authorities. I will return to this later.

After their birth, the babies were taken away from the camp and their confinement was thus extended into another space: a home. In spatial terms, they were 'transferred' (a revealing, albeit perturbing, expression since 'transfer' was the euphemism for 'murder' within the Argentine camps). These literal transfers did not imply death, but the sealing of the babies' disappearance as they were registered under other names. This also blurred state intervention and displaced responsibility into the private sphere.

In this attempt to grasp the purpose of the disappearance of children beyond the individual desire of a particular perpetrator to become a 'parent', it is possible to trace a precedent in the more explicit Spanish politics towards children of the Republicans. Under the Francoist dictatorship, pseudo-scientific 'research' was conducted on political prisoners, combining racist theories, the ideas of the positivist school of criminology and Catholic religion, with the aim of proving the relationship between mental inferiority, Marxism and atheism (Vinyes et al., 2002, pp.31–54). As a conclusion to these 'studies', the military psychiatrist Antonio Vallejo Nágera recommended that 'the segregation of these individuals from childhood might free society from such a frightening plague' (Vinyes et al., 2002, p.40, my translation). Following this proposal, more than 12,000 children of prisoners were taken under state guardianship and forcibly admitted into public and religious institutions, where they were subjected to abuse and humiliating treatment combined with a harsh Catholic education. More than 42,000 children sent to Republican colonies abroad were repatriated without the consent of their family and were also institutionalized. A law allowed the authorities to register those children who could not remember their surname with a new one, which 'legalized' the erasure of their origins. This politics of segregation, repatriation and fostering was exploited by official propaganda as acts of charity, but left no public (or at least no accessible) records. Despite many children being illegally given up for adoption or losing their names, this policy does not seem to have addressed their parentage on a massive scale. The Francoist dictatorship placed its trust in the process of institutionalization to turn these children against the political tendencies of their families and in favour of the regime.

The Argentine military shared a similar ideological matrix with their Spanish comrades-in-arms. Catholic 'integrismo' (integralism) and anti-Communism reappeared 40 years later almost unmodified. Vallejo Nágera's concept of a 'Hispanic race', based not on genetics but on the environment, shared features with the figure of the 'national being' promoted by the Argentine military. It is impossible to find more than a few oral statements that recognize the practice of the disappearance of children, but the public discourse of the military authorities concerning the family and society offers some clues. According to Judith Filc, this discourse

> traced a map of Argentinean society, establishing the limits between *Argentine* and *non-Argentine* and thus building an ideal nation, without social classes, in which national identity was determined by shared 'essential values' (...). The division of the nation had been generated by the 'foreign' subversive ideology (...). The National Reorganization Process wanted to restore this lost unit.
> (Filc, 1997, p.38, my translation, original emphasis)

Once the political arena was suppressed, atomized individuals were forced to return to private space, but a private space that from now on was placed under the surveillance of the state and thus politicized. The family, as a liminal space between public and private spheres, between natural and cultural, was the chosen target. The regime built a series of complementary, but also contradictory, metaphors about the family. It was defined as the basic cell of society – the latter conceived as an organism – in a biological image that gave a 'natural' character to social structures. It was presented as the only secure space, while at the same time susceptible to foreign penetration; for this very reason, parents were encouraged to step up vigilance of young people. On another level, the dictatorship insisted upon the image of the nation as a great family – from which 'subversives' were obviously excluded. Citizens were represented as 'immature children' who needed a strong father to lead them back to the right path: the armed forces reserved this role as 'state-father' for themselves (Filc, 1997, p.43, my translation). As a strong father, the dictatorship arrogated to itself the right to punish the families of the disappeared for not having raised them well: the disappearance of children also bears this exemplary feature.

Given this conception of the family (in addition to the secrecy around enforced disappearances), it is not surprising that the education of those babies considered to be potential 'subversives' did not take place in public institutions, but rather at home. The normalizing function was delegated to those families selected and the state stepped aside.

Since the disappearance of the children in the womb, their relatives and most notably the grandmothers associated with the non-governmental organization (NGO) 'Abuelas de Plaza de Mayo' (Grandmothers of the Plaza de Mayo) have consistently raised their voices to reclaim them. Despite the fact that the Grandmothers understood early on the nature of this practice at the level of the state, the narrative that they have since developed has rather reinforced the private dimension of the crimes committed. Expressed in their terms, those children – today men and women – were taken as 'spoils of war' and 'appropriated' by the so-called appropriators, a term which refers only to the people who illegally perform the parental function. The Grandmothers seek to 'restitute their identity'. The men and women that they find are called 'recovered grandchildren'. Despite the unquestionable role played by the Grandmothers in tracking down this population and generating public politics around this issue, it cannot be overlooked that expressions such as 'spoils', 'appropriation' and 'recovery' as well as the notion of identity as an attribute that someone else can impose upon and restore to another, reproduce a form of objectification. Referring to them as their 'grandchildren' meanwhile tends to obstruct a comprehension of the social dimension of this politics. Since 2003, this narrative has become official under the successive Kirchners governments. The Grandmothers of Plaza de Mayo and the so-called grandchildren, as well as other relatives of the disappeared and human rights NGOs, have been major participants in the politics of memory of the last three administrations. The 'grandchildren' in particular nowadays occupy a highly symbolic place in domestic politics.[3]

As stated above, it might be assumed that there were practical reasons for giving priority to the kidnapping of babies born in captivity. A wider approach, which takes into account the concentration camp as an institution intended to produce and spread terror throughout society, would, however, reveal more. In her classic study of the concentration camps in totalitarian regimes, Hannah Arendt acknowledges the fundamental role of 'killing the juridical person' on the road towards total domination. This requires placing certain categories of people outside the protection of the law, a procedure that should be arbitrary in that it has no relationship to any subjective action defined as a crime according to the normal penal system (Arendt, 1962, p.447). In the case of these babies, the killing of the juridical person was not necessary. Neither was it enough simply not to register their births. They were, therefore, left outside the protection of the law; they disappeared and 'reappeared' as if they came from nowhere into new families.

The well-known concept of biopolitics (coined by Michel Foucault and fundamental to Giorgio Agamben's approach to the concentration camp as a state of exception) is useful in grasping the social dimension of the disappearance of children as a peculiar economy of population which only acquires its full meaning within the framework of the more extensive biopolitics of 'national reorganization'. The Argentine dictatorship did not just take the life of inmates in the concentration camps; it also fostered life in a particular way: babies were forced to be born and live as children of the perpetrators. But if it had only been a measure of social hygiene, aimed at avoiding 'subversion' in the future, it would not have been limited to babies born inside the camps and would have included all children. This is where the notion of arbitrariness becomes indispensable. While in the concentration camps examined by Arendt 'the arbitrary selection of victims indicates the essential principle of the institution' (Arendt, 1962, p.450), in the Argentine camps the inmates were mostly political dissidents. As Pilar Calveiro asserts: 'Although the group of casual victims was a minority in numerical terms, it played an important role in the *spread of terror*, both inside and outside the camp. There was irrefutable proof as to the *arbitrariness* of the system and its true *omnipotence*' (Calveiro, 1998, p.45, my translation, original emphasis). In Calveiro's analysis, casual victims occupy a place that is analogous to that of the arbitrary or innocent victims discussed in Arendt's study. I wish to propose that it is not only these casual victims who fit with this figure but (and in many ways more so) also the children who are undoubtedly innocent and also a universal symbol of innocence. Arbitrariness was exercised on children in two different ways. On the one hand, arbitrary selection seems to be the only rule followed regarding the children who were already born and present during the kidnapping of adults; on the other hand, inside the concentration camps, they incarnated the figure of the innocent victim as no one else could. Considered from this point of view, the disappearance of children can be revealed as the most arbitrary, and thus most terrifying, biopolitical practice carried out by the dictatorship, which in addition extends the practice of enforced disappearance in space and time, beyond the walls of the concentration camp and into future generations.

In the totalizing utopia which inspired this biopolitics, the homes to which the children were transferred share intrinsic features with the camp. According to Arendt, the concentration camp is the only space in which it is possible to reduce men to a Pavlovian 'bundle of reactions' (Arendt, 1962, p.456). The Argentine dictatorship extended this attempt at totalization into another space that indeed shows certain continuities, but also differences, with it. The new confinement does not take place in an inviolable physical space. Many former disappeared children have recounted that they suffered restrictions on their freedoms. These ranged from the most severe, such as being taken abroad to avoid 'restitution' to their families of origin, to others less severe, such as surveillance of their activities and relationships, a harsh religious or military education, or the imposition of a certain career (the chosen parents usually responding to the more general expectation that the dictatorship instilled in all parents by building traditional patriarchal families with the kidnapped children). However, this kind of confinement is different and is achieved by erasing the original history and overprinting it with one that is false. In this variation of enforced disappearance, the victims are oblivious to their own condition, which decisively undermines their capacity of resistance and their possibilities of escape. The darkness, silence and immobility that Calveiro detects as common denominators in all Argentine camps find their correlate in concealment, obedience and submission at home. Just like the bodies that are arranged in the concentration camps like packages, the dictatorship expected these children to fill a place at home, as well as in society, and stay there forever. But beyond all similarities, the aspiration of turning children into eternal inmates of a camp without walls can be shown to be naïve. If the camp aims to empty out the subjectivity of its inmates, the disappearance of children directly supposes a vacuum of subjectivity upon which it would be possible to inscribe anything at will. This biopolitical practice expects to act on those babies as if nothing had happened, as if the kidnapping, torture inside the womb, birth in captivity, time shared with the mother and separation could leave no trace. The unconscious dimension and even the materiality of the body are denied, by assuming that neither the victims nor the people they will know in the future will ever note the physical differences with the supposed family. I am not suggesting that this concentrationary experiment is condemned to failure by definition. It has proved its effectiveness in the many cases in which, after the truth has been disclosed, victims remain bound to those they consider to be their parents, vindicating their kidnapping as an act of mercy and even going ahead with their careers in the security forces. But as Calveiro asserts, contradicting Arendt, there are always 'lines of escape' in a concentrationary space, which is particularly true in this case because, no matter how suffocating the 'family' environment may be, it could never be identical to a concentration camp.

If it is not a mere prolongation of the concentration camp, how then should we account for this space of the home in which the biopolitical foundation has left its imprint, while 'family' relationships following the strict pattern of traditional family roles have been growing for almost four decades? The contradiction contained in the Freudian notion of the 'uncanny' (*unheimlich* in German) and its link to the semantic field of the home make this concept the most fertile to describe it. Sigmund Freud developed this concept in order to refer to 'that species of the frightening that goes back to what was once well known and had long been familiar' (Freud, 2003, p.124). As Freud points out

> among the various shades of meaning that are recorded for the word *heimlich* there is one in which it merges with its formal antonym, *unheimlich* (...). [T]his word *heimlich* is not unambiguous, but belongs to two sets of ideas, which are not mutually contradictory, but very different from each other – the one relating to what is familiar and comfortable, the other to what is concealed and kept hidden. *Unheimlich* is the antonym of *heimlich* only in the latter's first sense, not in its second.
> (Freud, 2003, p.132, original emphasis)

Freud summarized it as follows: 'the uncanny derives from what was once familiar and then repressed' (Freud, 2003, p.153). He also accounts for a third meaning, especially suggestive for this issue: 'the term "uncanny" (*unheimlich*) applies to everything that was intended to remain secret, hidden away, and has come into the open' (Freud, 2003, p.132). The home to which the disappeared children were transferred condenses all these meanings of the uncanny into a single space. What seems to be familiar serves to keep something from sight, while what is most intimate has been repressed. Playing with the literal translation from German, we could say that they are 'unhomely homes', a paradoxical term for a paradoxical space. The third meaning of the uncanny as something that should remain hidden, but which has been revealed, arises when these men and women are identified: they are those beloved and searched-for kidnapped children, yet at the same time they resemble the people who raised them and in one sense they *are* their children. Neither the hegemonic narrative about enforced disappearance in Argentina nor the specialist knowledge that has engaged with the search, take this element of taboo into account. Theatre has, however, achieved this and it is for this reason that I will finish this article by examining three plays that explore the uncanny features of the 'unhomely home' in different ways.

The disappearance of children in post-dictatorship theatre: The dramatic space of the 'Unhomely Home'

There are different categorizations of space in theatre. For the purposes of this analysis, it will be enough to distinguish between stage space and dramatic space: the first corresponding to the physical space where the play takes place; the latter to the places represented by any process, including narration. It is considered that every play puts forward (or hides beneath) a spatial model that tends to organize two dramatic sub-spaces in binary opposition. This opposition describes conflicts between the characters or between the subjects and objects of the action; action that can often be translated into attempts to break this spatial layout or trespass across the border between the dramatic space actually represented and what constitutes 'off stage' (the places represented by non-dramatic means) (Jurii Lotman and Anne Ubersfeld as cited in Pavis 2005, p.170; Pavis, 2005, pp.169–176, 195; García Barrientos, 2003, p.128; Sanchis Sinisterra, 2003, pp.234–236, 295–296).

Many of the plays about the disappearance of children in Argentina (most of them written and premiered within the cycle entitled 'Teatroxlaidentidad' or Txi[4] (Theatre for Identity) locate the action within the dramatic space of the 'unhomely home'. Although there are more plays about already-born children who were kidnapped with their parents than about babies born in captivity, the homes to which they were transferred usually bear similar features to those of a concentration camp. This is more obvious in Txi plays. In addition, in these latter works the figure of the 'appropriator' is portrayed in a highly stereotyped way, as a mere perpetrator. *Una buena afeitada* (A Good Shave), by Juan Sasiaín (2005),[5] offers a good example of this kind of representation.

This play takes the form of the monologue of a barber who works in a concentration camp. He is referred to simply as 'Father'. The action is located a few years after the dictatorship, in the bathroom of the home to which the little 'Daughter' was transferred immediately after her birth. The off-stage space of the concentration camp is remembered in detail by the Father. He calls it poetically 'el oscuro' (the dark) and presents it as the opposite of another off-stage space: his sunny barber's shop located downtown on Libertad (Freedom) Street, where he provided shaving services before taking the job in the camp. He recalls his former work as an art – 'the art of shaving' – and his shop as a friendly place, replete with laughter and familiarity. On the contrary, in 'el oscuro'

> I had to learn how to work in bad light, almost in the darkness (...). Everything was more fenced in, utilitarian, mechanical (...). I was a fundamental part of the apparatus (...). I become a professional in the art of discipline and silence. The work became boring, sad, solitary.
>
> (Sasiaín, 2005: p.225, my translation)

The way in which the concentration camp is presented as oppressive not only for the prisoners the Father shaves, but also for himself, is suggestive. As Calveiro reminds us, the camp has its mechanisms that allow the perpetrators to do their 'jobs', such as the chain of command, the fragmentation of the process, the objectification of the inmates, among others (Calveiro, 1998). This part of the play insinuates that both perpetrators and the disappeared are affected by the dehumanizing machinery of the camp. But the play does not go further in this direction. After recalling his personal involvement in the delivery of the Daughter, cutting the umbilical cord with his razor, and the transfer of the baby to his home, he introduces the character of 'El Colo', a detained-disappeared man who was the father of the baby. He narrates how he masturbated 'El Colo' after shaving him and then killed him with his razor in order 'to freeze the instant and take the secret with me' (Sasiaín, 2005, p.227, my translation). So, he is not an ordinary man out of whom the concentration camp has made a perpetrator, but a sadist who finds pleasure in a tortured body and who takes the life of another for his own benefit. The story is more disturbing since he tells it in the presence of the Daughter, whose head is covered by a towel (which reminds spectators of the hoods that the disappeared were forced to wear in the camps), while he approaches the razor to her covered face. By doing so, it becomes a direct menace to the girl.

Both dramatic spaces – the camp and the home – are connected by 'an antique family mirror' in front of which he shaves. The mirror functions as a gate leading to other spaces and times which are open in the 'here and now'. From the depths of its reflection, the ghosts of two genuine fathers haunt the barber: his own – also a barber – who taught him to shave and 'El Colo'. The confrontation with the memory of his father suggests disapproval for having turned the 'art of shaving' into a mechanism of the concentration camp. The mirror also reinforces the simultaneous and paradoxical identity and contiguity between the camp and the home. It brings closer an 'absent or autonomous space' until the latter is turned into a 'latent or adjacent space' (García Barrientos, 2003, pp.137–141), demonstrating the biopolitical dimension of this seemly private place. The illusory depths of the mirror are supposed to chain the Daughter to the Father's genealogy, even in a physical sense: 'When she looks at it, I will be there (. . .). The same hands. The same smell' (Sasiaín, 2005, p.224). But at the end of the play, the Father confesses to being afraid that when the Daughter looks into the mirror in the future, she will not see him but rather 'El Colo'.

By presenting the perpetrator's home, condensed into the sordid space of a bathroom, as a continuation of the concentration camp, the play is illustrative of many aspects of the disappearance of children: the complicity of the so-called appropriators with the disappearance of the parents, the denial of the body, the haunting quality of the disappeared, a certain degree of sexual perversion sometimes involved in the coexistence between 'parents' and 'children',[6] and also the naivety of the assumption that the victims would never suspect their condition.

In the other two plays that I will consider (*Potestad*, by Eduardo Pavlovsky,[7] and *Chiquito*, by Luis Cano[8]) the space of the concentration camp is not so explicitly alluded to or compared. This space is not described as such, but its structural features arise in other ways.

At the beginning of *Potestad*, the character, who is simply called 'Man', establishes the dramatic space of his home in detail, tracing imaginary lines between the three members of his family (himself, his wife Ana María and their daughter Adriana), defining and reducing the space to that triangle. During the first half of the play, the Man tries to reconstruct the exact positions and movements of their three bodies on a particular Saturday afternoon, an attempt that becomes more and more grotesque, as if by doing so he would be able to restore the order which had been broken when a mysterious man rang the doorbell and took the girl away. From that moment on, the space of the home expands and becomes disgusting and depressing for both the Man and Ana María.

The reader-spectator has no information through which to understand who has taken Adriana away – nor why – until the end of the play, when the Man recalls the off-stage space of another home. He has gone to this other apartment, in his capacity as a doctor, to certify the death of a couple who have been savagely shot while in bed. He recalls the address off by heart and refers to the members of the security force who committed the murder as 'the guys', which demonstrates his knowledge and implication in the incident. The Man recalls his surprise and indignation when he discovered the girl in the other bedroom, but his outrage is addressed towards the victims: he describes this off-stage home as a dangerous place due to the young parents' 'fanaticism'. At that moment, according to the stage direction, 'blood should fall upon the character's face' (Pavlovsky, 1987, p.44, my translation). The blood has trespassed from off-stage to stage space, emphasizing his complicity.

The spatial layout of the play represents the disappearance of the girl as the transfer of an element of the drama from an off-stage space to the represented dramatic space of the Man and Ana María's home. In an analogous way, the presumed return of the girl to her family is presented as the transfer of that element from the home to another off-stage space, which remains uncertain and indeterminate. The agent of the first transfer is the Man; the agent of the second, the enigmatic man who turns out to be a judicial official. The 'unhomely home' is not shown as a continuation of the camp, but as a concentrationary device itself. It constitutes a reduced space within the confines of which bodies are forced to repeat the same movements over and over again, which recalls the Arendt's 'world of conditioned reflexes, of marionettes without a trace of spontaneity' (Arendt, 1962, p.456). There, the Man, Ana María and Adriana are trapped. Only the girl gets to escape, through the intervention of the justice system (which implies restitution of the juridical person in her, if not her identity, which is a much wider concept). At the end of the play, both the Man and Ana María are the only inmates left of this concentrationary device which they built at home. Their anguish over the absence of Adriana provocatively recalls the pain of the relatives of the disappeared. Home has become uncanny for them too. While the borders around this space of confinement have been revealed to be porous when Adriana is taken by the judicial official

> There is (...) an aesthetic harmony in the gliding of the two, no violence, no aggression, (...) it was intimacy not a violation of anything, everything glided along.
> (Pavlovsky, 1987, p.33, my translation)

For the Man and Ana María those borders seem, in contrast, to be as solid as walls.

The last play, *Chiquito* (Little One), also takes place within the dramatic space of the 'unhomely home'. Chiquito is a retired member of the military; he and his wife, the Nurse, have raised a boy – who is today an adult – to whom they give the strange name Cascarita (Scab). Cascarita's condition as a disappeared child is never made explicit as such. Chiquito and the Nurse refer to the fact that they found him on the doorstep, and talk about an adoption, but Cascarita does not believe them and neither does the reader-spectator.

The transfer of Cascarita from another space to this home remains hidden, although the confession made by Chiquito about having 'sent [someone] to the other side' when he was in the Army, recalls the concentration camps. In this play, the camp occupies the place encapsulating a secret, of a terrifying but never confirmed suspicion. If in *Una buena afeitada* the reader-spectator has a glimpse inside the concentration camp and in *Potestad* he or she is brought unbearably close to a concentrationary device within the home itself, in this play the camp functions as a latent menace.

Cascarita's confinement has two concentric circles: the home and the suburban neighbourhood of Sáenz Peña. The spatial layout of stage/off-stage counterpoises the home with two other spaces: on the one hand, the bar to which Chiquito insists on inviting Cascarita to play dice, seeking the young man's total identification with him; on the other hand, an unspecified place 'beyond Sáenz Peña' to which Cascarita escapes in his search for the truth of his origins. But his search is without success. This reflects one aspect of the problem of the disappearance of children which is usually disregarded. In the last decade, hundreds of men and women have responded to the doubt cast on their parentage by the appeals of the Grandmothers of Plaza de Mayo, but the resultant genetic tests have found no matches with the families who are searching for disappeared children. This seems to be the case for Cascarita, who returns to the 'unhomely home' looking for an answer, as well as to take revenge. When Cascarita rapes and/or kills Chiquito, the total identification between the two of them finally takes place:

> CASCARITA: Do you know what I have come to do? I came/To rescue what is left of Chiquito inside me/That is why I place on top/While his head falls to a side/It is the end/I am getting into him/Until disappearing inside him.
>
> (Cano, 2008, n.p.)

Chiquito's body becomes the space in which the biopolitical utopia of the dictatorship is realized, a spatial metaphor of the impossibility of escaping from the conditioning of the environment which, despite Cascarita's efforts, has turned him into a perpetrator. The borders or his confinement have been shown to be elastic: no matter how far from Sáenz Peña he goes, he takes Chiquito with him.

This pessimistic ending, as well as the end of *Potestad*, dares to raise questions that seem to remain taboo for other narratives: can a seemly private space, such as a 'family' home become a space of exception? Are the so-called appropriators merely a kind of perpetrator, or did the normalizing duty imposed on them by the state and accomplished through the patriarchal family model turn them into a new uncanny category which has yet to be accounted for? What are the extended effects of the biopolitics of fostering one life as another among the entire generation of disappeared children? Is it possible to escape from a space of confinement without walls such as the 'unhomely home'? If so, how?

Notes

The research leading to this chapter has received funding from the European Research Council under the European Union's Seventh Framework Program (FP/2007–2013)/ERC Grant Agreement n° 240984, 'NOT.'

1. I wish to express my gratitude to Prof. Dr. Aleida Assmann, who suggested the term 'unhomely home' to me at the conference during which the first version of this chapter was presented.
2. Interview with the group Colectivo de Hijos, Buenos Aires, March 2013.
3. To cite one example of their importance, the football tournament which is being played in Argentina as I write this article has been named in honour of the 'Recovered Grandchildren'.
4. Txi was created in Buenos Aires in 2001 to support the ongoing search carried out by the Grandmothers of Plaza de Mayo. Txi has promoted the writing of short pieces about 'identity' ever since and stages them with the aim of promoting doubt in the generation of the 'grandchildren'.
5. *Una buena afeitada*, written and performed by Sasiaín and directed by Federico Godfrid, was premiered in Buenos Aires in Txi 2002. It was staged again in Buenos Aires in 2003 and in Madrid in 2008, both times within the Txi series.

6. This sensitive 'open secret' was recently denounced by Carla Artés Company (Hauser, 2011) and María Ramírez ('It was like hell and it felt like I had been buried alive', *Página/12*, 18 March 2012, my translation), who both brought actions against their kidnappers and sexual abusers.
7. *Potestad* was premiered in Buenos Aires in 1985, performed by Pavlovsky and directed by Norman Brisky. Since then, it has been staged several times, directed by Pavlovsky. It is considered to be a classic play about disappearance. 'Potestad' in Spanish means not only parental guardianship but also power and authority.
8. The first version of this play was premiered in 1997 with the title *Ruleta Rusa* (Russian Roulette). The version I work with is the one staged in Buenos Aires between 2008 and 2010, directed by Analía Fedra García. It took part in national and international festivals and won several prizes.

Bibliography

Abuelas de Plaza de Mayo. 2013. http://abuelas.org.ar, date accessed 12 November 2013.
Arendt, Hannah. 1962. *The Origins of Totalitarianism*. Cleveland and New York: Meridian Books.
Calveiro, Pilar. 1998. *Poder y desaparición. Los campos de concentración en Argentina*. Buenos Aires: Ediciones Colihue.
Cano, Luis. 2008. *Chiquito* (unpublished).
Di María, Andrea and Mariana Eva Perez. 2007. 'La apropiación de niños por motivos políticos como práctica genocida'. In *Genocidio y Diferencia – Conference Proceedings*, V Encuentro sobre Genocidio, Grupo de Estudio de Genocidio del Centro Armenio and Cátedra Libre de Estudios Armenios, Faculty of Philosophy and Literature, University of Buenos Aires, Buenos Aires, 218–231.
Filc, Judith. 1997. *Entre el parentesco y la política. Familia y dictadura, 1976–1983*. Buenos Aires: Editorial Biblos.
Freud, Sigmund. 2003 (1919). *The Uncanny*. London: Penguin Books.
García Barrientos, José Luis. 2003. *Cómo se comenta una obra de teatro. Ensayo de método*. Madrid: Editorial Síntesis.
Hauser, Irina. 2011. 'Un represor con otro problema judicial'. *Página/12*, 27 July 2011, http://www.pagina12.com.ar/diario/elpais/1-173138-2011-07-27.html, date accessed 12 November 2013.
Pavis, Patrice. 2005. *Diccionario del teatro. Dramaturgia, estética, semiología*. Buenos Aires: Paidós.
Pavlovsky, Eduardo. 1987. *Potestad*. Buenos Aires: Ediciones Búsqueda.
Ramírez, María (interviewer unknown). 2012. 'Era un infierno y yo me sentía enterrada viva'. *Página/12*, 18 March 2012, http://www.pagina12.com.ar/diario/elpais/1-189888-2012-03-18.html, date accessed 12 November 2013.
Sanchis Sinisterra, José. 2003. *La escena sin límites. Fragmentos de un discurso teatral*. Ciudad Real: Ñaque Editora.
Sasiaín, Juan. 2005. 'Una buena afeitada'. In *Teatro x la identidad: obras de teatro de los ciclos 2002 y 2004*, edited by Abuelas de Plaza de Mayo. Buenos Aires: Ministerio de Educación, Ciencia y Tecnología and Abuelas de Playa de Mayo.
Vinyes, Ricard, Montse Armengou and Ricard Belis. 2002. *Los niños perdidos del franquismo*. Barcelona: Plaza & Janés.

Part III

Haunted Spaces, Irrupting Memories

9
'The Whole Country Is a Monument': Framing Places of Terror in Post-War Germany

Aleida Assmann

Introduction

When it comes to framing places of terror and disappearance, Germany unfortunately has a wide range of cases to offer. In the intense discussion preceding and framing the building of the central German Holocaust memorial in Berlin, which was dedicated in 2005, an interesting comment came from Jewish historian Marianne Awerbuch. She wrote: 'The whole country is a monument!' (Assmann, 2011, p.222). The new monument for the murdered Europeans Jews was built in the centre of Berlin on neutral ground. With her statement Awerbuch wanted to prevent this new site somehow eclipsing, devaluing and displacing the authentic historical sites in the attention and memory of the Germans. A special paragraph concerning the obligation to preserve and care for the former concentration camps, that had been turned into historical sites of memory after the end of the war, had been inscribed into the treaty of unification of the two German states after 1990. This state of affairs, however, in no way demonstrated that 'the whole country is a monument'. Hundreds and hundreds of less conspicuous sites had been made invisible after 1945, transforming them into nondescript places by deleting the traces of their history. If nobody intervenes, nature has a great capacity for de-historicizing places. 'I am the grass, let me work' is the tag line of a poem 'Grass' by Carl Sandburg (Sandburg, 2013) about the great battlefields of the nineteenth and twentieth centuries. When it comes to the built environment and architecture, the reuse of buildings has proven to be an effective way to drive the forgetting and effacement of historical knowledge. Even at the historical sites such as the former concentration camp of Dachau, for instance, central well-preserved and stately buildings were reused by the Allies immediately after the war and handed over to the German administration after their retreat. A clear demarcation line was thus drawn separating what was henceforth to be taken into safe-keeping, to be carefully preserved as tokens from a guilty past, from buildings of the same historical complex that were semantically neutralized and which returned to the normal cycle of everyday use in an ongoing present.

Marianne Awerbuch's statement that in Germany, 'the whole country is a monument', was therefore all but self-evident. It took a new generation of young people to rediscover the forgotten history that was buried under the transformations of modern life. What the parents had been eager to cover up in a pact of silence, the sons and daughters were eager to uncover and mark, thus restoring the past to memory. This material memory work was stimulated and carried out on a local level; the younger generation had neither an official mandate nor financial support when they turned the recovery of historical traces and the marking of sites and buildings into their own generational project. Much of what they started was eventually taken over by official institutions of cities, county and state; much, however, is still based on their individual investment, depending on their personal efforts and energy. This part of their memory work might therefore disappear again soon if it is not taken up and continued by younger members of the community.

Interestingly enough, in Germany it was an artist of the generation of 1968 (who challenged the complicit silence of their parents with the Nazi past) and not a research group of academic historians funded by the state, who stimulated a unique historical recovery project in 1996 that anticipated Awerbuch's statement about the whole country being a monument. Sigrid Sigurdsson (1999), an artist and activist of memory, who had become famous for her archival installations, created a map of Germany with the boundaries of 1937 with the title: 'Germany – a Monument – a Research Task' ('Deutschland – ein Denkmal – ein Forschungsauftrag') (Figure 9.1).[1] She was the first to notice that no map existed in which all the known Nazi concentration camps and detention sites from 1933 to 1945 were listed. This is why she called her work 'Forschungs*auftrag*' (research commission) rather than 'Forschungs*projekt*' (research project) – it was a reminder to the public and historians, pointing out to them a dimension that they had overlooked. Sigurdsson hired a historian and with her she created a map of the German topography of Nazi terror, visualizing for the first time in detail its extended and all encompassing network of power, destruction and death.

Sigurdsson's map had three important effects. The first was *visualization*. The map littered with black dots signifying larger and smaller sites of terror shows the extent of the bureaucratic system of repression, persecution, exploitation and death at one glance. It creates the impression of an epidemic disease covering the whole country. A second effect was *instruction*. The detailed map shows that the network of terror extended into all regions of the country, sparing none. The insight revealed by this map was that of a shocking proximity to the sites of terror. Suddenly the sites and traces of this past were no longer neatly contained in clearly marked areas but extended into the immediate neighbourhood, which could be reached from

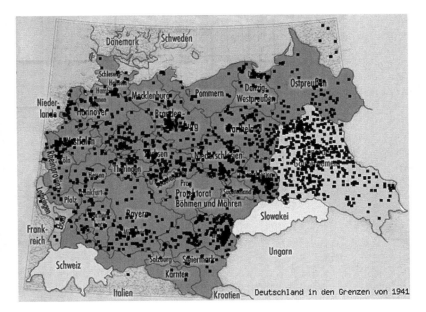

Figure 9.1 Map of Germany with the borders of 1937, showing the sites of concentration camps
Courtesy of Sigrid Sigurdsson.

everybody's front door. The third effect was *integrated research*. The visual artwork of the map was connected to a digital database into which all relevant information was to be fed. In this way, it became an innovative framework for co-operative research by linking museum and university, supporting existing activities and stimulating new ones. This individual initiative of an artist shows amazing institutional flexibility, taking part in different mediations, being part both of exhibitions and research projects. It also highlights the open-endedness of this ongoing encompassing 'monument' as a collective project and work in progress.

Recovering two topographies of terror in post-war Germany

'Great is the power of memory that resides in places' (Cicero, 1989, pp.394–396). This was the conviction of Cicero, the Latin master of mnemotechnics. He did not only invent artificial systems of imaginary memory places, using the technique of *loci* (the pigeon holes) and *imagines* (the images to be stored in these places), but also focused on historical sites, such as the site of Plato's academy in Greece. When he visited that site with his friends, there were no material traces left as reminders of its great history. This, however, was not a problem for the historical tourists from Rome who were well read and whose memory and imagination were stuffed with stimulating stories and images. Therefore they were struck by the particular aura of the authentic place that kindled their imagination and transformed the knowledge they had brought along into a 'lived experience' of the place.

There is a long cultural tradition of marking places where important events happened and singling them out for monumentalization and memorialization: birth places of political leaders and cultural heroes, battle fields where decisive victories or defeats happened, places that are connected with religious martyrs and miracles. The spatial practice of cultural and religious pilgrimage arose from the attraction of those sites, which were believed to retain something of the presence of former saints and heroes. It is this belief in the aura of authentic places that constitutes their mnemonic power and attraction for *HisTourism* (Mütter, 2009).

Of such places we may say that they retain and support a *voluntary memory*. They are selected and maintained by the society for their normative potential to reinforce heroic models and reproduce cultural values. I want to distinguish them here from places that are not intentionally chosen and embraced for a memorial purpose. They remain ignored and unmarked until they suddenly reappear and resurface unexpectedly. Then they confront the society with a history that it had preferred to forget.

I want to present here two examples of such involuntary places. The first is the so-called topography of terror in Berlin. What I find particularly striking about this place is the story of its involuntary recovery. After reunification, German memory was redesigned to integrate firmly its traumatic history. This development was confirmed with the opening of the holocaust monument in 2005, 60 years after the end of the Second World War. The marking of memorable places of Nazi history, however, was far from consensual until well into the 1980s: some memorial plaques had been put up on buildings by local initiatives to indicate their function in the administration of the Nazi regime, but many of these plaques like, for instance, the one designating the former Imperial War Court (Reichskriegsgericht) soon found their way into the waste-bin.[2]

The former headquarters of the Gestapo in the centre of Berlin offer a striking example of an involuntary place of memory (see Reichel, 1995). It was from here that the concentration camps were administered, that the records of the regime's opponents were kept, and thousands of the latter were detained and tortured before being sent to concentration camps. The buildings that had housed the former headquarters of the Gestapo secret police, the SS and the State Security Office between 1933 and 1945 were demolished in the 1950s. From then on, it was impossible to identify Prinz-Albrecht-Strasse 8 – the official address of their headquarters – either on the spot or on maps of the city. The most feared address in Berlin had thus silently disappeared. The East Germans had replaced this street with a new one, Niederkirchnerstrasse, named after the seamstress and Communist resistance fighter Käthe Niederkirchner, who was murdered at the concentration camp of Ravensbrück. On the West German side of the area, the land had been levelled out, and for many years the remnants of the buildings were used as rubble: *Erdverwertung* (reutilization of earth) was the technical term. In 1981, Bazon Brock seized on this term when he included the area as part of a cultural tour and reframed it for the historical imagination. He turned 'the reutilization of earth' into an eloquent metaphor for historical change: 'It was here that the ruins of what had been were and are piled up, sorted out, and re-designated' (Brock, 1986, p.194). A sizable part of this rubble from the Nazi ruins was used for the foundations of Tegel Airport. This combination of demolition, waste, and covering up was later conceived to be highly symbolic. Brock also noted that for decades the site had been used for driving without a driver's licence (*Führerschein*), and he could not resist a pun here: in stark contrast to the spatial practice of the Third Reich 'when the *Führer* (the leader, Adolf Hitler's title) and his *Unterführer* (sub-leaders), at least since 1938, were in possession of *Führerscheine* (a collective licence) issued by the German people' (Brock, 1986, p.195).

In 1983, a competition was announced to turn this area of wasteland into a 'memorial park for the victims of National Socialism'. A monument proposed by the Rumanian poet Oskar Pastior and garden architect Edelgard Jost was praised but not realized. It would have totally voided the place and sealed its surface with a layer of solid black plates of stone. The accompanying message of the artist was: 'Only an empty space can do justice to this place.' An additional design resembling a spider web was to indicate this point of origin of Nazi crimes, adding the word 'HERE' in the centre to establish a contact-zone between the historic site and later visitors to suggest the effect that 'HERE you yourself are the monument'.

Since this monument was never built, the status of the site as an historical place of memory remained officially unrecognized. An application by the opposition SPD (Social Democratic Party of Germany) to excavate the remnants of the buildings was rejected by the Berlin Parliament on 31 January 1985. A few months later, US President Ronald Reagan visited Germany on the occasion of the fortieth anniversary of the end of the Second World War. On 5 May 1985 together with Chancellor Helmut Kohl he held a ceremony at the military cemetery at Bitburg, which contains the graves of German soldiers, including those of SS troops. The Reagan-Kohl commemoration event at Bitburg triggered a symbolic counter-demonstration that took place in Berlin on the same day. A crowd of people armed with shovels began to dig wildly on an inconspicuous plot of land of the former Prinz Albrecht Strasse, firmly determined to contradict the popular opinion that 'there was no longer anything to seek or find at the site of the SS and Gestapo headquarters' (Figure 9.2) (Wirsing, 1986).

In the summer of 1985, a systematic examination of the site under the direction of the Berliner historian Reinhard Rürup uncovered the remains

Figure 9.2 Collective excavation at the site of the former Gestapo headquarters (1985) Photograph by Hans Peter Stiebing.

of a basement with washrooms and a kitchen area. This was a symbolic breakthrough which, in the very heart of Berlin, established material contact with the recent past and which was eventually put on display beneath a provisional roof under the heading 'Topography of Terror', also dubbed 'the silent place' in a later exhibition (Rürup, 2010).[3] After the provisional exhibition, a museum was opened on the site in May 2010 in the shape of a two-storey glass and steel rectangle. The present director of the museum, Andreas Nachama describes it as an exemplary place where party and state institutions were fused together, adding: 'It holds lessons about the workings of other dictatorships as well... The Pinochet dictatorship in Chile or the military junta in Argentina.' (*DIE WELT*, 6 May 2010)

This archaeological securing of evidence shows clearly what the status of an involuntary place of trauma is in the land of the perpetrators: placed materially in immediate proximity, but worlds away in terms of consciousness, visibility, memory. These 'stones of provocation' connected to the topography of terror were uncovered and brought to public view against considerable resistance (Spielmann, 1988). The power of memory in this case asserted itself from the bottom up against a strong desire to forget and to suppress. According to playwright Heiner Müller, traumas are mnemonic dynamite, which sooner or later will explode: 'The work of memory and of mourning proceeds from shocks', he said in an interview.[4] Like Nietzsche, Warburg and Freud he advocated a theory of memory as psychic energy that links lasting traces of memory to primal scenes of violence. For Müller as for Walter Benjamin, memory is a revolutionary force which 'brings to the fore the blood of forgotten ancestors' together with residual, unresolved issues from the past. Both Marxists considered this act of revolutionary remembering as a passionate objection to the suffering and injustice of history.

If the National Socialist administration had had its way, it would have followed up the Jewish genocide with a mnemocide. Forgetting is the strong desire of all perpetrators. After a regime change that also involves a radical change of cultural values, not all signs and messages are immediately reorganized in the society. In Germany it took a long time and a huge effort to turn the tables. The Nazi propaganda had of course fallen silent after 1945, but those formerly condemned to silence had not yet had a real chance to speak out. Forty years later, persecutor and persecuted had still not openly exchanged their roles and status.

There is a sequel to this story that brings us into the actual present, because it took place another three decades later. It shows how the non-recognition of involuntary places can be prolonged. This story is still evolving in Southern Germany in Stuttgart, capital of the federal state Baden-Württemberg. Its site is a building named 'Hotel Silber' after its former use. This imposing nineteenth-century building had housed the regional central office of the Gestapo from 1937 to 1945. It did not disappear after the war and received no historical mark whatsoever; instead, it was immediately reused as Stuttgart's central police station. In this case, it was not rupture and the effacement of the traces but a firm institutional continuation after 1945 that rendered the historical site fully invisible. Focus on the building was renewed by the intention to remove it in 2008, when the government of Baden-Württemberg together with a local investor planned to reconstruct a sizable part of the city centre to build the so-called Da Vinci Complex, an area with new grand hotels, business space and an expensive shopping mall. This economic redesign of the city centre was the context for the re-entry of Hotel Silber into public consciousness as a traumatic historic site. When it also became known that the building was to be torn down, a small number of citizens formed a protest group, trying to prevent the plan (Figure 9.3). They worked hard to reinsert this place on Germany's map of terror, but to no avail. The newspapers denigrated the protest as anti-modern and notoriously backward looking. In the end it was not protest that was successful but the intervention of the Japanese Tsunami, which damaged the nuclear reactor in Fukushima and effected a landslide in the German federal elections in 2011, producing unprecedented support for the environment-conscious Green Party. After 58 years of continuous rule the conservative CDU (Christian Democratic Union) was replaced by the 'green' politicians. When the latter took office they decided to leave the Hotel Silber untouched and transform it into a site of memory. In the coalition agreement between

Figure 9.3 Flyer of "Aktion Hotel Silber"
Courtesy of Elke Banabak, Initiative Hotel Silber.

the conservatives and the Green Party we can read: 'Places of memory are to be supported with conceptual and archival work. The memory culture that – thanks to many local and regional initiatives – has gained a new importance in public life needs continuation and reliability.'[5]

This recent development shows the extent to which a memory culture is contingent on contemporary interests and party politics. In a democratic society, memory places are always identified and supported by one group and ignored or even resisted by another. By themselves, the traumatic sites do not cry out: 'I am witness to a story that must not be forgotten!' On the contrary, if nobody tells and heeds their story, life evolves carelessly and effaces all traces. Historic buildings are torn down, reconstructed or transformed through new functions and uses. Nor is the memory of the inhabitants a reliable source but dissolves after three generations.[6] Public debates and contestation, on the other hand, are a powerful stimulus for memory. After 67 years, the Hotel Silber became a prominent place that has moved it into the centre of political interests, public attention, media information, internet blogging and personal commitments. This example also shows that the number of involuntary sites of memory is never closed, just as the work of memory that is always embedded into the changes of social life and open towards the future.

National and regional sites of memory

I have already introduced the distinction between voluntary and involuntary memory sites, which have a very different history of commemoration. Let me add here another distinction, which is equally important to further describe the specificity of these places: national and regional. Though this dimension is commonly overlooked, this framing context is of great importance for the organization, message and appeal of these places, including different forms of participation. According to the German constitution, the upkeep and care of regional sites of terror and trauma is a responsibility of the regional governments (*Bundesländer*), except for those sites which are deemed to be of national and international importance, representing certain forms of persecution in exemplary ways. To this group belong the sites of the former concentration camps, which, after German unification, became a national responsibility, including their conceptual articulation and steady financial support.[7]

The situation of the places administered by the regional governments is quite different. They lack a similar visibility, long-term-commitment and structure of support. They are to a large extent memory places from below, discovered, marked and maintained on a voluntary basis by personal commitment. Their designation and number is therefore largely dependent on the historical sensibility, the initiative and commitment of individual citizens. This double structure shows that in Germany, the culture of memory is not only a responsibility that is delegated to the state but also a democratic concern of civil society.[8]

This historical sensibility and interest in active participation required a generational change and took a long time to grow. When, after the war, survivors of the concentration and forced labour camps returned to visit the sites of their suffering and mark them with plaques and other memorial signs, they found little or no support among the German population for their commemorative activities. In this early phase, the memory of the historic trauma was the sole responsibility of the victims, while the former perpetrators left the burdened past behind and invested enthusiastically in the future. This has changed considerably, as Germany has now not only a number of national sites of trauma with high visibility and attracting international tourism, but also a rich memorial landscape of regional and local sites which are visited by neighbouring populations, school classes, affected survivors and their families. What is remarkable about these local places of terror and trauma, is the long temporal lag before they were established. Although they are relevant places for the whole society; lack of interest and resistance remain strong. But these local places are important for two reasons. One is that they reflect a more democratic form of participation in the memory culture than the national sites, which are far away and in the responsibility of the federal state. The other is that they tell a story that intersects with the memory of the respective populations, relating to their immediate environment in a well-known region. This local anchoring of the history of the Holocaust is an important complement to the trans-nationally standardized Holocaust education supported by the 'International Task Force for Holocaust Remembrance, Education and Research' (founded on the initiative of Swedish president Göran Persson at an international conference in Stockholm in 2000) which has become more and more independent from concrete places. An apt way to characterize the difference between national and regional sites of memory is to use Pierre Nora's distinction between 'milieu de mémoire' and 'lieu de mémoire' (Nora, 1989, p.7). In stark contrast to the national 'lieux de mémoire' that are neatly separated from their surroundings, marking a totally different and alien world that can be entered and left behind, the local sites of trauma are part of a 'milieu de mémoire'; they are situated literally before the front door; you need not look for them, you stumble on them unexpectedly. They are embedded in residential areas and much less conspicuous than the national sites. And, as the case of Hotel Silber shows, many of them are yet to be discovered.

These national and regional traumatic sites of memory elicit very different responses and have different functions for the victims and the succeeding generations of the perpetrators. For the victims, these authentic places retain a visible trace of the crime, triggering painful repercussions in their embodied traumatic memory. For the succeeding generations of Germans, they have become places of learning and commemoration. In this, they have a trans-historical effect: they make retrospectively visible what nobody wanted to see or know about at the time they were operating so efficiently. They reveal to today's Germans what their ancestors had not wanted to see, hear of feel: the irreparable loss that was caused when German Jewish citizens were 'disappeared' from the midst of the society, their cities and villages – 'from apartments, schools, hospitals, law firms, medical practices, universities, courtrooms' – and one should add: shops (Pflug et al., 2007, p.35).

Spatial practices: Decontamination and the transformative power of memory

The political transition from dictatorship to democracy is effected by the replacement of a complex framework of political and legal rules, but this remains ineffective if it is not supported by an important shift in the historical sensibility within the society. What is its background and motivation? How is it expressed in word and action? These are questions that I want to turn to in the last part of my chapter. My focus will be on new spatial practices that have emerged in dealing with inconspicuous and involuntary places of memory. In Germany after 1945, one way of getting rid of a violent history had for a long time been to ignore the traumatic past, just to wait and let the proverbial grass of forgetting do its work. A distance from the scenes of the crime was created by effacing traces, by allowing life to take its course and cover them up. Buildings were torn down like the central office of the Gestapo in Berlin or reused like that in Stuttgart. Former sites of the many regional KZs (concentration camps) were overgrown with grass and quickly disappeared from perception and consciousness. In these cases, the traumatic past was supposed to disappear more or less on its own, by the sheer force of the passing of time.

Over the last three decades we could observe a shift from forgetting to remembering in relation to involuntary traumatic places. The new spatial practice relating to traumatic sites is premised on remembering. It is based on the insight and experience that a traumatic past does not simply disappear by itself but tends to linger subliminally and refuses to go away. 'The past that does not pass' (Nolte, 1986) has become a standard formula for trauma which, at its core, is a 'state of exception' in the structure of our temporality. It applies, as we have learned since the 1980s, to three contexts in particular: juridical, medical and moral. In cases of excessive violence and trauma, the past does not automatically disappear but returns to be readdressed by lawyers, therapists and concerned citizens. The past returns, firstly, in the crimes against humanity that need to be prosecuted and indicted in the (inter)national law court. It returns, secondly, in the suffering of victims from post-traumatic stress disorder that needs to be therapeutically attended to, and it returns thirdly in the moral consciousness of a society that establishes commemoration places and practices for the victims. These have become regular forms of transition for states undergoing a transformation from an authoritarian society to a democratic one. In all of these contexts, it is remembering rather than forgetting that has become the general agenda. I will confine myself here to a few German examples of this shift from forgetting to remembering, showing how new practices of remembering were locally invented and enacted.

All of these new practices were invented by individuals introducing elements of art into social space. My first example are the 'stumbling stones' by Gunter Demnig which he has been inserting into the sidewalks of German and other cities since 2003. These small blocks of brass are inscribed with the names and fates of victims of Nazi terror – Jews as well as those that were persecuted for political reasons, Sinti and Roma, Jehovah's witnesses, homosexuals and victims of euthanasia – and placed in the ground in front of their last address from which they were 'disappeared'.[9]

This spatial practice is underpinned by local civic groups who cooperate by doing the extensive archival research that goes with the placing of the stumbling stones. They recover biographies of forgotten victims together with information about their families around the globe who are included in the commemoration process and often participate in the local events of dedicating the blocs. I see in this spatial practice an important local complement to the de-territorialized national holocaust monument in Berlin. While the one monument covers the space of a whole football field, the other fits on the palm of a hand. The un-inscribed vertical *stelae* of Peter Eisenman's monument differ greatly from the horizontal brass plates with their names and biographical information which, in order to read, one has to bow down to. Nor are the stumbling stones a monument that one intentionally goes to visit; on the contrary, they wait for us to stumble upon them unawared and to read them when we had not expected to do so.

Today members of the third and forth post-war generation live in houses the history of which they do not know. In a country where excessive crimes were perpetrated, some of its younger citizens might feel haunted by this unknown history that still lingers, even though time has seemingly effaced its traces. The urge to mark the houses in their city and to uncover this history may emerge from the desire for knowledge and the personal decision of individuals to distance themselves from a contaminating complicity with silent profiteers. The recovery of the history of the house is thus embraced as an act of solidarity with the victims, helping to 'de-contaminate' the social space.

In Vienna, where Demnig's stumbling stones were rejected by the city magistrate, a group of citizens has invented another spatial practice with a similar symbolic effect. The Servitengasse in the Alsergrund district was once a place inhabited by many Jewish families and lined with Jewish shops. In 2004 a group of younger tenants got together to find out who had once built and lived in the houses that they were now inhabiting. After four years of intense archival research this collective project in search of lost tracks led to an exhibition and a monument. The exhibition showed the stories of many former Jewish tenants, owners and shopkeepers of the Servitengasse. The monument was designed by the artist Julia Schulz and dedicated in 2008, 70 years after the annexation of Austria to Nazi-Germany. It consists of a square glass box, placed in the ground and illuminated during the night, containing the symbolic 462 keys and name-tags of Jewish citizens that had been expelled and deported from this district, most of them from this street (Miljkoviæ, 2008). Of the 377 Jews of the Servitengasse only seven survived the Nazi terror. These seven returned to the street for the first time on the occasion of this exhibition.[10]

My last example is Gusen, a small village in Austria where the artist Christoph Mayer was born in 1974. As he grew up there he slowly learned from indirect hints that this village was different from others. Gusen had been the site of a concentration camp during the Second World War where the inmates were exploited with forced labour in a nearby mine, 37,000 of whom were murdered in the process. After the war there was nothing left to remind outsiders of their suffering and the history of the place. The only carrier of this knowledge was the embodied memory of the survivors themselves who regularly returned to this site of trauma and built a monument in 1965. Their commemorative practices were not joined by the villagers, and these activities evolved largely unnoticed by the local community. With his memorial project, Christoph Mayer broke away from this solid post-war community of silence and repression. In another act of 'decontamination' he brought the historical site back into social memory – without moving a single stone. He created an audio installation that leads the visitors through the memorial landscape of Gusen. By listening to the audio guide, which constellates voices of survivors, bystanders and perpetrators, the visitors have to create their own images of what they do not see with their eyes as their feet walk on the authentic site (Figure 9.4) (Lebert, 2007).[11]

Conclusion

As Marianne Awerbuch insisted, after 12 years of Nazi rule, the whole of Germany has indeed become a 'monument'. What she meant was: a place littered with traumatic spaces, reaching from the former concentration camps to the extended transnational network of repression and terror up to the destroyed synagogues and various apartments from which Jewish citizens

Figure 9.4 'Audioweg Gusen'. The present Gartenstraße in Gusen in which, between 1940 and 1945, the Barracks from the camp Gusen I were located
Photograph by Chrispoth Mayer chm.

were forcibly deported and murdered. The artist Sigrid Sigurdsson transformed the 'monument' of the country into a map showing the multiple sites of terror, which covered the land like an infectious disease. As traumatic sites are places of an involuntary memory that shuns the confrontation with their history, they can easily be evaded by effacing traces or covering them up through new use and function. Nevertheless, these traumatic spaces also retain a kind of mnemonic energy that calls for a belated response, exerting a power to return to these places of haunting and unrest. Sites of traumatic memory differ considerably from monuments, memorials and museums in that they are never congruent with the meaning given to them in retrospect. While monuments can be defined as 'identity fictions of the survivors', traumatic sites generate an affective surplus of suffering and guilt which calls for later action (Koselleck, 1979). In spite of their sparse material relics, authentic historic sites are more than just symbols, because they are also themselves. While cultural symbols may be built up and pulled down, these places can never be totally appropriated or made to disappear completely in a new geopolitical order. Uncovering these traumatic places, marking them and inventing commemorative practices are responses to their mnemonic energy that reintroduce the forgotten into social consciousness and integrate what had been split off by assigning it a place in the memory of the community.

Notes

1. This project was done in cooperation with Cornelia Steinhauer. Since 2009: Extension of the database and integration into the 'architecture of remembering', Karl-Ernst Osthaus Museum, Hagen, curated by Michael Fehr; since 2011: cooperation with historians Bettina and Holger Sarnes. http://www.deutschland-ein-denkmal.de/ded/information/texts?textName=text-002, date accessed 4 December 2013.
2. For example, the memorial plaque at the former Reichskriegsgericht, Witzlebenstr. 4–5 (Reichel, 1995, pp.191–192).
3. See also the Internet page of the 'Stiftung Topographie des Terrors'.
4. 'Verwaltungsakte produzieren keine Erinnerungen', Interview given by Heiner Müller on 7 May 1995 in Berlin and done by Hendrik Werner, http://hydra.humanities.uci.edu/mueller/hendrik.html, date accessed 7 January 2014.
5. Election Program of the Green Party, 2013, p.261.
6. An open letter of the initiative Hotel Silber addressed to the Breuninger family clearly explains the plans: 'The building Dorotheenstraße ten must be preserved as a place of memory, of learning and research. Following the model of the cities Cologne, Berlin, Nuremberg, Dresden and Munich it shall house the long overdue Stuttgart and Württemberg NS-Center of Documentation.'
7. These national sites of trauma are: Bergen Belsen, Buchenwald, Neuengamme, Ravensbrück, Sachsenhausen and Dachau. See also Knigge and Frei, 2002.
8. 'To a large extent, the memory work at the regional places is in the hands and responsibility of committed men and women of the civil society' (Pflug et al., 2007, p.35).

9. For 120 Euro anybody can initiate a stumbling stone by funding its production and its placing in the ground. For further information see http://www.stolpersteine-leipzig.de/index.php?id=268, date accessed 7 January 2014.
10. *DER STANDARD*, 16. June 2010.
11. See also http://audioweg.gusen.org/, date accessed 7 January 2014.

Bibliography

Assmann, Aleida. 2011. *Der lange Schatten der Vergangenheit. Erinnerungskultur und Geschichtspolitik*. Munich: C.H. Beck.
Brock, Bazon. 1986. 'Geschichte als Differenz in der Gegenwart'. In *Ästhetik gegen erzwungene Unmittelbarkeit: die Gottsucherbande. Schriften 1978–1986.*, edited by Nicola von Velsen. Cologne: DuMont.
Cicero,
Knigge, Volkhard and Norbert Frei editors. 2002. *Verbrechen erinnern. Die Auseinandersetzung mit Holocaust und Völkermord*. Munich: C. H. Beck.
Koselleck, Reinhard. 1997. 'Kriegsdenkmale als Identitätsstiftungen der Überlebenden'. In *Identität. Poetik und Hermeneutik 8*, edited by Odo Marquard and Karlheinz Stierle. Munich: Fink Hareven, 255–276.
Lebert, Stephan. 2007. 'Ein Dorf und der Tod'. *Die Zeit*, 19 May 2012.
Marcus T. 1989. *De finibus bonorum et malorum. Über das höchste Gut und das größte Übel, Volume 1–2*, edited and translated by Harald Merklin. Stuttgart: Reclam.
Miljkoviæ, Marijana. 2008. 'Servitengasse: 426 Schlüssel gegen das Vergessen'. *DER STANDARD*, 9 April 2008.
Mütter, Bernd. 2009. *HisTourismus: Geschichte in der Erwachsenenbildung und auf Reisen*. Oldenburg: BIS-Verlag.
Nolte, Ernst. 1986. 'Vergangenheit, die nicht vergehen will. Eine Rede, die geschrieben, aber nicht gehalten werden konnte'. *FAZ* 6 June 1986.
Nora, Pierre. 1989. 'Between Memory and History: Les Lieux de Mémoire'. *Representations*, 26: 7–24.
Pflug, Konrad, Ulrike Raab-Nicolai and Reinhold Weber. 2007. 'Orte des Gedenkens und Erinnerns in Baden-Württemberg'. *Schriften zur politischen Landeskunde Baden-Württembergs* 35.
Reichel, Peter. 1995. *Politik mit der Erinnerung*. Munich: Carl HanserVerlag.
Rürup, Reinhard et al., eds. 2010. *Topographie des Terrors: Gestapo, SS und Reichssicherheitshauptamt auf dem 'Prinz-Albrecht-Gelände'. Eine Dokumentation*. Berlin: Arenhövel.
Sandburg, Carl. 2013. *Grass*. www.poetryfoundation.org, date accessed 13 December 2013.
Sigurdsson, Sigrid. 1999. 'Deutschland – ein Denkmal – ein Forschungsauftrag'. In *Deutschland – ein Denkmal – ein Forschungsauftrag: ein Projekt zur Erforschung der nationalsozialistischen Lager und Haftstätten sowie der Orte des Massenmords 1933 bis 1945*, edited by Michael Fehr, and Sigrid Sigurdsson. Karl Ernst Osthaus Museum. Hagen: Neuer Folkwang-Verlag.
Spielmann, Jochen. 1988. 'Steine des Anstosses – Denkmale in Erinnerung an den Nationalsozialismus in der Bundesrepublik Deutschland'. *Kritische Berichte*, 16/3: 5–16.
Wirsing, Sibylle. 1986. 'Die Freilegung des Gestapo-Geländes. "Der umschwiegene Ort" – eine Berliner Ausstellung'. *FAZ* 24 December 1986.

10
Haunted Houses, Horror Literature and the Space of Memory in Post-Dictatorship Argentine Literature

Silvana Mandolessi

In his well-known essay 'The Uncanny' (1919), Freud posits an intrinsic relationship between the experience of what he terms 'the uncanny' and spatiality. According to Freud's definition, the uncanny occupies a fundamental position in that it manifests itself in the alteration of a space which, having hitherto been perceived as familiar, becomes the opposite: an unhomely space inhabited by otherness; a space which loses its familiar quality because it has been invaded and altered. The uncanny is thus linked to the affect with which a subject relates to a given space: to the affect with which a space is charged and to the transformation of this affect into another – predictably its opposite.

At the same time, the category of space, which in Freud's essay may in principle seem easy to define, is revealed to be more complex and difficult to grasp. There exists, for example, an intimate interdependence between space and time which renders it more complex. According to Freud's formulation, space and memory appear to be intrinsically linked, as there is an invasion of a past experience into the present which manifests itself in the uncanny. Different temporalities coincide in the same place while the boundary between past and present becomes blurred, thus rendering space an ambiguous category. The ambiguity or indecipherability, uncertainty and impossibility of assured knowledge are in fact the most remarkable characteristics pertaining to the sensation of the uncanny. This intellectual uncertainty and the impossibility of dissociating what is familiar and what is not form the nucleus of the experience that Freud seeks to describe.

Even though Freud's formulation of the uncanny deals with individual subjectivity, the same characteristics are relevant when describing the political experience of terror, the focus of this chapter. There is a spectrum of emotions related to fear which comprises, among others, the uncanny, horror and terror. There also exists a long history of trying to adequately distinguish what nuances each of these emotions.

As David Punter points out, the main difference between 'horror' and 'terror' is precisely the political characteristic of the latter. In his entry on 'Terror' in *The Handbook to Gothic Literature* Punter emphasizes that terror has had, and indeed continues to have, a direct connection with the socio-political field. In this sense, it is no coincidence that the roots of Gothic fiction (the genre of terror par excellence) can be traced back to the period of revolution in Europe; one of its manifestations being the French 'Reign of Terror' (*La Terreur*). While horror has to do with what frightens or disgusts, terror is at once deeper and less total, offering the dual possibility of submerging us in political abjection and emerging from it having gained a certain sense of self (Punter, 1998, p.235). In short, the affective impact of horror is more direct, cruder and also simpler, whereas the affective impact of terror is more profound, indirect, potentially more complex and capable of affecting subjectivity, thus involving a socio-political dimension.

Returning to the aforementioned link between the affect of terror and the importance of spatiality as established by Freud, I will approach political terror in terms of space, focusing on the dictatorship that gripped Argentina between 1976 and 1983. My analysis will focus on literature that narrates this socio-political experience. Thirty years on, the topic is still omnipresent in Argentine literature, albeit now written for the most part by a generation that did not directly experience it. What such literature processes, therefore, are the effects of terror and its memory. In recent novels that deal with the effects of state terrorism, what catches the reader's attention is an extended use of conventions drawn from the fantastic and gothic genres in order to narrate the social and subjective experiences of disappearance. This will not seem so strange if we consider that the closest cultural representation to the figure of the disappeared is that of the ghost: someone in between life and death; a liminal figure located between presence and absence, past and future. Jacques Derrida suggests that 'the spectral is that which is *neither* alive *nor* dead' (Wolfreys, 2002, p.x, original emphasis). The disappeared are indeed spectres of Argentine collective memory. Following Avery Gordon's line of argument it is possible to reaffirm that, despite every effort to produce concrete knowledge of the disappeared and dispel their spectral status, spectrality is still the form in which they inhabit the collective memory (Gordon, 2008). This is frequently approached in narrative terms via the classic literary genre of terror. Comparing historical events with the well-known fantastical story *The Monkeys' Paw*, by William Wymark Jacobs, the narrator of Guillermo Saccomanno's novel *77* (2008) states:

> Our reality was no less terrifying than this tale. The dictatorship referred to its victims as *desaparecidos* [disappeared]. The prefix '*des*' suggested that, in the event that they were found, what these mothers were going to

receive would then be *aparecidos* [appeared]. However many explanations and psychological theories were invented to overcome the grief, the disappeared would always be phantoms circling them just as *they* circled the *Plaza* demanding that pink building for their appearance. Perhaps terror was the most apt genre to recount our national history.

(Saccomanno, 2008, p.65, my translation and emphasis)

The genre of the fantastic – and that of the gothic in particular – has often been conceived as a genre of evasion; a genre scarcely entering into contact with reality. The images of ghosts, supernatural events, haunted houses, monstrous creatures and exotic locations suggest, in principle, a type of narrative that would not be well suited to reflection upon political violence. However, numerous critics have questioned the classification of the gothic as a genre of evasion, drawing attention instead to its capacity to refer to the socio-political reality in which the work is produced, even though this reference may not be made by means of the most direct or transparent realism. Furthermore, since the publication of Derrida's influential work *Specters of Marx* (1994) the notion of spectrality and in particular the concept of 'haunting' – direct derivatives of the gothic tradition – have taken on a dimension which transforms them into critical instruments with which to think politically. To this effect, Andrew Smith affirms that 'whilst it would be banal to state that ghosts bring the past back to life, spectrality does become a means through which to explore history' (Smith, 2007, p.153). The metaphor of ghosts that literally bring the past into the present transforms them into a powerful image of what a culture has tried to silence within itself: this oblique character of the ghost lingers by signalling what a culture can express only in indirect terms. In line with what certain critics have termed the 'spectral turn', I would like to concentrate here on the representation of two paradigmatic spatialities in post-dictatorship Argentine literature; paradigmatic in the sense that they symbolize two key elements – or experiences – under the regime established by the Argentine dictatorship. The first is the affectivity of terror and the second is the affectivity evoked by absence (not any absence, but rather a particular experience of absence resulting from the repressive technique of disappearance). I would like to put forward the hypothesis that spatially these two affectivities express themselves in opposite ways: in the first case, the terror that dominates the social body is rendered figurative by means of a maximum concentration of space which in literature is represented by the haunted house; in the second, the experience of absence that causes disappearance. In contrast to the maximum spatial concentration that terror provokes, disappearance is identified with evanescence or dissolution – within the space and of the space itself. More specifically, disappearance is determined by the impossibility of assigning a particular location to the body. Absence and spatiality mutually convoke one another, which is why spatiality becomes a key category for understanding – and on occasions 'coming to terms with' – the functioning and effects of military dictatorship.

The haunted house

The military dictatorship in Argentina carried out its repressive practices via the installation, across the entire national territory, of more than 300 concentration/extermination camps. The victims were kidnapped in their houses or on the street and taken to one of these centres. Once inside, they were deprived of everything and subjected to torture in order to extract information and subsequently 'disappeared'. In her examination of the way in which these camps functioned, Pilar Calveiro underlines that one of the keys to understanding the regime's oppression is the fact that these spaces were not – as was the case in other repressive regimes – located outside and far away from the city, but rather within the confines of urban public space (Calveiro, 2006). She explains that the location of Clandestine Detention Centers (Centro Clandestino de Detención – CCD) in the heart of the city constituted an 'open secret':

> The problem of the secret appears to be directly linked to the question of legality. The secret – what is hidden, and/or underground – is part of the centrality of power (...). The concentration camps were secret and so were the bodies interred *Nomen Nominandum* in the cemeteries. However, in order for the mechanism of disappearance to function, these secrets had to be open; such camps needed to be known about in order to disseminate the terror (...). Secrets which need to be known, albeit remaining unspoken, but which everyone knows.
> (Calveiro, 2006, pp.78–79, my translation)

The neighbours knew and did not know what was happening there. They could hear voices, see fragments, but were not entirely sure about the crimes that were being committed. This mechanism was essential to spreading terror across the entire society. All space becomes contaminated with terror via the spectral presence of this 'secret' right in the middle of public space. Space which was once familiar now becomes haunted by the presence of a secret which threatens its inhabitants. Thus, the insertion of the concentration camp into the middle of the city does not effectively transform the entire city into a camp, but rather affectively transforms the relationship of the city to its inhabitants. The experience of this space becomes figurative in post-dictatorship novels as the closed space of a haunted house. The haunted house awakens widespread terror and the threat of feeling pursued in a closed space, from which it is impossible to escape; a sensation which is identified with the paranoia that terror produces. The classic or exotic haunted house does not appear in the novels to which I refer here, but rather in common spaces: ordinary houses, public spaces, such as schools, or larger spaces such as small provincial towns. They are, above all, spaces closed off in themselves, with no contact whatsoever with the outside. This lack of contact with the world outside is one of the characteristics that differentiates the welcoming quality of a familiar space from the oppressive character of a space of imprisonment. Contact with the outside world is not necessarily forbidden or closed off in a way that might indicate the fact that the house now represents a sign of threat rather than familiarity: it is the secret that inhabits it that is the centre of gravity attracting its inhabitants, preventing them from leaving. The house possesses a blind centre, installs a conflict with such intensity that it causes everything outside to pale and dissolve. The space turns in on itself precisely because what should be *outside* has been situated *inside*, at the heart of the familiar.

La casa de los conejos (The Rabbit House) by Laura Alcoba (2008) is narrated from the point of view of a young girl and recounts her confinement, alongside her mother and other members of the Montoneros, inside a house in which they are all living secretly during the dictatorship. The girl lives with the fear of accidently betraying the secret of the house – the secret in this case being the existence of the house itself. Although she and her mother manage to escape, the house will eventually be blown up and those inhabiting it will die. In *Ciencias morales* (Moral Sciences) by Martín Kohan (2007), the claustrophobic space is that of the renowned Colegio Nacional (one of Argentina's most prestigious public high schools) in Buenos Aires. Here, a similar plot is inverted: the space of the school shuts itself off in order to protect its pupils from being contaminated by the surrounding social chaos. A strict disciplinary regime is established, one which prevents any contact with this exterior space which the conservative forces within the school perceive to be dangerous. Other novels reproduce the pattern of closed space, extending it from the home or school to a town. In *El colectivo* (The Bus) by Eugenia Almeida (2009), the setting that is chosen to narrate the oppressive atmosphere of the dictatorship is a small town in the province of Córdoba in the 1970s. If small towns are usually oppressive in themselves, then this image is reinforced because the town's contact with the world outside is all but cut off. The only bus to pass through the town, thus linking it with other towns, is stopped by the military because they are looking for a couple, deemed to be 'subversives', who are supposedly hiding there. Confinement and silence are the two topics that dominate the narration. In the end the couple is found and murdered and thus the town returns to 'normality'. A similar, albeit more complex, image forms the basis for Carlos Gamerro's *El secreto y las voces* (The Secret and the Voices) published in 2002. This novel is also set in a small town – this time in the province of Buenos Aires – and describes the search undertaken by Fefe, who years later returns to the town in which he spent her childhood in order to find out what really happened to the town's only 'desaparecido', who turns out to be his father, something the reader only discovers at the end. In this case, the oppressive atmosphere is derived from the reconstruction of the voices, rather than the silence which reigns over the characters in *El colectivo*. The protagonist speaks to each of the town's inhabitants who, instead of holding their tongues, are keen to recount what happened. These voices, which despite their differences end up speaking in unison, become oppressive in precisely the opposite way to the silence discussed above: because they do not hold their tongues and because the chorus of murmurs repeats itself from different angles, what emerges is a discourse of complicity in which everyone ends up being responsible for the disappearance of someone innocent.

As can be observed, the pattern of closed space is repeated in the novels. Furthermore, in each case this closed space functions in the same way as that of a haunted house, which can be read as a metaphor for the way in which social space functions during a military dictatorship. Each one of these spaces is a haunted space, because behind the appearance of a normal course of life lurks the secret of a crime.

In *La casa de los conejos*, the house is blown up because someone reveals its whereabouts, and this someone turns out to be one of the members who is hidden in the house. In *Ciencias morales* the supposedly unpolluted space of the school, which claims to protect its students from social violence, is revealed to be inhabited by violence on the inside. This inner violence in the novel comes from the school's Chief Custodian, who is in charge of looking after the safety of its members but who rapes the Hall Monitor. *El colectivo* tells of how the relationships between the neighbours are shot through with old hatreds, social inequalities and misunderstandings that do not have anything to do with the 'subversive' couple and, as certain secrets remain incomprehensible to the reader even as the novel draws to a close, they determine the life of the town and render its inhabitants incapable of reacting. This is a social space that is 'contaminated' beyond what happens with the disappeared couple. Finally, the town in *El secreto y las voces* is an illustration of civilian complicity with the military dictatorship. As the protagonist discovers, the whole town knew that his father would become one of the 'disappeared', because the policeman in charge told everyone in the hope that someone would prevent it happening, but no one did anything. The imminent disappearance of the main character's father was once again an open secret; a secret of ambiguous character that associated it with generating terror.

These novels may all stage terror, but I would particularly like to point out that spatiality introduces an important distinction with regard to a common idea that terror comes from being at the mercy of alien forces, from the possible threat that otherness poses. In contrast to this classic conceptualization, according to which an Other – or that which is other – invades our innocent and unpolluted space, the space of the haunted house in contrast indicates that the source of terror lies inside the social body and is the uncontrollable eruption of underlying social conflicts. The home – a metaphor for public space – collapses, not because of the invasion and violence exercised upon it by an alien force, but rather because it becomes terrifying with the weight of unresolved crimes which have been silenced for so long. The theme of the haunted house invites the reader to renounce any simplistic version of political conflict and revise the historical genealogies that lead to terror in the present, albeit in a different way in each of these texts. The idea that the 'outside' does not exist and that the origin of conflict needs necessarily to be traced inside the house – the social body – prevents comfortable readings of society as innocent; simple spectators of two alien forces that debate with one another beyond the bounds of their responsibility.

The materiality of absence

The second form of spatiality does not specifically concern literary thematics – such as the haunted house – but the manner in which the affective experience of absence is inscribed into a space. If the experience of absence – and the affectivity that it incites – is obviously present in the death of a loved one, in the case of forced disappearance it takes on an intensity that is exceptional, being derived from the uncertainty surrounding the location of the body. Traditionally, the ritual of burial enables the body of the deceased to be attributed a resting place. Giving him or her a place means that the domains of the living and the dead can be differentiated and enables the place of the living to be protected and cocooned. But in the case of disappearance, the impossibility of granting a place to the absent body 'extends' this absence to all spaces. A painting by South African artist William Kentridge illustrates this effectively: in it there is a small figure with his back turned, facing an inscription that occupies almost all the space of the painting, and which reads '[h]er absence filled the world'. Gabrielle Schwab sees a perfect emblem of traumatic loss in Kentridge's painting because

> the mood of Kentridge's drawing captures the affects that aggregate around disappearances: the absence becomes a totalizing force, swallowing all life and energies. It is as if the world is gradually emptied out by the disappeared, leaving nothing behind but the ghostly traces of past memories. Disappearance drains the world's vitality and color, creating the death-in-life quality of a shadow world.
>
> (Schwab, 2013, p.7)

Absence cannot therefore be considered simply as the opposite of presence. Lars Frers insists on this in his article 'The Matter of Absence' (Frers, 2013, pp.433–434) in which he argues that absence, or rather the experience of absence, is always a relational phenomenon. A person has to miss something or someone in order for him, her or it to be absent. There was a farm here and now there is not; someone was here with me in this place, but died of cancer two years ago and now I am here alone. The perception of absence thus emerges in the comparison with the way in which space and time are lived and, in particular, from the difference between past and present within the same space. It is in this difference that *absence* becomes *presence*.

The question posed by much post-dictatorship fiction is *how* to represent – make visible or present – this absence, in particular the affective aspect of absence that results from disappearance and its principle characteristic: the impossibility of assigning a place (of rest) to the body. It is no coincidence that many works of fiction resort to a spatial matrix in their attempt to represent and reflect upon the affectivity induced by disappearance. This absence that is present – or omnipresent – translates spatially in many works of fiction in their representation of paradoxical spaces and, by not occupying any place, ends up occupying all space. Among these, it is worth mentioning *La costa ciega* (The Blind Coast) by Carlos María Domínguez (2010), *Memorias del río inmóvil* (Memories of the Immobile River), by Cristina Feijoó (2001), *El lugar perdido* (The Lost Place) by Norma Huidobro (2007) or *Purgatorio* (Purgatory) by Tomás Eloy Martínez (2008).

The very titles of these novels highlight these paradoxical and anomalous spaces: because they are anthropomorphized (*La costa ciega*); because what should flow is in fact static (*Memorias del río inmóvil*); because the lost space is in reality the only one that is permanently inhabited (Huidobro's novel); or because they call directly upon spaces that have traditionally been represented as intermediary, suspended and generally associated with their not being easy to inhabit, as is the case in *Purgatorio*. These novels may all stand out because they grant space a central role, but one in particular stands out because it positions space at the centre of the scenario, converting it into a significant instrument by which the feeling of absence that is typical of disappearance is translated symbolically: *Los planetas* (The Planets) by Sergio Chejfec, published in 1999, in which the narrator who is simply called 'S' recalls his disappeared friend 'M' by remembering the walks they took together across the city. The geography of the city is visited and revisited through this memory and the perception of space becomes one of the principle objectives of the narration, alongside the relationship that these friends have with their surroundings – a defamiliarized space that is rendered strange. In this sense, Chejfec's novel belongs to what Wolfgang Hallet would call 'fictions of space' or 'spatial fictions'; fictions that thematize perception and spatial practice as a key element in their narration (Hallet, 2009, p.108).

Los planetas neither reconstructs the terror of the era nor investigates the socio-political causes of violence. Instead, it takes the form of an intimate narrative evoking time shared between friends and above all dwelling on the effect that M's disappearance has had on S. Space in the novel is not only the stage on which events take place, but itself becomes a specific theme.

It becomes the key to measuring, or giving meaning to, the effects of disappearance. As S affirms, this is because the defining feature of disappearance is spatial: the impossibility of assigning a place to an absent body. The narrator states in one passage of the novel:

> If the fatefulness of his absence exaggerated what had happened, the lack of a space, a site, as I said, made it incomprehensible. It might have been a matter of just one person, as was the case, but it was infinite in scope.
> (Chejfec, 2012, p.108)

The impossibility of precisely locating an absent body distorts, in various ways, the manner in which space is both perceived and inhabited. One of the ways in which this is thematized in the novel is through the idea of disorientation or spatial dislocation: things are not in the place in which they seem to be. They occupy one space, while also occupying another.

A second metaphor for spatial distortion and dislocation is that of disorientation; the impossibility of orientating oneself correctly in space. This can be read as a means of expressing the loss not only of spatial but also cultural coordinates (Hallet, 2009, p.82). According to Hallet, this undermines a human's ability to 'cognitively to map its position in a mappable external world' (Jameson cited in Hallet, 2009, p.82); a loss of cultural coordinates brought on, in this case, by the catastrophe of meaning established by the practice of forced disappearance.[1] The novel habitually adopts the strategy of attributing the impossibility of self-orientation to disappeared friend M, rather than describing it as a sensation experienced by S. S states that

> M had always had a poor sense of direction; this led to a complete detachment from the geography of the city. It took him the same torturous effort to locate a point five blocks away, as fifty. (...) To his mind, space was a question without a clear answer.
> (Chejfec, 2012, p.23, emphasis added)

What remains significant is that, in his consciousness, space is 'a question without a clear answer'.

The most significant spatial anomaly is, however, without a doubt that which refers to the dialectic between absence and presence. Against the abundance of a realist text – and by this I mean of a space filled with meaningful objects – the city in *Los planetas* appears in contrast to be marked by absence. That is not to say that the objects (buildings, streets, houses) are not there – although Chejfec often situates the reader in places that are unpopulated and uninhabited (liminal spaces, vacant lots, roads, parks) – but rather that the most tangible or monumental presence is not one marked by abundance, but in the most radical way by emptiness. In a passage from *Los planetas*, S describes a football stadium that occupies the centre of the neighbourhood in which M once lived. Rather than *filling* the space and acting as a point of reference, the stadium is portrayed as a *hole* in the real:

> [D]espite its size, the shadow it cast, and the matches that were played within it, the field was not really the center of anything. The noise that swells up from the grounds and the silence –despite the match – beneath which everything seems submerged and that allows no indication from inside to pass, demonstrate the ambiguity of the gaping space, at once receptive and manifest, that is the stadium. The funereal silences that fill the air when the stands suddenly fall quiet imbues [sic] its rudimentary architecture with a sense of absence proportional, though inversely, to its size. At first one thinks about it and says, for example, [sic] Well of course the stadium is the center of the neighborhood, the place that gives life to its surroundings, the building that gives the neighborhood its character, and things like that, referring to the green patch of turf toward which all the surrounding streets and sidewalks seem to be orientated. But the opposite is actually true – the crust of the field is precisely that: an empty space erected on an arbitrary site.
>
> (Chejfec, 2012, p.31, original emphasis)

In another passage from the novel, the narrator states: 'Years later that same place (...); that same place would contain M's sudden absence as it had once contained his body, as contradictory as this might sound' (Chejfec, 2012, p.32).

In other words, the city is presented as an anomalous space paradoxically inhabited by a vacuum. Rosemary Jackson comments on fantastical spaces: '[u]nlike marvellous secondary worlds, which construct alternative realities, the shady worlds of the fantastic construct nothing. They are empty, emptying, dissolving' (Jackson, 1981, p.45). The text does not construct anything, or perhaps a more appropriate analysis would be that instead it builds nothingness. It bestows a place upon emptiness which in turn *gives M his place*.

The act of giving M *his* place equates to a testimony of absence, or to producing an absence in a way that renders it visible, tangible; in a way in which it can be experienced as a loss without becoming diluted over time. There was a time when M and S would walk together through a shared space: the city of Buenos Aires. The here and now of the narration takes place in this same city, albeit one that is irremediably other. *Los planetas* obsessively works to bear testimony to the tenuous difference between two cities which relies on this relationship to lived space and time. Space not only becomes a witness and metaphor – merely the static mise-en-scène within which the action takes place – but the figure of absence. Its distortions and spatial anomalies enable representation of the distortions and anomalies that the practice of terror and forced disappearance under the military dictatorship in Argentina imprinted upon society.

To conclude, when space in these novels is read figuratively, a series of spatial anomalies come to the fore, drawing attention to the significance of the following point: that both the haunted house and the spectral spaces of absence amount to a symbolization of affectivities and affect. Affect is not synonymous with sentiment or emotion, because as the theory of affect has clearly demonstrated, it transcends subjectivity: it does not presuppose a subject that is at the centre (Gregg and Seigworth, 2010). In this sense, to speak about the affect of terror or the affect exuded by absence does not imply that a subject is terrorized or experiences loss on a private level: rather it refers to forces and intensities that traverse bodies without necessarily emerging from them. Therefore, the affectivities of terror or the absence that such spaces conjure up are political, enabling us to reflect in a more complex manner upon the intensities and forces that become mobilized – or indeed inversely become immobilized – via the bodies that make up social space.

Notes

The research leading to this chapter has received funding from the European Research Council under the European Union's Seventh Framework Program (FP/2007–2013)/ERC Grant Agreement n° 240984, 'NOT.'

1. For further discussion of forced disappearance as a 'catastrophe of meaning' see Gatti, Gabriel. 2014. *Surviving Forced Disappearance in Argentina and Uruguay: Identity and Meaning*. New York: Palgrave Macmillan.

Bibliography

Alcoba, Laura. 2008. *La casa de los conejos*, translated by Leopoldo Brizuela. Buenos Aires: Edhasa.
Almeida, Eugenia. 2009. *El colectivo*. Buenos Aires: Edhasa.
Calveiro, Pilar. 2006 (1998). *Poder y desaparición: los campos de concentración en Argentina*. Buenos Aires: Colihue.
Chejfec, Sergio. 2012. *The Planets*, translated by Heather Cleary. Rochester: Open Letter.
Derrida, Jacques. 1994 (1993). *Specters of Marx: The State of the Debt, the Work of Mourning and the New International*. New York: Routledge.
Domínguez, Carlos M. 2010. *La costa ciega*. Buenos Aires: Mondadori.
Feijoó, Cristina. 2001. *Memorias del río inmóvil*. Buenos Aires: Clarín/Alfaguara.
Frers, Lars. 2013. 'The Matter of Absence'. *Cultural Geographies*, 20/4: 431–445.
Gamerro, Carlos. 2002. *El secreto y las voces*. Buenos Aires: Norma.
Gatti, Gabriel. 2014. *Surviving Forced Disappearing in Argentina and Uruguay: Identity and Meaning*. Basingstoke: Palgrave Macmillan.
Gordon, Avery F. 2008 (1997). *Ghostly Matters: Haunting and the Sociological Imagination*. Minneapolis: University of Minnesota Press.
Gregg, Melissa and Gregory J. Seigworth. eds. 2010. *The Affect Theory Reader*. Durham and London: Duke University Press.

Hallet, Wolfgang. 2009. 'Fictions of Space: Zeitgenössische Romane als fiktionale Modelle semiotischer Raumkonstitution'. In *Raum und Bewegung in der Literatur. Die Literaturwissenschaften und der Spatial Turn*, edited by Wolfgang Hallet and Birgit Neumann. Bielefeld: Transcript, 81–115.
Huidobro, Norma. 2007. *El lugar perdido*. Buenos Aires: Alfaguara.
Jackson, Rosemary. 1981. *Fantasy: The Literature of Subversion*. London: Methuen.
Kohan, Martín. 2007. *Ciencias morales*. Barcelona: Anagrama.
Martínez, Tomás E. 2008. *Purgatorio*. Buenos Aires: Alfaguara.
Mulvey-Roberts, Marie. ed. 1998. *The Handbook to Gothic Literature*. Basingstoke: Palgrave Macmillan.
Punter, David. 1998. 'Terror'. In *The Handbook to Gothic Literature*, edited by Marie Mulvey-Roberts. Basingstoke: Macmillan.
Saccomanno, Guillermo. 2008. *77*. Buenos Aires: Planeta.
Schwab, Gabriele. 2013. 'Ghostly Transferences: On Memory and Haunting'. Lecture delivered at the University of Konstanz on 29 January 2013. Unpublished manuscript.
Smith, Andrew. 2007. 'Hauntings'. In *The Routledge Companion to Gothic*, edited by Catherine Spooner and Emma McEvoy. London and New York: Routledge, 147–154.
Wolfreys, Julian. 2002. *Victorian Hauntings: Spectrality, Gothic, the Uncanny and Literature*. Basingstoke: Palgrave Macmillan.

11
Counter-Movement, Space and Politics: How the Saturday Mothers of Turkey Make Enforced Disappearances Visible

Meltem Ahıska

In the light of the contemporary

'What is the contemporary?' Reflecting on this question Agamben argues that one who is contemporary should actively perceive 'the darkness of his time as something that concerns him, as something that never ceases to engage him [sic]' (Agamben, 2009, p.45). The protests that started in late May 2013 in Turkey, now referred to as the *Gezi Resistance* produced a radical conception of contemporaneity in this respect, as opposed to the concept of contemporaneity much emphasized in the hegemonic discourses of modernization and progress. By creatively engaging with the darkness of its present the event has to a great extent destroyed the closure of history in Turkey. I contend that this has a significant impact on the way we think of politics in relation to time and space.

In this chapter, I will first explore the trope of *counter-movement* as a political capacity inspired by the Gezi Resistance. Then I will look at how counter-movement plays a vital role not only in producing a new space for politics, but also in enacting political memory in the particular case of the Saturday Mothers – the mothers of the disappeared in Turkey, who since 1995 have been silently demonstrating by holding aloft the photographs of their disappeared kin every Saturday in Galatasaray, Istanbul. By employing Erin Manning's discussion about time and politics (Manning, 2004), I would argue that the politics of the Saturday Mothers that made the enforced disappearances visible was possible by a counter-movement. A movement that re-casts time and creates a new space, and re-moves the subject from the space of violence 'naturalized' within the national temporality.

But why *counter*-movement and not just movement? The Gezi Resistance provides some meaningful clues. Let us look at some instances of the resistance that I regard to be signs of counter-movement. The initial aim of the resistance seemed simple: the protestors were against the cutting down of trees and the illegal confiscation of a public park in Taksim, at the heart of Istanbul. The trees were being cut down in order to resurrect an Ottoman military barracks, now to be transformed into a hotel and a shopping mall. The project of rebuilding the barracks carried symbolic political meanings evoking continuity with the past – by adding the attributed grandiosity of Ottoman Islamic rule to the popular appeal of the government. However, the project was also one of disjuncture, being part and parcel of the so-called urban transformation in line with the profit oriented neo-liberal policies of the AKP (Justice and Development Party) regime from 2002 onwards.

The resistance against the project soon spread to other parts of Turkey with differing political agendas and was attacked with brutal police violence causing severe injuries and deaths. What I find most significant for this chapter in the upheavals that took place during May–June 2013 is the political portability of place, expressed poignantly in the widely employed slogan 'Everywhere is Taksim, everywhere there is resistance...!'[1] It was this very portability that allowed for the movement to spread throughout Turkey. The slogan is powerful, yet enigmatic, and requires further thinking with regard to how place is moved for making politics. This, I would argue, constitutes a counter-movement of place informed by a different conception of temporality as opposed to the hegemonic construction of space and time in capitalist-national politics.

By blasting the continuum of time structured by the violent state practices and the capitalist 'modernization' of Turkey since the nineteenth century, the Gezi Resistance has brought different fragments of the past and of national space into the time and place of 'the now', that is, into a new contemporaneity. In other words, the repressed histories within the national frame were brought into a dialogue in the present through the prism of a particular place – Taksim Square, generally praised as the heart of public life, commerce and tourism. Various issues generated by the state or state-sponsored violence, and usually taken in isolation in oppositional politics, for example regarding Kurds, non-Muslim minorities as well as Islamic dissidents, socialists, women and LGBTQI (lesbian, gay, bisexual, transgender, queer and intersex) people, were reactivated in the political encounter of the protestors in a way never experienced before.[2] The Gezi Resistance not only generated its own memories, particularly around the commemoration of the protestors who had been killed, but also re-enacted the memories of the past. The encounter has revealed different moments of loss in the building of the nation. For example, the resistance rendered visible the now absent presence of an Armenian cemetery in the surroundings of Gezi Park, and connected this repressed history of destruction in the 1930s[3] to present political concerns. An organization of Turkey's Armenians, *Nor Zartonk* (New Awakening), set up gravestone replicas in the occupied park reading, 'You took our cemetery, you won't have our park!' According to Bieberstein and Tataryan this was not only 'a critique of AKP's neo-Ottomanism. It also unsettled common perceptions of the park as unmarked green-space. It posed the question of how this "public space" came into being, asking passer-bys and co-occupants to face history' (Bieberstein and Tartaryan, 2013). It is this new contemporaneity that allowed for a counter-movement of place by joining diverse temporalities and spatialities in one political moment.

We already confront here a series of theoretically and politically important questions regarding space, time, and memory. If space is socially constructed, then temporality, informed by global and local social dynamics, is an integral element in the construction of space as Massey has argued (Massey, 1992). Yet the space–time in Massey's terms is also a product of differential movements initiated and controlled by power structures that make and represent both space and time. We know that in the homogenized temporality of the nation, the movement of people, objects and land enables government and the accumulation of capital. In this movement called 'progress', McQuire argues that the scope and rapidity of change has caused an immense disjunction (McQuire, 1998, p.119), producing a particular violence of displacement and loss disguised as modern development. 'The possibility of loss – whether loss of knowledge, of species, of culture, of the past in general – remains anathema to the ideology of progress' (McQuire, 1998, p.123). It is within this hegemonic rationale of modern development that the prime minister of Turkey has mocked the political concerns of Gezi protesters about the trees, by offering Europe as a model: 'It is common practice in the EU that you uproot the trees if necessary, and then transplant them to another place...The environmental technologies are highly developed now'.[4] In this steady movement, not only trees but also people are to be removed from their place to be 'transplanted' to other places, if they are not already annihilated during the process, as can be seen in several instances in Turkish history. Then, how could the memory of loss, whose traces are always to be found in particular places, be politicized? I contend that the portability of place as an emergent political capacity in Gezi casts a new light by which to understand differential histories and moments of loss that are denied by the violent time of progress in Turkey.

I will argue that the still unresolved question of the enforced disappearances in Turkey is related to the displacement of people and things for the sake of sustaining a particular power regime. Avery Gordon's reflection on disappearances in Argentina in the late 1970s is thought-provoking:

Disappearance is a complex system of repression, a thing in itself. With less noise than expected, it *removes* people – including and significantly

those it never tortures or kills – from their familiar world, with all its small joys and pains, and transports them to an unfamiliar place, where certain principles of social reality are absent.
(Gordon, 2008, p.112, emphasis added)

Then, the politics against disappearance, for example in the case of the Mothers of the Disappeared can be revisited by thinking about the desire to retransport the disappeared unto another space – the counter-movement of place – to give them a second life while making loss visible and political. 'Loss' has been the key theme of the movement of the mothers of the disappeared in Turkey too. However, in order to understand how the counter-movement reveals the memory of loss, we need to first understand how different regions of the national space are made 'exceptional' and timeless. The exceptional places contain 'memory knots' (Milton, 2011) of entangled traumas, which are at the same time knots of violence naturalized and rendered invisible in the hegemonic logic of national progress. Both the memory knots of entangled traumas and the state violence that weaves them are *embedded* in these places creating zones of indistinction between law and fact (Agamben, 2005).

'Disappearance under surveillance' and the anonymity of the 'missing' citizen in Turkey

One can list many events that could be associated with 'social traumas' in Turkish history from the Armenian genocide to the violent crushing of various rebellions; from military coups to the attacks on non-Muslim minorities; from the war against the Kurds to the massacres of Alevi populations. Each has its own perpetrators and victims in a specific context, yet all seem to be connected to each other in a historical pattern leading to a certain entanglement of social traumas. The impact of the entanglement can be captured in the image of 'memory knots' that make the engagement with the past and the memorialization of traumas intensely difficult (Milton, 2011). Milton argues that 'the image of knots invokes the pain inflicted on bodies by traumatic events (and more quotidian knots in the stomach or the throat), and the potential limitations this pain poses to language in the aftermath of violence' (Milton, 2011, p.193).

I would argue that the particular shape that the 'memory knots' take in the Turkish context is associated with what Stoler and McGranahan discuss as 'imperial formations' (Stoler and McGranahan, 2007). Very different from a focus on the bounded temporal and spatial frame of the nation, the study of imperial formations routes us in other, less visible paths that address various continuities within discontinuities, and their different materializations in space, as survival or ruination.

> Imperial formations are polities of dislocation, processes of dispersion, appropriation, and displacement. They are dependent on both moving categories and populations. As states of deferral, imperial formations manage and produce their own exceptions, which can be easily named: conditions of delayed sovereignty, temporary intervention, conditional tutelage, military takeover in the name of humanitarian intervention, or violent intervention in the name of human rights.
>
> (Stoler and McGranahan, 2007, p.8)

The first aspect of the memory knots in Turkey, then, is informed by the long and continuing history of the imperial formation: the embeddedness of violence in specific geographical areas. The memory knots are localized, yet they also bear the traces of movement – the manoeuvres of the state in violently populating and de-populating these areas throughout history. Historian Fuat Dündar claims that the ciphers to modern Turkey should be sought in the *ethnic engineering* that started with the Committee of Union and Progress in the early-twentieth-century Ottoman Empire, and aimed to Turkify and militarize the nation through policies of displacement and resettlement – policies that concerned and affected Armenians, Greeks, Jewish, Bulgarians and Kurds among other communities (Dündar, 2008). The formation of the dispersed and localized geographies of state violence, in this context, should be thought together with the accumulating repertoire of tactics and strategies that the state constantly modifies and implements in different cases through time.

The second aspect of the memory knots concerns the lack of language for the people afflicted by violence since the violent and mostly fatal strategies of displacement are enacted by defining 'exceptional situations' thereby constituting a pact of public secrets to use Taussig's terms (cited in Gordon, 2008, p.75) – something known but unspoken and unacknowledged – which is not only hard but also extremely dangerous to break. The violence in the exceptional zones constitutes a shocking parallel universe to 'normal national life': 'Everyone must know just enough to be terrified, but not enough either to have a clear sense of what is going on or to acquire the proof that is usually required by legal tribunals or other governments for sanction' (Gordon, 2008, p.110).

Enforced disappearance as one strategy of the state, when viewed in this broader historical frame, is more than an individual-targeted act; it aims to eradicate a certain community of people, their movement and life networks. The cases of enforced disappearances that are partly known in public today, thanks to the struggles of the Saturday Mothers, mostly belong to the period after the 1980 military coup, although it is becoming more apparent now that enforced disappearance as a violent strategy of the state was used much earlier, especially during the Armenian Genocide in 1915. Yet 1980 constitutes a significant rupture, during which earlier strategies of the state were selectively appropriated, condensed and reimplemented. After the 1980 coup, the Grand National Assembly of Turkey was closed down; the constitution was abolished, political parties and organizations were disbanded. Thousands of people were detained; secret intelligence files were assembled on more than one million people; 517 people were sentenced to death and 50 of these sentences were carried out. 14,000 people were deprived of citizenship rights; 171 people were documented to have been killed by torture; a total of 299 people died in prisons (Göral et al., 2013, p.15). The coup had a major impact in crushing the existing, albeit limited, forms of democratic participation and resistance, and violently continued the Turkification and militarization process of the society that had begun much earlier. However, the social and economic context was quite different now, with Turkey stepping into a neo-liberal regime of government with processes of privatization of public goods and services, the proliferation of news media and a 'contemporary' discourse of liberal market and individualization. A double reality was created with dissidents and opposition repressed through violent means on one side and a fast growing middle class enjoying the opportunities of the new regime.[5] The divide was also more or less a geographical one between the east and west of the country.

The Kurdish Resistance, which grew particularly in the southeastern parts of Turkey against the violent acts of the military state after the coup, was first presented with the help of media to the rest of the society as 'a handful of bandits' ('*3–5 çapulcu*' in Turkish, interestingly a term that was used to downplay the Dersim massacres in 1938, and again for the Gezi protestors in 2013). But soon the Turkish state started a 'low intensity war' against the Kurdish guerillas, declaring a state of emergency and martial law in many Kurdish areas (including 14 cities). In these 'exceptional zones' a State of Emergency Regional Governorship was established with extremely broad powers:

> These powers included the evacuation of certain settlements, the prohibition of settlement, the restriction of entry to and exit from certain settlements, the suspension of education at all levels, the restriction or suspension of entry and exit of all food stuffs and animal fodder in the region, the right to use all means and tools of communication within the borders of the region, and to confiscate them if deemed necessary.
> (Göral et al., 2013, p.16)

These powers resonate with the ethnic engineering within the imperial formation that I have discussed before, and the main target has been the control of the movement of people and objects within the designated region.[6]

Similar to Judith Butler's conceptualization of the prison as the limit case of the public sphere,[7] what is at stake in the contained 'exceptional zones' is the seizure of the public and its privatization. Through the extra-legal networks of the regional government, the state enacts a privatized system of violence. Privatization of the public in this context has two seemingly contradictory yet interdependent consequences: one is 'embedding the practices of violence in the space' (Göral et al., 2013) and making it familiar to the inhabitants, and the second is creating anonymity in the wider realm of law and 'democracy'. I contend that the fabrication of both *familiarity* and *anonymity* of violence has intricate links to Agamben's depiction of the state of exception (Agamben, 2005). The modern state of exception, according to Agamben, includes 'the exception itself within the juridical order by creating a zone of indistinction in which fact and law coincide' (Agamben, 2005, p.26). The indistinction holds a central place for understanding the case of enforced disappearances.

The enforced disappearances which reached their highest numbers in the 1990s, particularly in the eastern parts of the country, had been a public secret until the Saturday Mothers initiated their silent demonstrations in Galatasaray Square, Istanbul in 1995, which I will discuss in the next section. The reported number of disappearances is between 1000 and 2000, yet the lists prepared by human rights organizations are tentative, as there are no official records available. Furthermore, although many of the perpetrators are known because of the testimonies of local witnesses, criminal justice is not efficiently carried out.[8] Given these circumstances, the term widely used by the authorities, journalists and even some human rights activists to refer to enforced disappearances, *gözaltında kayıp* (literally, 'disappearance under surveillance') is highly symptomatic. A similarly mysterious term, *faili meçhul* (agent unknown), is employed for the perpetrators of political murders, the numbers of which exceed 10,000 by now. But how can one disappear under surveillance? Or, how is it possible that murderers are never identified and captured? The anonymity produced for both the perpetrators and the victims is not simply exceptional but contributes to defining the socio-political environment in which the state rules in Turkey. People are reduced to objects that are removable, and their removal is obscured in euphemistic terms. In 1992, in an interview with visiting journalists, a brigadier general who had spent several years in Şırnak (a city under the state of emergency) said: 'I am trying to create a beautiful painting here. If they try to besmirch this painting with even the smallest *stain*, I will break this painting over the heads of the people of Şırnak. And that is precisely what I *eventually* did' (cited in Göral et al., 2013, p.30, emphasis added). The statement truly captures how facts and law eventually blur into each other in order to distinguish 'loyal' citizens from disturbing and removable 'stains'.

As argued above, the other aspect that is integral to the production of anonymity is the familiarization of violence, which is produced by embedding the violence in the designated space. The Turkish Armed Forces restructured for the purposes of 'low intensity warfare' created a network of personalized alliances to enforce their *de facto* law in the exceptional zones. One of the most significant alliances has been the one forged with the villagers. They tempted the guerillas to confess to help the armed forces, and the villagers to become village guards with material benefits to fight against the Kurdish guerillas. For this they required a very detailed knowledge of local networks. The enmities between families and tribes were manipulated to set some people against the others and villagers who refused to cooperate with the state were forced to migrate; their villages were burnt down; many were killed or disappeared. The embedding of violence in the space transformed the lived space into one of death and destruction, and enveloped it within the discourse of 'fighting against the Kurdish terrorists' for the rest of the country. The space embedded with violence appears timeless under its subjection to the hegemonic movement of progress, and is dislocated from history and memory.

Time that makes politics

Erin Manning proposes that politics is about time – making time and taking time (Manning, 2004, p.73). A 'pre-determined space cannot house the political' she argues (Manning, 2004, p.75); we must make space for a timely politics that evokes the contingency of time and place. The temporal dimension of politics emphasized in Manning's approach significantly contributes to understanding what is at stake in fighting against violent human rights violations. The conception of temporality is vital for finding and revealing narratives that are made in and with time. It also underscores the particular spaces of crime that are codified as exceptional within national time, thus relegated to 'out of time'. In Turkey, the human right organizations mostly have a tendency to file the numbers of the disappeared, which are obscured by the authorities, but the price of listing numbers is the elimination of not only the personal but also the temporal and spatial dimensions of the enforced disappearances. The report *The Unspoken Truth: Enforced Disappearances* (Göral et al., 2013) by Truth, Justice, Memory Center is a pioneering work in that sense; it contains a detailed conceptual, spatial and historical map of the networks of violence, and presents interviews conducted with the relatives of the disappeared. Conducted in the zones of exception, for example in Şırnak and Cizre, the interviews presented clearly reveal that violence has been embedded in space and produced timelessness together with fear, anxiety and hopelessness. The report also shows that the desperate families in search of their disappeared kin first sought help from the local authorities – from the prosecutors, the gendarmerie, and the village guards – with a faint hope that the authorities, who were *in fact* the perpetrators, would help. However, each time they were confronted with lies, denial, or open threats. The legal discourse that the state should protect the rights of people has been very much infused with an extra-legality that functioned through the localization and privatization of state violence. A very striking example comes from a woman in search of her disappeared husband:

> We did not know what to do, we waited, and eventually we went to the prosecutor's office and said, 'we have a complaint, we have a problem'. And the prosecutor told us, 'go back to your homes.' He then added, *'the whole world is like this'*, and he did not let us do anything.
> (Göral et al., 2013, p.52, emphasis added)

But we also understand from the accounts of the families of the disappeared that the hope that there was another possibility, that there was *another world* was never totally eradicated.

Avery Gordon claims that the disappeared continue to haunt us, and 'haunting recognition is a special way of knowing what has happened or is happening' (Gordon, 2008, p.63). In other words there is another reality to disappearances, the knowledge of which is not possible by merely demanding 'rights' and exposing facts and numbers. If the 'state shuts all doors' to the search for legal rights (cited in Göral et al., 2013, p.51) there must be 'another door' to enter. This was possible by blasting the continuum of time that has sentenced the 'exceptional' spaces of violence into timelessness. 'Blasting might be conceived as entering through a different door, the door of the uncanny, the door of the fragment, the door of the shocking parallel' (Gordon, 2008, p.66). Gordon claims that the Mothers of the Disappeared in Argentina precisely did this by rendering the haunting presence of the disappeared publicly visible in their demonstrations. They evoked an oppositional political imaginary by carrying the photographs of the disappeared and insisting that they should be brought back with life. *Aparición con vida* was an impossible yet politically meaningful demand, which crossed the boundaries of reality and fantasy that the state violence had already blurred through the very concept of the disappeared. 'The mothers insisted on *Aparición con vida* because they sought not to bury and forget the dead, but rather a "dynamic reintegration of the dead and disappeared into *contemporaneity*"' (Gordon, 2008, p.115).[9]

The weekly silent demonstrations of the Saturday Mothers in Galatasaray, not more than 30 people at that time, holding the photographs of their disappeared relatives, and demanding that 'those missing under custody be found, and those responsible be tried', were initiated in 27 May 1995 after the discovery of the tortured body of Hasan Ocak in a mass grave, 55 days after he had 'disappeared'. The mothers already had a model of protest for them that had travelled a long way from Argentina. Travelling forms of protest present a very interesting theme in our 'globalized' world, which I cannot possibly address within the scope of this chapter. However, the movement, or rather the counter-movement of protest models already has an affinity with how the emotions of suffering, fear, and anxiety of the families of the disappeared in the 'exceptional zones' have travelled to Istanbul, transforming the space of normality bridging it to the 'exceptional zone', with the hope that 'this is the way to make our voices heard to the world' (Göral et al., 2013, p.55). A new space and time was being made for politics.

The movement of the Saturday Mothers managed to evoke the uncanny world that was the other, yet integral part of the dominant 'normal reality' reigning in Istanbul. However, the political meaning of the movement was soon explained away with references to 'Kurdish terrorism' in the media mobilizing national enmity against the Kurds. The movement suffered intense attacks from the police. The Saturday Mothers' movement had to be suspended in 1999 due to increasing police violence, and recommenced only ten years later, in 2009.

Most Saturday Mothers were women from the families of forced migration that had come to Istanbul in the early 1990s.[10] They did not have any particular disposition for politics. They had to leave 'home', their most familiar environment to take to the street. They were politicized through the very experience of doing politics during which their womanhood also underwent significant transformation. They learned to struggle with the police and to raise their voice. There was a certain 'disidentification' in Rancière's terms (Rancière, 1999), with their predetermined gender roles and spaces, which allowed the making of time for politics. And they did so, by radically transforming the meaning of motherhood that is constantly utilized by national ideology. The Saturday Mothers showed practically that caring for the other has political meaning.

The created space for politics, which overlaps with a given public space, fused with many symbols of government, entertainment and consumption in Galatasaray, at the centre of Istanbul, is only temporary. However, the temporality that is constructed by the rhythm of the movement – meeting every Saturday in the same place at noon for 19 years now – creates a different space, a space opened up by 'time made by politics' (Manning, 2004). In that particular space they permit '*history* to arise where *immediate understanding* may not' (Caruth, 1996, p.11, original emphasis). The Saturday Mothers have cut the 'memory knot' by demonstrating a certain enigma that evades immediate understanding, that of the 'disappearance' of their loved ones. They expand the passing time to transform the given space and infuse it with the memories of loss. Holding the photographs as evidence of both life and loss, they seem to silently ask, as Butler says, 'Who "am" I, without you? [...] On one level, I think I have lost "you" only to discover that "I" have gone missing as well' (Butler, 2004, p.22).

The Saturday Mothers make a time–space for relocating the 'missing' through their social and political stories/histories, names and images; as well as a space for relocating and condemning the so-called unknown perpetrators with their specific names and images. For example, in their 350th week (in 2011) the Mothers posted the photocopied images of politicians, officers and police chiefs that were responsible for the disappearances on a monument in Galatasaray (built for the fiftieth anniversary of the Republic and entitled 'The Bright Face of the Republic') to reveal not only the dark side of the Turkish Republic, but a longer and a continuous history of state violence. It is significant in this respect that the Saturday Mothers have included 'disappeared' people from other times and spaces in their political agenda including those who were disappeared during the Armenian Genocide.[11]

The Saturday Mothers are reported to say in a meeting, 'We will be here until the perpetrators are found. We will be here even if a thousand years pass'.[12] I would say, then, that the struggle of the Saturday Mothers is not merely a struggle for 'rights' registered within the space of national sovereignty or within a particular understanding of the *present* esteemed by modernity. Instead it is a struggle for justice that is articulated through a different conception of time–space, that goes back to distant remembered times informed by the imperial formation and reaches to a future that has not yet come to pass. I contend that the appearance of the Saturday Mothers within the space they create demonstrates that the national space is haunted not only by the particular memories of the disappeared but also by the past and future threats to dislocate people under the guise of 'contemporary' development.

The Saturday Mothers' movement[13] has been influential in making visible the haunting of the disappeared in Turkey. With the significant political achievements of the Kurdish movement in the last years, the Saturday demonstrations have also moved back to eastern parts of Turkey to take place in Diyarbakır, Batman and Cizre. In 2013 the Saturday Mothers were awarded with the Hrant Dink Award commemorating the Turkish-Armenian journalist Hrant Dink assassinated in 2007. So far, neither the perpetrators responsible for the disappearances nor for the assassination of Hrant Dink have been publicly identified and charged for their crimes. Many Mothers who joined the movement in 1995 are absent now because of death or illness. After 19 years, the hopes are more concentrated on finding the bones and having a gravestone rather than demanding that the disappeared return alive. The mothers are forced to take a more 'realistic' position as the counter-movement has difficulties in resisting the passing of hegemonic time. In other words, the past is in constant danger of disappearing from *contemporaneity*. In a recent panel, a member of the Saturday Mothers' movement, Maside Ocak, said: 'The Gezi Resistance was perhaps the dream of our disappeared. Yet the number of people who are joining us on Saturdays has radically decreased since the Gezi Resistance began'.[14] It is thought-provoking that the Gezi Resistance, which engaged with the darkness of its time also created a dazzling light in the present that can blind one to 'the shadows in those lights' (Agamben, 2009, p.45). It is in this gap between light and obscurity, present passions and past dreams that time has to be made to *constantly* create and sustain a new space in which the haunting loss can be acknowledged. This is a challenge to the resistance movements now.

Notes

1. Versions of this slogan had been used in different oppositional movements in Turkey before, yet it was with the Gezi Resistance that the adaptable format of the slogan was popularized.
2. There is a growing literature on Gezi events now both in Turkey and outside. For a brief yet diverse and rich collection of essays, see for example, Navaro-Yashin and Umut Yıldırım (2013).
3. Nalcı and Dağlıoğlu (2011) give a detailed account of how the large piece of land on which an Armenian cemetery existed was taken over in 1939 by the Istanbul Municipality through a long and dubious legal process. Gezi Park was then built on a section of this land utilizing the marble gravestones for building the stairs of the park.
4. Erdogan's talk at the International Ombudsman Symposium held in Ankara on September 3, 2013, as reported in the newspaper *Radikal* the same day. http://www.radikal.com.tr/politika/erdogan_avrupaya_fransiz_degiliz_avru payi_da_biliriz-1149043, date accessed 22 October 2014.
5. For a discussion of the socio-cultural trends and tensions of this period, see Gürbilek (2010).
6. Üngör claims that the massive state-sponsored violence in the Kurdish region is a highly entangled one, since the Kurds have been both perpetrators backed by the state (that is, in the Armenian genocide) and victims of state violence. The violence 'can be traced back to Ottoman-Turkish militarism' and triggered by 'the traumatisation that runs through the Ottoman fin de siècle' (Üngör, 2011, p.193), Thus the continuing history of violence and ruination in the form of destroyed lives and villages that afflicts the Kurds in the region can be regarded as 'imperial effects' (Stoler, 2008, p.95).
7. 'Freedom of Assembly or Who are the People?' Lecture at Boğaziçi University, 15 September 2013.
8. According to recent reporting of Truth, Justice, and Memory Center in Turkey 89% of the court cases concerning enforced disappearances have been continuing for more than 18 years now. This strategic prolongment is likely to push these cases into the 'statute of limitations' that sets in after 20 years. Of the court cases concluded thus far 7% ended with a verdict of non-prosecution, 2% with the statute of limitations, 2% with acquittal, and only 1% with conviction. 'İnsan Hakları Gününde Kaybedilenler İçin Adalet Yok', Hafıza Merkezi, http://www.hakikatadalethafiza.org/duyuru.aspx?NewsId=326&LngID=1, date accessed 2 March 2014.
9. For a detailed account of the movement of the mothers, and their disputes and struggles with the state and other groups about the 'status' of the disappeared in Argentina, see Bouvard (2002).
10. For a comprehensive research on forced migration in Turkey, see Kurban et al. (2007).
11. In their meeting on 27 April 2013 the mothers asked what happened to 220 Armenian intellectuals who were deported from Istanbul on 24 April 1915 and hence 'disappeared'.

12. 'Failler Bulunana Kadar Bin Yıl Geçse de Buradayız' *Bianet*, http://www.bianet.org/biamag/insan-haklari/130158-failler-bulunana-kadar-bin-yil-gecse-de-buradayiz, 23 May 2011, date accessed 2 March 2014.
13. As other activists and supporters joined the movement over the years the name 'Saturday People' is also used to refer to the movement.
14. From the panel 'Türkiye Kadınlarının Sesleri' Sabancı University Gender and Women's Studies Forum and Women's Voices Now, Minerva Han, 28 September 2013.

Bibliography

Agamben, Giorgio. 2005. *State of Exception*, translated by Kevin Attell. Chicago: University of Chicago Press.

Agamben, Giorgio. 2009. 'What Is the Contemporary?' In *What Is an Apparatus? And Other Essays*, translated by David Kishik and Stefan Pedatella. Stanford: Stanford University Press.

Bieberstein, Alice von and Nora Tataryan. 2013. 'The What of Occupation: "You Took Our Cemetery, You Won't Have Our Park!"', http://www.culanth.org/fieldsights/394-the-what-of-occupation-you-took-our-cemetery-you-won-t-have-our-park, 31 October 2013, date accessed 2 March 2014.

Bouvard, Marguerite Guzman. 2002. *Revolutionizing Motherhood: The Mothers of the Plaza de Mayo*. Lanham: Rowman and Littlefield Publishers.

Butler, Judith. 2004. *Precarious Life: The Powers of Mourning and Violence*. London: Verso.

Caruth, Cathy. 1996. *Unclaimed Experience: Trauma, Narrative, and History*. Baltimore: The Johns Hopkins University Press.

Dündar, Fuat. 2008. *Modern Türkiye'nin Şifresi: İttihat ve Terakki'nin Etnisite Mühendisliği (1913–1918)*. Istanbul: İletişim Yayınları.

'Failler Bulunana Kadar Bin Yıl Geçse de Buradayız'. *Bianet*, http://www.bianet.org/biamag/insan-haklari/130158-failler-bulunana-kadar-bin-yil-gecse-de-buradayiz, 23 May 2011, date accessed 2 March 2014.

Göral, Özgür Sevgi, Ayhan Işık and Özlem Kaya. 2013. *The Unspoken Truth: Enforced Disappearances*, translated by Nazım Dikbaş. Istanbul: Truth, Justice, Memory Center.

Gordon, Avery. 2008. *Ghostly Matters: Haunting and the Sociological Imagination*. Minneapolis: University of Minnesota Press.

Gürbilek, Nurdan. 2010. *The New Cultural Climate in Turkey: Living in a Shop Window*. London: Zed Books.

'İnsan Hakları Gününde Kaybedilenler İçin Adalet Yok'. Hafıza Merkezi., http://www.hakikatadalethafiza.org/duyuru.aspx?NewsId=326&LngID=1, date accessed 2 March 2014.

Kurban, Dilek, Deniz Yükseker, Ayşe Betül Çelik, Turgay Ünalan and A.Tamer Aker. 2007. *Coming to Terms with Forced Migration: Post-Displacement Restitution of Citizenship Rights in Turkey*. TESEV Publications: e-book.

Manning, Erin. 2004. 'Time for Politics'. In *Sovereign Lives: Power in Global Politics*, edited by Jenny Edkins, Véronique Pin-Fat and Michael J. Shapiro. New York: Routledge.

Massey, Doreen. 1992. 'Politics and Space/Time'. *New Left Review*, 1/196: 65–84.

McQuire, Scott. 1998. *Visions of Modernity: Representation, Memory, Time and Space in the Age of the Camera*. London: Sage.

Milton, Cynthia E. 2011. 'Defacing Memory: (Un)tying Peru's Memory Knots'. *Memory Studies*, 2011/4: 190–205.
Nalcı, Tamar and Emre Can Dağlıoğlu. 2011. 'Bir Gasp Hikayesi'. *Agos*, 26 August 2011.
Navaro-Yashin, Yael and Umut Yıldırım eds. 2013. *Cultural Anthropology*, Hot Spots, http://www.culanth.org/fieldsights/391-an-impromptu-uprising-ethnographic-reflections-on-the-gezi-park-protests-in-turkey, 31 October 2013, date accessed 2 March 2014.
Rancière, Jacques. 1999. *Disagreements: Politics and Philosophy*, translated by Julie Rose. Minneapolis: University of Minnesota Press.
Stoler, Ann Laura. 2008. 'Imperial Debris: Reflection on Ruins and Ruination'. *Cultural Anthropology*, 23/2: 191–219.
Stoler, Ann Laura and Carole McGranahan. 2007. 'Introduction: Refiguring Imperial Terrains'. In *Imperial Formations*, edited by Ann Laura Stoler, Carole McGranahan and Peter C. Perdue. Santa Fe: School for Advanced Research Press.
Üngör, Uğur Ümit. 2011. 'Recalling the Appalling: Mass Violence in Eastern Turkey in the Twentieth Century'. In *Memories of Mass Repression*, edited by Nanci Adler, Selma Leydesdorff, Mary Chamberlain and Leyla Neyzi. New Brunswick: Transaction Publishers.

12
An Orderly Landscape of Remnants: Notes for Reflecting on the Spatiality of the Disappeared

Gabriel Gatti

Music filters through the ruins: *Treme* in greater Buenos Aires

We first witnessed David Simon's analytical capacity a few years ago in *The Wire* (Simon, 2002). In that HBO series, the city of Baltimore was neatly dissected to reveal an intricate web formed by inner-city residents, police officers, trade unions, the media, government agencies, politicians... that snares the lives (both everyday and not-so-everyday, public and private) of all these subjects, linking them together in interdependencies almost impossible to escape. Some years after completing *The Wire*, Simon teamed up with Eric Overmayer to write and produce another series, *Treme* (Simon and Overmayer, 2010). In this new series, which has also gained a cult following, the same dissecting skills applied to Baltimore are now deployed for the city of New Orleans.

There are, however, some substantial differences, and these differences have to do with more than just the fact that the city dissected in each series is different. Whereas in *The Wire* the focus was on routine (however corrupt and degraded it was nonetheless routine, and the fascination was in the mechanical repetitiveness that ensnared those who lived it), in *Treme*, Simon and Overmayer's sharply psychological eye pierces bone-deep into the logical opposite of routine, the fracture caused by a devastating catastrophe that hit the city in 2005: Hurricane Katrina. One series – *The Wire* – portrays the tragedy of the normal; the other – *Treme* – depicts life in the state of exception, the meanings that a loosely connected group of musicians, or citizens, carve out for their lives when the grounds that gave life its meaning are pulled out from under them. *Treme* offers something that is not at all easy to depict: the different ways of constructing things with meaning in a universe suddenly hurled into the realm of absence of meaning.

In August 2005, a catastrophe defined time and space in New Orleans: space became a landscape of remains (in the form of ruins of the city's worst-hit neighbourhoods, such as the one the series takes its name from, or of the useless remnants of the state and its social services, or of the support networks formed by family and friends now disarticulated by absences, deaths, people who fled, suicides...); time is broken, marked by a calendar that begins anew *after* (three months after Katrina in the first season, 14 months after Katrina in the second season).

In the first season, the storylines focus on the options available for life after a disaster. Every episode begins with the same reminder: catastrophe is not far off, the water marks have not yet dried. There are mould stains on the ceilings of the houses that were flooded and buried under water, there are wet tracks on the walls, there are signs spray painted by rescue workers on the fronts of houses indicating that they had been searched and whether they were cleared for occupation. Places that were formerly occupied by life are now occupied by the void. And yet the survivors remake (or try to remake) their lives after the catastrophe. There is a bit of everything: people who have fled, some who committed suicide, others who embrace new options... Life after the disaster. The landscape, meanwhile, is scarred with marks, traces in the memory of the space that is gradually, slowly, built, like a landscape of remains.

Fourteen months after. In the second season it is no longer about survival, but about repairing what has been destroyed and stabilizing the catastrophe situation. The ruins are permanent. The mark left traces on the landscape and they cannot be erased; it *is* the landscape. Reconstructing, repairing, restarting... Remaking what is gone and is no longer is what marks the rhythm of daily life, as the memory of the disaster marks it. Every episode begins with the same presentation: first, the flood marks; then, signs of the rebuilding efforts and the institutional actions deployed to recover the city; lastly, life in the ruins, which moves to the rhythm of the music of All Souls' Day, the Day of the Dead. It is no longer about filling ground zero, but about living in it. The aim is not to obliterate the ruins, but to live in them (in one scene, a man who had fled after the hurricane comes back to find his home occupied by friends who have cleaned it, returning it to its previous state, and he wants to know what they have done with his mark).

While there are obvious differences between post-Katrina New Orleans and post-military dictatorship Argentina, I think the elements they have in common are more significant. I would like to briefly highlight three of these shared elements: the first is that in both cases a catastrophe determines time and space; second, that catastrophe filled the space with remains; and, third, a life, a universe, a whole world is organized around that catastrophe. That is certainly what happened in Argentina, at least in the social worlds that formed around the figure of the detained-disappeared. With the catastrophe, the conventional order of things is shaken by an earthquake so great that the disarray that ensues can no longer be interpreted with the words we have. Our cognitive structures crack, the cognitive structures we use to think of the living, the dead, and the normal meaning of things. And the abnormal too. Because we are faced with a figure that is thought of as placeless; a figure that does not fit into any recognizable entity; a figure that is absent and present at the same time; a figure without logic; a *bodiless* figure. Nothingness. Something terrible.

And a strange, in the sense of inconsistent and unusual, order of things emerges to shape, to give meaning to that absence of meaning: the order of remains. At least, that is my hypothesis: the remnants, what remains, the waste even, lend their peculiar texture to the figure of the detained-disappeared, to the manner in which their biography is constructed, to the way of thinking about what is left of their community life and their history. The remnants, the remains, the ruins are of things that no longer exist, but they comprise the materiality of the detained-disappeared.

I am thinking of remnants of many different orders: immaterial, like the remnants of a story, the scattered bits and pieces of the passage through a dark clandestine centre, or the remnants of a broken biography that has not been recomposed. Also, the many fractured psyches that the catastrophe left in its wake. But here I am thinking above all of tangible remnants, material remnants: bodily remains, remnants of spaces, scraps of files. Corpses, ruins, and dust. In this chapter I will consider only such remnants.

After the individual goes through the machinery of disappearance what is left are scraps, remains, residues. Very little is left: some information about the individual before he or she acquired the condition of detained-disappeared, perhaps accounts (incomplete, uncertain, and sparse) of the individual's passage through the clandestine detention centre. Physically there is, sometimes, although rarely, a body without an identity; most often there is an identity without a body, a name of someone who is known to *be* a detained-disappeared person but of whom little else is known. Some bureaucratic traces might remain but, more often than not, even these will be absent, and the only available information will be that which indicates that others have previously asked for information on those who have now disappeared. Such are records of habeas corpus requests made by mothers, copies of disappearance reports filed by partners unable to go before the state as subjects of law with legal standing to inherit, purchase, or sell community property because their partners have an impossible status (neither alive nor dead) which prevents such recourse.

And there are also the remnants of the buildings where everything took place, of the operators of the devastation, the places where it all happened. But what is left of most of the places that were devoted – many for a short time – to the task of extermination is either in ruins or yields just a vague memory of what they contained. What can be done now with these places that have become ruins or voids after so many years of being abandoned?

Broadly speaking, in what I would generically call the social field of the detained-disappeared (Gatti, 2012), two broad strategies for working with what remains can be identified. Two narratives (Ricœur, 1990) – two ways of telling and living – organize the field of the detained-disappeared. The first is harsh, typical of a time of conceptions, tragic, and is associated with older discourses; the second is also harsh, but it belongs more to a time of things already conceived, a more negotiating approach than the first. The first goes well with situations typically found in times of regime change, the type that political scientists and common sense call 'transitional', and also fits in with forms of representation that seek to exorcise the horror and recover what is hidden by a recent, ignominious past. The second, on the other hand, develops under conditions in which the impossible phenomenon is naturalized as such and in which the challenge is not so much to demand something, but to manage it. It involves finding ways of managing a life that unfolds within impossibility.

The first strategy is an attempt to put order among remnants. The second takes a different approach, leaving everything in its place.

Turning remnants into heritage (or the regeneration of disaster)

> I'm going to defend the museum. Look, it's very simple. I think we have to build a new museum. A huge one... The museum has to be pure. And it has to be in a neutral place. And it has to be pretty... it can be a museum of painful memories, but it has to be pretty. And there has to be someone who says, 'Listen: Horrible things happened here, sinister things, and now we've overcome it... now we have a contemporary art museum.' It's ultramodern... And why is it so white? Well, to move away a bit from that aesthetics of pain... And, so, you go into the museum wanting to know who those people who were held prisoner, or who died, were. Then they usher you into a room full of Apple computers. It has to be an Apple computer, mind you... And you can go into one of those computers and see the lists of people who went through that place and the people who died. And you can click on a name and learn everything about that person. You can see pictures of her as a young girl, of her family, you can find out about the boys who liked her, whether she drank hot chocolate before going to class when she was in high school, if as she walked back from the store she'd start eating the bread her mom sent her to buy, and all those little details of everyday life, which are a way of recovering the victim's biography.
>
> (Calderón, 2012)[1]

Ruins are interesting places. In the short history of the social sciences they are one of the first forms of the catastrophe of meaning that caught the attention of social scientists. In a 1911 article, Georg Simmel dared to reflect on the seductive yet disturbing status of ruins. 'The ruin of a building', Simmel said, 'means that where the [building] is dying, other forces and forms... have grown... [and] a new meaning seizes on this incident' (Simmel, 1959, p.259). In other words, ruins have a meaning: their lack of meaning. This ambiguity gives ruins their uniqueness, their condition as both places of life and places without the life they once had: 'Such places, sinking from life, still strike us as settings of a life' (Simmel, 1959, p.260). Situated between the formed and the unformed, located in a place halfway between what is and what is not ('between the "not-yet" and the "no-longer"' (Simmel, 1959, p.260)), ruins have a unique materiality, neither totally in nor totally out of the circle that gathers the *things that are*, near the place of waste – that is, of what radically no longer is – but maintaining, nonetheless, the trace of what they were (Figure 12.1).

We can adopt several strategies to deal with ruins. One is to leave them in the state we find them and work with them from there. Another is to fill them with representation, to take that space out of its ruinous condition, that is, to give meaning back to it, to recover it. Here the aim is to re-establish the bond that those things – that are now ruins – have with meaning, to facilitate their reconciliation following a period of bad relations. This is what archaeologists do and although they do not deny that those spaces are in a state of ruin, what they try to do is overcome that state, be it by reconstructing the spaces or by showing the moment at which they gave

Figure 12.1 Scale model of the 'Casa Grimaldi' clandestine detention centre, Santiago de Chile, December 2007
Photograph by Gabriel Gatti.

materiality to something with a specific meaning: they represent, they build scale models, they draw up maps and figures... 'Things regain their meaning',[2] a young Argentine archaeologist said to me as she worked to retrieve an object from the rubble of a clandestine detention centre.

Archaeologists can thus be called activists of meaning, since their activity is guided by the following axiom: if forced disappearance of persons destroyed identity, then archaeologists rebuild it, they provide identity; if forced disappearance of persons occurred in that space – the clandestine detention centre – then they reconstruct it, and they reconstruct what happened in it ('We have to work on the identity [of the clandestine detention centre]'). They go into the hole where the catastrophe occurred, where bodies were separated from names, where the disappeared became such. And they fill it:

> We're going to try to make a small scale model. Some people need to see it like that, and we're going to reconstruct it, so that they at least have a scale model for reference.
>
> The way we see it, in the state of ruin this is in, [if we were to leave it as it is] we would be left without a part of the explanation. We're recovering it so we can say 'it existed here'....

Situating the clandestine detention centre in history, giving meaning to the operator of devastation, that is the objective. Stripping that ominous space of its ominous quality: it is not hell, it is not something beyond anything we know. It is a place that is explicable. But the price of this effort to provide meaning may be high, very high: an overexposure to meaning avoids the question of what else the clandestine detention centre was, a place where representation itself failed, a place that did not fit into any series. Turned into heritage, into a place with identity, this space becomes part of a series, a piece in a continuum. It becomes part of a history and it is no longer singular – no longer a brutal, immense singularity. Its unfathomable singularity is broken.

Continuity prevails over disruption. What is more, if there were any trace of the latter, its insertion in the former would annul it. The strategy is to give the place back its meaning, to make it an 'anthropological place' (Augé, 1995), a space that is presumed to be full of identity, which is supposed to be bursting with history, a space which we know allows social relations to be deployed within it. It is irrelevant if those three – identity, history, social relations – are overflowing with perversity; the important thing is to bring them out of obscurity, illuminate them, situate them in a linear, continuous, causal timeline...

> We can't isolate this clandestine detention center without taking into account its connection with the other clandestine detention centers... in the area. Neither should we... place it out of time and work with it that

way, because we will fail to understand these continuities. So [this project] works on what this clandestine detention center is, observing the causes, why it came to be specifically a detention center, but also discovering how we got to what the deployment of State terrorism meant, and in that same analysis we observe its continuities in the present.

...and give meaning back to them; that is, restore the relationship that *this thing* – the clandestine detention centre and its universe – had with its corresponding words:

The clandestine detention center obviously means something to us. The thing is that we think that in order to have a historical reconstruction we have to link a historical process that involved different events, and one event perhaps leads to the explanation of the next one... We have to understand the before and the after.

It would be reasonable to think of the works that focus on turning these spaces into a memorial, a reminder, part of a 'map of pain', or a landmark in an expository tour of Buenos Aires' clandestine detention centres, as only a part of the representations of the recent past, as not imposing the truth but merely proposing one interpretation among many. They are, an archaeologist says, 'excuses to start thinking... I'm not going to reveal "the truth" '. But it would not be unreasonable either to think that these proposals shape, or, why not say it, abuse, those places and saturate them with meaning, that is, denaturalize them, transforming them into part of a collective identity and memory, *one* identity and *one* memory ('Our general objective today would be to recover a space for the reconstruction of memories, of an identity.').

These activists of meaning work from their professional expertise against the devastating effects caused by forced disappearance of persons: if forced disappearance destroyed, they build. Where it broke something into pieces, they reassemble. If it separated things from meanings, they give new meaning, they resignify, even at the risk of excess ('The purpose [of our work] is to always try to unite [object and meaning] and add even more meaning'.) With their work, they tell me, things 'come back here with some meaning'. Archaeologists, in sum, patch up materials that have been torn and incorporate them into an account: they give materiality to a memory; they turn the clandestine detention centre into heritage, no less.

Settled into the landscape of remnants: Living within disaster

If I had the money I would build everything down to the tiniest detail. Not only in terms of architectural fidelity. Everything. I would reconstruct the silence, that terrible stench, the screaming, the chains, the engines at night, the loud music...the feel of the place. And I would make it look old. I'd paint the walls with dirty water, I'd use a different color palette for the background. Shades of sepia. And I'd buy the paraphernalia. I'd buy a metal bed, I'd buy cables and plugs, I'd buy uniforms, I'd buy shirts with wide lapels, I'd buy the smell of shit. To create a sort of Disneyland of a realistic reality. So that people will think, 'This is what the people who went through this must have felt.' And I would make the public feel like prisoners. I would make them wait, I would asked them their names, I would separate the women from the men. I would give them numbers, and I would call out to them, 'Hey, you! Number 234.' In short, I would make them suffer. And I would get some survivors to act as guides to Hell. Like Virgil. And I would ask these guides to pause when they reach the place that recreates where they were locked up or where they screamed the most. As if they were unable to go on speaking and were choking back tears. And I would ask them to very softly say, 'This is where I last saw my wife.'

(Calderón, 2012)

In the psyche, catastrophe produces traumas. In some material spaces it also produced deep marks that are revealed today under the sordid, dirty form of ruins or of a dusty archive. When faced with one or the other, the conventional strategy revolves around three actions: cleaning, recovering and situating. That is, restoring the glow, remaking the lost fullness and explaining what the ruins were before they were what they are now, almost nothing, nothing with meaning. That is, the aim is to return those objects to meaning.

However, whether because of aesthetic conviction, theoretical concern or professional rigour, another option is available. That option is to show them as they are, to consider – however strange or uncomfortable it may be – that ruins or dusty archives are a possible state, and thus to understand that maintaining their current condition of absence of meaning, their dark, dirty condition, *makes sense*, is not meaningless. This also involves adopting a certain position: believing that doing the opposite (cleaning, recovering, situating) distorts the way the ruins are now and hides the essence, the terrible essence of what turned them into this, the catastrophe.

The dilemma that these people face is a powerful one: these workers of meaning, agents of a logic – that of modern representation that cannot confront the void – must explain things that are broken, traumatized. Taking those things out of those places is the first possibility, the one we turn to most often, in fact. The other is leaving them there. This other possibility entails that they...we...be forced to think of something that is radically disrupting for a modern scientist: that the meaning of these phenomena is to be found in the absence of meaning itself. If that is correct, what better way to explain them than in terms of a certain aesthetics of the unfinished? It is not about – or not only about – proposing styles of writing and representation that aim for, as Jean Griffet calls it, 'the suggestive power of uncertain images' (Griffet, 1991, p.360). That is certainly part of it: finding narratives whose textures fit well with those of entities and situations of such a strange nature. But beyond that stylistic aim, there is another one that is analytical: being rigorous with what could be called the mandate of representation, namely, the correspondence between the thing and the word that refers to it. Thus, with things such as 'trauma', 'ruins', 'waste', 'void', 'remnants' or 'absence', is it not best, even in the name of something as cold as 'scientific rigour' and 'professional ethics', to devise strategies that fit well with those things? That is what has been suggested by French sociologist and economist Yves Barel, a keen observer of moments in which social life is left without meaning: 'We need fluid words for such versatile phenomena' (Barel, 1984, p.31).

That is what this second approach, which I illustrate in the epigraph, is about: taking on the representation of those things and figures, including that of the detained-disappeared, accepting the very impossibility of representing and the resulting need to find means and languages to work with that impossibility. Leaving them in their current state, thinking of them as remnants, taking things in a ruinous state – waste – seriously can be a useful way of reflecting on it.

Because, naturally, not all representations are the same and it is possible to think that for some kind of phenomena the evidence of their existence is, precisely, something that is not recorded. That is in part the case with the disappeared: no record of their existence was meant to have been left behind, and none was left; that is to a large extent its most atrocious characteristic, its enormity and its inexistence. It happened, that much we know; they are dead, we know; we also know who is responsible. But there are no data, no evidence... Only remnants. Or if there is, it does not fit well with the logic of data and evidence. It is a part of the *data* – these data, the data of this catastrophe – the fact that there are no data is part of the data. The magnitude of this extermination was such that in addition to the obvious – bodies and lives – what was also annihilated here was representation itself, its possibility. The question posed by Jean-Luc Nancy (how to go about 'making what is not of the order of presence come to presence' (Nancy, 2005, p.34)) can thus be reformulated as an answer: *the only data are the absence of data*.

A priori we could say that that answer renders impossible any elucidation of what happened in the clandestine detention centres, that it is a trick answer, as it precludes all other answers. But only a priori: if taken literally, by asserting that 'the only data are the absence of data' what is being proposed is the opposite of immobility or silence, what is being suggested is a strategy for articulating in a precise way the representation of what happened. It is a very practical strategy, typical of a professional concerned with representing accurately. In the face of *this*, the professional will propose that we assume that 'data have a different nature there' and accept that, consequently, we need to think about them differently. This is what archive professionals do, subjects who, we must bear in mind, are eminently pragmatic: 'In these cases, when we make our annotations, we usually write that we found the index card but we didn't find the files. We record precisely that: that there are no data.'

Thus, while in a strange way, fact and representation do come together again, if the machinery of disappearance sought to produce that void ('They knew full well that there were things that were illegal and they didn't record them'; 'This, which was conceived from the institutional system, would not be recorded'), the archive gives evidence of that fact with a record that matches its condition: we have no data, the record is absent. A resounding absence, that absence. Very much present, in fact.

Ordinary garbage, extraordinary waste, technical rationality and humanitarian morality: Brief inconclusive notes

Ours are the years of the explosion of waste: we are brimful of garbage. Ours are also the years of the explosion of the management of that waste and of its professions: restorers, recyclers, ecologists... Ours are, lastly, the years of humanitarian morality (Fassin, 2011), of the proliferation of professions associated with humanitarian morality or focused on it: forensic anthropology, psychological aid in catastrophe situations, archaeology of the recovery of spaces of terror...

I think I am not wrong in proposing these connections, as all these spheres, that is, those of ordinary garbage and those of extraordinary waste, are not only connected by the use of the same nouns, but above all by the deployment of similar expertise, their techniques applied in this case to the recovery of remnants. The connection does exist, as in what is most essential, the remnants of memory, the ruins of the concentration camps, the waste sites, the ground zeroes, the topologies of horror, the dumping grounds, the archives of horror, the mass graves... are all structured around the same thing: they are all things that are no longer what they were, but things that nonetheless retain part of what they were. They are, in sum, remnants.

And also, in what is most essential, the trades deployed to address these entities and situations, both those of ordinary garbage and those of *extraordinary* waste, have enormous associations.

Identifying three of them will serve, if not as a conclusion to this chapter, at least as a way of raising some questions to reflect on:

(1) The first has to do with the linguistic regime of these trades, which deal with their objects by deploying actions that involve the prefix *re*: they *re*cycle, *re*cover, *re*arrange, *re*generate, *re*incorporate, *re*trieve, *re*deem, *re*pair... They turn a discarded object that has been stripped of meaning into

something with meaning. They redeem it. But, in that process, do they not also turn it into something else?

(2) The second suggests that all of these professions make facts hard (Latour, 1985, p.10), that is, they turn soft, diffuse realities with limits that are indefinite, sometimes even unrepresentable, certainly, always formless or deformed, into proven facts, into hard objects, into transportable and comparable matter, into singular objects and above all, certainly too, into matter that has a definite form and is very tangible. With the detained-disappeared, with their worlds, is that really relevant?

(3) And the third points to their moral regime. These trades work with convictions that are typical of instrumental rationality, or, in other words, they operate by transforming political problems into technical problems (Piper, 2005). When, like now, in the worlds of forced disappearance of persons, there is a proliferation of trades driven by the powerful gears of humanitarian rationality, and when such trades are deployed with the morally admirable, but analytically questionable conviction that they operate to achieve good, it is perhaps advisable to stop and take a critical look. That is the case here: an entity (the detained-disappeared) with an unsettling consistency, around which a social landscape filled with remains has been created, has generated policies, efforts, trades... that regulate the remnants, that bring order to their landscape. And they have become so stylized that they seem to speak of something else.

Notes

Parts of this chapter have been previously published in Spanish in Gatti (2011) and in English in Gatti (2014). I would like to thank Laura Pérez Carrara for her thorough translation work.

1. This and another fragment included below are part of the play *Villa* that Guillermo Calderón first staged in 2011 and which appeared in print in 2012. I quote the Uruguayan adaptation of the manuscript, edited by Carla Larrobla and Mariana Risso. At one point in the play, which is nothing short of brilliant, Calderón puts three characters in the ruins of a clandestine detention centre and has them discuss what they should do with those ruins. One of the characters, Alejandra, suggests building an 'ultramodern museum'; another, also called Alejandra, suggests a 'sinister mansion'...
2. These quotations and others that follow are from field work carried out in Argentina between 2005 and 2008, whose precise details can be found in Gatti (2012, 2014). All were done with people connected to the world of forced disappearance, in this case with archaeologists from the GAAMI (Archaeological and Anthropological Group of Memory and Identity) who work on the recovery of the remains of different clandestine centres of detention in Buenos Aires, and later with workers on archives recovered from various police and military installations that operated during the Argentine dictatorship of 1976–1983, basically in the Provincial Commission for Memory in the city of La Plata.

Bibliography

Augé, Marc. 1995. *Non-Places: Introduction to an Anthropology of Supermodernity*. London and New York: Verso.
Barel, Yves. 1984. 'La dissidence sociale'. *Actions et recherches sociales*, 16/3: 29–50.
Calderón, Guillermo. 2012. *Teatro II: Villa/Discurso/Beben*. Santiago de Chile: LOM.
Fassin, Didier. 2011. *Humanitarian Reason: A Moral History of the Present*. Berkeley: University of California Press.
Gatti, Gabriel. 2012. *Identidades desaparecidas. Peleas por el sentido en los mundos de la desaparición forzada de personas*. Buenos Aires: Prometeo.
Gatti, Gabriel. 2014. *Surviving Forced Disappearance in Argentina and Uruguay: Identity and Meaning*. New York: Palgrave Macmillan.
Griffet, Jean. 1991. 'La sensibilité aux limites'. *Sociétés*, 34: 359–366.
Latour, Bruno. 1985. 'Les vues de l'esprit. Une introduction à l'anthropologie des sciences et des techniques'. *Culture Technique*, 14: 5–29.
Nancy, Jean-Luc. 2005. *The Ground of the Image (Perspectives in Continental Philosophy)*. New York: Fordham University Press.
Piper, Isabel. 2005. *Obstinaciones de la memoria*. PhD dissertation. Universidad Autónoma de Barcelona. Unpublished.
Ricœur, Paul. 1990. 'Individuo e identidad personal'. In *Sobre el individuo*, edited by Paul Veyne et al. Barcelona: Paidós.
Simmel, Georg. 1959. 'The Ruin'. In *1858–1918: A Collection of Essays, with Translations and a Bibliography*, edited by Kurt H. Wolff. Columbus: Ohio State University Press.
Simon, David. 2002. *The Wire*. TV series. Los Angeles: HBO.
Simon, David and Eric Overmayer. 2010. *Treme*. TV series. Los Angeles: HBO.

13
A Limitless Grave: Memory and Abjection of the Río de la Plata

Estela Schindel

Emerging from the brown, turbid waters of the Río de la Plata,[1] a few metres away from the shore at the north of the city of Buenos Aires, a figure with human form can be seen floating. It is a life-size sculpture and its polished metallic surface reflects the water, with which it blends. The figure has its back turned to us and thus we are unable to catch its eye from the river bank. The impossibility of seeing the face evokes an anxiety at its incompleteness. There is a truth that will never be known in its entirety; a history that will never be completed. The work is part of the *Parque de la Memoria* (Memory Park) located on the banks of the river in commemoration of the victims of state terrorism in Argentina. Claudia Fontes, creator of the sculpture, carefully positioned the work so that its face cannot be seen. The sculpture is called 'Reconstruction of the Portrait of Pablo Míguez', and evokes a disappeared 14-year old (Figure 13.1). Fontes studied available documentation in detail in order to reconstruct the figure as faithfully as possible: she looked at available photographs, talked to members of the victim's family and researched the kind of clothing a teenager from that time might have been wearing, as well as the gestures that he may have adopted. Then she prevents us from seeing this. To cite the artist's own words: 'I like to think that the final image (...) is created in the mind of the spectator, by means of the evocation of his trace. This, for me, is the condition of the *desaparecido*: s/he is present, but we are prohibited from seeing him or her' (Claudia Fontes, quoted in Battiti, 2012, p.33, my translation).

This impossibility refers to the uncertain condition of the *desaparecido*. The lack of precise knowledge as to the circumstances, time and place of murder means that most of the history remains obscured. The artist perceives this with mastery and returns the anxiety of not knowing to the spectator. She suggests that something of the disappearance will always remain out of grasp, without a visible face, and instead invites our look to linger on the river.

Figure 13.1 Reconstruction of the Portrait of Pablo Míguez, by Claudia Fontes
Courtesy of Parque de la Memoria, Buenos Aires.

The evocation of the *desaparecidos* of the Argentine dictatorship in this sculpture merges with the open and uncomfortable question over the place that the Río de la Plata occupies in the Argentine social and cultural imaginary. During the last dictatorship (1976–83) thousands of disappeared were thrown from planes, while still alive, into this river or the Atlantic Ocean. How can such a crime be accounted for? How can society work through it and how can it continue to live next to this same river? How can its ominous presence next to an impassive city be understood? These questions are so wide that, like the huge river itself, they do not allow the other shore to be glimpsed, hence the calming vision of terra firma to be discerned. As a space without place – a mass of water that never stays the same – the river challenges attempts to attach memories to it. The liquid territory of the Río de la Plata cannot provide the stability that the earth offers to the deceased who are buried. Its silent presence by the city, however, is itself a reminder of the crime; at once a limitless, unmarked grave and a device to hide the evidence.

In what follows, I explore this sinister legacy of the river and link it to the ambiguity with which the city of Buenos Aires has related to its river and which goes back to its foundational narratives. I analyse efforts made, especially in the arts, in order to make the memory of what are referred to as the 'death flights' visible and create instances of remembrance in this space that is always in flow. If, however, a collective elaboration of the meaning and legacy of the Río de la Plata is still pending, I argue, this is because its very presence embodies, for Argentine society, a manifestation of the abject: that which has been externalized from the self, but which nevertheless remains an intimate and constitutive part of it, as is the case for the disappeared.

The death flights: Execution and concealment

Murder in the death flights was not the only means by which the *desaparecidos* were annihilated by the military as part of the Argentine state terror in the 1970s. However, the military's use of this execution method was both systematic and widespread. Numerous accounts bear testimony to its use in the former clandestine detention centre in the ESMA (Navy School of Mechanics or Escuela de Mecánica de la Armada), where on a set day of the week a group of abductees would be injected with a sleeping drug, taken to a plane, and then thrown still alive into the waters of the Río de la Plata or the Atlantic Ocean. Less is known about similar procedures from other clandestine centres, although numerous flights were reported to have left Campo de Mayo on a regular basis (Almirón, 1999). The death flights would allow the military to perform massive clandestine killings and, at the same time, make the bodies disappear. Prisoners were not informed of their imminent execution, nor were their relatives, and the bodies – evidence of the crime – were meant to sink along with any memory of them. No written documentation has been found, but testimonies indicate that high-ranking members of the Argentine Catholic church had approved the method and considered it to be a 'Christian form of death'.[2] The flights were at once a mechanism for assassination and for concealment of the corpses: an instrument for a concise and consolidated clandestine execution and for the erasure of any traces; state crime administered with a maximum economy of resources and efficiency. This method of extermination fitted into the context of the regime's goal of re-founding Argentine society in the long term. The dictatorship aimed at reconfiguring society by expelling what it deemed to be its undesirable elements – defined as 'subversive' – associated with the social and political activism that had contributed to an intense politicization in the country. Zygmunt Bauman considers this operation to be typical of the modern 'gardening' state that cultivates and designs the desired society by putting aside what is undesirable (Bauman, 1989). By hiding and rendering the traces of death invisible, the military aimed at generating the illusion of cleanliness and order.

The river did, however, soon begin to give up the dead and offer signs of what was happening. In May 1976, two months after the coup, reports emerged in local newspapers of bodies mysteriously discovered on the Argentine and Uruguayan banks of the river. In a matter of only a few weeks, the toll came to over a dozen, all carrying personal effects that would identify them as Argentine (Schindel, 2012, pp.177–181). The press reported 'the macabre appearance of mutilated, naked corpses with their hands tied' in the waters to the east of Montevideo, which caused 'the widest of speculation as to the identity of the victims and the reason for their assassination' (Schindel, 2012, p.178). These 'speculations' implied a complex game of interpretation and deciphering of the bodies, based, for example, on their possessions or tattoos. Some were even led to surmise that they are Asian citizens because of the 'yellowish pigmentation' of the corpses. But these bodies turned up, hands and feet bound, bearing signs of torture and mutilation, carrying documents and personal effects that are characteristically Argentine. Who were they? Who killed them and why? Why were these young bodies washing up on the shore on both sides of the Río de la Plata? The enigma eventually dissipated in the press. It reappeared in September, but shortly afterwards such news ceased to be published; quite possibly due to more radical measures taken to obliterate the traces of disappearance.[3]

The Argentine artist, León Ferrari, recorded the early presence of these news in his work entitled *We Did Not Know*, a compilation of newspaper headlines that were already reporting the appearance of bodies at the time the flights were taking place. The title of the work alludes to the belated excuse that circulated socially in Argentina, where supposedly people were unaware as to what was going on, while the country's principal daily newspapers gave indications to the contrary. Former detainee Miriam Lewin remembers, however, that the death flights were so difficult to imagine that they even spawned disbelief among abductees themselves. She recalls that rumours circulated inside the ESMA detention centre about the death flights, although the detainee-disappeared could not really believe them. 'We denied it', Lewin says, 'or at least we avoided talking about it explicitly in words. Like many other things that took place inside, we knew what was going on but couldn't show or express it'.[4] Many survivors do, however, agree in pointing to the nervousness that reigned in the ESMA prior to the transfers on Wednesdays (Calveiro, 1998, p.30).

In 1977, the bodies of several women washed up on Argentina's Atlantic coast, among them two mothers of the Plaza de Mayo, a French nun who had shown solidarity with relatives of the disappeared and an activist who was accompanying them at the time. These women had been seen alive in the ESMA and their bodies showed signs of having fallen into the water from a great height. Their bodies had been buried in anonymous graves in a cemetery close by and in 2005 they were finally identified by the Argentine Team of Forensic Anthropology. The discovery of these remains enabled the circuit of kidnapping by security forces, disappearance, torture and murder in the form of the death flight to be pieced together and demonstrated.

In the meantime, the continuing trials of the personnel involved in the death flights had begun, but the accused continued to deny their participation or provide information that could ease the anguish of the victims' relatives. Only one sergeant dared to declare publicly what he had seen of the flights leaving the Campo de Mayo army detention centre (Almirón, 1999), along with a ship's captain who, tormented by his troubled conscience, confessed his involvement in the crime to journalist Horacio Verbitsky (1996). It was precisely after this marine's declarations in 2005 that the matter was given significant space in the media and received widespread public recognition.

The issue of the death flights was then granted a presence in the public sphere because of the declarations made by a repressor and at the whim of a capricious and ephemeral media agenda, despite the fact that survivors had borne witness to the flights several years before, as in the trial of the military juntas in 1985, and their testimonies had been recorded in the Report of the Commission about the Enforced Disappearances set up by presidential decree after the return to constitutional order in 1983 (CONADEP, 1984). Moreover, this brief public discussion fell far short of a more thorough reflection upon or debate about the legacy of this massive crime. The problem of how to continue living alongside this ominous legacy of the river was not really raised publically and the Río de la Plata continued to be a silent, haunting presence.

An impoverished imagination: The elusive images of the death flights

'Our imagination is impoverished by comparison with that of the perpetrators. They imagined things that in our minds were impossible to envisage', reflects Verbitsky – himself a leftist activist in the 1970s – with regard to the rationale that led to the death flights. This difficulty in 'imagining' or conceiving such a method of execution also translates to the problematic process of acknowledging it in socio-cultural terms. But as Georges Didi-Huberman states, in his lengthy meditation on the capacity to imagine and give images to the Holocaust, if something took place and existed in the world, it was because it was and continues to be possible and needs to be imagined 'in spite of everything', precisely because it challenges the imagination (Didi-Huberman, 2008).

In 1999 popular Argentine rock musician, Charly García, made a bold move towards providing images for this unimaginable crime. The City Government of Buenos Aires invited him to give an open-air concert in the area close to the river in the newly remodelled port. García immediately associated the place with the disappeared and decided to perform a dramatic re-enactment of the death flights by incorporating them symbolically into the show. The artist said that he would accompany his recital with an orchestra playing onboard a boat and helicopters flying overhead, from which mannequins were to be thrown into the river in remembrance of the disappeared. The idea horrified the relatives of the disappeared and provoked anxious requests to cancel it. An artists' group close to the association

Madres de Plaza de Mayo (Mothers of the Plaza de Mayo) suggested that García change the profile of the act and instead of throwing mannequins from a great height, enable them to 'emerge from the waters of the river as if they were being revived'.[5] Finally, García decided to cancel any artistic intervention additional to the music, and instead invited the mothers of the disappeared to take to the stage during the concert. The episode was soon forgotten, but is worth retrieving here as a symptom of the most profound uneasiness that for a few weeks became publically visible. Both the proposal to imitate the fall from the flights, and that to stage a sort of resurrection of the disappeared from the water, express a mimetic, literal and almost naïve representational gesture. What was underlying García's idea to stage the death flights was, however, more than a provocation: it revealed a disavowed need to turn what had happened into images and make something of the unimaginable in the death flights manifest. Repressed anxieties needed an escape valve and as an artist with a sharp eye for detecting the sensitive points of the Argentine 'collective unconscious' (the title of one of his songs), he was recognizing the discomfort posed by the proximity to the river.

Another case, which differs from Charly García's initiative but is likewise symptomatic, is that of an inexplicable full-page advert for Diesel jeans, which had appeared in an Argentine magazine a few months before the concert. It consists of a photographic image of eight youths submerged in the ocean, their hands tied together and their feet tied to concrete blocks. A caption in English states: 'They're not your first jeans, but they could be your last. At least you'll leave a beautiful corpse.' It was published in the magazine *Gente* on 9 April 1998. The advert immediately incited fervent repudiation and complaints on the part of human rights organizations and was quickly withdrawn. According to the company, the advert had been designed by a British agency within the context of an international campaign distributed in 80 countries, without having been rejected when checked in Argentina with certain groups and without anyone having shown any opposition.[6] In the political climate of 1998, dominated by neo-liberalism and discourses stressing the need to 'forget the past', impunity seemed to have become permanent and there was reason to believe that public treatment of state terrorism would not return to the political agenda. Which images occupy, in such a context, the place of a collective trauma that is not recognized as such? How does collective denial of such a massive crime work? What went through the minds of those who managed and published this advert? Do they mean to suggest that blue jean fabric is more resistant than the disappeared and their ideals? In a context that was prone to silence and oblivion, Charly García's idea and the withdrawal of the advert brought the issue into the public eye and demonstrated that the death flights were still far from being worked through collectively. Whether parapraxes or instances of recklessness, these incidents touched on what had been removed from the image and even the imagination in the evocation of the death flights: the fall, the blind moment of death, the sinking of the bodies, which no one survived.

A film released shortly after these episodes contributed perhaps one of the most accomplished and perturbing visual approaches to the evocation of the death flights. In the final sequence of Marco Bechis's *Garage Olimpo* (1999), a film that recreates the concentrationary universe of the Argentine dictatorship with brutal realism, we see a military jet flying over the edge of the land and then a sea of muddy waters, the tailgate of the plane eventually opening. In a powerful sensory condensation, the shot juxtaposes the instrument of crime and the vision of the river, with the allusion to national symbols, such as the Argentine rosette on the wing of the military airplane and a song in honour of the national flag as the only background music. Artifice abounds in the sequence: it takes place in the middle of the day while, according to testimonies, the flights took place at night; the plane used is not a Skyvan, the type of plane mainly used to carry out this procedure; and, according to the credits, filming took place in California. The value of truth invested in the image does not, however, necessarily bear any relation to its authenticity. It is more a case of turning what is both inconceivable and difficult to imagine into an image. These pictures do not directly represent, but instead skirt around, the image of the final instance of disappearance.

In his passionate plea for a difficult aesthetic of the image that requires us to visualize the horror of the Holocaust 'despite everything', Georges Didi-Huberman criticizes the generalizing statements about an alleged invisibility, unfigurability or unrepresentability when it comes to the horrors of genocide. He instead advocates the possibility of confronting the extreme through images which are nothing but a 'simple image: inadequate but necessary, inexact but true' (Didi-Huberman, 2008, p.39). Although it is not a testimonial image, the final sequence of this film accompanies the spectator in the effort to imagine it and confirms that, in the face of a 'generalised obliteration' of the camps, *'each apparition* – however fragmentary, however difficult to look at and to interpret – in which a single cog of this enterprise is visually suggested to us becomes all the more necessary' (Didi-Huberman, 2008, p.26, original emphasis).

Words, like images – however incomplete or inexact they may be – work to piece together the fragments in spite of, or precisely because of, the 'inexpressability' or 'incommunicability' of the genocidal experience. A brutally direct and, at the same time, nauseating attempt at representing the death flights in Argentine literature features in Rodolfo Fogwill's *Los Pichiciegos* (1983), a novel considered by critics to be visionary in more than one sense. Written in just a few weeks during the war with Great Britain in the South Atlantic in 1982, it portrays a group of soldiers who have deserted and who survive underground. The author inserts a reference to the crimes committed by the military a few years prior into the dialogue between them: 'I heard they were thrown out of planes into the River Plate', says one. 'That's impossible', replies another. A third one adds that he also heard that they were dropped into the river from planes: 'If you hit the water from twelve thousand meters, you turn into thick mush that won't float and gets pulled down beneath the surface by the current' (Fogwill, 2007, p.42). The dialogue continues between those who try to imagine this and those who dismiss the practice as implausible: how can they take planes up to throw people into the sea? Fogwill places the effort to conceive this intolerable moment of death and the destroyed body into words that – much like the re-enactment in *Garage Olimpo* – do not recreate a factual truth,[7] but point to the core of the problem: how to lend words or pictures to what is unbearable to conceive and finds no place to which it can be attached.

Attempts at recognizing the flights in artistic work, such as this literary scene, aim rather at alluding to what can be sensed, but nevertheless remains, beyond the frame of the image. Fernando Reati has analysed the way in which the death flights are indirectly evoked in some recent works of literature, theatre and popular music: in these pieces the river is depicted as a calm surface that is hiding an invisible danger, smooth waters conceal an unknown threat (Reati, 2012). Attempts to represent the flights in the visual arts also recur to metonymic operations, by representing the surface of something that cannot be completely grasped. The photographer, Marcelo Brodsky, registered the river's muddy waters, imprinting upon them the statement: 'The river became a non-existent grave'. He accompanied it with a photograph of his disappeared brother sailing as a child and a portrait of an immigrant uncle on the deck of a ship bringing him up the same river to Argentina. The juxtaposition of images brings a family's path together with that of society as a collective: the river of the promises of progress and childhood playtime gives way to an impossible grave. The photographs of other visual artists, such as Fernando Gutiérrez and Helen Zout, sketch out the hazy interiors and the austere silhouettes of planes used in the flights in black and white, or simply portray the fog that hovers over the enigmatic waters of the river. Jonathan Perel's cinematographic meditation presents an immobile river for eight minutes, with a sole shot of water and nothing else. All these images aim outside the frame, to what is not seen: the water hides more than it shows.[8] As in the sculpture portraying Pablo Míguez, we can never see the whole face.

Artist, activist and sailor, Jorge Velarde, was obsessed by the character of the river as a territory without place, reflecting on how to create places on a vast surface where all traces disappear. He dismissed the installation of fixed and static objects as a reflection of his murdered comrades whom he instead remembers happy and full of life: 'I could not evoke them with a dead object. What is more, the river is merciless with anything that is put there.'[9] He decided instead to trace a line with the prow of his sailing boat, opening up a furrow – albeit ephemeral – and marking out an imaginary point where the bodies might have impacted upon falling. Between 1998 and 2005, Velarde undertook a series of trips on the Río de la Plata and its boundary with the Atlantic Ocean, some with relatives of the disappeared, making 'drawings on the river' (the name given to the act) with the trail left by his sailing boat (Figure 13.2). He traced the form of an 'X' and declared the centre of the cross as the central point of his memory. 'That would be the point at which the bodies made impact with the water.' They threw flowers into the water on

Figure 13.2 Drawings on the River, by Jorge Velarde
Courtesy of Jorge Velarde.

this spot, a gesture which can be found in the old traditions of fishermen in honour of the victims of a shipwreck. Once the journey was over, he recalled: 'I looked at this area, this territory and all I saw was the texture of the waves, nothing. However, the change, the transformation had occurred.' The work left only the signs of the nautical cartography, audiovisual recordings and a narrative of the action. Matter was not modified. An ephemeral trace had been created for an instant in these places in the form of a cross, which is as much a sign of someone who leaves a mark as a figure of an unknown quality: the unknown figure of an equation. An element, much like the face of Pablo Miguez's portrait, that we cannot discern.

How to live next to a limitless grave? Memory and abjection

In his essay about water and forgetfulness, Ivan Illich suggests thinking of the primordial liquid, like space itself, as material and imbued with a historical and cultural character. Substance, he states, is also a social construction and cities are made up of two types of material: urban space and water (Illich, 1985). Therefore, for Illich, the way in which both relate to one another can reveal information about a given society. Water, like memory, emanates from deep wells and our relationship to the aquatic substance is inextricably linked to the way in which we inhabit and remember. 'To dwell means to inhabit the traces left by one's own living' (Illich, 1985, p.8), and hence our environment bears our footprints. If it does not, then dwelling and remembering become alienated.

When the urbanist, Le Corbusier, visited Buenos Aires in 1929 he was dismayed to see a metropolis that, unlike most European cities, turns its back on the river. He hoped to rectify this gesture of the city turning in on itself and averting its gaze from the monumental mass of water by making the river the central element of his master plan for Buenos Aires, which never materialized (Fedele, 2012). A certain ambivalence towards the river, perceived as an unclassifiable liquid mass, has accompanied the inhabitants of its Argentine coast since the Spanish conquerors in the sixteenth century, taken aback by its breadth, named it *Mar Dulce* (Sweet Sea). According to Simon Schama the myths and memories attached to the rivers 'carry us back to the first watery element of our existence in the womb': for this reason, along those streams are borne 'some of the most intense of our social and animal passions: the mysterious transmutations of blood and water; the vitality and mortality of heroes, empires, nations, and gods' (Schama, 1996, p.247). However, the unclassifiable quality and unmeasurable dimension of the Río de la Plata provided for a paradoxical sign of identity. Jorge Luis Borges (Borges, 1923) alluded to the dissonance between the epic of any foundational narrative and the less than heroic substance of these turbid waters when, in his 'Mythical Founding of Buenos Aires' he inquired: 'And was it along this torpid muddy river/that the prows came to found my native city?' (cited in

Vicuña and Livan-Grosman, 2009, p.202). The ambivalent character of the river likewise confounds geographers, as they cannot agree as to whether the Río de la Plata is a river (it would be the widest in the world), an outlet to the sea, or – most probably – an estuary.[10] Its shallowness, erratic course and cross currents make navigation dangerous and mean that it constantly has to be dredged. It constitutes an enormous aquatic mass in which different categories come together and transmute, where the banks are so far apart that one cannot be seen from the other: fresh and salt water blend; river and sea amalgamate; frontier and territory converge. Juan José Saer refers to a river that reflects and replicates the never-ending plains of the limitless pampas to the point of indistinction (Saer, 1991). The cradle of a nation and its tomb, at once the object of positive identification and rejection, the city of Buenos Aires maintains an aloof and estranged relationship to its river. This double condition of identification and rejection provided the frame and perhaps also the condition of possibility for the death flights. It can therefore be interpreted in terms of abjection, a concept related to what is polyvalent and ambiguous: something that attracts and repels at the same time.

The category of abjection was especially developed by Julia Kristeva (Kristeva, 1982), who originally related it to the constitution of subjectivity, but later also extended it to the social and political fields (Mandolessi, 2012). Abjection is identified with the process of rejecting, expelling or, in Kristeva's critical terms, abjecting what is considered to be 'other' to the self. But that which is expelled is in reality a part of the self which, through rejection, is transformed into something alien. The abject manifests itself in objects or situations that challenge the establishment of precise limits, such as the corpse as it marks the frontier between life and death (Kristeva, 1988, p.10, quoted in Mandolessi, 2012, p.33). The abject is characterized as a shapeless substance which cannot be differentiated, such as ambiguity and frontier, where elements that should remain separate become confused and identities fall to pieces. Like the river of muddied waters and uncertain course, the abject applies to objects of indefinite status or paradoxical cultural significance. Itself an immense, never-ending grave, the river is since the death flights also a carrier of corpses and a reminder of death. But its abject character, I suggest, is manifold and refers not only to the bodies as liminal objects. Beyond these eschatological associations, the river embodies the abject because it stirs the conscience of a limit that has been erased.

The processes of individual and national identity construction operate in an analogical form. Historically, the nation state is established via the upheaval of the political body that rejects those parts of itself that are defined as other or in excess, a rejected otherness that engenders the consolidation of national identity (Mandolessi, 2012, p.175). The massive disappearances under the Argentine dictatorship were perpetrated as a way of expelling from the national collective a part of itself that nevertheless belongs intimately to it. A long campaign of stigmatization had, prior to the disappearances, constructed the social and political activists targeted by the regime as 'subversives' different and alien to Argentine society. No matter how symbolically and effectively rejected, however, the river also reminds us that they always did and will belong: the abjected is our own. Yael Navaro-Yashin has written about the 'abjected space' as a border area that becomes what a collective wanted to abject out of itself (Navaro-Yashin, 2012, p.148). The abject, which in her case study is the experience of Greek Cypriots expelled from Northern Cyprus in 1974, can be extrapolated to the Argentine case in the way in which the dictatorship aimed at reconfiguring society by expelling an imaginary other, constructed as such through decades of antileftist rhetoric (Schindel, 2012). The river, as an abjected space, carries the remembrance of those whom the criminal state had excluded from the national community. Furthermore, a transgression has been made that surpassed all cultural boundaries by violating the mandate to bury the dead and by leaving the abjected other – the *desaparecido* – inhabiting an ambiguous zone in between life and death.

In the 1990s the landscaping of the riverside where Le Corbusier had envisioned a 'city of *affaires*' eventually took place. It happened under the sign of private capital and neo-liberal policy in the form of huge real estate development projects and postmodern recycling of old deposits in the port area. But instead of reconciling the river with its people, giving the city back the view over the water, the new neighbourhood of Puerto Madero offered a paradoxical reincorporation: with its skyscrapers and luxurious infrastructure, it integrates the river only to ignore it once again, leaving its waters trapped within the canals that have been reconstructed for the purposes of tourism and business. Far from recomposing the denaturalized relationship that the *porteños*[11] have with their river, the new urbanization at once establishes and cuts off contact with the water. Rather than allowing a harmonic cohabitation with it, the river is both suggested and hidden; its vision from the public spaces remains distant and fragmented. One of the streets created in the new design of this neighbourhood carries the name of Azucena Villaflor de Devicenzi, one of the founding Mothers of Plaza de Mayo kidnapped and later murdered on a death flight, whose body was found in 2005 and served to prove the crime. This can be labelled ironic, or also symptomatic of an urban model opposed to the ideals that mobilized the disappeared activists, that is consecrated at the very place which bore witness to their deaths; a new city built 'cynically and spectacularly in front of *a river of death*' (Santangelo and D'Iorio, 2007, p.21, my translation, original emphasis).

There is no single answer to the question as to how to incorporate the daily, unsettling presence of this huge collective grave into modes of inhabiting the city. But by opening up spaces in which the question can be formulated, Argentine society can devise the means of confronting what has been forced out, embracing the absences and taking them back. North of the new area of Puerto Madero the Memory Park, to which the 'Reconstruction of the portrait of Pablo Míguez' belongs, is in fact one of the few urban areas from which the river, in its breadth, can be contemplated at a short distance. There stands the only monument to be erected in Argentina that names all the known victims of state terrorism. The plaques without a grave and the waters that bear no names meet at a geographical and affective point. As one of only a few public spaces that enable contact with the river to be regained, it formulates a double invitation: to recover enjoyment of the coastal area, refreshing oneself from the stifling city and gaining the vision of the water, while recognizing this abjected part of Argentine society as its own, even if we will never manage to see its complete face.

Notes

The research leading to this chapter has received funding from the European Research Council under the European Union's Seventh Framework Program (FP/2007–2013)/ERC Grant Agreement n° 240984, 'NOT.' The interviews with Miriam Lewin, Carlos Somigliana, Jorge Velarde and Horacio Verbitsky quoted here took place in the context of this research in Buenos Aires in February and March of 2011.

1. I have chosen to use the Spanish name for the River Plate throughout the chapter in order to maintain the affective connotations of the original.
2. Interview with the author, 8 February 2011. See also Verbitsky, 1996.
3. A former Sergeant claims to have heard that, due to these appearances, prisoners were administered an incision that would produce a haemorrhage, causing them to sink rather than float in the water. Moreover, the flights were sent much further south over the Atlantic so that the current would not bring them back to shore (Almirón, 1999, p.183).
4. Interview with the author, 18 February 2011.
5. The controversy can be traced in the press coverage at the time. See, for example, the editions of *Página/12* dated 16, 19 and 28 February 1999.
6. See Página/12, 5 May 1998, http://www.pagina12.com.ar/1998/98-05/98-05-05/pag18.htm, date accessed 18 March 2014.
7. According to the forensic anthropologist C. Somigliana the bodies did not pulverize, but fractured upon impact with the water. They were not thrown from 12,000 meters, but from a much lower height to avoid a drop in air pressure inside the plane when the tailgate was opened which would have killed everyone. Interview carried out on 16 February 2011.
8. Jonathan Perel. 2013. *Las Aguas del Olvido*.
9. Interview carried out on 11 February 2011. All subsequent quotations from Velarde are taken from this interview.
10. See: http://www.britannica.com/EBchecked/topic/463804/Rio-de-la-Plata, date accessed 17 March 2014.
11. Inhabitants of Buenos Aires, a word derived from *puerto* (port).

Bibliography

Almirón, Fernando. 1999. *Campo santo. Los asesinatos del Ejército en Campo de Mayo. Testimonios del ex-sargento Víctor Ibañez*. Buenos Aires: Editorial 21.
Battiti, Florencia. 2012. 'El arte ante las paradojas de la representación'. *Cuadernos del Centro de Estudios en Diseño y Comunicación*, 41: 29–40.
Bauman, Zygmunt. 1989. *Modernity and the Holocaust*. Cambridge: Polity Press.

Borges, Jorge Luis. 1923. 'The Mythical Founding of Buenos Aires', translated by Alistair Reid. In *The Oxford Book of Latin American Poetry*, edited by Cecilia Vicuña and Ernesto Livon-Grosman 2009. Oxford: Oxford University Press.
Calveiro, Pilar. 1998. *Poder y desaparición. Los campos de concentración en Argentina*. Buenos Aires: Colihue.
CONADEP. 1984. *Nunca Más*. Buenos Aires: Eudeba.
Didi-Huberman, Georges. 2008. *Images in Spite of All: Four Photographs from Auschwitz*. Chicago: University of Chicago Press.
Fedele, Javier. 2012. 'City and River: Urban Plans in the Argentina of the First Half of the 20th Century'. Lecture to the 15th International Planning History Society Conference. http://www.fau.usp.br/iphs/abstractsAndPapersFiles/Sessions/05/FEDELE.pdf, date accessed 14 March 2014.
Fogwill, Rodolfo. 2007 (1983). *Malvinas Requiem. Visions of an Underground War*, translated by Nic Caistor. London: Serpent's Tail.
Illich, Ivan. 1985. *H$_2$O and the Waters of Forgetfulness: Reflections on the Historicity of 'Stuff'*. Dallas: The Dallas Institute of Humanities and Culture.
Kristeva, Julia. 1982. *Powers of Horror: An Essay on Abjection*. New York: Columbia University Press.
Le Corbusier. 1947. *Proposición de un Plan Director para Buenos Aires*. Buenos Aires: Muncipalidad de Buenos Aires.
Mandolessi, Silvana. 2012. *Una literatura abyecta. Witold Gombrowicz en la tradición argentina*. Amsterdam and New York: Rodopi.
Navaro-Yashin, Yael. 2012. *The Make-Believe Space: Affective Geography in a Postwar-Polity*. Durham: Duke University Press.
Reati, Fernando. 2012. 'Cuídame de las aguas mansas...Terrorismo de estado y lo fantástico en "El lago" y "Los niños transparentes"'. *Revista iberoamericana*, LXXVIII/238–239: 293–310.
Saer, Juan José. 1991. *El río sin orillas. Tratado imaginario*. Buenos Aires: Alianza.
Santángelo, Mariana and Gabriel D'Iorio. 2007. 'Buenos Aires, la experiencia desquiciante'. En *El río sin orillas*, 1/1:18–26.
Schama, Simon. 1996. *Landscape and Memory*. London: Fontana Press.
Schindel, Estela. 2012. *La desaparición a diario. Sociedad, prensa y dictadura (1975–1978)*. Villa María: Eduvim.
Verbitsky, Horacio. 1996. *The Flight: Confessions of an Argentine Dirty Warrior*, translated by Esther Allen. New York: The New Press.

Part IV

Spaces of Exception, Power and Resistance

14
Spatialities of Exception

Pilar Calveiro

The construction of notions of time, space and movement has over time been modified in conjunction with evolving forms of organization in societies. Certainly, the way in which time and space are conceptualized corresponds to a hegemonic vision of the world and is linked directly to the social organization of both, as well as to their utilization as indispensable instruments in the exercise of power. In this sense, the classification, reticulation and stratification of spaces to control flows and movement have been characteristics of power in modernity, although this has been undertaken by varying means, depending on the political system.

In general, it has been characterized by an extreme form of territorialization which creates marginal spaces of exclusion and confinement, such as the ghetto, that are necessarily in opposition to spaces of power that are defined by their centrality. However, in the passage to late modernity the location of power has become unclear, since 'it is both everywhere and nowhere' (Hardt and Negri, 2000, p.191), becoming defined as a non-place. In its turn, the resistance that has always attempted to de-territorialize and decode is met with a power that emulates and disconcerts it. When trying to exit a deviant grid, agenda or routine, this resistance has difficulty finding a peripheral location that has yet to be thought of. It increasingly seeks more lateral or underground positions (that it does not find), particularly in those places in which the multiple and proliferating powers are either invisible or impotent.

Following this idea, I will analyse the particularities of and transformations in the way in which space is treated in three repressive models, each a product of *states of exception* which either suspend the rule of law or superimpose upon it a right of exception that violates every guarantee for certain sectors of the population. In this article, I will refer first of all to the concentrationary models operated in the Nazi Lagers, then to the clandestine detention centres operating during the Argentine 'dirty war', and finally to Guantánamo and the black sites of the Central Intelligence Agency (CIA) in the so-called War on Terror. In my opinion, this sequence demonstrates the passage from a totalitarian state with global pretensions to an authentically global power that could be termed 'globalitarian' (Tassin, 2002) on account of its resonance with some of the main features of the totalitarian experience.

The saturation of space in the Nazi concentration camp

The Nazi Lager formed an extra-national concentrationary complex that, although managed by the German State, extended beyond the national borders to reach other territories annexed during the Second World War – as was the case with Auschwitz. In analysing this, I will draw mainly on Primo Levi's account of Monowitz. This place was a slave labour camp at the service of the company IG Farben, a 'private' Lager which, together with the extermination camp at Birkenau and a further 40 camps, formed the concentrationary complex at Auschwitz. Monowitz alone comprised a complex of Lagers (intended for different types of prisoners – prisoners of war (POW), women, French volunteers) surrounding the Buna, a kind of industrial city where according to Levi's description not even a blade of grass would grow and where streets and buildings were designated, as indeed were the prisoners, by numbers and letters.

The Lager where Levi lived might appear, rather paradoxically, to be a version or adaptation of German military life (Levi, 2013). For example, it had at its centre a vast open parade ground, where squads of prisoners were lined up to the beat of a military band in columns of five as they went to and from work. This would be done marching, cap in hand, stiff-necked and without talking, always under the supervision of the Schutzstaffel (*Protection Squadron*) (SS). This routine, undertaken in military formation, did not represent the disciplining of an army willing to die, but something much more profound and humiliating: a discipline exercised even on those who are destined to be exterminated.

The topography of the Lager consisted of a square measuring approximately 600m on each side, surrounded by electrified barbed wire. Inside, there were 60 wooden barracks distributed according to their respective functions: the infirmary, a canteen for Germans and Kapos, administrative offices, kitchens, a pilot plant, a camp brothel and those barrack blocks allocated to housing the prisoners. The blocks reserved for 'prominent' prisoners and those for housing Aryan Germans, whether politicians or criminals, were differentiated from those that housed the Kapos. The blocks assigned to common prisoners were in turn divided into two areas: a living room for the barrack chief and his friends, and the general dormitory with 148 three-storey bunk beds. One in every six or eight of these blocks housed the showers or latrines. What has been described so far had – in appearance at least – a structure similar to that of military quarters, with space organized according to function and distributed hierarchically. However, there were certain features that differentiated it significantly: the electrified fence and the control towers signalled a different and much more radical type of enclosed order. Likewise, the patch of grass in front of the central parade ground, although remaining empty when not in use, marked the spot where the gallows were erected for public executions. But in addition to these defining aspects, what distinguished the inner functioning of this space was one feature in particular: its extreme saturation.

The way in which the concentrationary universe functioned created spaces that were completely saturated with life and death from the initial contact. Transportation had already occurred in freight wagons, sealed and closed from the outside, containing up to 120 'men, women and children pressed together without pity, like cheap merchandise', 'pieces' in SS language (Levi, 2004, p.17). Levi recalls: 'fifty persons in a freight car are most uncomfortable' but they can in this instance lie down next to one another. When there are 100 or more, however, 'one must take turns standing or squatting' (Levi, 2013, p.119). Tired, hungry, thirsty and afraid, lying on the floor of those wagons, the prisoners formed 'an obscure agitation, a human mass, extended across the floor, confused and continuous, clumsy and aching' (Levi, 2004, p.24), forced to 'lie days and days on their own filth' (Levi, 2004, p.216).

Once they arrived at the camp and the selection took place between those who were to be murdered immediately and those who would die later, the conditions of overcrowding did not change radically. Within the camp barrack blocks, bunk beds were arranged tightly from floor to ceiling, 'like the *cells of a beehive*' (Levi, 2004, p.38, emphasis added) so that full advantage was taken of every last cubic metre. Overpopulation was such that two people had to sleep on most of the bunk beds. The corridors that separated them were so narrow that two people could hardly pass at the same time, and, according to Levi, *'inhabitants of the same Block cannot all stay there at the same time unless at least half are lying on their bunks'* (2004, p.35, emphasis added). In Birkenau, conditions were even worse: up to nine women could sleep on a plank measuring 1.8 by 2m (Levi, 2004, p.434). Under these conditions, sleep is not rest even while sleeping, and this is precisely the point: it is a space that gives no respite.

The confusion of bodies was echoed in the mixture of languages, in a 'perpetual Babel, in which everyone shouts (...) no one listens to you', recounts Levi (2004, p.41). Communication was difficult and interrupted in the tangle of bodies that were animalized and in the disarray of tongues that stripped the Other of any distinguishing feature of the human condition, such as speech. Roars, grunts and punches took the place of the spoken word. The crowding of bodies was a central part of the treatment to such an extent that punishment cells of one square metre used in Auschwitz 1 were at times used to hold up to five prisoners at the same time.

The infirmary in Monowitz was composed of eight barracks, separated from the rest by wire fences. In spite of this apparent distinction, inside they had a similar disposition: three-storey bunk beds were lined up along the barrack, always insufficient in number, which is why the sick had to share them and those on the highest level were effectively crushed against the ceiling, without room even to be able to sit up. However, in spite of the overcrowding, life in the infirmary meant significant differences: one did not work there, it was not cold and, unless a serious fault was committed, people were not physically punished. Being free from these misfortunes meant a substantial difference: prisoners could attempt to communicate and speak about something other than hunger or work. Hence, they could reflect upon what they had been turned into (Levi, 2004, pp.48–62).

In every place, 'on the scaffolding, on the trains being switched about, on the roads, in the pits, in the offices, men and more' worked like 'horses' under the whip of the Kapos (Levi, 2004, pp.46 and 75). 'Livestock, waste, filth' with the same 'mark [on the skin] used for cattle', licking the soup plates 'like dogs' and finally exterminated with 'the same poisonous gas' that was used in ships against bedbugs and lice; thousands of people animalized, locked and starved, always below their most elemental needs, and finally eliminated as part of the superfluous humanity within mass society.

Levi recounts that in the northeastern corner of the Lager, the most distant that the SS occupied, a kind of tumultuous inner clandestine market was organized: the black market – always active and where the currency of exchange was the very scarce bread. The black market was one of the most important connections to the outside through goods that entered and exited based on their more favourable price inside the camp or within the industrial zone of the Buna. From these exchanges and many others, in spite of the confinement, the Lager was not a completely closed-off place. From inside you could see the surrounding nature and, above all, some prisoners entered and exited the camp itself, always in formation. Those who worked in the industrial establishments had contact with civilians, who were alarmed by their deplorable condition. But these civilians, alongside those who observed the prisoners as they moved in formation through the streets, were in the end witnesses to what was going on, albeit at a distance. Auschwitz was an industrial–concentrationary complex where a large number of civilian personnel worked, coexisting with a situation that was only half-concealed. In this sense, it must be said that hiding the huge apparatus of the concentration camps from the German people was not possible or desirable for the Nazis, as is shown in different testimonies (Levi, 2004, p.196).

The chimney at Birkenau was another distinctive feature, which affected the inner and outer space of Auschwitz. Through the windows of the barracks in Birkenau you could see 'the flames issuing from the chimney' so that when Giuliana Tedeschi asked her fellow prisoners about that fire, they answered: 'It is we who are burning' (Levi, 2004, p.434). Although the chimney was not visible from Monowitz, it became increasingly present for everyone through the expression, which was cryptic at first and later desperate: 'This is a German Lager (...) and no one leaves except through the chimney' (Levi, 2004, p.218). The centrality of the chimney inside the camp wire was a reminder not only of death, but also of the total dissolution of the person as final objective.

The concentrationary universe of the Third Reich was thus played out in an extra-national space, in accordance with its political aspirations of world control. It was designed as a kind of industrial/military complex that brought mass production together in the same area with an equally mass programme of extermination; both elements specific to war capitalism. The internal disposition of the camp was similar to that of a military quarter, as was its modus operandi with the use of military uniforms, formation, commando units, chains of command and discipline. However, distinctive features within the space signalled its specificity as a place of extermination. In this sense, the gallows and the chimney at Auschwitz were particularly significant, occupying the very centre of the space.

Transportation of prisoners in cattle wagons and in conditions similar to those of animals, numerical markings on flesh, housing in saturated spaces where overcrowding of bodies led to the irritation of the senses, all contributed to the dehumanization and, above all, animalization of the Other. The physical containment of camps with regards to their environment was nevertheless relative. Although surrounded by electrified fences that prevented any escape, there were exchanges and a certain degree of reciprocal visibility across the camp boundaries that denote the civilian population's 'knowledge' of the prisoners' situation and the latter's awareness of social indifference.

Finally, it was a repressive constellation of classification and selection, where the distinction between work camps and extermination camps marked the difference between two forms of elimination: causing death and leaving to die. In this regard, Levi notes that out of 97 Italians who arrived in Auschwitz in February 1944 almost 80% had died by October that year, although only 8% had been victims of a 'selection'. 'Death by hunger, or by diseases induced by hunger, was the prisoner's normal destiny' (Levi, 2013, p.37) rather than selections. In effect, within the military industrial space, whatever was deemed to be useless or burdensome was discarded, while at the same time everything that was of use was extracted from individuals until their utter exhaustion. This is a kind of existence designed for the Other, whose death is considered irrelevant; a biopolitical experience based on the selection-production-extraction of mass society.

The fragmentary space: Clandestine detention centres in Argentina

In the case of Argentina, clandestine detention centres also comprised an interconnected network of camps – in this case at a national level – with passing of prisoners between them. However, the scale of the phenomenon was much smaller than in the Nazi case, not only in absolute terms but also in proportion to the general population. The question of scale is by no means irrelevant as it has to do with a different and much more selective repressive process. In this case, the enemy to be exterminated was reduced by his or her condition as a political opponent instead of massively affecting large human groups defined exclusively by their belonging to a certain community, as was the case of the millions of Jews and Gypsies. Instead of genocide, what was practiced could be called a politicide; a more discriminating type of repression, albeit with the levels of arbitrariness singular to any type of extermination process and with the consequent climate of terror that immobilizes society. The repressive modality and its dimensions in quantitative terms determined characteristics that are also different in spatial terms. Another substantial difference from the Nazi case is that in large part the clandestine centres were located in the middle of cities; yet even when they were to be found in the most important urban centres, their existence was concealed and denied in official discourse. For the most part, they operated in existing police, military or even civilian offices which were adapted expressly to function as clandestine centres. 'All of them were dependent upon the military authority with jurisdiction over each area' (*Nunca más*, 1991, p.58, my translation). They were not, however, recognized by the authorities but rather constituted 'a clandestine and parallel structure' (*Nunca más*, 1991, p.56, my translation), superimposing an illegal repressive circuit onto the legal one. In this sense, they were kept in much stricter isolation from the surrounding space which implied the suppression of any connection to the outside. The occasional excursion of some prisoners outside the camp was exceptional and the entry and transfer of people were concealed, although in more than one case neighbouring residents declared that they had suspected or found evidence of what was occurring inside. However, visibility and contact between the inside and outside worlds were severely interrupted in both directions. Arrival and reception at the clandestine centre was individual and although it adhered to a general procedure, it was always applied on an individual basis and in an isolated manner.

The structure of the camps varied, although each contained a reception area for prisoners, torture or interrogation rooms, offices allocated to intelligence work and the tasks of military personnel, space assigned to prisoner housing and the exit area through which prisoners were taken to their execution: the final transfer. In the case of the largest centres, such as the Argentine Navy Mechanics School (Escuela Superior de Mecánica de la Armada – ESMA), there were workshops and designated work areas for a very small number of prisoners. Captives were housed according to a system of classification: pregnant women; prisoners from other camps housed temporarily at the ESMA; prisoners with certain privileges relating to their usefulness, their alleged 'recuperation' or their open collaboration with the system. However, this all coexisted within the same isolated construction, sometimes underground and generally dark: a hole in the space resembling more a pit inside a barrack than a barrack as such, or a city. Although the total space of the camps included these different sections – later identified by some survivors – for most of those seized, given the virtual lack of movement, the only places identifiable were the torture room and the block in which they were held pending their transfer.

In contrast to the Nazi concentration camps, where torture was constituted by daily life itself, in the Argentine camps alongside the daily anguish of incarceration there was also a space specifically designated to torment as part of the entry process: the interrogation rooms – or 'operating theatres' – and the intelligence offices where the information obtained was processed. The specialization of space as an interrogation area and its centrality in testimonies mark a difference between this mechanism and that of the Nazis. This can be attributed to a shift from the extraction of a person's entire living strength to the extraction of only what is of interest in him/her: the information s/he possesses.

The general treatment given to the majority of those detained in the Argentine camps consisted of concentrating prisoners into the same barrack block, although separated by partition walls, individual bunk beds or cells, depending on the case.

> The bunk beds were conglomerate wood compartments, without a roof, 80cm wide by 2m long, where a person could fit lying down on a foam rubber mattress. The lateral partition walls were around 80 centimeters high, so that they impeded the visibility of the person housed inside (...). They left a small opening at the front, through which the prisoner could be pulled out.
>
> (Calveiro, 1998, p.46, my translation)

The cells or tubes were of approximately the same size. The sketches of the major clandestine centres (El Olimpo, La Perla, ESMA, Campo de Mayo, Pozo de Bánfield, Club Atlético, Vesubio, el Banco, el Atlético) drawn by survivors show that the space was organized into adjacent, isolated compartments: one for each body.

Inside them, people remained seated, handcuffed, hooded, in absolute silence and totally inactive for the whole day. At night, they slept in the same spot and under the same conditions, next to, although segregated from, their fellow prisoners and prohibited from talking amongst themselves or communicating in any way. It was a system of compartments or containers – whether manufactured or made out of wood – in which to deposit bodies that were treated as objects: faceless, hooded beings, immobile and mute, identifiable by a number, resembling a package more than a person or animal. These bodies/packages were temporarily stored until the mechanism became saturated and required their disposal in order to make room for others in an identical situation. The organization of space into long sequences of compartments corresponded to the compartmentalization of the repressive process itself, of the camps with regards to society, and even of subjectivity: containers within containers.

The practices of hooding and enforced silence should be highlighted as marks of the principle of sensory and communicative isolation, correlating in turn with the enclosing of the clandestine centre with regard to the outside. The hood also has the function of impeding recognition of and placement within space. In turn, chaining and forced immobility interrupt all movement within the camp, other than going to the toilet once or twice a day, sometimes in a group. Survivor Liliana Callizo evokes the sensation of spatial disorientation when she recalls that 'at first the person seized has no idea about the place around him. Some of us had imagined it as round. Others as a football stadium (. . .). We did not know in what direction our bodies were facing' (*Nunca más*, 1991, p.60, my translation). The prisoners were each given a number, as in the Nazi camps, but instead of it being tattooed onto their skin like cattle, it became their identification code for tracking their every movement similar to the barcode on a package, especially for the final transfer.

In some of these centres which today serve as memorial sites, such as the ESMA or La Perla, the point of exit and subsequent transfer of prisoners to their death is marked in a special way. The elimination of people usually took place outside the camp, save in the exceptional cases of a prisoner who had died during torture. In some instances the prisoners were transported far from the camp, tied and gagged, executed by firearm, their remains then buried or cremated in places that thus far remain unknown. However, the method that was massively adopted was to inject the person with sleep-inducing drugs prior to him or her being thrown into the ocean in the same way an unwanted parcel might be discarded. The death and disappearance of bodies occurred therefore outside the confines of the concentrationary space and yet the last site on which they were present is recorded in testimonies and stands out in a way that is meaningful in current space.

To conclude, the Argentine concentrationary universe unravels in a national space, although it also depends on a repressive network at regional level. Its structure and spatial characteristics show a much more selective process of extermination that could be considered as extensive yet not massive. It is for this same reason that the organization of the site does not deal with masses but shows rather a dual process: on the one hand, concentration of the detained in the so-called LRD (Lugar de Reunión de Detenidos – literally, the Meeting Place for Detainees) and on the other, their strict separation from one another, especially in terms of communication, within the confines of the concentrationary space itself. It could thus be argued that they function simultaneously as both concentration and isolation camps. A fragmentary space is created that also accounts for a fragmentary organization of power and society. Its rigorously closed nature with regard to external space, linked to the superposition of legal and illegal repressive circuits (of which no explanation is given) also emphasizes the isolation of some spaces with regard to others. Internally, the camp is not organized in accordance with the productive industrial model, but rather as a deposit for dangerous waste. For nothing other than useful information is expected to be extracted from the prisoners. Once this objective has been achieved they are deposited, like toxic material, until the time of their elimination. This is why the space is relatively simple and contains places for obtaining and processing information (torture and intelligence rooms), a place for depositing (barracks or quarters), and a place of exit. What follows is the suppression of the senses as opposed to their irritation, which in conjunction with immobilization within the space and numbering means that prisoners are treated as objects or 'packages', rather than animalized. It is a form of power that does not leave inmates to die – it feeds and heals bodies while they remain inside the mechanism – but rather causes death, albeit expelling said death to an external place outside the camp. It gets rid of people while they are still alive by casting them into the ocean as if it wanted to avoid the act of committing murder directly. It even claims to foster living, as in the case of the children born in confinement. It is a biopolitical experience based on the selection-isolation-casting aside of a dysfunctional Other who is understood to be 'dangerous material'.

The black hole and vacuum in the global concentrationary network

One of the 'novelties' that the anti-terrorist war has brought with it is the existence of clandestine detention centres, such as Guantánamo, that evoke the imaginary of the concentration camp almost automatically. In January 2002, Camp X Ray – the first premises of Guantánamo – was opened and the first prisoners arrived there, hooded, in shackles and chained to one another. Initially, cages were set up outdoors within which the first 300 seized were held like captured animals without disclosing their identity.

Towards the middle of 2002, the so-called Delta camp was built on the same Guantánamo base. This was the place to which the prisoners who had so far been caged were transferred as well as where those who arrived later – also handcuffed and blindfolded – were installed. This new camp originally had some 408 cells each measuring 1.8m wide by 2.4m long. Each was fitted with a sink, a latrine and a foam rubber mattress, all encased within solid walls to block visibility and stop communication between inmates, adhering to the schemes of radical isolation operated in maximum security prisons. Given the basic facilities provided in each cell, the aim was that there should be no need to remove them from their lodgings. Those detained remained almost the whole day in individual cells, illuminated by some natural light although without being able to see outside. Shortly afterwards, the new Delta 6 camp was built. It was very similar to Delta 5 and was based on the layout of a high-security prison in the state of Indiana, its design characterized by heavy use of concrete, metal and bulletproof glass, with special isolation cells, zero personal contact and electronic systems controlling everything. Here, persons remained 22 hours a day in windowless individual steel cells, lit 24 hours a day with fluorescent lamps. Finally, a third camp called the Echo, with the same characteristics yet tougher still, kept prisoners locked up for 23 or 24 hours a day. Each cell housed one person, completely isolated from the rest, in a system of confinement close to that of 'modern' maximum security prisons. It is important to draw attention to the similarity between what are allegedly 'modern' prisons, which hold a growing percentage of people, and the concentrationary model.

In its 2008 Report, Amnesty International confirmed the passage of around 800 detainees through Guantánamo alone. It also indicated that hundreds of people were detained under *'indefinite* military custody', without being charged or put on trial, not only in Guantánamo but also in Afghanistan, not to mention thousands in Iraq. A third level of clandestine confinement (read: concentration) within the framework of the 'War on Terror' was integrated into what Amnesty International described as a real 'archipelago of prisons in the world, many of them secret' (*La Jornada*, 6 June 2005, my translation), *black holes* where 'people literally *disappear*, are detained indefinitely in secret' (William Schulz quoted in *La Jornada*, 6 June 2005, my translation and emphasis). This is a universe of exceptionality on the margins of national and international rules and of the global laws of war because of both its location and the powers that support it: a repressive mechanism on a planetary scale which means that there is no external space in which to be safe.

The location of these black sites is completely unknown, even to those who have been locked up inside them and survived. Some could be military bases or facilities managed by the CIA. Their hermetic nature seems to be absolute. Analysis of their inside space will be based on the account given by Muhammad al-Assad and other prisoners, gathered by Amnesty International. They recount that they were in:

> a facility designed specifically for imprisonment within a regime of solitary confinement: there were no decorations or illustrations of any type on the walls, the floor was stripped, there were no windows, and no

natural light. The men were *confined in absolute isolation and never spoke to anyone except their interrogators*. The guards were silent and dressed in black from head to toe – Muhammad Basmillah (another of those seized) described them as 'ninjas' – and they communicated through hand gestures (which leads us to assume that they did not want their language or country of origin identified). Inside the cells, *loudspeakers produced white noise,*[1] *a constant whirring of low intensity*. Sometimes they would reproduce Western music as well as verses of the Qur'an during the last part of the seclusion period. The electric light was kept on for 24 hours a day (...). For a whole year, they did not know what country they were in (...). In the first six to eight months, they spent almost all the time they were not asleep facing the four naked walls of their cells, which they did not leave except for interrogation. None of the men ever saw the other two, or any other detainee (...). Muhammad Bashmillah estimated that around 20 people were taken to the showers each week in the section where he was, but he does not know how many sections there were in the center.

(Amnistia Internacional, 2005, my translation and emphasis)

A prisoner also stated that the pressure of isolation was so strong that 'each time I saw a fly in my cell, I was filled with joy'. On the other hand, Mamdouh Habib recalls that Mauhammad al-Madni,[2] imprisoned for years and housed in Guantánamo in a cell close to his, 'had completely lost his mind' and heard him say: 'Speak to me, please, speak to me (...). I'm depressed (...). I need to speak with someone (...). Nobody trusts me' (Amnistia Internacional, 2006, p.5, my translation). The preparation of the space to guarantee complete spatial disorientation is remarkable, since the person does not even know what country he is in, which together with the most absolute isolation and lack of communication is known to lead to psychological unhinging.

In addition to this form of isolation, there is also the one derived from obstructing and essentially sealing off the senses – using earflaps, blinders, masks, hoods, gloves – that enforce an even more radical spatial disorientation and lack of communication. Seymour Hersh recalls that in mid-2002 a detainee considered to be

recalcitrant (...) would be fitted with a kind of straight jacket, with arms tied to the back and legs held with straps. Their eyes were covered with goggles and their heads with caps. The prisoner was later led to something similar to a kennel (...) and they were given one hour of recess. The straight jacket forced him to move, if he decided to do so, on his knees and bent at a 45 degree angle. Most would limit themselves to remain seated and withstand the heat.

(Hersh, 2004, p.34, my translation)

It is difficult to think of a more absolute restriction of movement than this.

Scarce or absent mobility in space, disorientation from the obstruction of sight and isolation of prisoners from others hold certain affinities with the techniques used in the Argentine clandestine centres. Contemporary accounts suggest a much more radical treatment in the manner and extent to which communication and movement are restricted. At the same time, other uses of the space are also incorporated. Saturation by means of *white noise* or loud music and intermittent lighting, as is mentioned in some testimonies, are forms of simultaneous disturbance of sight and hearing which increase spatial disorientation. They cause psychological unhinging through procedures for disorientation and lack of communication by blocking, altering or saturating the senses, in accordance with the passage from a disciplinary society to a society that interweaves discipline and control (Hardt and Negri, 2000, p.330).

Death happens inside the camp and, although it is caused in a direct manner, it favours leaving to die over emptying out of the subject. When on occasions, however, the corpse does appear, what is presented is not the body but rather a photograph of it. Such is the case with one of the most famous images captured in Abu Ghraib by Sabina Harmon, where she appears, smiling and giving a thumbs-up next to a corpse bearing signs of torture. Death is no longer at the centre as something sinister, but instead is trivialized like a theatrical work, as if the real were barely more than fiction.

To conclude, concentration in the so-called war against terror takes place in a global space that does not recognize any sort of 'outside'. It is managed by the legal intelligence services that themselves create illegal underground networks in order to establish a permanent state of exception that coexists with forms of state governed by the rule of law. It is not massive or multitudinous, as in the previous case studies, but operates on those sectors of the population considered to be 'dangerous' and defined as 'terrorists' wherever they may be on the planet. It is a mechanism for radical isolation with regards to the society that surrounds it, the natural environment, between prisoners and their captors, and among prisoners themselves. Concrete, metal, bulletproof glass and technology are interposed between people. They create spaces of radical confinement, both with regard to the outside and in its internal organization, forming a sort of black hole – a non-place – without specific localization. It is a space that 'creates neither singular identity nor relations; only solitude and similitude' (Augé, 1995, p.103). There is no communication within it, individuals are not identified, socialized or localized beyond entry or exit from this hole. It is a space prepared for the disconnection of inmates from one another and between them and the outside, while the mechanism itself remains perfectly connected to the power networks that feed it. It could be considered a space that selectively handles processes of connection and disconnection.

Likewise, for those who are trapped inside, by undergoing an almost absolute restriction of movement and communication, the subject is stripped of his or her human condition; reduced merely to his or her biological condition. S/he is also attacked in that (biological) condition, via the sealing off or saturation of the senses, completely disorienting and unhinging him or her both physically and psychologically. It is a power that is not interested in using the physical power of the prisoner, or even the information s/he may possess, since it can keep people in this way even when s/he does not have anything useful to contribute. It is directed at the pre-emptive emptying out of the Other – a stranger who *could* be dangerous – by spoiling bodies and minds leading to the dissolution of the person. It can kill, but above all it leaves to die. In this sense, it is the consummation of what Hannah Arendt foresaw as the aim of totalitarianism. It is a biopolitical experience based on the isolation – emptying out of an Other who is barely potentially 'dangerous'.

Concentrationary models have therefore gone from a lack of communication as a result of a diversity of languages, to a lack of communication owing to prohibition of the spoken word, and then to a lack of communication in terms of any verbal, physical or visual contact whatsoever. The degree of isolation increases, a sign not only of its own transformation, but also of those societies that maintain them. There is a shift from the mass model of the factory-quarter to the fragmentation of the pit-deposit, to the black hole of a non-place.

There is also a transition from causing death to simply leaving to die; from the treatment of the subject as animal to his or her treatment as a disposable object and finally to the detainee as an empty shell, whose death is completely trivialized. These are all diverse forms of construction and extermination of the Other who is unremittingly excluded and eliminated, whether s/he represents a real threat or is subject to a pre-emptive course of action.

Notes

1. White noise consists of a type of signal that can be used both to disorient people and as a technique for sensory privation.
2. This is a person detained in Indonesia in 2002 and later transferred to Egypt, where he 'disappeared'. He reappeared in Guantánamo in 2004. He lacks written representation and news of him came from other prisoners who had been liberated.

Bibliography

Amnistía Internacional (AI). 2005. 'Documento – Estados Unidos/Yemen. Reclusión secreta en los "lugares negros" de la CIA'. AI Index: AMR 51/177/2005. http://www.amnesty.org/es/library/asset/AMR51/177/2005/es/47fa9b47-d493-11dd-8a23-d58a49c0d652/amr511772005es.html, date accessed 15 March 2014.

Amnistía Internacional (AI). 2006. 'Estados Unidos. Guantánamo: Vidas desgarradas'. AI Index: AMR 51/007/2006. https://doc.es.amnesty.org/cgi-bin/ai/BRSCGI?CMD= VERDOC&BASE=SIAI&SORT=-FPUB&DOCR=1&RNG=10&FMT=SIAIWEB3.fmt& SEPARADOR=&&TITU=VIDAS+DESGARRADAS, date accessed 15 March 2014.
Augé, Marc. 1995. *Non-Places: An Introduction to Supermodernity*. London: Verso.
Calveiro, Pilar. 1998. *Poder y desaparición*. Buenos Aires: Colihue.
Conadep. 1991. *Nunca más*. Buenos Aires: Eudeba.
Hardt, Michael and Antonio Negri. 2000. *Empire*. Cambridge: Harvard University Press.
Hersh, Seymour. 2004. *Obediencia debida*. Mexico: Aguilar.
La Jornada. 2005. 'Estados Unidos ha creado un archipiélago de centro de detención, denuncia AI'. 6 June 2005. México. http://www.jornada.unam.mx/2005/06/06/index.php?section=mundo&article=032n1mun, date accessed 13 March 2014.
Levi, Primo. 2004 (1958). *If This Is a Man and The Truce*, translated by Stuart Wolf. London: Abacus.
Levi, Primo. 2013. (1986). *The Drowned and the Saved*, translated by Raymond Rosenthal. London: Abacus.
Musitano, Adriana. 1991. *Poéticas de lo cadavérico*. Córdoba: Ediciones Comunicarte.
Tassin, Étienne. 2002. 'Totalitarisme'. In *Dictionnaire critique de la mondialisation (GERM)*, edited by Cynthia Ghorra-Gobin. Paris: Le Pré aux Clercs.

15
Imaginary Cities, Violence and Memory: A Literary Mapping

Gudrun Rath

The city and the imaginary

Imaginary cities, cities which do not exist as concrete geographical places, enjoy a long tradition in the history of Latin America. Juan Rulfo's eerie ghost town of Comala, which formed the setting for *Pedro Páramo* in 1955, is part of this tradition and stands alongside cities of unparalleled international repute, such as Macondo in *Cien años de soledad* (One Hundred Years of Solitude) by Gabriel García Márquez. The powerful reach of Macondo extended as far as the outskirts of Vienna, where its name was given to a housing estate inhabited by former refugees.[1] The imaginary map of Latin America also contains such cities as Juan Carlos Onetti's Santa María, which is located to the south of Buenos Aires and forms the common spatial context for his trilogy of novels *La vida breve* (A Brief Life), *El astillero* (The Shipyard) and *Juntacadáveres* (Body Snatcher), or Rodrigo Fresán's Canciones Tristes, the city with no fixed position on the map. Of course, imaginary cities are not restricted exclusively to Latin America.[2] As Mabel Moraña points out it is quite possible that, since its violent colonization, Latin America has been a *locus of desire*, a space that has conjured up not only utopias of a longed-for Arcadia, but also imaginary places of rejection which reveal more about the constitution of European societies at that particular time than about the so-called newly discovered continent (Moraña, 2006, p.32). Nevertheless, the density of imaginary cities on the map of Latin America raises a variety of questions, questions associated especially with the functions of imaginary space, the relationship between real, imaginary and symbolic space, as well as the anatomy of art and its role in society. These questions become increasingly demanding when they involve scenarios of violence and repression. If we follow Cornelius Castoriadis and view imaginary cities as part of the 'social imaginary' (Castoriadis, 1994), then they are to be understood not as something that opposes social reality but as a fundamental and creative part of it. They can be understood as what he referred to as the 'radical imagination' (Castoriadis, 1994, p.136 onwards) – unprecedentedly novel ideas emerging from the human psyche – which is not limited to the representation, reproduction or reshaping of the already given. Consequently, this chapter will focus on the following questions: what are the functions of an imaginary city that condenses violence and repression? Can it conceptualize resistance to repressive systems? How can such a *mapping* be understood in a larger cultural and historical context, insofar as it is not confined to the mimetic function of literature, but also includes 'the right to the city' (Harvey, 2012) in aesthetic production? So now, let's embark on our first voyage.

Sleepless in the non-city

In 1985, just two years after the end of the military dictatorship in Argentina, the Argentine author Marcelo Cohen published his novel *Insomnio* in exile in Barcelona. The setting is the imaginary city of Bardas de Krámer in Patagonia, named after its tycoon founder. But the age of industry has long since passed for Bardas. Spies populate the public space that, reduced to places of transition, have become non-places (Augé, 1995). Decay and economic depression shape the city alongside the sleeplessness that defines the title and is also largely responsible for its urban dreariness. In addition to this, Bardas de Krámer is unquestionably a city with no way out. It is sealed off by the *fuerza interamericana* (the Inter-American Military Forces), and the only chance of leaving lies in a daily mass media event: a television lottery with the telling name of *El Parte* promises the winner a ticket into exile.

So far, so fantastic. For in the case of Cohen's Bardas de Krámer, it is undeniably the use of 'reality shifting' strategies which decisively shapes what he calls the 'realistic uncertainty', the 'realismo incierto' (Chiani, 2001, p.1) and moves his novel in the direction of science fiction. Nevertheless, the powerful oppressiveness triggered by *Insomnio* is based on the novel's explicit proximity to the 'real'. After all, everything could well have been like this and, especially in the light of its appearance shortly after the end of Argentina's military dictatorship, the novel reads like a commentary on the country's history of politically motivated state repression. And even though the latter is not explicitly named, the cultural 'continuity of repressive signs' (Chiani, 2001, p.1) forms a constant trail in Marcelo Cohen's texts.

So the question is: based on Cohen's Bardas de Krámer, how can we conceive the function of imaginary space within the context of societal violence? A glance at the map of imaginary cities in Latin America reveals a clear continuous presence of – individual or state motivated – violence which makes the imaginary cities palpable as social narratives. In Juan Carlos Onetti's *La vida breve*, for example, the spatial doubling between Santa María and Buenos Aires is heightened through the split personality of the protagonist. While using a different name he feels free to unleash his violent fantasies on his female neighbour, so that the construction of the imaginary space is accompanied by a sketch of a society that is even more strongly shaped by gender hierarchies and hegemonic masculinity than the actual social order. Similarly, in Juan Villoro's 1991 novel *El disparo de Argón* (The Argon Shot) a whole new imaginary district was added to the extant area of Mexico City, and in it the human organ Mafia pursues its illegal activities in an eye clinic. This can be read as a commentary framed in spatial categories that validly applies to experiences of social violence in Mexico – violence that is still virulent to this day. In our final example, Juan Rulfo's *Pedro Páramo*, this correlation between the spatial imaginary and societal violence prompted a psychoanalytical investigation of the text's imaginary space, the city of Comala, which is entirely inhabited by dead people (and the narrator). This approach is based on psychoanalytical parameters and investigates both the individual and the collective level in society. In the first case, Comala was viewed as an example of an oedipal mother–son relationship, while in the second, society's overall experience of violence during the Mexican Revolution formed the key collective focus (Bastos and Molloy, 1977; Martín, 2001).[3] In both cases the basic point of departure was a condensation of social constellations in the imaginary space, and the imaginary city became a microcosm of the 'imagined community' (Anderson, 1991).[4] In this sense, imaginary cities can be understood as spatial models which condense social, political, historical or literary debates (Heffes, 2008, p.22).[5]

The most recent example in this context is probably Roberto Bolaño's counterpart to Ciudad Juárez, the imaginary city of Santa Teresa in his novel *2666*, which focuses on the endless series of femicides (*femicidios*) targeting women factory workers on the Mexican-North American border.[6] *2666* condenses the savage murders into a 'forensic report' which provides such vividly precise and accurately detailed descriptions of the tortured female bodies that it makes the fact that these murders are invariably perpetrated without prosecution even more incomprehensible. While the name of the imaginary city to which these murders are transferred alludes to a surplus of neighbourly love via the reference to Mother Teresa, some of the corpses are dumped on mountains of rubbish, thus representing the bloody, penalty-free 'trash' production of global capitalism. Consequently, *2666* plays out all the possibilities of the crime novel within the protected space of the imaginary Santa Teresa in order to deal with the utterly inconceivable nature of the events in its counterpart Ciudad Juárez.

But the possibilities of imaginary cities extend far beyond this mimetic function. They are not merely restricted to pure problems of representation, nor do they simply depict society in, for instance, allegorical or mythical terms; they also fulfil more concrete social functions, as I would now like to discuss.[7] Again, in the concrete case of *2666* these social functions can be outlined with the concepts of 'denuncia' (accusation) and 'testimonio' (testimony) which have become increasingly relevant in society over the past decades in view of the human rights violations committed by military dictatorships throughout the continent, and have become established as a genre that dissolves the borders between fiction and factuality in favour of a space that for the first time actually creates the possibility of witness testimonies.[8]

This function of articulation and accusation can also be applied to non-contemporary social conflicts. In fact, the translation of a problem into spatial categories has existed as one of the best-known mnemonic techniques since antiquity.[9] Cicero already mentioned memorizing in spatial parameters in *De oratore*. In the case of Comala, Jörg Dünne has plausibly argued that the conception of an imaginary space not only fulfils a memorizing function but also one that, by use of the imagination, creates a *compositio loci*, as formulated in the *Spiritual Exercises* of Ignatius Loyola in the sixteenth century (Dünne, 2008, p.94). According to Loyola, the purpose of the *compositio loci* does not lie in the exact reconstruction of a geographical place, but in the imaginative composition which, departing from the visual level, promotes the development of the senses, such as touch, smell, voice and so on. With this in mind, the conception of imaginary cities can, like classical and early modern mnemonic techniques, be seen as a visualization strategy that transposes the articulation of social problems to a visual level.[10]

According to Rosalba Campra these mnemonic techniques and imaginative concepts can also be understood as attempts to imagine social order, for which spatial visualization – and especially the constantly recurring rectangular grid layout in Latin American urban design – is particularly suitable as a rationalization strategy (Campra, 1994, p.33). However, viewed from a historical perspective, it appears in this context that such imaginary schemata for the establishment of order are not only relevant as individual mnemonic techniques of social processes, but were already in process of implementation in connection with power and hierarchy from the very beginning of colonization in America. In his classic study *La ciudad letrada* (The Lettered City), Ángel Rama stressed the connections between urban planning and the creation of order in the Latin American context. In contrast to the organically developed European cities of the Middle Ages, the colonial urban designers rigorously applied a new model in the Americas which was based on strictly ordered geometric patterns (Rama, 1984, p.17 onwards). As Rama demonstrates in his study, these represented the transposition of power relationships into the public space where the geometrical order directly reflected the imposition of a strict, hierarchical social order.[11] Consequently, social 'discipline' had its counterpart in urban planning measures which openly demonstrated the power relationships for all of the inhabitants. These measures laid down the social structures in a 'regime of transmission' (Rama, 1998, p.21) – from top to bottom, from Spain to America. In this way, geometrical urban alignment was implemented in order to preclude the development of any kind of social 'disorder'. In this context, Rama ascribes a central role to symbolic representation by means of which the hegemonic groups of the *letrados* – the colonial apparatus of civil servants, clerics and writers who commanded the skills of reading and writing – clearly stipulated urban power relationships through written and graphic depictions on maps prior to their actual existence. In so doing, the 'order of signs' superimposed their potency over the real and left their traces upon it (Rama, 1998, p.24).[12] According to this historical perspective, the possibility of 'thinking the city' was determined by the distribution of power in the colonial system and was closely linked with the 'ownership' of letters. In contrast to these early modern imaginings of the city later imaginary cities that emerged in the context of state motivated repression – such as Marcelo Cohen's Bardas de Krámer – can be read as societal counter-concepts that demand their 'right to the city' in this way.

But before we come to these aspects of resistance, we need to address another aspect in connection with the visual character of imaginary cities. Beyond the above-mentioned imaginary and rationalizing functions, the visual character that is inherent in imaginary cities also initiates other processes, especially of collective memory. In this sense they fulfil the function of an archive based on visual parameters. In the case of Marcelo Cohen's *Insomnio*, it could be argued in keeping with Michel Butor that here 'the city as text' primarily functions as an 'archive city' (Butor, 1992) translating the collective memory of the Argentine military junta's repression into spatial and thus visual parameters, that is, not by precise mimetic reproduction and documentation of the situation at that time, but by the spatial condensation of a social climate of repression and permanent surveillance. This archive function is strengthened by the fact that the protagonist in Cohen's novel, Ezequiel, is one of the few inhabitants of the city who has not forgotten how to read or write. He earns his living from reading and writing assignments, thus personifying the interrelationships and the significance of memory and writing to which Jan and Aleida Assmann have repeatedly drawn attention.[13]

Patagonia rebelde: Memory, resistance and the future

In the case of *Insomnio* the archive aspect is also present in another respect. Although Bardas de Krámer is an imaginary city, it is nevertheless set in the real Patagonia and thus in a space that is multiply occupied through Argentina's history. The location of the city invokes historical political events within that space, ranging from the violent suppression of the indigenous population and the distribution of the latifundias among financial investors from abroad, in the so-called desert campaign of 1879, to anarchist resistance activities (Bergero, 2002, p.36). As Adriana Bergero has convincingly shown, the latter are especially interwoven with Patagonia as a space of the imagination which, after all, was the starting point of anarchist groupings in the nineteenth century that were crushed with brutal state repression (Bergero, 2002, p.37).

Even though Bardas de Krámer lies in a space that is seemingly detached from the Argentine capital of Buenos Aires, it is precisely this 'outside' that can only be filled with meaning when understood in its relationship to the events on the 'inside'. The locating of Bardas de Krámer in Patagonia recalls a kind of historical dualism that was already present in Sarmiento's 1845 text, *Facundo: Civilización y barbarie*, since it portrayed the social disparities between the supposedly civilized capital and the supposedly barbaric pampa. In addition to this, Bardas de Krámer is depicted as a city which, during its era of industrial prosperity, acted as a magnet for migrants from around the globe. As a result, other cities in the novel dissociate themselves from Bardas de Krámer as a 'diaspora city'. Consequently, these phenomena should be read against the historical context of Argentina's immigrant society which, according to the intentions of statesmen such as Sarmiento, would bring about the 'civilizing' of Patagonia by 'genuine' Europeans following the genocide of the indigenous population. However, contrary to this vision, Argentine immigration policy above all attracted the poorest social classes from the south of Europe and political activists (Copertari, 2009, p.118; Grimson, 2007). So *Insomnio* also taps into this layer of collective memory while updating it within the context of neoliberalism and repression. The fact that Bardas de Krámer is set in a space that is simultaneously occupied by numerous layers of Argentina's historical memory indicates how crucial it is to consider references to repression and resistance.

Echoes of this are present in *Insomnio*, for instance in the sketches of practices of urban resistance, the most obvious of which is the visible practice of graffiti that most likely could only be deciphered by the few inhabitants capable of reading. This practice, which since its inception has been closely linked with urban space, emphasizes – just like the writer Ezequiel – the resistance potential of writing as a medium that unites the ability to criticize and think autonomously within discourse in the written form.[14] The repressive order that characterizes Bardas de Krámer is inundated with graffiti messages that have no clearly interpretable meaning. Resistance in the 'enclave' (Bergero, 2002, p.35) is conceived as an invasion of signs in the regimented order of the city, signs which defy any clear connotations with *langue* and *parole*.

But it is also apparent that precisely these aspects articulate the special temporality of imaginary cities, a temporality that focuses equally on the past and the future. In the case of *Insomnio*, attention has repeatedly been drawn to the neoliberal tendencies of de-industrialization and de-individualization, the tension between global and local, and the parallel mounting surveillance of civil society, which the novel already anticipates in the mid-1980s (Bergero, 2002, p.35). So, besides fulfilling the archive and memory functions that have already been mentioned, the novel also fulfils a prophetic function (see also Logie, 2008).[15]

Hence, imaginary cities not only condense spatial conceptions but are also distinguished by superimposed temporal layers, which particularly accentuate their model character. In this respect they function as a specific variant of the chronotope with a connection to real political circumstances, as Mikhail Bakhtin has amply emphasized (Bakhtin, 2008).

But one thing in particular distinguishes the model character of imaginary cities, and this aspect can also be traced within the theme of resistance: on the one hand, imaginary cities bring together theory and practice by conceptually sketching the imaginary space, while on the other hand making it accessible and visualizable. Thus, in Lefebvre's sense, they produce the space that they theoretically present, and consequently these model cities display a high level of performativity (Heffes, 2008, p.15). However, the immediacy of this performativity manifests itself not only through the text cities themselves, but above all through their role within society, which I will now examine as intervention.

The imaginary city as intervention

The discussion in urban studies surrounding the role of the 'urban imaginary' (*imaginarios urbanos*) already dates back some years. In the case of Néstor García Canclini, one of the most well-known exponents in this field, *imaginarios urbanos* represents an area of the imaginary – which Canclini understands more in the socio-cultural than in the Lacanian sense – which extends beyond empirical traceability and is thus located in the niches and ambivalent zones of knowledge (García Canclini, 2007, p.90).[16] The question about which role can be ascribed to these *imaginarios urbanos*, when they involve forms of aesthetic-artistic articulation, was last most productively addressed by Joaquín Barriendos Rodríguez who highlighted the connections between aesthetic-artistic articulations and the immediate social effects of the *imaginarios urbanos* (Barriendos Rodríguez, 2009). In the context of social problems in the growing metropolises of Latin America, Barriendos Rodríguez sees the *imaginarios urbanos* as a strategy of political appropriation which should be considered against the background of increasing social inequality and social exclusion. In this respect Barriendos Rodríguez sees aesthetic-political practices as practical tools that can be applied in the metropolises as counter interventions against capitalist and gentrification mechanisms:

> Nevertheless, niches appear where the fields of reflection in visual studies, the political dimension of the *imaginarios urbanos* and the strategies of critical confrontation with contemporary artistic practices intersect, niches to imagine, propose and realise more balanced living conditions.

[...] If one avoids all forms of aesthetic idealisation, it is possible to re-articulate new forms of representing public space from the field of art, so that it functions as a hinge between the micro-political action of the *imaginarios urbanos* and the tactics of appropriating 'places' by the citizenry. In this sense, the *imaginarios urbanos* can function as elements in which not only expectations, habits and users of the public space are reflected, but also the micro-urban or micro-political practices to which Michel de Certeau referred in relation to the awareness of everyday life.

(Barriendos Rodríguez, 2009)

Even though in the case of repressive systems, 'more balanced living conditions' seem less important than political overthrow, I would nevertheless like to read the conception of imaginary cities as a form of aesthetic-political production and, in the sense of Barriendos Rodríguez, as a possibility of intervention, which not only depicts the social inequalities but also intervenes in social discussions as a performative element. For Rodríguez 'the aesthetic micro-politics are [...] thus epistemological motors on a small scale which can become the source of powerful social transformations' (Barriendos Rodríguez, 2009). Let us hope that hegemonic urban designers are also able to read these micro-political signs. By producing and traversing imaginary cities, writers assert 'the right to the city' that David Harvey so vehemently demanded (Harvey, 2012) but in aesthetic space.

Notes

1. See http://nachbarschaftsgartenmacondo.blogspot.com. This also includes the passionate Anti-Macondo Manifesto of the 'McOndo' generation, but also Anna Jagdmann's account of the discovery of a map of Macondo, see Jagdmann (2006). Villoro (2007) addresses the relevance of Macondo as a construct.
2. Two examples that spring to mind are Italo Calvino's *Le città invisibile* or William Faulkner's imaginary county of Yoknapatawpha. Interestingly, Onetti also translated Faulkner, which leads to intertextual aspects in Onetti's own imaginary cities. But as Sylvia Molloy (1991) has skilfully shown in the case of Borges's Buenos Aires, such processes not only affect imaginary cities, as understood in this contribution, but also extend to other concepts of the city. In her examination of the development of urban fiction in Latin America, Beatrix Ta (2007) detected a process that moves from representations with 'realistic' nineteenth-century aspirations to what Ta calls 'virtual' city imaginations. And, despite their differing terminology, this is where the twentieth-century texts examined in this chapter can be located.
3. Indeed, in Martín's view (2001, p.128) this correlation between psychological and topical space also explodes the differentiation between reality and fiction: 'El paisaje físico deviene ficción, paisaje mental y afectivo. Éste, a su vez, deviene reflejo del mundo externo. Ficción y realidad llegan a ser términos que, en definitiva, se incluyen mutuamente; de ahí que la narrativa rulfiana escape a los cánones literarios de la corriente regionalista'.
4. Also in this context see Jean Franco (1997).

5. In contrast to the title of her study, Heffes does not concentrate exclusively on imaginary cities, but also includes urban utopias of the nineteenth century.
6. On Bolaño's *2666* see Cánovas (2009).
7. On allegory and myth in this context, see Logie (2008) and Campra (1994).
8. In this respect Edgardo Berg (2009) stresses the function of imaginary cities in the sense of Roberto Arlt's 'máquina simbólica' which permanently oscillates between the poles of 'deseo' (desire), 'testimonio' and 'denuncia'.
9. See also Mahlke in this volume.
10. It is in this sense that Isabel Quintano (2004, p.249) refers to the significance of visuality for urban space in the context of Juan Villoro's *El disparo de argón*.
11. On this topic Rama (Rama, 1984/1998, p.19) remarks:

> La palabra clave de todo este sistema es la palabra *orden*, ambigua en español como un dios Jano (el/la), activamente desarrollada por las tres mayores estructuras institucionalizadas (la Iglesia, el Ejército, la Administración) y de obligado manejo en cualquiera de los sistemas clasificatorios (historia natural, arquitectura, geometría) de conformidad con las definiciones recibidas del término [...].

See also Jorge Luis Romero's study *La ciudad y las ideas* for a similar argument from a historical perspective.

12. In his study on the geopoetics of Latin America, Fernando Aínsa describes this process in the sense of an 'aesthetic appropriation' of American topography (Aínsa, 2005, p.6).
13. See for example Assmann (2001). Incidentally, a similar constellation can be found not only in Cohen's *Insomnio* but also in García Marquez' *Cien años de soledad*, where the most severe symptom of the erupting 'insomnia plague' is the inhabitants' loss of memory. Here again, the loss of memory, which develops gradually with the loss of childhood memories, names and things, finally to end in the loss of memory about oneself as a person, is linked up with the theme of the written form:

> Este cruel destino obliga a colocar letreros a todo. De ahí el cartel que ponen a la entrada del pueblo con la leyenda de *Macondo* y el que colocan en la calle principal y que pregona que *Dios existe*. Lo que los atribulados habitantes del pueblo no podían prever era que se trataba de una realidad escurridiza, capturada fugazmente por las palabras, 'pero que había de fugarse sin remedio cuando olvidaran los valores de la letra escrita'. Y es Melquíades, quien regresó de la muerte porque no pudo soportar la soledad y 'decide refugiarse en aquel rincón del mundo todavía no descubierto por la muerte', el que libera a Macondo de la peste del insomnio. El pueblo recupera sus recuerdos y José Arcadio Buendía y el gitano renuevan su amistad.
> (Zuluaga 2004/2007, online resource)

Similarly, in Juan Carlos Onetti's Santa María the construction of the imaginary city is linked at a meta-level with the ownership of writing. See Becerra (1991).

14. Cf. Baudrillard (1978), and for a specific history of graffito in Argentina see Claudia Kozak's study *Contra la pared* (2004).
15. In this respect it can, as Ilse Logie (2008) aptly remarks, be ranked among the 'Postales del porvenir', the 'postcards from the future', which Fernando Reati (2006) analyses in his book of the same title. According to Reati's categorization, Bardas de Krámer has post-apocalyptic traits and can thus be included

among a series of texts which in the 1980s already anticipate the consequences of neoliberalism under Carlos Menem.
16. For a critical review of the discussion see Gorelik (2002).

Bibliography

Aínsa, Fernando. 2005. 'Propuestas para una geopoética latinoamericana'. *Archipielago*, 13/50: 4–10.
Anderson, Benedict. 1991. *Imagined Communities*. London: Verso.
Assmann, Aleida. 2001. 'Speichern oder erinnern? Das kulturelle Gedächtnis zwischen Archiv und Kanon'. In *Speicher des Gedächtnisses: Bibliotheken, Museen, Archive*, edited by Moritz Csáky and Peter Stachel. Vienna: Passagen, 15–29. On-line at: Kakanien Revisited http://www.kakanien.ac.at/beitr/theorie/AAssmann1/, date accessed 1 March 2013.
Augé, Marc. 1995. *Non-Places: Introduction to an Anthropology of Supermodernity*. London and New York: Verso.
Bakhtin, Mikhail. 2008. *Chronotopos*, translated by M. Dewey. Berlin: Suhrkamp.
Barriendos Rodríguez, Joaquín. 2009. 'Kunst im Stadtraum und die Politisierung der imaginarios urbanos in lateinamerikanischen Großstädten'. *Symbolische Barrikaden. Bildpunkt*, http://www.igbildendekunst.at/bildpunkt/2009/symbolischebarrikaden/rodriguez.htm, date accessed 1 October 2013.
Bastos, Maria Luisa and Silvia Molloy. 1977. 'La estrella junto a la luna: variantes de la figura materna en Pedro Páramo'. *MLN*, 92/2: 246–268.
Baudrillard, Jean. 1978. *Kool Killer oder der Aufstand der Zeichen*, translated by Hans-Joachim Metzger. Berlin: Merve.
Becerra, Eduardo. 1991. 'Santa María de Onetti: Autodestrucción y ficción literaria'. *Anales de literatura hispanoamericana*, 20: 219–241. On-line at: revistas.ucm.es/fll/02104547/articulos/ALHI9191110219A.PDF, date accessed 1 March 2013.
Berg, Edgardo H. 2009. 'Los relatos de la ciudad: papeles de trabajo'. *Espéculo: Revista de Estudios Literarios*, 42. On-line at: https://pendientedemigracion.ucm.es/info/especulo/numero42/relaciud.html, date accessed 1 March 2013.
Bergero, Andrea. 2002. 'Desindustrialización, espacio global y gestión colectiva en *Insomnio* de Marcelo Cohen'. *Hispamerica*, 31/93: 35–47.
Bolaño, Roberto. 2005 (2004). *2666*. Barcelona: Anagrama.
Butor, Michel. 1992. *Die Stadt als Text*. Graz et al: Literaturverlag Droschl.
Campra, Rosalba. 1994. 'La ciudad en el discurso literario'. *SYC*, 5: 19–39.
Cánovas, Rodrigo. 2009. 'Fichando "La parte de los crímenes", de Roberto Bolaño, incluido en su libro postumo 2666'. *Anales de la literatura chilena*, 10/11: 241–249. On-line at: http://analesliteraturachilena.cl/wp-content/uploads/2011/05/a11_14.pdf, date accessed 1 March 2013.
Castoriadis, Cornelius. 1994. 'Radical Imagination and the Social Instituting Imaginary'. In *Rethinking Imagination: Culture and Creativity*, edited by Gillian Robinson and John Rundell. London: Routledge, 136–154.
Certeau, Michel. 2006. 'Praktiken im Raum'. In *Raumtheorie. Grundlagentexte aus Philosophie und Kulturwissenschaften*, edited by Jörg Dünne and Stephan Günzel. Frankfurt a.M.: Suhrkamp, 343–353.
Chiani, Miriam. 2001. 'Represión, exilio, utopía y contrautopía: Sobre Marcelo Cohen'. *Orbis Tertius*, 4. On-line at: http://www.orbistertius.unlp.edu.ar/numeros/numero-8/articulos/01-chiani, date accessed 1 October 2013.

Cohen, Marcelo. 1986. *Insomnio*. Barcelona: Muchnik Editores.
Copertari, Gabriela. 2009. *Desintegración y justicia en el cine argentino contemporáneo*. Woodbridge: Támesis.
Dünne, Jörg. 2008. 'Entre *compositio loci* y fotografía: Juan Rulfo y las imagenes'. In *Ficciones de los medios en la periferia. Técnicas de comunicacioìn en la literatura hispanoamericana moderna*, edited by Wolfram Nitsch, Matei Chihaia and Alejandra Torres. Köln, Universitäts- und Stadtbibliothek Köln (Kölner elektronische Schriftenreihe, 1), 85–98.
Foucault, Michel. 2006. 'Von anderen Räumen'. In *Raumtheorie. Grundlagentexte aus Philosophie und Kulturwissenschaften*, edited by Jörg Dünne and Stephan Günzel. Frankfurt a.M.: Suhrkamp, 317–329.
Franco, Jean. 1997. 'The Nation as Imagined Community'. *Cultural Politics*, 11: 130–140.
García Canclini, Néstor. 1999. *Imaginarios urbanos*. Buenos Aires: Eudeba.
García Márquez, Gabriel. 1971. *Cien años de soledad*. Buenos Aires: Editorial Sudamericana.
Gorelik, Adrián. 2002. 'Imaginarios urbanos e imaginación urbana: Para un recorrido por los lugares comunes de los estudios culturales urbanos'. *EURE* (Santiago), 28/83: 125–136.
Grimson, Alejandro. 2007. 'Migration: The Experience of Argentina'. In *Cultures and Globalization: Conflicts and Tensions*, edited by Helmut Anheier and Yudhishthir Raj Isar. Wiltshire: Sage, 264–271.
Harvey, David. 2012. *Rebel Cities: From the Right to the City to the Urban Revolution*. New York: Verso Books.
Heffes, Gisela. 2008. *Las ciudades imaginarias en la literatura latinoamericana*. Rosario: Beatriz Viterbo.
Jagdmann, Anna. 2006. 'Diario del hallazgo del mapa de Macondo. Santafé de Bogotá, 19 a 25 de septiembre de 2003'. *Revista de Crítica Literaria Latinoamericana*, 32/63–64: 283–295.
Kozak, Claudia. 1998. 'Ciudades bajo palabra. Literatura y memoria en el fin de siglo'. http://www.celarg.org/int/arch_publi/kosakb6.pdf, date accessed 1October 2013.
Kozak, C. 2004. *Contra la pared. Sobre grafitis, pintadas y otras intervenciones urbanas*. Buenos Aires: Libros del Rojas.
Lefebvre, Henri. 2006. 'Die Produktion des Raums'. In *Raumtheorie. Grundlagentexte aus Philosophie und Kulturwissenschaften*, edited by Jörg Dünne and Stephan Günzel. Frankfurt a.M.: Suhrkamp, 330–342.
Lindón, Alicia. 2007. 'Diálogo con Néstor García Canclini¿ 'Qué son los imaginarios y cómo actúan en la ciudad?'. *Eure*, 33/99: 89–99.
Logie, I. 2008. 'Avatares de un mito: manifestaciones del apocalipsis en la literatura rioplatense contemporánea: el caso de Insomnio de Marcelo Cohen'. In *Les sujets contemporains et leurs mythes en Espagne et en Amérique Latine*, edited by P. Petrich, J. Premat, M. Llombart. Paris: Paris 8 Université, 1–10. On-line at: http://www.cervantesvirtual.com/obra/avatares-de-un-mito-manifestaciones-del-apocalipsis-en-la-literatura-contempornea-rioplatense-el-caso-de-insomnio-de-marcelo-cohen-0/, date accessed 1 October 2013.
Martín, Marina. 2001. 'Espacio urbano y espacio "psíquico" en Juan Rulfo'. *Revista Hispánica Moderna*, 54/1: 126–139.
Molloy, Silvia. 1999. 'Flâneries textuales: Borges, Benjamin y Baudelaire'. *Variaciones Borges*, 8. http://www.borges.pitt.edu/bsol/documents/0803.pdf, date accessed 1 March 2013.

Moraña, Mabel. 2006. 'Latin American Cultural Studies: When, Where, Why?' In *Debating Hispanic Studies: Reflections on Our Disciplines*, edited by Luis Martín-Estudillo, Francisco Ocampo and Nicholas Spadaccini. Hispanic Issues On Line: 1 (Fall 2006). http://spanport.cla.umn.edu/publications/HispanicIssues/hispanic-issues-online/hispanic, date accessed I October 2013.

Onetti, Juan Carlos. 1950. *La vida breve*. Buenos Aires: Sudamericana.

Quintana, Isabel. 2004. 'Topografías urbanas de fin de siglo: Las formas de la mirada en la literatura mexicana'. *Revista de Crítica Literaria Latinoamericana*, 30/59: 249–266.

Rama, Angel. 1998 (1984). *La ciudad letrada*. Montevideo: Arca.

Reati, Fernando. 2006. *Postales del porvenir: la literatura de anticipación en la Argentina neoliberal (1985–1999)*. Buenos Aires: Editorial Biblos.

Romero, José Luis. 1976. *Latinoamérica: las ciudades y las ideas*. México, Madrid and Buenos Aires: Siglo Veintiuno Editores.

Ta, Beatrix. 2007. *Von Städten des Realen zu Städten des Imaginären. Entwicklungstendenzen im hispanoamerikanischen Stadtroman des 20. Jahrhunderts*. München: Martin Meidenbauer.

Villoro, Juan. 2007. 'Lección de arena: "Pedro Páramo" '. On-line at: http://www.casamerica.es/txt/casa-de-america-madrid/agenda/literatura/ciudades-imaginadas/leccion-de-arena-pedro-paramo, date accessed 1 March 2013.

Zuluaga, Conrado. 2004/2007. 'Macondo, geografía y novela'. On-line at: http://www.casamerica.es/txt/casa-de-america-madrid/agenda/literatura/ciudades-imaginadas/macondo-geografia-y-novela, date accessed 1 March 2013.

16
Occupied Squares and the Urban 'State of Exception': In, Against and Beyond the City of Enclaves

Stavros Stavrides

What has been described as the 'Squares Movement' (Giovanopoulos and Mitropoulos, 2011) has emerged almost unexpectedly in many metropolises throughout the world. People gathered in central city squares, in many cases stayed there for days and used these spaces as spaces of protest and action. At the beginning there was the eruption of dissident social movements in the Arab world. The Tunisian revolt against Ben Ali's dictatorship was followed by a similar uprising in Egypt and in other countries in North Africa and Middle East. People created encampments in important city squares and defended their right to demand democracy against usually very violent police attacks.

Encampments as a form of prolonged and generalized protest against corrupt and unjust governments soon spread to many large cities of the rest of the world. In Madrid, Barcelona, Athens, New York, London, Tel Aviv, Nicosia but also Montreal and Rio de Janeiro, people occupied squares in an effort to fight devastating austerity policies and economic and social inequality. What these movements shared was a remarkable horizontality in forms of decision making and organization as well as an explicit effort to defend citizen rights in the name of a sought-after 'real democracy'. The Squares Movement took many forms during 2011 and had differing results in the corresponding countries. But it has managed through collective acts of coordinated protest and self-management to re-invent dissident politics.

What seems to have connected those acts, which were nevertheless highly inventive and differentiated, was a generalized demand for justice and democracy, along with a common will to establish new forms of egalitarian collective action. This movement emerged as an inherently urban expression of dissident politics which developed new forms of reclaiming and performing public space as common, that is as a space which is created and maintained through practices of collective sharing (Stavrides, 2014, p.58). In the occupied squares, acts of protest and outrage were combined with important collective experiments in search of potential forms of collective action and organized everydayness based on direct democracy and equality. And these experiments were directly expressed in and through urban space. They actually created new and paradigmatic, albeit ephemeral, forms of egalitarian urban coexistence.

Even though they were exceptional and short lived, the urban experiments of the Squares Movement have produced an interesting counterexample to the prevailing urban model of the 'city of enclaves'. What this chapter will attempt to trace is the way this counterexample developed in relation to a crucial characteristic of the enclave city: the inherently urban 'state of exception' which today produces a specific form of urban order based on the situated suspension of specific citizen rights and obligations. In, against and beyond the enclave city (to borrow Holloway's phrase), dissident squares created glimpses of a possible 'city of thresholds'. Might this be one of the forms a 'real state of emergency' would take were it to reverse and transcend the process by which the dominant state of emergency becomes the rule (Benjamin, 1992, p.248)?

Contemporary urban order

Despite postmodernist praise for the alleged randomness of the contemporary urban environment and attempts to think of today's cities as aleatory combinations of spaces and multiple spatialities, contemporary metropolises are characterized by a dominant spatial order. True, we no longer experience the clearly defined spatial hierarchies of pre-industrial and industrial cities, but contemporary cities develop and are controlled through a distinct spatial logic which contributes to the reproduction of current capitalist societies. This logic is clearly distinguished from modernist zoning logic, which prescribed a form of urban order based on the idea of a structured arrangement of the different basic functions which supposedly constitute the city. Compared to this modernist logic, which managed partially to control the modern city form (exemplary cases are Brasilia as prototype city, British New Towns and various satellite cities throughout the world including the former 'Eastern Block' cities), today's urban 'chaos' seems to present the paradigmatic opposite to urban order. However, behind the image of chaos and pure contingency lies a different form of spatial order: the order of an urban archipelago.

If the image of an archipelago is valid in describing a new type of urban order, how does this image correspond to existing urban arrangements? Bearing in mind that this image attempts merely to construct a model that is meant to capture the crucial characteristics of contemporary cities in terms of their spatial organization, we should recognize in this image a foundational distinction; urban 'islands' are distinct from urban 'sea'. As in an archipelago, urban islands are self-contained worlds with recognizable boundaries, which communicate in various ways and in various degrees through the sea than extends between them. Whereas, however, the sea of a geographical archipelago remains a natural medium, which is humanized through use, in the urban archipelago the urban sea is an important and integral part of urban order. Urban sea is the space of flows that surrounds and connects urban islands, urban sea is what makes the city work as a whole, no matter how divided urban space is.

There must be an organizing principle that maintains the distinction between urban islands and urban sea. This principle must have its roots in the very raison d' être of any spatial order which is to ensure and express the reproduction of the corresponding social order. If contemporary capitalist societies are being reproduced through forms of government based on biopolitics, then the organizing principle of urban order must necessarily be compatible with biopolitical premises.

Biopolitics marks for Foucault a period in which state power is expressed and reproduced through practices aimed at the control of a population that is extensively studied and classified, and is under constant surveillance. Biopolitics extends the realm of politics to the very biological processes through which human life is made possible, reproducible and, thus, socially productive (Foucault, 2008, p.21 and 2007, pp.449–451).

Biopolitics separates, classifies, and controls different types of individuals in order to make them productive and obedient. Thus, biopolitics is not simply expressed in spatial ordering but necessarily employs specific spatial arrangements to impose its rules, and to ensure the exercise of a specific form of power: biopower. According to Foucault, biopower is a 'set of mechanisms through which the basic biological features of the human species became the object of a political strategy, of a general strategy of power' (Foucault, 2007, p.16). We could say that biopolitics gives new meaning to the age-old techniques of power which aim at controlling subjects through separation and spatial enclosure. Biopower is disciplinary and productive because, to borrow Deleuze's description of Foucault's essential discovery, it manages 'to concentrate; to distribute in space; to order in time; to compose a productive force within the dimension of space-time, whose effect will be greater than the sum of its component forces' (Deleuze, 1992, p.3).

The peculiar islands of the urban archipelago come into existence as biopolitical enclosures, as biopolitical enclaves: closed and controlled environments in which specific types of individuals and behaviours are moulded. Urban islands are defined as specific locations which correspond to a vast organizing taxonomy of 'types of life' that are compatible with the logic of the corresponding society. The city of enclaves is 'an archipelago of "normalized enclosures"' (Soja, 2000, p.299). This results in a taxonomy of essentially discontinuous urban spaces. Between the urban islands there remains a not easily definable and controllable medium, the urban sea, on which spatial discontinuity is projected and through which it is maintained.

Foucault has brilliantly studied the prison, the hospital, the army barracks, the school and the factory as characteristic enclosures of the disciplinary society. But he has not directed his attention to those spaces of flow that constitute the very organizing tissue of contemporary and modern cities: streets, squares and residual and abandoned urban spaces. Those spaces are not outside the reach of biopower. Power, however, is exercised in them in a different way. Control is metastatic and usually assumes the form of a test. Police road blocks, for example, normally search for deviant behaviours through sampling, that is, acts of selective scrutiny. If urban enclaves are shaped and controlled through explicit protocols of use that bind their inhabitants, the urban sea is shaped and controlled by acts of sampling that attempt to impose regulated forms of public behaviour (Stavrides, 2010).

The urban archipelago is thus a complex form of spatial order which is reproduced by biopolitical techniques of government. Because of its complexity this kind of spatial order is not obvious nor is it permanent. It is (as perhaps any kind of spatial order is), a project rather than an accomplished state. Island enclaves are constantly being formed and their perimeter is secured by various systems of control, as their entrances-exits are symbolically supervised by regulating rituals. Urban islands can be closed neighbourhoods (gated communities or ghettos), corporate towers, large sports stadiums, shopping centres and shopping malls and airports.

Perhaps what Deleuze defines as a passage from disciplinary societies to societies of control (Deleuze, 1992) is rather a new biopolitical synthesis which further elaborates techniques of social discipline by combining enclosures (characteristic of disciplinary power) with modulating regulations which mould flows through metastasis. In societies of control, according to Deleuze, one faces 'metastable states coexisting in one and the same modulation, like a universal system of deformation' (Deleuze, 1992, p.5). These metastable states are indeed characteristic of the systems of control (and, therefore, creation) of the urban sea. Urban islands, however, are still being produced and maintained in the form of urban disciplinary enclosures.

It seems that Foucault and Agamben have provided us with different but compatible (or even complementary) models through which we can recognize the hidden matrix of biopower. This hidden matrix appears to have been developed through the mechanism of exception: although biopower aims at the support of normality, it does so by recourse to the definition of the abnormal and its paradigmatic separation and confinement (Dreyfus and Rabinow, 1983, p.195). This claim constitutes the main thread that connects Foucault's studies and research. According to this reasoning, the control of the abnormal and the corresponding reproduction of the normal permeate all forms of biopolitics. Agamben, on the other hand, defines exception as the hidden mechanism through which power is established as sovereignty.

Sovereign power is the power which can declare a state of exception, and sovereign power is exercised and legitimized through this act (Agamben, 2005, p.35).

The importance of the mechanism of exception as a propelling force of biopolitics can be shown in the comparison of two spatial models through which Foucault and Agamben respectively try to think about biopower and biopolitics. For Foucault, the 'plague stricken town' (Foucault, 1995, pp.195–198) became the laboratory of ascendant biopower: in a situation of emergency, to control the plague, authorities had to control the population, had to know where everybody was, in what conditions, and with what kinds of symptoms. The state was legitimized to invade the private domain of *oikos* and there to extend its regulating power. People's lives were directly and forcefully connected to the mechanisms of biopolitics.

Agamben revisits the image of the plague stricken city considered as a biopolitical matrix, in a short article he has written on the 'red zones' constructed to close off the centre of Genoa during the meeting of G8 leaders in 2001. Genoa's red zone literally produced a temporary urban enclave, a contemporary 'forbidden city' inside the city (Agamben, 2001). As in the case of the plague-stricken city, he says, in Genoa authorities sought to secure those parts of the city that were important for the exercise of power (in the case of plague, those parts had been rich neighbourhoods and the civic centre), while leaving the rest of the city more or less unguarded (as the authorities left the poor neighbourhoods largely unprotected during the plague's spread). Under such circumstances of exception Genoa was temporarily transformed into a paradigmatic biopolitical spatial matrix in which the creation of an enormous enclave citadel was combined with the metastatic sampling control prevailing over the rest of the city.

In both Agamben's and Foucault's use of the model of the plague stricken city, exceptional circumstances play a crucial role. In both, authorities exercise power in the name of the protection of society. And because the threat appears sudden and exceptional, authorities are legitimized in taking extra measures to override collective and individual rights: to suspend the law.

As we know, Agamben has explicitly focused on the state of exception which he considers, as 'a space devoid of law, a zone of anomie in which all legal determinations – and above all the very distinction between public and private – are deactivated' (Agamben, 2005, p.50). Both the plague-stricken and the riot-stricken cities are instantiations of such a 'space devoid of law'. Biopower systematically destroyed (and keeps on destroying) the distinction between public and private.

Although Agamben has been rightly criticized for constructing an ontology of the state of exception considered as the generative mechanism of sovereign power (Ek, 2006 and Mills, 2008) a claim that leads to the assumption, that 'politics is always already biopolitics' (Lemke, 2005, p.6), his contribution to the understanding of the mechanism of exception is very important. He has clearly discerned that the state of exception is neither outside the law nor inside it. Law is present in its suspension, exception is established in the name of law, order is broken in order to be saved (Agamben, 2005, p.46).

Biopower, therefore, is not some kind of total and absolute power, it is power that is exercised upon subjects who have partially or totally lost their rights, but only temporarily or under circumstances which are definable. The mechanism of exception is used to create processes that limit as well as distribute rights. The subjects of biopower are not only those who are reduced to 'bare life' (Agamben, 1998, p.7) but also those who are defined as subjects-citizens through various processes of exclusion. Exclusion is always an exception and, to generalize Holston's observations on Brazilian society, 'a differentiated citizenship... is universally inclusive in membership and massively inegalitarian in distribution' (Holston, 2008, pp.5 and 193).

If the limit figure of biopolitical project is 'bare life', then the 'absolute biopolitical space' (Agamben, 2000, p.41) is the Nazi extermination camp. According to Agamben, in this spatial arrangement, in which humans were reduced to biological life without rights and, were therefore 'abandoned by law' (Agamben, 1998, p.28) exception became the rule. The camp is not a space of exception (Agamben, 2005, p.170) but a space of normalized exception. This can only mean that inside the camp a state of exception has produced a new, localized normality. Because this kind of normality is based on the suspension of law, it does not take the form of law. It is rather being constructed through a ruthless administrative reason which supervises an 'abnormal normality', to use a paradoxical phrase. It is because the camp materializes the state of exception in the form of a secluded enclave (in which rules appear to be based on administrative reason alone without recourse to general rights), that the camp can expose the mechanisms that sustain today's enclave spatiality. In every urban enclave general laws and rights are suspended and special kinds of rules apply. The force of law passes over to protocols of use (actually protocols of behaviour). To be in any urban enclave one has to follow those protocols. In gated communities, for example, there exist specific 'legal agreements which tie the residents to a common code of conduct' (Atkinson and Blandy, 2005, p.178).

Biopower sustains the urban archipelago as a discontinuous and highly complex spatial order, which contains urban enclaves as well as the vast sea of urban flows. The mechanism of exception helps to maintain the secluded life of each and every enclave, without letting the city disintegrate into an agglomerate of rival micro-worlds. Centralized, not dispersed, political decisions still constitute the body of biopolitics and major power centres, such as national states and international corporations, still define the general rules of this society's reproduction. The city itself may appear as 'splintered' (Graham and Marvin, 2001) but it does not dissolve into an 'incoherent overall structure' that contains 'solipsistic enclaves' (Diken and Bagge Lautsten, 2005, p.96).

Contemporary city-dwellers learn to inhabit exception, they learn to adapt to exception. Enclaves of dwelling, leisure and work define those who inhabit them temporarily or permanently by shaping their habits and behaviour. Importantly, those who are forced to live on the borders of bare life can barely escape the enclaves in which they are trapped (refugee detention centres, isolated sweat-shops, and so on). Biopolitical choices may even create literal camps in the form of non-urban locations ('black sites' such as the secret CIA prisons or Guantánamo) in which people with no rights at all are exposed to bare, unmediated power (Minca, 2007, p.94). These spaces, however, cannot be taken as paradigmatic 'urban' enclaves but as the extreme case at the far end of a discontinuous spectrum of different spatializations of exception.

Identity crisis in the occupied squares: Beyond enclave-defined citizenship

Enclave spatiality does not merely ensure the controlled distribution of urban 'functions' (or 'uses') and urban 'users'. Enclave inhabitants, those, that is, who are allowed or forced under certain conditions to spend their lives in specific enclaves, are defined and classified by the very process which creates and sustains the complex order of the urban archipelago. Enclaves identify and classify citizens. The mechanism of normalized exception moulds and distributes different social roles as well as different social life forms.

The Squares Movement has put into crisis this spatially imposed and reproduced system of classification which supports the biopolitical government of urban populations. By producing a different kind of spatiotemporal exception, this movement created an important crisis in dominant identity reproduction mechanisms.

Holloway has, in a way, pre-figured this crisis in his criticism of identity politics. 'Identity', he maintains, 'is an illusion really generated by the struggle [of dominant capitalist power] to identify the non-identical. We, the non-identical, fight against this identification' (Holloway, 2002, p.10). In the context of contemporary biopower, social identities as well as political identities (even those that are being created in the process of struggle) tend to be trapped in the classificatory matrix of biopolitical control. When resistances are named and circumscribed in this taxonomy they cease to be fundamentally threatening to the reproduction of social order. Holloway goes as far as to say that 'identity is the reproduction of capital within anti-capitalist struggle' (Holloway, 2010, p.113). Identification of the subjects of political actions is thus considered as a process which creates the necessary conditions for the neutralization of such actions.

Hardt and Negri also attack identity politics but with the aim to 'work through it and learn from it' (Hardt and Negri, 2009, p.326) in order to go beyond it towards an 'abolition of identity' (Hardt and Negri, 2009, p.326). Their analysis of the potential tasks of a struggle against the dominant systems of identity classifications meets Holloway's ideas on the struggle against identifications. Both theories maintain that the very process of circumscribing the actions and representations which differentiate people into a stable and recognizable set of identities depends upon the logic of domination. Hardt and Negri, through the concept of 'singularities', which (as opposed to identities) are inherently multiple and oriented towards multiplicity (Hardt and Negri, 2009, p.339) and Holloway through the concept of the 'flow of doing' (Holloway, 2002 and 2010) which transcends any form of identification of the doer, try to propose a potential politics beyond identity.

Different life experiences, different life histories and different pre-existing identities (based on profession, political choices, descent, ideologies and so on) intersected in the occupied squares. But people neither did simply perform those identities, nor did they simply reproduce their personal life narratives. People discovered common needs and aspirations as well as a will to go beyond what had defined them so far. As if in a melting pot of identities people experienced powerful, albeit fleeting, combinations of identifying expressions that sometimes shattered deeply rooted convictions. For example, was the waving of the national flag in the occupied squares a simple and straightforward expression of nationalism? For people humiliated by authoritarian governments and violently unjust policies, a national flag might appear as an object which emblematizes collective dignity and struggle. A person, who literally wore a Greek flag in Syntagma square occupation, had written on it: 'Please don't sell my country'. In Tahrir Square, Cairo, after Mubarak's fall spontaneous festivities included lots of flag waving and dancing (Alexander, 2011, p.65). Weren't those people reclaiming their country rather than trying to express a national identity?

In the squares encounters took place between people who did not share an already established common world (a world defined by common interests or ideologies). According to Rancière, for politics to happen, this world should be 'a polemical distribution of modes of being and "occupations" in a space of possibilities' (Rancière, 2006, p.42). Politics in the squares has moved beyond the barriers of the consensus that biopolitics neatly crafts day after day. Politics has resurfaced as the contested terrain which brings into view 'newcomers' (Rancière, 2010, pp.59–60), those who were excluded from dominant taxonomies of roles and identities, those who had no voice or 'legitimate' opinions. Rancière's newcomers were clearly visible in the occupied squares. Not only because some people entered the central scene of politics for the first time (as, for example, women in the squares of the Arab Spring) but because some people found ways to transcend their identities: a doctor in the medical centre of Syntagma Square was more than a doctor, a student participating in the media team more than a student, a member of the 'organized groups of underprivileged football fans' who fought against the police in defence of the Tahrir Square occupation was no longer a mere 'hooligan' (Abul-Magd, 2012, p.566).

Occupied squares as thresholds

Those who occupied the squares, ordinary people as well as activists, created a different kind of a space of exception. In the process of protesting against the dominant rules that define citizenship, the occupiers experimented with new rules of collective organization meant to re-create direct democracy. If those rules had remained trapped in a well-defined urban enclave and had been established with no regulating mechanisms to ensure equal participation, they would have been transformed into one more enclave-bound use protocol. In the squares, however, exactly because rules of coordination and cooperation were constantly assessed and collectively created, they rather opened occupied space to newcomers and to new ideas. In urban enclaves exception creates a trap: local rules describe users who abandon certain rights or acquire certain privileges (in both cases certain general laws are suspended). Exception encloses, exception defines, exception separates. In the squares, exception opens boundaries, exception acquires a metastasizing power, exception upsets dominant taxonomies and spatial order.

In the occupied squares a common space was invented through those very practices which attempted to experiment with forms of a new emergent public culture of cooperation and solidarity. Common space thus was always a stake rather than an accomplished state of spatial relations. Common space happened in the squares. Common space came into existence when occupiers tried to construct their temporary tent cities with their many micro-centres and their corresponding micro-communities. In Syntagma Square,

> [e]ach micro-square had its own group of people who lived there for some days, in their tents, people who focused their actions and their micro-urban environment on a specific task: a children's playground, a free reading and meditation area, a homeless campaign meeting point, a 'time bank'... a first aid center, a multimedia group, a translation group stand and so on
>
> (Stavrides, 2012, p.588)

Every such microcosm became part of a larger one which was inclusive and always under construction. According to a commentator, the Occupy Wall Street area 'has become many things. Public square. Carnival. Place to get news. Daycare centre. Health care centre. Concert venue. Library. Performance space. School' (Stoller, 2011 as quoted in Castañeda, 2012).

In Barcelona, 'Once the Plaza de Cataluña was "occupied", a small semi-autonomous town was born within it...Walking through the camp, one would see single and collective tents as well as booths hosting commissions, libraries and book sales' (Castañeda, 2012, p.312).

If enclave spatiality prevails in the contemporary biopolitical city, threshold spatiality characterizes the emerging common spaces of the occupied squares. Threshold spaces are in-between spaces, spaces that come into existence because they permit crossings and create relations of comparison between adjacent areas. Urban thresholds connect and separate at the same time, and thus create areas that are not defined by their perimeter but are always open to relational and dynamic definitions.

Threshold spaces, as we know from anthropology, mediate, express and symbolize transitions, transformations, changes in status and identity for those who cross them (Turner, 1974 and 1977, Van Gennep, 1960). Societies have constructed and imagined thresholds in order to mark rites of passage, to exorcise external threats, and to supervise regular role changes for their members. But societies have always known that in the experience and the imaginary of threshold crossing the potentiality of change is emphatically present. That is why societies try to control thresholds. People who experience in-betweenness may defy the rules of controlled belonging and may discover the power of comparison which opens established identities to otherness. On thresholds classificatory power trembles, on thresholds biopolitics falters.

Common space emerged in the occupied squares as threshold space. Projecting their practices and their temporary spatial arrangements on to the monumental spaces of authorized publicness, the occupiers of the squares created crossings rather than strongholds. They produced spatial relations that were in a constant clash with the imposed routines of the central public space they chose to occupy. Common space thus became the locus, the expression and the necessary ingredient of an emerging public life which was striving to go beyond dominant urban order (Stavrides, 2014, pp.58–59). In the middle of urban archipelagos, common space created proliferating connections, osmotic gestures that defied established spatial boundaries.

Occupied squares implicitly opened thresholds in social time too. Upsetting the normalizing routines of public space they opened possibilities for new collective habits: everyday life in the tent cities produced opportunities for festive events, discussions, creative acts and collective initiatives of organized co-habitation. Walter Benjamin suggests that revolutionary classes are characterized by 'the awareness that they are about to make the continuum of history explode' (Benjamin, 1992, p.253). Maybe this awareness was not emphatically present in the occupied squares. Or maybe it was present at least to some, especially in the squares of the Arab Spring where people openly defined what they did as revolution (in Tunisia the uprising was called 'the Jasmine Revolution'). However, historical continuity as a narrative of progress was explicitly challenged in the squares. As a highly publicized placard held up in Madrid's Puerta del Sol Square said: 'Nobody expects the #Spanish Revolution'.[1] By introducing new ways of understanding the past, by reclaiming and reinterpreting past struggles for dignity and democracy, the Squares Movement understood its present as a threshold, a possible turning point in history, in which people demand a change of course. Giving new meaning to spaces marked by the traces of important public events, the Squares Movement opened the past to the future.

Conclusion

In contemporary biopolitical urban environments, the mechanism of exception produces barriers of separation and enclaves governed through local specific rules. A state of exception is declared in periods of crisis in contemporary cities and this justifies extra measures to control space. But the state of exception characterizes the everyday normality that is reproduced in contemporary urban enclosures. Exceptional normality is presented as normalized exception and is justified as necessary through a functional administrative discourse. In our times people must learn to inhabit exception as if it were normality.

In the Squares Movement a different form of urban exception emerged. Occupied squares threatened the urban normality of the biopolitical city which is founded on the urban state of exception. Occupied squares produced a perhaps precarious and fleeting but also powerful and promising state of exception that looks very much like that envisaged by Benjamin: a real state of exception, a deep and uncompromising suspension of those dominant laws which guarantee the reproduction of social order. During this brief, exceptional period citizenship was exposed as inherently exclusionary and selective. A true state of spatiotemporal exception, thus, reversed the characteristics of the dominant exception. In place of the latter's ordering and disciplinary mechanisms, occupied squares produced mechanisms of sharing and cooperation. Enclave spatiality was confronted with a threshold spatiality which sustains encounters and mutual awareness. In the squares exception opened history and space to the possibility of change and to the dynamics of transformation. Instead of binding exception to normality, the Squares Movement opened exception to possibility, to the creative forms of collective inventiveness. In such a prospect 'exception destroys normality instead of becoming normality's supporting mechanism' (Stavrides, 2010, p.37).

An emerging city of thresholds is against and beyond the city of enclaves. An emerging history of thresholds is created by people who defy dominant historical narratives. Was the experiment of occupied squares which erupted in 2011 only a series of examples of popular unrest or a turning point in the history of contemporary biopolitical spatiotemporal and social order? It remains to be seen.

As this text was being written, people have flooded the squares of São Paulo and Rio, demanding that the increase in bus fares be cancelled. Maybe their most impressive slogan can be taken to hint towards a possible answer to the question just posed: 'It is not about 20 cents'. Maybe it was about everything, everything that obstructs the emergence of a just world.

Note

1. The photo is available at http://boingboing.net/2011/05/17/nobody-expects-the-s.html, accessed 2 May 2014.

Bibliography

Abul-Magd, Zeinab. 2012. 'Occupying Tahrir Square: The Myths and the Realities of the Egyptian Revolution'. *South Atlantic Quarterly*, 111/3 (Summer): 585–596.
Agamben, Giorgio. 1998. *Homo Sacer: Sovereign Power and Bare Life*. Stanford: Stanford University Press.
Agamben, Giorgio. 2000. *Means Without End: Notes on Politics*. Minneapolis: University of Minnesota Press.
Agamben, Giorgio. 2001. 'Genova e il Nuovo Ordine Mondiale'. *Il Manifesto*, 25 July 2001.
Agamben, Giorgio. 2005. *State of Exception*. Chicago: The University of Chicago Press.
Alexander, Jeffrey C. 2011. *Performative Revolution in Egypt: An Essay in Cultural Power*. New York: Bloomsbury Academic.
Atkinson, Rowland and Sarah Blandy. 2005. 'Introduction: International Perspectives on the New Enclavism and the Rise of Gated Communities'. *Housing Studies*, 20/2: 177–186.
Benjamin, Walter. 1992. 'Theses on the Philosophy of History'. In *Illuminations*, edited by Walter Benjamin. London: Fontana Press.
Castañeda, Ernesto. 2012. 'The Indignados of Spain: A Precedent to Occupy Wall Street'. *Social Movement Studies*, 11/3-4: 309–319.
Deleuze, Gilles. 1992. 'Postscript on the Societies of Control'. *October*, 59: 3–7.
Diken, Bülent and Carsten Bagge Laustsen. 2005. *The Culture of Exception: Sociology Facing the Camp*. London: Routledge.
Dreyfus, Hubert L. and Paul Rabinow. 1983. *Michel Foucault: Beyond Structuralism and Hermeneutics*. Chicago: The University of Chicago Press.
Ek, Richard. 2006. 'Giorgio Agamben and the Spatialities of the Camp: An Introduction'. *Geografiska Annaler*, 88/B (4): 363–386.
Foucault, Michel. 1995. *Discipline and Punish: The Birth of the Prison*. New York: Vintage Books.
Foucault, Michel. 2007. *Security, Territory, Population: Lectures at the College de France, 1977–1978*. Basingstoke: Palgrave Macmillan.
Foucault, Michel. 2008. *The Birth of Biopolitics: Lectures at the College de France, 1978–1979*. Basingstoke: Palgrave Macmillan.
Giovanopoulos, Christos and Dimitris Mitropoulos. eds. 2011. *Democracy Under Construction*. Athens: A/synexeia Editions, in Greek.

Graham, Stephen and Simon Marvin. 2001. *Splintering Urbanism: Networked Infrastructures, Technological Mobilities and the Urban Condition*. London: Routledge.
Hardt, Michael and Antonio Negri. 2009. *Commonwealth*. Cambridge: Harvard University Press.
Holloway, John. 2002. *Change the World Without Taking Power*. London: Pluto Press.
Holloway, John. 2010. *Crack Capitalism*. London: Pluto Press.
Holston, James. 2008. *Insurgent Citizenship: Disjunctions of Democracy and Modernity in Brazil*. Princeton: Princeton University Press.
Lemke, Thomas. 2005. 'A Zone of Indistinction. A Critique of Giorgio Agamben's Concept of Biopolitics'. *Outlines*, 1: 3–13.
Mills, Catherine. 2008. *The Philosophy of Agamben*. Montreal: McGill-Queen's University Press.
Minca, Claudio. 2007. 'Agamben's Geographies of Modernity'. *Political Geography*, 26: 78–97.
Rancière, Jacques. 2006. *The Politics of Aesthetics*. London: Continuum.
Rancière, Jacques. 2010. *Dissensus: On Politics and Aesthetics*. London: Continuum.
Soja, Edward W. 2000. *Postmetropolis: Critical Studies of Cities and Regions*. Malden: Blackwell.
Stavrides, Stavros. 2010. *Towards the City of Thresholds*. Trento: Professionaldreamers.
Stavrides, Stavros. 2012. 'Squares in Movement'. *South Atlantic Quarterly*, 111/3 (Summer): 585–596.
Stavrides, Stavros. 2013. 'Contested Urban Rhythms: From the Industrial City to the Post Industrial Urban Archipelago'. In *Urban Rhythms: Mobilities, Space and Interaction in the Contemporary City*, edited by Robin J. Smith and Kevin Hetherington. London: Wiley-Blackwell.
Stavrides, Stavros. 2014. 'Open Space Appropriations and the Potentialities of a "City of Thresholds"'. In *Terrain Vague: Interstices at the Edge of Pale*, edited by Manuela Mariani and Patrick Barron. New York: Routledge.
Stoller, Matt. 2011. 'The Anti-Politics of #OccupyWallStreet', http://www.nakedcapitalism.com/2011/10/matt-stoller-the-anti-politics-of-occupywallstreet.html, date accessed 25 February 2014.
Turner, Victor W. 1974. *Dramas, Fields and Metaphors: Symbolic Action in Human Society*. Ithaca: Cornell University Press.
Turner, Victor W. 1977. *The Ritual Process*. Ithaca: Cornell University Press.
Van Gennep, Arnold. 1960. *The Rites of Passage*. London: Routledge and Kegan Paul.
Zibechi, Raul. 2010. *Dispersing Power: Social Movements as Anti-State Forces*. Oakland: AK Press.

17
'Memory, that Powerful Political Force'

Interview with David Harvey

Estela Schindel: *One of the subjects we are particularly interested in discussing with you is the relation between violence and the unequal distribution of space. How do you relate the spatial inequalities with violence – not only structural violence or economic violence, but also explicit forms of state violence – like state terror as it was deployed in Argentina in the 1970s?*

David Harvey: There are various ways in which you can understand violence. I tend to honour Marx's idea that the daily violence that is done to working people is at the root of a lot of difficulties and particularly at the root of alienation and frustration, and that daily violence can occur in two ways: one is through the economy of exploitation in the labour process, but there is also what I call the economy of accumulation by dispossession, which occurs very much in the living space. Historically there has been a very important relation between these two forms. For instance, if workers are strong and can start to get higher wages and better working conditions, then one of the ways in which capital recuperates what it gives workers at the point of production is by extracting much more in the way of rent, of financial services, costs and so on in their living space. One of the theses that I work with is the idea that the production of value may occur at the point of production, but the realization of that value for a capitalist class can occur in production or it can occur in the store, it can occur in the living space and capital will substitute one for the other. There is a violence that exists in the labour process but there is also a violence which exists in terms of the relationship between, for instance, landlords and tenants, between shop keepers and merchant capitalists and people who are forced to purchase their products in order to live.

The nature of violence for me is very much about different economies of appropriation, which does not necessarily involve the kind of violence that consists of hitting people over the head, although it may, of course, come to that. The state is very heavily involved in orchestrating the structures of violence, both in the work place and in the living space. Therefore, we have a state-engineered regulation of that violence to the degree that people are strong in the community and are strong in the working space. The state can be forced to be more generous as it were. But on the other hand, the capitalist class typically through financial means controls the state apparatus. Over the last 30 years we have seen an increasing way in which the state is being pushed by the forces of the capitalist class to withdraw from support for social reproduction. Basically it says to the working class: 'It is your problem how you take care of your education, it is your problem how you take care of health care, how the sick are taken care of. It is your problem; it has nothing to do with us'. We see an increasing shift of violence into state administration of that violence by the increasing withdrawal of the state in provision of public facilities, public spaces and the like and increasing privatization of much of social life. The structures of economic violence have changed very much in that direction over the last 30 or 40 years. Neo-liberalism means many different things, but one of the things it means is a shift in the form of violence, so that it becomes increasingly oppressive, both in the work place and in the living space. You have to see these joined forms of oppression and joined forms of administering violence with the state apparatus now increasingly captive to upper class and bourgeois interests and essentially doing the bidding of the wealthy, who can essentially buy politics. There is a joke in the United States that we have the best Congress that money can buy and it has become even truer than it was when Mark Twain said it a hundred years ago.

ES: *Do you think that authoritarian regimes or totalitarian regimes also display some forms of spatial politics or spatial violence? They certainly may enact policies of unequal redistribution of space, like favouring an unjust housing market, but do you think that there is also something specific about the urban policies and the design of space under authoritarian or totalitarian regimes?*

DH: Any regime of governmentality, whether it is the left or the right, is bound to have some kind of territorial policy and territorial project. In Chile in the years of the government of socialist president Salvador Allende, for instance, the neighbourhood health clinics were very important centres of militant association and there was a territoriality of what the left was doing. When Pinochet came to power they substituted that territoriality with one of hierarchical control and so destroyed the former structures of territoriality. As a general rule I would suggest that any regime would seek that structure of territoriality which is most suited to its particular political project. Just to go to the British example, Margaret Thatcher was faced with considerable resistance to her neo-liberal project by municipal governments. So she had to reform municipal government and in the end she had to abolish things like the Greater London Council because they were such centres of political opposition. She came up with a completely different structure of territoriality, which was more suited to her being able to control things. The same applies to the relationship between decentralization and centralization. There is a little bit of a myth about decentralization being a left project but it seems to me that actually capitalists have used decentralization as a means to establish centralized power. For instance the decentralization of governments in Buenos Aires seems to have been a way to make sure that power can control things much better. This is what Margaret Thatcher did to London, because the Greater London Council was controlled by the socialists, by Marxists actually, Ken Livingstone.[1] So they abolished it and then reduced power to lots of decentralized kind of units. It is interesting that in Bolivia the group that is now claiming autonomy is the bourgeoisie. Regional autonomy is now their call, because they figure that it is in their interest. One has to be careful about saying decentralization is a left strategy. In fact, whoever can find the spaces which are best suited to exert control will take the corresponding territorial strategy and that is how territorial strategies should be regarded.

ES: *In Argentina the dictatorship used policies like the modification of location contracts law, which conferred more rights to landlords or the massive eradication of shanty towns, which are also very territorialized policies of reshaping the space. But this was accompanied by a net of detention centres which served to irradiate terror into all sorts of spaces of social life. These clandestine detention centres where in some cases located next door to 'normal' family houses. Terror was thus at work not only inside but also outside of these detention facilities. The whole city was permeated by terror. Do you think that there is any specific trait particular to our cities, or to Latin American cities – or may be to the capitalist city as such – which allows concentrationary spaces to grow in the middle of the city? Pilar Calveiro for instance wrote that not every society can create the conditions for the existence of concentration camps. Can we say the same about the cities? Are there certain urban features which allow the existence of a network of clandestine torture centres in its midst? And if yes, what would a city need to be like, in order for such concentrationary spaces not to be possible?*

DH: When you think about the uneven geographical development that occurs within cities it is very difficult to generalize about it, you have to take each specific case. But when you start to look closer there are some general principles that emerge. For example, the city I lived in for many years, Baltimore, went through a process of deindustrialization and major jobs were lost. When I went to the city in 1969 more than 30,000 were employed in the steel works there. By 1990 about 5,000 people were employed in the steel works producing the same amount of steel. Just recently the steel works has finally closed down.

Now, politically when we wanted to do things, say in 1970, we would go to the steel workers. And if the steel workers and a few other big unions supported you, a lot of politics happened. Now that does not exist. Those jobs have disappeared. Blue-collar jobs have essentially disappeared from the city. The result is that you have a void in terms of what can be done in the city. The result is that there is a large sector of the population of the city that has no access to decent jobs at all. So something else they can do is turn to the drug trade. There is this famous TV series, 'The Wire', whose background is the deindustrialization of Baltimore and how it produces those spaces. And then of course those spaces become troublesome. So, the strategy becomes to seal them off in some way and then to criminalize them and turn them into spaces of oppression and control in which certain things do go on and other things cannot. This is the production of a certain kind of space. And by criminalizing the space you start to have a world in which a large number of the youth end up in prison. In the United States we have got a huge prison population now which has arisen out of this deindustrialization of the United States. And then the question arises: how can you pacify and control those areas which have become desolate and have actually become captive to the drug trade and other forms of illegal activity? And these strategies start to become generalized. So when you say 'Well in Argentina in the military period there was an attempt to pacify them, deal with them in certain ways', I would suggest that we look at it more broadly and ask the question: how is that different from what is happening in Rio's *favelas* right now with the militarization, the pacification program? It is being presented as a progressive attempt to integrate the *favela* population into the broader world when in fact it is very much about gaining access to those sites. It is also about the problem the authorities have with the Olympic Games and all those kinds of events coming up. This pacification agenda has been pioneered in Rio and is being suddenly exported to India and other places. The big question in the world right now is: how do you exercise social control over large segments of the population that have no access to decent jobs? And this has become a problem in certain parts of the world where it was not a problem before, because of deindustrialization and the like. About a fifth of the population of the United States does not have access to decent jobs now. This is a very unusual situation historically and it is being addressed by these 'pacification programs'. This gets mixed up with anti-terror surveillance, the attempt to suppress all forms of political protest, which are seen and treated in essence as potentially terrorist acts. This sort of mentality goes back to the militarism which, some people had argued, was abolished when we got rid of the military dictatorships. But it seems to me that the same processes are being repeated with a very different kind of legitimation.

ES: *Some authors are working on this proliferation of control or surveillance spaces you mention, and some would also place the CIA detention site of Guantánamo or the maquiladoras as spaces of exception or enclaves. What do you think of this approach? Do you connect that with the phenomenon you were describing?*

DH: I actually do not like Agamben's work about states of exception. What we are really looking at is the dynamics of class struggle, how the dynamics of class struggle are unfolding, not only in working spaces but also in living spaces. Living spaces are becoming sites of conflict and sites of class struggle of various kinds. That is why we are beginning to see more interest in themes like the rights of the city, because this is more about daily life in the city and what is happening to living conditions of populations in the city. There is a tendency at any one particular historical moment to find some 'continental philosopher' who has got a new wrinkle and say 'everything fits into that'. I do not think that Agamben himself actually meant it this way and I think it has been taken far too far. There is no question that what we are seeing is the militarization of urban space and the policing of urban space now becoming a very big political question and also becoming a technological question. We are seeing a lot of militaristic technologies being devoted to questions of this sort. The Israeli architect Eyal Weizman,[2] for example, studies how the Israeli Defence Force intervened in Ramallah and how it dealt with an urbanized revolt (the US military also found itself in that problem in Baghdad and Fallujah). So, there is now recognition in the military apparatus that conflicts of the future are less likely to be between territories, 'place A fighting against place B'. It is more likely to be urban revolutions and urban uprisings, urban discontent. And how do you pacify those restive urban areas? So, yes, there is a shift of that sort, but I do not think it is helped by creating a new language about states of exception. I think working people have always been 'exceptional' in some way. So that is not the way I would go with it. I would suggest that we look at the dynamics of political struggle and see how that struggle is being militarized, and how governmentality is being restructured around the control of larger and larger segments of an urban population that have no access to decent jobs and decent living environments. That is going to be a huge political problem in years to come.

ES: *Do you think that this might be the reason why in general Marxist theory did not pay much attention to the concentrationary spaces as such? Because they cannot be traced back so directly to class relations or class struggle?*

DH: I have had a struggle with the Marxists over the question of urbanization. Most of my life I have been working on a Marxist approach to urban questions. And I have always taken very seriously that most revolutionary movements have an urban dimension: the Paris Commune, or the revolution of 1848, the uprising known as the 'Cordobazo' in Argentina in 1969 or wherever. Actually most Marxists have never taken me very seriously – not until recently. I think if you said the Marxist tradition has missed out very badly by failing to see that class struggle is as much an urban phenomenon as a factory-based phenomenon, I would agree entirely and say: Look, this is what I have been trying to say since *Social Justice and the City* (1973). For the last 40 years I have been trying to say that: you have to see how these forms of struggle relate to each other, how exploitation in the work place and in the living place are related. And actually, the interesting thing about the class struggle is that even factory struggles succeed best when they are supported entirely by the surrounding community. But there is a tendency in Marxist history to write about the factory worker and to take no account of the way the women in the community were, for example, baking the food that supported them. There is a very interesting book by Margaret Kohn about radical spaces in which she argues that everybody talks about the factory councils, but nobody talks about the Houses of the People (*Casa del popolo*) which were the places where the community organized in support.[3] And that is where a lot of the politics occurred, because the gender politics in the Houses of the People were relevantly different from those in the work place. But the tendency in Marxist history is to actually concentrate on the factory worker. We should be thinking about the proletariat as all those people who produce and reproduce city life. That gives you a completely different definition of who the proletariat is and it gives you a completely different definition of what a revolutionary movement might look like. So if you said to me 'Look, the Marxist tradition has been defective', my answer would be 'Yes, I have been fighting that tradition all along and finally now they are beginning to listen to me'. But even now it is still very interesting that because I am an urbanist they say 'Well, he is one of these people over there who deal with the urban; the real stuff is over here'. That is completely wrong and I am trying to correct that. When people say 'Well, because the Marxist tradition has been rather sexist and concentrated on the male factory workers being the centre of the politics and has been place-bound in the sense that it is about the factory, not about the city; because of all of that we go off into some postmodern, or some identity politics kind of stuff or some more philosophical kind of thought' you abandon the key insights that come from Marx's theory. I think this is the wrong way to go. So, I have been trying to preserve the key insights that come from Marx's theory by arguing that it has got to become a much broader thing, that our conception of class and what class struggle says that a rent strike is a form of class struggle, a crucial form of class struggle, and a fight over health care and health clinics in neighbourhoods is a crucial form of class struggle. The unions are not necessarily involved in that in the same way, but for me the significant thing is putting all that together.

Urban social movements are often interpreted by the left as somehow rather being not political or not class struggle. What I am saying is 'No, that's not the case'. On the other hand, I think there is a difficulty in persuading an urban social movement, say, around homelessness or affordable housing or something of that kind, to see themselves in potential alliance with trade unions and people in the work place and to also have modes of organizing which politically articulate a class perspective. Many of the extant urban social movements are about their own particular problem. This is a challenge which has to be faced right now. We have to therefore start to argue for a broader based understanding of what these urban social movements might be about and this is why I think these broader ideas about, for instance, the right to the city as a collective right, the right to take back the city for the whole population, so the city can be restructured around a different kind of notion of what the labour process will be (that would produce and reproduce the city), those are the key questions which need to be approached. There is an organizational gap, but experience is growing around how to deal with that gap.

ES: *Your reflections on spaces of hope or spaces of resistance have been very inspiring to many. Going once again to the question of spatial deployment of violence and those other spaces, the places of control and surveillance: How do you think that spaces of hope can arise amidst such militarized or heavily controlled spaces?*

DH: First of all it would be entirely wrong ever to imagine that some omniscient or omnipotent power has complete control over a whole population. It never does and there are always subversive elements. As we know from what happened even within the most vicious of dictatorships there are ways of resisting, people make jokes or they sing songs or they do something else which everybody knows is subversive and so life can never be completely controlled. There are always spaces where something different is likely to be going on and something subversive is going on. The important thing about this idea of subversion is precisely that it is subversive. The left has historically found ways to subvert even through the most brutal dictatorships. And often in the process by the way it has used urban life as an organizing principle. For instance, the way in which much of the left organized against Franco in Spain was through the community organizations and the neighbourhood associations. They didn't organize it in the work place because they knew they would get killed if they did that. But you can organize. Actually the Communist Party was better in the neighbourhood organizations than it was in the work place. There you find a space in which your work becomes less suspicious and it is less easily challenged.

I think that the problem right now is not the qualities of the repressive apparatus. I think that the difficulty right now is that many of the populations that we are talking about (for instance we mentioned the case of 'The Wire': I have some problems with how things get depicted in 'The Wire', but a lot of it nevertheless has a certain truth to it) are simply caught up in the drug trade, and are drug takers and not very political. I think that the drug trade is the most sinister way of controlling political activism because that world does not want to create a socialist alternative. It wants to make a living and is making a very good one, some of it out of embedding itself within the illegality which is connected to this capitalist world. To me one of the biggest problems that exist right now is the nature of life which has arisen in the territory of 'The Wire', or the territory of the inner cities and the *favelas* and so on and is now so captive to this form of illegal capitalism. Everything is then postulated in a 'war on drugs' which can also be, of course, a political war as well as a war on drugs. But it is put in a kind of frame which seems to me to have nowhere to go politically, and is not progressive in any way whatsoever.

ES: *Speaking about the political legacies of the past, and linking it to the possible ways of identifying their traces in the city, there is this contested question about what to do with the former sites of terror, where murder and torture took place. I heard that you visited the former ESMA detention camp here in Buenos Aires. What can you tell about the experience of visiting this place?*

DH: Well, I have always valued very much this comment from Balzac: 'Hope is a memory that desires'. I think that the power of collective memory is politically very important, provided it is connected also to this notion of desiring something different. I have always been very attracted to this phrase of Balzac because it points immediately to the significance of collective memory in political action. For me, there is a great distinction between the politics based on nostalgia and a mourning of what is being lost, which I find very negative, and the politics which approaches historical memory by saying: 'We desire something different and it is on the basis on that historical memory and in honour of that historical memory that we do something very different'. What I liked about the presentation of the Disappeared in one of the spaces at the former ESMA, was that the gallery in which you see the pictures of the Disappeared is not called 'The Gallery of the Disappeared' but 'The Gallery of the Revolutionaries'.[4] This says to us that we do not have to mourn the deaths of these people and feel sad for what happened to them. Rather we have to honour what it was that they died for and we have to connect it to our own desire to complete the project that they never fulfilled. That is a very powerful idea and when it is mobilized becomes very significant. And it does get mobilized historically in certain situations. I am always very impressed with the capacity of the French to go out on the streets and stop the city. It is a historical memory and there is a French revolutionary tradition that goes back to the French revolution of 1848, the Paris Commune, and everything else. When something happens, then people respond and pick up that historical memory and say: 'Well, we can go out there and we can actually do things in a radically different way'. We have seen some of that in French political life over the last 20 years in ways we have not seen in other places. So I am thinking of the cultivation of this historical memory, of keeping this historical memory alive and attaching it to places through memorials and through things of this sort. Walter Benjamin has a very interesting way of looking at that. He distinguishes between memory and history. For him history organizes things and makes everything appear as a narrative. But memory is always unstable. He says that it flashes up at moments of danger in creative ways. I think that memory is therefore a very powerful political force. And collective memory is a very powerful political force too. So we should do everything to encourage it even though we can not manage it. And it is not history. History tries to tame memory, and guide it in certain ways. So you write the history of the United States so every school child knows the history of the United States, but it is not actually about what happened. When Howard Zinn wrote *A People's History of the United States* he was trying to say that there is a different historical memory, upon which his book is based.[5] Or when the subalterns in India started to write what it was like to be part of the subaltern classes, I think that you start to see a different history writing which is about trying to recreate possibilities for different kinds of historical memory.[6] And I think there is no way in which we could have a hope for the future that does not have some point or rather reside in some sort of conception of our historical memory of what might be possible from the past. That is an individual thing but I think that it is also collective, and it transcends generations. But it is sometimes hard to get the next generation to absorb what that collective memory was really about. And that it is one of the things that it seems to me people have to relearn for themselves in the process of struggle: that there is this collective memory. It is very interesting to go to demonstrations in the United States where you find young 18-year-olds talking to people like me and ask what was it like in the 1960s when people were revolutionary in the streets and there was social control of the cities and tanks controlling the centre of Baltimore because of the riots. 'What was it really like?' Then this historical memory comes back which is very important.

ES: *There are big discussions about the memorialization processes and how these collective memories are to be inscribed in the cities. Many people think that memorials could help us as a transmission between generations, as you* said, while others say that they can in the end act as the opposite: memorials can neutralize this desire to change things in society and just work as a 'deposit' for past memories.

DH: I think that it can be both and that is the interesting thing about it. There is no such thing as a memorial that does not have that ambivalence. On the one hand, it tries to state what it was and at the same time, in doing so, it invites to us reflect on what it really was as opposed to what it seemed to be. Having said that, I think that there are some memorials that really do work in this ambivalent way. One of my favourites is the Vietnam Memorial in Washington, which, by being underground and not heroic and posing the question in the way it does, it is troubling. I do not think anybody can go into it and not come out feeling a little bit awkward as opposed to the classical memorial of the heroic soldier with the rifle in the air or a Iwo Jima flag or something like that which turns out to be staged anyway. So, I think it is always ambivalent and that is the interesting thing about memories, that they are uncontrollable and that you never know when they are going to erupt and around what they are going to erupt.

The interview took place in Buenos Aires on 5 October 2011.

Notes

1. A member of the Left of the Labour Party, Ken Livingstone was elected as Leader of the Greater London Council in 1981. This council was abolished by Margaret Thatcher's government in 1986.
2. Eyal Weizman is an architect, Professor of Visual Cultures and Director of the Centre for Research Architecture at Goldsmiths, University of London.
3. Kohn, Margaret. 2003. *Radical Space. Building the House of the People*. Ithaca and London: Cornell University Press.
4. Harvey refers here to one of the many institutional spaces operating at the location of the former ESMA in Buenos Aires, namely the ECUNHI (Espacio Cultural Nuestros Hijos), run by the Asociación Madres de Plaza de Mayo (one of the two organizations of the Mothers of the Disappeared in Argentina).
5. Zinn, Howard. 1980. *A People's History of the United States*. New York: Harper & Row Publishers.
6. The Subaltern Studies group was formed in 1979–80 by historian Ranajit Guha and others, who developed a revisionist historiography of colonial India; they were critical of the elitist biases of dominant history writing which, in their view, distorted the historical portrayal of the subalterns or the 'people' and neglected their role in the anti-colonial struggle.

Index

Note: Locators followed by the letter 'n' refer to notes.

abject/abjection, 151, 198–9
absence and spatiality, 152–3, 156–60
absolute power, 236
'Abuelas de Plaza de Mayo' (Grandmothers of the Plaza de Mayo), 122, 129, 130n4
accumulation by dispossession, 11, 57–8
economy of, 244
active forgetting, 37
activists/activism, 136, 168, 174n13, 181–2, 191–2, 195, 198–9, 224, 239
Adorno, Theodor W., 106
aerial bombardment, 77–8, 81–4, 86, 88
aesthetic framing, 34, 38, 44
Afghanistan, 59n10, 214
Agamben, Giorgio, 5–6, 64, 123, 162, 165, 168, 172, 234–6, 248
Ahıska, Meltem, 5, 7, 9–10, 12, 162–74
air power/air raids, 77–8, 81–4, 86, 88
AKP (Justice and Development Party), Turkey, 163–4
Aktion Reinhardt, 39
Alcoba, Laura, 154
Alderman, D. H., 23, 27
Alexander, Jeffrey C., 238
Algeria, 108, 115
Allende, Salvador, 245
All-Polish Youth, 37
Almirón, Fernando, 190, 192, 200
al-Qaeda, 51
American Civil War, 77
American Jewish Committee, 41
Amnesty International, 214–15
am s'ridai charev ('the survivors of the sword'), 80
anarchist resistance activities, 223–4
Anderson, Benedict, 221
Angkorian Kingdom, 24
animalization, 207–9, 212–13, 217
anti-colonialism, 253n6
anti-monuments, 80

anti-Semitism, 37, 44
anti-terrorism, 213
anti-terror surveillance, 247
Anzacs, 88
Arab Spring, 238, 240–1
Arab world, social movements in, 231
archaeological research, 41, 43, 45n6, 140
archipelago model, 232–4
architecture, abstract elements, 86
archival installations, 136
Arendt, Hannah, 31, 123–4, 128, 217
Argentina
dictatorship (1976–83), 6, 8–9, 12, 48–56, 108, 123–4, 151–3, 155, 157, 159, 177, 186n2, 189–91, 194, 198–220, 222, 246–7, 250; appropriators, 6, 122, 126–127, 130; *Nunca más* (Never Again), 107–8, 111, 210, 212
displacement of population during dictatorship, 53–5
forced disappearance, 48–49, 52, 54, 159, 176–86
post-dictatorship fiction, 150–60
repressive practices/torture techniques, 114, 153
secret detention centres: arrival and reception of individuals, 210; chaining and forced immobility, 211–12; disappearance of children, 119–26; forms of elimination, 190–7, 200n3, 200n7, 212; fragmentary space, 210–13; haunted house, literary thematic, 153–6; identification number of prisoners, 212; isolated compartments, 211–12; located in the middle of cities, 210; remnants and recovery of the remains, 176–86; sensory and communicative isolation, 212–13;

structure and spatial characteristics, 210–13; torture and interrogation rooms, 211, 213; torture of Jewish detainees, 114
testimonial literature, 150–60, 219–26
theatre, Txi plays, 126–30
see also Tucumán *monte*
Argentine Navy Mechanics School, *see* ESMA detention centre, Argentina
Argentine Team of Forensic Anthropology, 59n7, 191
Arlt, Roberto, 227n8
armed conflict, 4, 64, 78
Armenia, Turkish policy of displacement and resettlement, 166
Armenian cemetery, 163, 173n3
Armenian Genocide, 78, 82–3, 165–6, 172, 173n6
ashes of victims, 35, 40, 42, 45n1, 46n13
assembly-line destruction/murder, 77, 88
Assmann, Aleida, viii, x, 5–6, 9, 12, 130n1, 135–49, 223, 227n13
associative afterlives, 67–8
asylums, 55
Athens, 10, 97, 231
atomic bombs, 78
Augé, Marc, 181, 216, 220
'authentic' spaces, 6, 12, 25–6, 135, 138, 144, 147–8
authoritarianism, 93, 145, 238, 245
Awerbuch, Marianne, 135–6, 147

Bakhtin, Mikhail, 106, 225
chronotope, concept of, 106–8, 113–14, 116, 117n4, 225
Bal, Mieke, 38, 45n5
Baltimore
deindustrialization of, 246–7
depicted in *The Wire*, 176
riots, 252
banality of evil, 31
barbarism, 83–4
bare life, 236–7
barracks, military, 163, 206–9, 211, 213, 234
Battiti, Florencia, 188
battlefields, 23, 62, 77, 109, 135

battle of Somme (1916), 80
Baudrillard, Jean, 227n14
Bauman, Zygmunt, 5, 190
Beckett, Samuel, 106
Benjamin, Walter, 7, 59n9, 64–5, 71n2, 83, 141, 232, 240–1, 252
Bergen Belsen Memorial, 148n7
Berlin
former Gestapo headquarters, 138–41
Holocaust memorial, 135, 146
involuntary recovery, 138–41
Jewish Museum, 79, 86–8
Prinz Albrecht Strasse, 138–9
Topography of Terror, 138–40
Bettelheim, Bruno, 107, 110–12, 114, 116
Beuys, Joseph, 84
biological transnational citizenship, 70
biopolitics, 66, 70, 119, 123–5, 127, 130, 209, 213, 217, 233–8, 240–2
biopower, 233–7
Bitburg military cemetery, 139
body(ies), the
afterlives, 67–71
'body-centred regime' of evidence and truth, 70
denial of, 127
heaped up, 61
overcrowding of, 207–9
tortured, 127, 165, 170, 191, 195, 212, 221
unveiled, 64–7
without identity, 178
Bohemia, Protectorate of, 45n3
Bolaño, Roberto, 221, 227n6
Bolivia, 52, 89, 246
bombing of civilians, 77–8
Borges, Jorge Luis, 197, 226n2
Boxer rebellion, 77
Brenner, Neil, 58
British government
Baldwin's government, 81
strategic hamlets project in Malaysia, 59n10
Thatcher's government, 245–6, 253n1
British New Towns, 232
Brodsky, Marcelo, 195
Bronfen, Elisabeth, 22
brothel, camp, 206

Buck-Morss, Susan, 64
Buenos Aires
  clandestine detention centres, *see* clandestine detention centres (Argentina)
  Le Corbusier's master plan for, 197, 199
  Parque de la Memoria (Memory Park), 188, 199
  Provincial Commission for Memory, 186n2
Bulgarians, 166
Buna, 206, 208
burial, ritual of, 156
burial grounds, 23, 42–4, 67, 115
Butler, Judith, 38–9, 44, 167, 171

Calveiro, Pilar, 5–6, 13, 107, 110, 112, 114, 123–4, 127, 153, 191, 205–17, 246
Cambodian genocide, 21–32
  as an 'autogenocide,' 25
  Choeung Ek Center for Genocide Crimes, 21, 27, 30–2
  collapse of Phnom Penh, 26–7
  CPK leadership, 25
  Democratic Kampuchea, 24, 26–7, 32
  the Khmer Rouge, 21–7, 29–32
  PRK leadership, 26–7, 29–30, 32
  S-21, Tuol Sleng Security Center, 27
  Tuol Sleng Museum of Genocide Crimes, 27, 30–1
  Vietnam's intervention, 26
Campra, Rosalba, 222, 227n7
Cano, Luis, 128, 130, 227n6
capitalism
  global, 221
  illegal, 251
  industrial, 23
  merchant, 23
  urban, 3
  war, 209
cartography, 2, 6, 51, 89, 92, 197
Caruth, Cathy, 105, 107, 171
Castells, Manuel, 61, 66
Castoriadis, Cornelius, 219
cell, 10, 29, 110–11, 208, 211, 213–15
Chandler, David P., 27–9
Chejfec, Sergio, 157–9

Chile
  Casa Grimaldi clandestine detention centre, 180
  Pinochet dictatorship, 9, 140, 245
China
  Boxer rebellion, 77
  and Cambodia, 26
  Japanese invasion of 1931, 88
  People's Republic of China, 30
  victims of poison gas warfare, 78
chronotope model, *see* Bakhtin, Mikhail
CIA, 89, 205
  Alice-in-Wonderland method, 111
  black sites, 6, 9, 13, 214–15, 237, 248
  (*see also* Guantánamo detention camp)
  Handbook of Torture, 108, 111, 116
Ciudad Juárez, 221
clandestine detention centres (Argentina)
  Automotores Orletti, 113
  Campo de Mayo, ix, 190, 192
  Club Atlético, 211
  el Atlético, 211
  el Banco, 211
  El Olimpo, 211
  ESMA, 113–14, 190–1, 211–12, 251
  La Perla, 211; memorial site, 212
  Pozo de Bánfield, 211
  Vesubio, 211
coercive techniques, 110–11, 117n3
Cohen, Marcelo, 220, 223, 227n13
collective memory, 2–3, 9, 32, 116, 151, 223–4, 251–2
Colombia, 4
Colombo, Pamela, 1–14, 48–59, 106, 115, 117n4
colonialism, 8, 24, 62, 223
common space, 69, 154, 239, 240
communication, restriction in camps, 207–8, 211–17
Communist guerrillas, 55
Communist Party, 30, 250
Compañía de Monte Ramón Rosa Jiménez, Argentina, 51
CONADEP (Comisión nacional sobre la desaparición de personas, 1984), 108, 114, 192
concentration camps, *see* Nazi concentration/extermination camps

Condor Legion, 80, 82
conventional warfare, 49
Corbusier, Le, 197, 199
Cordobazo uprising, 249
counterinsurgency, 55–6, 59n11, 108
counter-movement, 12, 162–5, 170, 172
cultural politics of grief, 38–41

Das, Veena, 8
death by hunger/starvation, 31, 208–9
death camps, 34, 39–40, 41, 43, 45n7, 107
see also Nazi concentration/extermination camps
death flights, 13, 190–9
de Certeau, Michel, 4, 226
dehumanization, 127, 209
Deleuze, Gilles, 51–2, 233–4
democracy, 58n2, 61, 63–4, 142–5, 167–8, 231–2, 241
direct, 232, 239
real, 231
Derrida, Jacques, 8, 36, 45n2, 151–2
'desaparecido' (the disappeared), 1, 107, 115, 151, 154, 188–9, 190, 199
disappearance of children in Argentina, 119–30; 'Abuelas de Plaza de Mayo' (Grandmothers of the Plaza de Mayo), 122, 129, 130n4; biopolitical practice on children, 123–4 (see also biopolitics); politics of segregation, repatriation and fostering, 121–30
remnants and recovery of the remains, 176–86
in Río de la Plata, 188–200
in Turkey, 162–73; gözaltında kayıp (disappearance under surveillance), 168
deterritorialization, 4, 11, 49, 51–2, 57, 66
Didi-Huberman, Georges, 34–5, 192, 194
Dink, Hrant, 172
'dirty war,' 205
'disappeared,' the, see 'desaparecido' (the disappeared)
Dix, Otto, 78–9, 81–2, 84
DNA profiling, 70

Dorfman, Ariel, 69
Dünne, Jörg, 222
Dziuban, Zuzanna, 5–8, 10, 34–46

Ejército Revolucionario del Pueblo (ERP), Argentina, 48
Ek, Richard, 5, 21, 235
Elden, Stuart, 4, 51–2, 58
empathy, 25, 44, 69, 110, 116
encampments, 231
enclaves, 5, 13, 224, 232–7, 239–41, 248
enforced disappearances, see 'desaparecido' (the disappeared)
ethnic engineering, 166–7
Europe, 88–9, 164, 197, 222, 224
aerial bombardment, 78, 81–4
period of revolution, 151
European Court of Human Rights, 69
exception
Agamben's definition, 234
archipelago of, 5
state of, 5–6, 13, 123, 145, 168, 176, 216, 231–41
exceptional spaces, 5–7, 166
extermination camps, see Nazi concentration/extermination camps
extraterritorial zones, 5

face and figure, war representations of human, 77–90
factory struggles, 249
fantastic genre, 12, 112–13, 117n5, 151–2
Fassin, Didier, 185
favelas, 247, 251
Feierstein, Daniel, 6
Feijoó, Cristina, 157
Felman, Shoshana, 105
femicides, 221
Ferrándiz, Francisco, 5–6, 9, 11, 61–71
Ferrari, León, 191
Filc, Judith, 121–2
First World War (1914–18) in popular culture, 79, 81–2, 84
Fogwill, Rodolfo, 194–5
Fontes, Claudia, 188, 189
forced labour camps, 31, 143, 147
forensic architecture, 4
forensic sciences, 13, 30, 69–70, 185, 221

Foucault, Michel, 5, 55–6, 66, 70, 123, 233–5
France, 45n3, 82
Franco, Jean, 226n4
Franco/Francoist regime, 1, 61, 62–3, 65, 68, 70–1, 119–21, 250
Frank, Anne, 79
Frei, Norbert, 148n7
French colonialism, 24
French revolution of 1848, 249, 252
French volunteers, 206
Fresán, Rodrigo, 219
Freud, Sigmund, 125, 140, 150–1
Friedlander, Saul, 116
fuerza interamericana (the Inter-American Military Forces), 220
Fuerzas Armadas Peronistas (Peronist Armed Forces – FAP), 59n4
funerary dislocation, 64

GAAMI (Archaeological and Anthropological Group of Memory and Identity), 186n2
Gamerro, Carlos, 154
García, Charly, 192–3
García Canclini, Néstor, 225
García Márquez, Gabriel, 219, 227n13
gated communities, 234, 236
Gatti, Gabriel, 5–6, 10, 12, 108, 112–14, 160n1, 176–86
gender, 70
  hierarchies, 221
  politics, 249
  roles, 171
Genoa's red zone, 235
genocide
  Armenian, 78, 82–3, 165–6, 172, 173n6
  Cambodian, 10, 21–32
  Jewish, 78, 84, 141, 194, 210
  Yugoslavia, 78
Germany
  attack on Guernica, 80, 82
  Condor Legion, 80, 82
  former headquarters of the Gestapo in Berlin, 138–41
  Gusen memorial, 146–7
  National Socialists, 10, 34–5, 37, 139, 141

new spatial practices of memory, 144–7
regional and local memorial sites, 143–4
stumbling stones, Demnig's, 145–6
Stuttgart, Baden-Württemberg, 141–3, 148n6; Hotel Silber as memorial site, 141–3
Gestapo, 114, 138–41, 145
ghetto, 6, 37, 91, 92, 96–7, 101–4, 205, 234
ghosts, metaphor of, 151–2
globalitarian power, 206
Gordon, Avery, 8, 151, 164–6, 170
Gorelik, Adrián, 228n16
gothic fiction, 12, 151–2
graffiti, 224
Graham, Stephen, 4, 236
Grandmothers of the Plaza de Mayo, Argentina, *see* 'Abuelas de Plaza de Mayo'
Greece, 10, 83, 137, 141, 166, 199, 238
Gregory, Derek, 7, 51
grievability, notion of, 38–41, 44–5
ground zero, 24, 177, 185
Guantánamo detention camp
  black sites, CIA, 214–15, 216
  Camp X Ray, 213
  death in, 216–17
  Delta camp, 213–14
  Echo camp, 214
  testimonies of former detainees, 214–15; Mamdouh Habib, 215; Mauhammad al-Madni, 215; Muhammad al-Assad, 214; Muhammad Basmillah, 215
  torture techniques, 213–17
  white noise, 215–16, 217n1
Guattari, Félix, 51–2
Guernica, attack in, 80
guerrillas, 11, 48–58
Guevara, Che, 89
Gypsies, 45n4, 210

Hardt, Michael, 70, 205, 216, 238
Harvey, David, 2–3, 5, 7, 10–11, 13–14, 50, 57, 66, 220, 226, 244–53
hauntology, 8, 152
historical memory, 14, 66, 68, 224, 251–2

HisTourism (Mütter), 138
Hitler, Adolf, 79, 89, 139
Holloway, John, 232, 237–8
Holocaust, 25, 78, 192, 194
  archives, 80, 89
  autobiographical writings of, 107
  memorials, 135, 138, 146
  memory in Poland, 34–46
  post-Holocaust art, 79–80, 84–9
  survivors, 80, 89, 146
human rights, 66, 69–70, 119–20, 166, 168
human rights organizations, 122, 168, 193
human rights violations, 64, 70, 169, 222

iconographies, 66, 69
identification number/code, prisoner, 183, 206, 212–13
Ignatieff, Michael, 69
imaginary cities, in Latin American literature, 219–26
Imperial War Court (Reichskriegsgericht), 138
India, 97, 247, 252, 253n6
indigenous population, 223–4
inequality, 3, 155, 225–6, 231, 244
injustice, 2, 3, 93, 141
interrogation, 21, 29, 78, 110–11, 210–11, 215
interwar years, 77–8, 80, 88–9
involuntary memory, 4, 138, 140–1, 143, 145, 148
isolation, 5, 10, 30, 54–5, 163, 181, 210–17, 237
Israeli Defence Force, 248
Istanbul, 10, 162–3, 168, 171, 173n3
Iwo Jima flag, 253

Jackson, Rosemary, 117, 159
Janicka, Elżbieta, 35–8, 44, 45n1
Japan
  invasion of China, 1931, 88
  Tsunami, 141
Jasmine Revolution, 241
JC Royal corporation, 30
Jehovah's witnesses, 145
Jelin, Elizabeth, 7

Jeremiah, book of, 80
Jewish genocide, *see* genocide
Jewish Museum, Berlin, 79, 86, 87
Jewish mysticism, 84
Jews
  extermination of, 39
  Polish anti-Semitism, 36–7
  Turkish policy of displacement and resettlement, 166
  violence against, 37, 89, 135, 145–6, 210
Job, book of, 42
judicial afterlives, 68–9

Kabbalah, 85–6
Khmer Rouge, 21–2, 24–7, 29–32
kidnapping, 48, 115, 120, 122–6, 131n6, 153, 191, 199
Kiefer, Anselm, 78, 79, 84–86, 88
killing fields, 21, 27, 30
  see also Choeung Ek
Kohan, Martín, 154
Kohl, Helmut, 139
Kohn, Margaret, 4–5, 249
Koh Sla Dam, Cambodia, 31
Koselleck, Reinhard, 148
Kristeva, Julia, 198
Kubark manual, 110
Kurds, 163, 165–6, 171, 173n6
Kwon, Heonik, 8

labour camps, 143, 206, 208–9
labour process, 244, 250
LaCapra, Dominic, 35, 105
Lam, Mai, 27, 29
Lanzmann, Claude, 34, 80
Latin America, imaginary cities, *see* imaginary cities
Latour, Bruno, 186
Laub, Dori, 105
Lefebvre, Henri, 2, 7, 23–4, 39, 50, 225
Lerman, Miles, 45n6
Levi, Primo, 80, 88, 206–9
Levinas, Emmanuel, 79
Lewin, Miriam, 117, 191, 200
LGBTQI (lesbian, gay, bisexual, transgender, queer and intersex), 163
Libeskind, Daniel, 79, 86

'lieux de mémoire,' 7, 144
'lived experience,' 138
loci, technique of, 137
London, 86, 108, 231
   Greater London Council, 246, 253n1
   Ken Livingstone, 246, 253n1
Lorca, Federico García, 1, 13
Lyotard, Jean-François, 66

Madrid, 9, 91, 130n5, 231
   Puerta del Sol Square, 241
   Residencia de Estudiantes (Students' Residency), 1
Mahlke, Kirsten, viii, xiii, 5–6, 11, 105–17
Maitland, Sarah, 11, 91
Malaysia, 59n10
Mandolessi, Silvana, 5–6, 8, 12, 150–60, 198
Manning, Erin, 162, 169, 171
maps, 7, 11, 40, 44, 53–4, 68, 91–3, 95, 97–104, 121, 136–8, 141, 148, 158, 169, 181–182, 192, 219–20, 223, 226n1
maquiladoras, 248
Martínez, Tomás Eloy, 157
Martínez Estrada, Ezequiel, 224
Marxism, 25, 121, 244
Marxists, 2, 51, 141, 246, 248–9
massacres
   Alevi populations, 165
   Dersim, 167
Massey, Doreen, 2, 164
mass graves, 11, 30, 40–4, 45n6, 170, 185
   abandoned graves, 61–71
   anonymous graves, 191
   cunetas (roadside graves in Spain), 65
   excavations, 30, 63, 68–70, 139–40
   'grave-robbers,' 40
   massacre sites, 7, 9, 11, 165
   unnamed graves, 64
   unidentified bodies, 64
mass murder, 3, 8, 78, 80
mass production, 209
Mate, Reyes, viii, 64–5, 71n2
material memory, 136
Mayer, Christoph, 146–7
Mayorga, Juan, 5–8, 11, 91–104

Mbembe, Achille, 66, 70
media, 10–11, 39, 63, 66–7, 69, 71, 143, 167, 171, 176, 192, 220, 239
memorial plaques, 42, 45n4, 138, 143, 148n2, 200
memorials, 1, 7, 10, 12, 14, 21–3, 27, 30–2, 37, 39–45, 45n7, 46nn12–13, 62–3, 96, 135, 138–9, 143, 147–8, 165, 182, 212, 252–3
   see also individual memorials
memory
   collective, 2–3, 9, 32, 116, 151, 223–4, 251–2
   as complex process, 7–8
   cultural, 39
   historical, 14, 66, 68, 224, 251–2
   knots, 165–6, 171
   'milieu de mémoire' and 'lieu de mémoire,' 144
   multidirectional, 9
   official, 39–40
   political, 12, 162
   powerful political force of, 244–53
   power of, 137, 140–1, 144–8
   as psychic energy, 140–1
   revolutionary force of, 141
   social, 1–2, 147
   theory of, 140–1
   traumatic, 144, 148
Memory Trail, 43
metaphors, 5, 29, 49, 65, 109, 122, 130, 139, 152, 155–6, 158–9
metonymization, 79–80, 109–10, 195
Mexican Revolution, 221
Mexico, 97, 221
migration, forced, 169, 171
mnemocide, 141
modernity, 5, 65–6, 172, 205
modernization theory, 59n11
'modern' prisons, 214
modern warfare, 105–6, 108–11
   coercive/interrogation techniques, 110–11
   'the enemy,' 109
   metaphor and metonymy, 108–9
   psychological weapons, 116
   spatio-temporal distortions, 109–15
   territory of war, 109–10
   and the torture cellar, 110–11

Molloy, Silvia, 221, 226n2
Montevideo, 191
Montreal, 231
monuments, 12, 23, 30, 39–42, 46n11, 63, 65, 79–80, 135–48, 158, 172, 197, 200, 240
Mothers of the Disappeared, 162, 165–6, 170–3, 193, 253n4
  Azucena Villaflor de Devicenzi, 199
Mother Teresa, 221
Mubarak, Hosni, 238
Müller, Heiner, 140–1, 148n4

Nachama, Andreas, 140
Nacht und Nebel (Night and Fog), 115
Nágera, Antonio Vallejo, 121
name-tags, 146
Nancy, Jean-Luc, 184
national identity, 121, 198, 238
nationalism, 238
National Salvation Front, Cambodia, 26
nation state, 66, 198
nautical cartography, 197
Navaro-Yashin, Yael, 5, 173n2, 199
Nazi concentration/extermination camps
  Auschwitz I, 80, 206, 208–9
  Auschwitz II Birkenau, 35–8, 206–9
  Bełżec: 41–45
  Buchenwald, 107, 110, 148n7
  Dachau, 107, 110–11, 135, 148n7; memorial site, 148n7
  electrified fences and control towers, 206–7, 209
  gas chambers, 37, 42–3
  Gusen, 146–7
  industrial/military complex, 208–9
  labour camps, 143, 206, 208–9
  Majdanek, 35, 39–41; photographs representing, 35–8
  Monowitz, 206, 208–9
  Neuengamme, 148n7
  Ravensbrück, 139; memorial, 148n7
  Sachsenhausen, 148n7
  selection of prisoners, 207, 209
  Sobibór, 34–5
  Treblinka, 35, 103

Nazis/Nazi regime, 37, 40, 78, 208, 211
  Nacht und Nebel (Night and Fog) decree, 1941, 115
  pogrom of 8 November 1938, 85–6
necropolitics, 66, 70
Negri, Antonio, 70, 205, 216, 238
neo-liberalism, 14, 163, 167, 193, 199, 224, 228n15, 245
Neuengamme, *see* Nazi concentration/extermination camps
New York, 231
Nolte, Ernst, 145
non-governmental organization (NGO), 122
Nora, Pierre, 7, 65, 67, 114, 144
North–South divide, 9
Nuremberg, 148n6

occupied squares, 239–41
  identity crisis, 237–9
  as threshold spaces, 239–41
Occupy Wall Street, 239
Onetti, Juan Carlos, 219–20, 226n2, 227n13
'open secret,' 131n6, 153, 155
Oslender, Ulrich, 4, 54
Ottoman Empire, 166, 173n6

pacification programs, 247
pan-Latin American rebellion, 52
parergon, Derridean, 36, 45n2
Paris Commune, 248, 252
Partido Revolucionario de los Trabajadores (PRT), 48
Partnoy, Alicia, 114
Patagonia, 220, 223–4
Pavlovsky, Eduardo, 128–9, 129, 131, 131n7
Pécaut, Daniel, 4
People's Republic of Kampuchea (PRK), 26–7, 29–30
Perel, Jonathan, 195
Perez, Mariana Eva, 5–6, 11, 119–31
Peronismo de Base (Grassroots Peronism – PB), 59n4
perpetrators, 12, 65, 108, 110, 120, 123, 126–7, 130, 140–1, 143–4, 147, 165, 168–9, 171–2, 173n6, 192
Pflug, Konrad, 144, 149n8
Phnom Penh, Cambodia, 24, 26–8, 30–1

Picasso, Pablo, 78–9, 83–4
Pile, Steve, 8
Pinochet dictatorship, *see* Chile
Piper, Isabel, 102, 186
placelessness, 24–6
plague, 121, 227n13, 235
plaques, memorial, 42, 45n4, 138, 143, 148n2, 200
Plato, 137
Poland, Holocaust memory, 34–46
　aesthetic framings of camp sites, 34–8
　anti-Semitism, anti-Jewish policies, 37
　archaeological research, 41, 43, 45n6
　architectural and sculptural projects, 41–5
　Foundation for Polish-German Reconciliation, 41
　grievability, commemorative art and, 38–41
police, 234
　attacks, 110, 163, 171, 231, 239
political activism, 190, 198–9, 224, 251
political afterlives, 67–8
political mourning, 70
political prisoners, 107, 120–1
post-dictatorship Argentine fiction, 150–60
post-Holocaust art, 79–80, 84–9
postmodernism, 199, 232, 249
Pot, Pol, 25, 27, 30, 32
power relations, 23, 222, 223
Preston, Paul, 62
prisoners of war (POW), 89, 206
private spaces, 66–7, 121, 130
production, labour process, 244
production of space, 1–2, 5, 23
Provincial Commission for Memory, Buenos Aires, 186n2
psychological approaches, 69–70, 105, 107–8, 110–12, 116n2, 117n5, 119, 152, 176, 185, 215–17
public executions, 9, 207
public grieving, 38–41

Qur'an, 215

rabbinical law, 41
Rabinow, Paul, 234
racist theories, 121
radical confinement, 214, 216

radical imagination, 219–20
Radstone, Susannah, 9
Rama, Angel, 222–3, 227n11, 248
Ramallah, 248
Rancière, Jacques, 35, 171, 238
rape, 21, 130, 155
Rape of Nanjing in 1937, 78
Rath, Gudrun, 5, 8, 13, 219–28
Reagan, Ronald, 139
reappearance of bodies, 64
Reati, Fernando, 195, 227n15
reburial, 44, 62–3, 68
'Recovered Grandchildren,' 122, 130n3
refugees, 219, 237
regression, 110–11, 113–14, 116
Reichskriegsgericht, 138, 148n2
remembering, 39, 141, 145, 148n1, 197
remnants, landscape of, 176–86
Report of the Commission about the Enforced Disappearances, *see* CONADEP
resistance, 7–9, 13, 88–9, 93, 97, 110, 116, 124, 139, 140, 144, 162–3, 167, 172–3, 205, 220, 223–5
reterritorialization, 4, 11, 51–2, 57–8, 61, 63, 67, 69, 71
revolutionary movements, 248–9
revolutions, 7, 11, 23–7, 48, 51–2, 56–8, 66, 141, 151, 221, 240–1, 248–9, 252
Ricoeur, Paul, 179
Rio de Janeiro, 231, 242, 247
Río de la Plata (River Plate), 188–200
　appearance of bodies, 190–1, 200n3, 200n7
　concealment of the death flights, 190–2
　Puerto Madero, 192, 199
　Velarde's 'drawings on the river,' 195–7
riots, 235, 252
rituals, 23, 63, 67–8, 156, 234
Robben, Antonius, 64
Rodrigo, Javier, 62, 219
Roma, 45n3, 145
Rome, 137–8
Romero, José Luis, 227n11
Rose, Gillian, 8
Rose, Nikolas, 70
Rothberg, Michael, 9, 105, 107

ruins, 64, 80, 96, 139, 176–80, 183–5, 186n1
Rulfo, Juan, 219, 221
rural guerrillas, 48–9, 51–4, 56
Rürup, Reinhard, 139–40
Russia, 82
Rwanda, 25

Saccomanno, Guillermo, 151–2
Saer, Juan José, 198
Samphan, Khieu, 30
Sanchis Sinisterra, José, 126
Sandburg, Carl, 135
São Paulo, 242
Sary, Ieng, 25, 30, 32
Sasiaín, Juan, 126, 130n5
satellite cities, 232
saturation of experience, 66
Saturday Mothers' movement, *see* Turkey
Schama, Simon, 197
Schindel, Estela, 1–14, 188–200, 244–53
Schlögel, Karl, 2–3
Schofield, John, 4
schools, 55, 144, 154
Schwab, Gabriele, 8, 156
Second World War (1939–45) in popular culture, 35, 78, 82, 83
secret intelligence files, 167
selection of prisoners, 123, 207, 209
senses, suppression of the, 209, 213, 215–17
sexual abuse, 127, 131n6
Sherman, William, 77
Shoah, the, 78, 80, 88, 105, 115–16
Shoah (Lanzmann), 34, 80
showers, 206, 215
Sigurdsson, Sigrid, 136–7, 148
Simmel, Georg, 179–80
Simon, David, 176
Sinti, 45n3, 145
slaughterhouse, 80
slavery, 8, 23, 37, 206
sleeping drug, 190, 212
Slovakia, 45n3
Śmiechowska, Teresa, 37
Smith, Andrew, 152
Sofsky, Wolfgang, 5
Soja, Edward, 2, 233
solidarity, 146, 191, 239
Sophal, Keat, 21–2, 27, 29

South America, 108, 115
sovereign power/sovereignty, 5, 7, 166, 172, 234–5
Soviet Union, 45n3
'spaces of hope,' 14, 250, 251
space-time (distortion), 11, 51, 65–6, 105–17, 158, 164, 205–17, 233
'here and now,' 114, 127, 157, 159
Spain/Spanish Civil War, 61–71
afterlives, new spatialities beyond the mass grave, 67–71
Audiencia Nacional, 68
Condor legion's attack on Guernica, 80, 82
cunetas (roadside graves), 65
forensic manifestation, 69–70
funerary legislation, 65
reterritorialization, processes of, 61, 63, 67, 69, 71
Spanish Supreme Court, 68
transformed landscapes, 65–6, 69
spatial disorientation, *see* space–time (distortion)
spectrality, 151–2
Squares Movement, 231–42
starvation, 31, 208, 209
state of exception, *see* exception, state of
Stavrides, Stavros, 5, 7, 10, 13, 231–42
Stockholm conference, 144
strategic hamlets project, 55–6, 59n9
Strejilevich, Nora, 114
Sturdy Colls, Caroline, 4
sugar industry, 48, 51, 54, 59n7, 59n12
surveillance, 55, 121, 124, 165, 168, 223–4, 233, 247–8, 250
suspension of law, 235–6
sweat-shops, 237
synagogue, 79, 86, 91–2, 95–6, 147
Syntagma square, Athens, 238–9

Tahrir Square, Cairo, 238–9
Taksim Square, Istanbul, 12, 163
tangible remnants, 12, 178
Taussig, Michael, 62, 65, 106, 113
technological revolutions, 66–70, 81, 88–9, 164, 216, 248
Tel Aviv, 231
territorial policy, 245

terror
  artistic configurations of, 77–90
  chronotope of, 106–8, 113–14, 116, 117n4, 225
  effects of, 6, 7, 117n4, 152, 160
  and horror, difference between, 151
  mapping of, 61, 64
  methods, 108, 110, 117n4, 159
  war against, 214, 216
  testimonies of survivors, 111–15
  'Artichoke' operation, 116n2
  Bettelheim's, 111–12
  Eichmann trial, 112
  ESMA survivors', 113–14, 190
  initial shock of arrest, 110, 111
  Liliana Gardella's, 115
  narratives of disappearance, 115
  Orletti's, 113
  spatio-temporal distortions, 111–15
  subject/object dimension, 112–13
Tet offensive, 89
Thatcher, Margaret, 245–6, 253n1
Thrift, Nigel, 4
Till, Karen, 6, 8
time knots of violence, *see* violence
Tokyo, 78
topography, 2, 4–5, 45n6, 136–8, 140, 206, 227n12
'Topography of Terror,' 138, 140
torture, 6, 21, 27, 29, 31, 65, 70, 93, 108, 110–11, 114–16, 124, 127, 138, 153, 165, 167, 170, 190–1, 210–13, 216, 221, 246, 251
totalitarian regimes, 2, 123, 206, 217, 245
transcultural memory, 9
transformation, 4–5, 10, 22, 24, 41, 66, 69, 81, 86, 109, 136, 145, 150, 163, 171, 197, 205, 217, 226, 240–1
transitional justice, 66
transnational human rights, 69
transnational memory, 9
transportation/transfer of prisoners, 119–20, 124–9, 191, 207, 209–13, 217n2, 221
trauma, 2–3, 9, 11, 105, 107, 114, 140–1, 143–5, 147, 148n7, 165, 183, 184, 193
traumatic realism, 107, 113, 116

Trigg, Dylan, 8
Trinquier, Roger, 105, 108–10
Truth, Justice, Memory Center, 169, 173n8
Tucumán *monte*, Argentina, 48–59
  Antonio Domingo Bussi, 55
  clandestine detention centres, 48–9, 52
  confrontation, spaces of, 49–51
  displacement and relocalization of population, 48–9, 52–6
  founding of new villages, 53–5
  Operativo Independencia (Operation Independence), 48, 53–5
  PRT-ERP militants, 48, 51
  reterritorialization, 51–2, 57–8
Tunisia
  Jasmine Revolution, 241
  revolt against Ben Ali, 231
Tuol Sleng Museum of Genocide Crimes, Cambodia, 21, 27–32
Turkey
  AKP regime (Justice and Development Party), 163, 164
  Armenian cemetery, Gezi Park, 163
  Committee of Union and Progress, 166
  Diyarbakır, 172
  enforced disappearances, 165–9
  Galatasaray, 162, 168, 170–2
  Gezi Resistance, 162–4, 167, 172
  Grand National Assembly of Turkey, 167
  Kurdish Resistance, 167
  Ottoman military barracks, project of rebuilding, 163
  Saturday Mothers' movement, 12, 162, 166, 168, 170–3
  Şırnak, 168–9
  Truth, Justice, Memory Center, 169, 173n8
Turkish Armed Forces, 168–9
Turner, Victor W., 240
Twain, Mark, 245
Txi plays (Teatroxlaidentidad; Theatre for Identity), 126–30, 130nn4–5
Tyner, James A., 5–6, 10, 21–32, 55

uncanny, the, 8, 12, 86, 119, 125, 129–30, 150, 170–1
unhomely home, 12, 119, 125–30

Index

United Nations, 26, 69
United States
  deindustrialization of, 246–7
  Holocaust Memorial Museum, 41
  military in Baghdad and Fallujah, 248
  Provincial Reconstruction Team (PRT) in Afghanistan, 59n10
  strategic hamlet project in Vietnam, 55–6
urban archipelago, 232–4, 236–7, 240
Urbanek, Marcin, 41, 43
urban imaginary *(imaginarios urbanos)*, 225–6
urban islands, 232–4
urbanism/urbanization, 3, 199, 248
urban order, contemporary, 232–7
  archipelago approach, 232–4
  biopolitics, 233–7
  spatial organization, 232–3
urban sea, 233–4
urban social movements, 250

Van Gennep, Arnold, 240
Verbitsky, Horacio, 192, 200
victimization, 70
  see also torture
Vienna, 146, 219
Vietnam
  Communist Party, 30
  intervention in the Cambodian genocide, 26
  strategic hamlets project, 55–6, 59n10
Villaflor de Devicenzi, Azucena, 199
Villoro, Juan, 221, 226n1, 227n10
Vinyes, Ricard, 121

violence
  daily, 244
  disputed and resisted spaces of, 205–42
  economic, 244–5
  genocidal, *see* genocide
  Harvey on, 244–5
  memories of traumatic pasts, 135–200
  time knots of, 165
voluntary memory, 138

war
  changing nature of, 77–8, 83
  conventional vocabulary of, 109
  global laws of war, 214
  modern warfare, 105–6, 108–11
  temporal dimension of, 109
war on drugs, 251
War on Terror, 51, 205, 214, 216
Weizman, Eyal, 4–6, 248, 253n2
Werner, Hendrik, 148n4
White, Hayden, 106
Winter, Jay, 5, 7–8, 11, 77–90
women
  in concentration camps, 25, 31, 80, 89, 119, 125, 129, 163, 191, 206–7, 211
  femicides of factory workers, 221
  in Marxist history, 249
  in the squares of the Arab Spring, 238
  survivors, 108

Young, James, 44, 46n11, 80
Yugoslavia, 25, 78

Zamora, José Antonio, viii, 64
Zinn, Howard, 252
Zout, Helen, 195

9781137380906